Environmental Reporting and Recordkeeping Requirements

Third Edition

Editor

Theodore W. Firetog

Contributors

Richard W. Bale
June C. Bolstridge
Lawrence B. Cahill
Lisa I. Cooper
Theodore W. Firetog
Wayne T. Halbleib
G. Vinson Hellwig
John C. Knoepfler
Martha E. Pellegrini
David G. Sarvadi

 Government Institutes, Inc.
Rockville, Maryland

Government Institutes, Inc.
4 Research Place, Suite 200
Rockville, Maryland 20850

ISBN: 0-86587-412-3

Printed in the United States of America.

ENVIRONMENTAL REPORTING AND RECORDKEEPING REQUIREMENTS

TABLE OF CONTENTS

(Environmental Reporting & Recordkeeping Table of Contents, continued)

ABOUT THE AUTHORS

Richard W. Bale
Associate
General Litigation Department
Robins, Kaplan, Miller & Ciresi
Minneapolis, Minnesota

Richard W. Bale is a fourth-year associate in the General Litigation Department at Robins, Kaplan, Miller & Ciresi, where he represents corporate clients in federal and state courts and before agencies such as the Minnesota Public Utilities Commission, the Minnesota Pollution Control Agency and the United States Environmental Protection Agency. Mr. Bale represented clients in highly-regulated industries such as transportation, telecommunications, and chemical manufacturing in litigation that involved contract obligations as well as state and federal regulatory issues. Mr. Bale has extensive experience advising companies in both litigation and regulatory compliance, particularly in the complex field of environmental law.

June C. Bolstridge
President
GAIA Corporation
Silver Spring, Maryland

Ms. Bolstridge is president of the GAIA Corporation of Silver Spring, Maryland, which provides environmental and computer services to industry and government agencies. During the past ten years, she has designed, developed, and implemented numerous environmental information management systems. She has provided demonstrations and training on environmental computer systems through the National Safety Council, Government Institutes, Georgia Tech Research Institute, the Air and Waste Management Association, and other organizations.

Previously a senior environmental engineer with ICF Incorporated, Ms. Bolstridge developed a computerized guidance system for the EPA's section 313 requirements and a complete data management system to assist industry with EPCRA reporting. Ms. Bolstridge prepared a comprehensive review document identifying commercially available computer systems with capabilities in emergency planning. As an environmental engineer on the staff of Martin Marietta, Ms. Bolstridge developed computerized systems to track *Federal Register* notices and provide information on the regulatory requirements for PCBs. She also designed, developed, and implemented systems to track, manage, and manifest hazardous wastes and document compliance with environmental permits associated with the space shuttle launch site at Vandenberg Air Force Base, California.

She holds a B.S. with honors from the State University of New York, College of Environmental Science and Forestry, and a M.S. in environmental engineering from the University of Washington.

Lawrence B. Cahill
Senior Program Manager
ERM, Inc.
855 Springdale Drive
Exton, Pennsylvania 19341

Mr. Cahill is a senior program manager for ERM, Incorporated in Exton, Pennsylvania. He was formerly a vice-president at McLaren/Hart Environmental Engineering Corporation in Lester, Pennsylvania. He is an skilled environmental auditor with more than 12 years of field audit experience. He has performed audit assignments for the U.S. Army and Air Force, several chemical companies (Dow, Celanese), and other manufacturers. As an engineer with Exxon, he audited facilities in the U.S., Canada and Europe.

Prior to joining McLaren/Hart, Mr. Cahill was with Roy F. Weston, Booz Allen & Hamilton, and Exxon Research & Engineering. He is the former environmental commissioner for Camden, New Jersey, and is the co-author of *Environmental Audits, 6th Edition* published by Government Institutes.

Mr. Cahill received his MBA from the Wharton School, his MS in Environmental Engineering from Northwestern University, and his BSME from Northeastern.

(About the Authors, continued)

Theodore W. Firetog
Environmental Counsel
Jaspan, Ginsberg, Schlesinger, Silverman & Hoffman
300 Garden City Plaza
Garden City, NY 11530-3324
(516) 746-8000

Mr. Firetog is currently environmental counsel to the Environmental Practice Group of Jaspan, Ginsberg, Schlesinger, Silverman & Hoffman, where he provides a wide range of legal counseling on all aspects of environmental law. He has been in practice of environmental law for over 13 years including counseling clients on compliance with environmental laws, rules and regulations, securing permits and variances, coordinating environmental audits, providing advice on the impact of environmental laws on real estate and other business transactions, and providing legal counseling with respect to hazardous waste litigation and insurance/coverage issues.

His environmental law expertise has been built on the practical experience that he received as a Staff Attorney with the Environmental Law Institute and as an Attorney-Advisor with the U.S. Environmental Protection Agency in Washington, D.C.

Just prior to coming to Jaspan, Ginsberg, Schlesinger, Silverman & Hoffman, Mr. Firetog was environmental counsel to the New York City law firm of Shea & Gould. He has authored various articles for environmental law symposiums and conferences.

Mr. Firetog received his B.S. degree in Natural Resources and his M.S. degree in Natural Resource Policy and Management from the University of Michigan. He obtained his Juris Doctor degree the State University of New York at Buffalo, where he was also a Sea Grant Law Fellow. He is a member of the Natural Resources Section of the American Bar Association and the Environmental Law Section of the New York Bar Association. He is listed in *Who's Who in American Law*.

Wayne T. Halbleib
Counsel
Energy & Environment Practice Group
Mays & Valentine
NationsBank Center
1111 East Main Street
Post Office Box 1122
Richmond, Virginia 23208-1122

Wayne T. Halbleib is counsel to the Energy & Environment Practice Group of the Richmond-based law firm of Mays & Valentine. His practice concentrates on providing environmental and occupational safety and health compliance and enforcement counseling, as well as litigation services for corporations, trade associations, banks, and small businesses in Virginia.

Mr. Halbleib currently serves as the Secretary of the Environmental Law Section of the Virginia State Bar. Prior to joining Mays & Valentine, Mr. Halbleib served as the first State Director of the SARA Title III Office within the Virginia Department of Environmental Quality. He served as Director of Virginia's SARA Title III Office from 1987 through July 1990. Mr. Halbleib served as an Assistant Attorney General for the Commonwealth of Virginia from 1980-1986. In that capacity, he defended actions brought against the Commonwealth and brought numerous enforcement actions on behalf of the Commonwealth against several corporations and the officers and directors for violations of both state and federal laws. Before joining the Virginia Attorney General's Office, Mr. Halbleib served as a law clerk to Senior U.S. District Judge Richard B. Kellam in the U.S. District Court for the Eastern District of Virginia in 1979.

Mr. Halbleib received his law degree from the University of Richmond School of Law, his M.S. in Public Administration from the University of Virginia, and his B.S. in American Government from the University of Virginia. He regularly lectures and writes on a wide variety of environmental issues.

(About the Authors, continued)

G. Vinson Hellwig
Vice President and Manager, Air Division
TRC Environmental Corporation, Inc.
5 Waterside Crossing
Winsor, Connecticut 06095

G. Vinson Hellwig is manager of TRC's Air Division where his responsibilities include project management of permitting and air engineering projects. Mr. Hellwig also serves as senior project manager on a number of air projects including emissions measurements, permitting, SARA Title III inventories, and control equipment engineering.

Prior to joining TRC, Mr. Hellwig was senior environmental engineer in the North Carolina office of a major environmental engineering firm. Responsibilities included regulatory analyses and air program development, as well as data systems management. He was the technical advisor for the BACT/LAER Information System and for an update of the SIP Tracking System. He also managed projects dealing with SIP development, NSPS, and NESHAP.

Mr. Hellwig also authored the *Good Practices Manual for the Delegation of NSPS and NESHAP Regulations*. While working for the U.S. EPA Region IV, Air Enforcement Branch, he was responsible for coordinating reporting requirements for compliance with the eight states in Region IV, conducting inspections of facilities in a variety of industries, developing compliance strategies for specific types of sources, providing guidance to state and local air pollution agencies, and interpreting EPA policy. He was also previously employed by the Alabama Air Pollution Control Commission and the Ampex Corporation Magnetic Tape Division.

Mr. Hellwig received his B.S. in Chemistry from Shorter College, and pursued graduate study at Clemson University and Auburn University, where he received his M.S. in Chemistry.

John C. Knoepfler
Attorney
Robins, Kaplan, Miller & Ciresi
Minneapolis, Minnesota

John C. Knoepfler is an attorney with the national law firm of Robins, Kaplan, Miller & Ciresi, headquartered in Minneapolis. Specializing in environmental law, Mr. Knoepfler represents and advises major industrial clients on a broad range of environmental matters throughout the United States, including Superfund remediation and litigation, RCRA compliance matters, asbestos abatement, insurance issues, environmental audits and recordkeeping. He is an instructor on underground storage tank requirements in conjunction with training conducted by the Minnesota Pollution Control Agency, and has spoken at various environmental and trade seminars on CERCLA requirements.

Prior to joining Robins, Kaplan, Miller & Ciresi, Mr. Knoepfler begin his career as an attorney in the United States Navy Judge Advocate General's Corps. He received his J.D. *cum laude* from the University of Minnesota.

(About the Authors, continued)

David G. Sarvadi
Associate
Keller and Heckman
1001 G Street, N.W.
Washington, DC 20001
202-434-4249

David G. Sarvadi, J.D., C.I.H., is an associate with the Washington, D.C. law firm of Keller and Heckman. Mr. Sarvadi recently joined the firm in the practice area of Occupational and Environmental Health and Safety.

Prior to joining the firm, he practiced industrial hygiene in a number of different environments. He has been a principal in a small consulting firm in the health and safety area, with particular responsibility for operations and administration. Occupational health and safety, toxic substance management, and product safety have been areas of his professional responsibility.

Mr. Sarvadi received his B.S./B.A. from Pennsylvania State University; his M.S. in Hygiene from the University of Pittsburgh; and his J.D. from George Mason University.

Environmental Reporting and Recordkeeping Requirements

Chapter 1

INTRODUCTION

THEODORE W. FIRETOG
Environmental Counsel
Jaspan, Ginsberg, Schlesinger, Silverman & Hoffman

Since the publication of the first two editions of Environmental Reporting and Recordkeeping, it seems that the regulated community is diverting more of its resources and devoting greater attention to understanding and complying with the plethora of environmental reporting and recordkeeping requirements contained in the volumes of environmental and health-related laws and regulations. Indeed, environmental records managers are now being employed by major companies, environmental records consultants are finding a niche for themselves in this rapidly growing field, and environmental attorneys, such as myself, are spending more time counselling and defending clients on matters relating to environmental reporting and recordkeeping.

Although corporations, companies, and other organizations have always had to contend with the production, compilation, administration, submission and retention of business records (including employment and personnel records, tax records, contracts, invoices, etc.), environmental reporting and recordkeeping have not always been among the foremost concerns of the regulated community. For the most part, compliance with environmental laws in the past has focused on controlling the discharge of pollutants and contaminants into the environment. Indeed, the primary thrust of the early environmental statutes was directed at mandating pollution control equipment or other technology to abate contamination and to protect human health and safety. This has led to a predictable course of events with the passage of each new statute and the promulgation of its implementing regulations.

As new environmental laws became enacted, or existing laws were amended, the regulated community would quickly focus its attention on the substantive pollution control requirements of the new or amended statute, and brace itself for the wave of regulations that would inevitably follow. Once a new environmental law or amendment became effective, and its regulations promulgated, federal, state and local environmental enforcement agencies promptly began to draft new enforcement policies, strategies, and penalty guidelines. The regulated community, in turn, responded -- usually by resorting to litigation that either challenged the new regulations or defended against Agency enforcement actions.

Indeed, this cycle of regulations and litigation (or other reactions by the regulated community) resulting from the enactment or amendment of federal environmental statutes over the past 24 years, has often been described as a series of waves, similar to the waves of any ocean or major body of water. Each wave of the environmental movement has had its crests or moving swells, undulating with the concerns of the nation as a whole.

There was, for example, a wave of regulations and litigation following the enactment of the Occupational Safety and Health Act of 1970 (29

2

U.S.C. § 651 *et seq.*); another wave resulted from the passage of the Toxic Substances Control Act ("TSCA," 15 U.S.C. § 2601 *et seq.*); and yet another wave was created by the enactment of the Resource Conservation and Recovery Act ("RCRA," 42 U.S.C. § 6901 *et seq.*), which has not altogether subsided. There was a virtual tidal wave of reaction and litigation when the Comprehensive Environmental Response, Compensation, and Liability Act of 1980 ("CERCLA," 42 U.S.C. § 9601 *et seq.*) became law. There is still an ongoing wave of reaction from the regulated community in response to the 1990 Clean Air Act Amendments (Pub. L. 101-549), as well as to the Oil Pollution Act of 1990 (33 U.S.C. § 2701 *et seq.*).

The vast majority of environmental articles, papers, and educational courses have focused on, and continue to deal with, the nature, extent, and ramifications of these "waves." Few have explored and charted the less obvious "undertow" that is present in all the major environmental statutes. Part of this undertow, common to all the statutes, is the existence of environmental reporting and recordkeeping requirements.

Although some environmental writings, as well as a few courses or seminars, have touched upon this subject in their treatment and analysis of a particular statute, this publication is devoted entirely to the study of environmental reporting and recordkeeping. This is propitious, since many of those in the regulated community have begun to realize that if the "waves" do not soak you, the undertow probably will.

Clearly, the regulated community is now appropriately focusing more of its resources on environmental reporting and recordkeeping requirements. This may be due to the following four reasons:

- The Increase in Reporting and Recordkeeping Requirements Which has Paralleled the Evolution of Environmental Laws;

- The Increase in Enforcement Activities Relating to Environmental Reporting and Recordkeeping;

- The Emergence of Non-Governmental Pressures Relating to Environmental Reporting and Recordkeeping; and

- The Regulated Community's Recognition of the Importance and Benefits of an Effective Reporting and Recordkeeping System.

Although reporting and recordkeeping requirements have always been included to some extent in the environmental statutes enacted following the creation of the Environmental Protection Agency ("EPA") in 1970 (*e.g.*, some notification and recordkeeping provisions were included in the 1970 Clean Air Act (42 U.S.C. § 7401 *et seq.*), as well as the 1972 Clean Water Act (33 U.S.C. § 1251 *et seq.*)), the fundamental importance of such provisions has increased dramatically with the passage of subsequent environmental laws and the reauthorization or amendment of existing statutes.

In 1976, for example, there was the passage of TSCA and RCRA, whose basic regulatory structures rely heavily upon the numerous provisions for reporting and recordkeeping relating to chemical substances and hazardous waste. The "Superfund Amendments and Reauthorization Act of 1986" ("SARA," Pub. L. 99-499), which amended CERCLA, added a new freestanding title (Title III), otherwise known as the Emergency Planning and Community Right-To-Know Act of 1986, which is essentially a reporting and

4

notification statute. Most recently, additional reporting and recordkeeping requirements were added to, and made an integral part of, the Clean Air Act Amendments of 1990.

The increase in statutory provisions relating to reporting and recordkeeping is reflected in the EPA's policies, program strategies, and enforcement actions. While the EPA had always engaged in some limited enforcement of reporting and recordkeeping requirements, it had generally done so in conjunction with actions brought for violations relating to other provisions of a particular statute. For example, the failure to file annual reports under RCRA may have been included as a lesser charge to a violation of illegally disposing of hazardous wastes.

The EPA, however, soon began to realize that environmental reporting and recordkeeping requirements are essential for ensuring that the basic regulatory scheme of each of the environmental statutes remains intact. Such requirements not only provide the Agency with the ability to effectively respond to emergency releases of hazardous or toxic chemicals, but they also provide the EPA with a cost-effective means of tracking compliance with its regulations and of evaluating their effectiveness, by, in essence, having the regulated community report on itself.

Accordingly, the EPA's attitude with respect to reporting and recordkeeping violations has changed. Currently, the Agency is directing more of its resources and personnel solely to the enforcement of reporting and recordkeeping violations. Armed with a wide arsenal of civil and criminal sanctions, the EPA has begun sending a message to the regulated community that the failure to keep appropriate records or to report required information will result in enforcement actions -- administrative, judicial and criminal.

Coupled with the increase in the environmental reporting and recordkeeping provisions and the increase in EPA enforcement activities, the emergence of non-governmental pressures have caused the regulated community to focus on the importance of such requirements. Certainly, any business transaction that involves real property will now need to address issues relating to "Environmental Due Diligence." The availability and completeness of environmental records and of reports submitted to regulatory agencies will be an integral and indispensable part of such due diligence.

Spurred by nongovernmental pressures, as well as the rise in the EPA enforcement activities relating to reporting and recordkeeping violations, the regulated community has increased its commitment to ensure compliance with the multitude and complexity of those requirements. In doing so, the regulated community has also recognized and realized important benefits of having an effective recordkeeping and reporting management system.

Apart from avoiding potential (and substantial) liability, fines, and criminal sanctions, business entities have discovered at least four additional benefits from complying with environmental reporting and recordkeeping requirements:

- Improved Environmental Management;

- An Increase in the Company's Level of Comfort
  and Security;

6

- Easier Compilation of Information for the Support or Defense of Litigation; and

- Facilitation in Assembling Information for Certain Business Transactions.

Compliance with reporting and recordkeeping requirements can improve the ability of a company to manage environmental issues effectively. A comprehensive reporting and recordkeeping compliance program can identify weaknesses or gaps which may exist within a company's existing informational and administrative network. By addressing those "blind spots," the company can develop a more effective and efficient approach towards managing its environmental activities, which in turn, will improve the company's overall compliance record and its ability to respond in the event of an environmental emergency.

Another significant benefit of complying with environmental reporting and recordkeeping requirements is the increased level of comfort and security derived from knowing that the company has reduced its exposure to potential civil and criminal liability. By reducing such exposure a company can also enhance its corporate environmental image within the community. An effective reporting and recordkeeping management system will also ensure that the company complies with the legal retention requirements for keeping or destroying its records and documents, and that a system for protecting vital records is established.

An effective reporting and recordkeeping system will also assist a company to compile and assemble information needed in the support or defense of litigation or for various business transactions, and reduce the associated costs of doing so. Without the ability to produce the necessary documents, many a court case, administrative enforcement action, or multi-million dollar business deal has been lost.

The primary objectives of the chapters that follow are to present the major environmental reporting and recordkeeping requirements in a single volume, and to explore some of the ancillary issues associated with such requirements. Among these additional issues is how to evaluate your company's reporting and recordkeeping procedures through the use of an environmental audit, and how to establish an effective document retention and destruction policy for your company.

Our focus initially is on the specific reporting and recordkeeping requirements pertaining to each of the major environmental statutes and regulations promulgated thereunder. The chapters that follow will examine these requirements, as well as the associated issues of environmental auditing and document management.

Chapter 2

CLEAN AIR ACT

G. Vinson Hellwig
Vice President and Manager, Air Division
TRC Environmental Consultants, inc.
East Hartford, Connecticut

1.0 INTRODUCTION

Under the Clean Air Act Amendments (CAAA), recordkeeping and reporting are required for sources subject to New Source Performance Standards (NSPS), National Emissions Standards for Hazardous Air Pollutants (HAPs), Prevention of Significant Deterioration (PSD), New Source Review (NSR), compliance orders and specific permit conditions. The Clean Air Act Amendments of 1990 extended reporting and recordkeeping requirements of all "major" sources. Each area has separate recordkeeping and reporting requirements, and we will review record types and whether they are subject to federal, state or local agency regulations.

There are few EPA suggested forms for reporting and recordkeeping under the air regulations. It is left up to the state regulatory agency or the company or facility to determine format. The contents of the reporting and recordkeeping requirements vary greatly with the regulation and source category. Typically, the specific requirements are listed under a specific source category and each one should be reviewed in detail.

Recordkeeping and reporting requirements are basically used by the agencies as an enforcement tool to document continuing compliance. The documentation must be as accurate as possible; tampering with any type of reporting or recordkeeping is not permitted and can result in legal prosecution.

2.0 RECORD TYPES AND FORMAT

Administrative and technical reporting and recordkeeping is mandated by the CAAA and the regulations under that act. There are various types of information that must be maintained including continuous emission monitoring records, usage quantities such as volatile organic chemicals (VOCs), tank throughput records, equipment leak and maintenance records, ambient air quality monitoring data, and process or control equipment operating data.

2.1 Record Types

The record or type of information that must be maintained is varied and the records to be maintained do not have specific requirements for detailed information in most cases. We will discuss the type of information, and provide examples of recordkeeping requirements.

2.2 NSPS and NESHAP Requirements

NSPS and NESHAPs are covered under Section 111 and Section 112, respectively, of the CAA Amendments of 1977.

2.2.1 NSPS

Section 111 of the CAA provides for the development and implementation of regulations under New Source Performance Standards (NSPS). These standards establish certain categories of air pollution sources which, after proper notification to the public, require that emission standards be established. As part of these NSPS, certain recordkeeping requirements are implemented to assure that the standards are being met.

Previously promulgated standards are found in the Code of Federal Regulations, Title 40, Part 60 (40CFR60). The Code of Federal Regulations is published each July, with any NSPS promulgated since the previous July included. 40CFR60 sets out the requirements and general provisions as they apply to the owner/operator of any stationary source which contains an affected facility. Any facility where construction or modification began after the date of proposal in the Code of Federal Regulations will be subject to the standard listed. NSPS promulgated after July will appear in the Federal Register (FR); potentially affected facilities must review the FR for any applicable NSPS revisions.

Most of the actual compliance and enforcement for NSPS has been delegated to the state agencies at the present time, while the EPA has reserved some authority.

There is a general provision under 40CFR60.7, "Notification and Recordkeeping", which deals with the installation and operation of Continuous Emission Monitoring Systems (CEMS). Any owner/operator that is required to have a CEMS must meet specific reporting requirements. Additional monitoring requirements are found as part of 40CFR60.13, and other reporting requirements are found under the individual NSPS categories.

CEMS Requirements

New Source Performance Standards (NSPS) require that any owner/operator subject to the provisions of mandatory continuous emission monitoring maintain those operating records, as well as records of any startup, shutdown or malfunction of an affected facility's air pollution control equipment during any period in which a continuous monitoring system or device is inoperative. In addition, every source that is required to install a CEMS must submit a written report of excess emissions, as defined in applicable portions of the regulations. These reports must be submitted every calendar quarter, and they must be postmarked by the 30th day of the end of each calendar quarter. The report must include certain information:

1. The magnitude of the excess emissions computed in accordance with 40CFR60.13(h), any conversion factors used, the date and time of the commencement and completion of each time period of excess emissions.

2. Specific identification of each period of excess emissions that occurs during the startup/shutdown malfunctions, the nature and cause of the malfunction, and, if known, the corrective actions that took place.

3. The date and time identifying each period when the continuous monitoring system was inoperative, except for zero/span checks, and the nature of repairs or adjustments.

4. If no excess emissions have occurred or the monitors have not been inoperative, repaired or adjusted, the report should state this.

The owner/operator subject to these provisions has to maintain a file of all measurements, source testing, CEMS performance evaluations, calibration checks, adjustments and maintenance performed on the system, and any other information required under a specific Subpart of the regulations. If subject to specific Subsection, these files must be retained for at least two (2) years following the date any such measurements are reported.

All CEMS must meet the performance specifications as listed under 40CFR60 Appendix B. If they are used to demonstrate compliance with emission limits on a continuous basis, they are also subject to 40CFR60 Appendix F.

Other Recordkeeping Requirements

Many categories of NSPS require keeping other records. Most of these deal with production records; however, in the area of coating and volatile organic compound (VOC) control, the requirements for records and tracking are far more complex. These deal with the quantity of solvent and calculation of solvent usage in estimating what is emitted into the atmosphere.

There are other reporting requirements that deal with VOC recordkeeping. For example, Subpart K and Subpart Ka, referring to VOC storage vessels, require that data be maintained on the Reid vapor pressure, and the quantity of material that is retained in these vessels.

There are a number of NSPS standards that require process monitoring and recordkeeping; for instance, the phosphate fertilizer industry has several NSPS that it is subject to, each with specific recordkeeping requirements. As stated earlier, all of these records must be maintained for a minimum of two (2) years. The recordkeeping and reporting requirements for leaks in the synthetic organic chemical manufacturing industry and petroleum refineries are very specific as to what types of records must be maintained when performing leak checks from the various points within the refinery operations such as valves, seals, pumps, etc. Although this is not a continuous monitoring activity, it is an ongoing program for which records must be maintained at any of the facilities that are subject to these regulations.

A company that is subject to NSPS should carefully review the applicable regulations and determine what records must be maintained and what must be reported to the agencies. If your facility is a NSPS source and you were reporting the required information, you should be aware that EPA amended a number of the reporting and recordkeeping requirements in the December 13, 1990 Federal Register. EPA states in that Federal Register notice that they are reducing the reporting burden placed on the facility.

Table 1 lists the current NSPS subparts that require R&R. There are presently 65 NSPS standards that require CEMS or some other form of R&R.

2.2.2 Hazardous Air Pollutants (HAPs)

Title III of the Clean Air Act Amendments of 1990 redefines the approach that must be taken to deal with HAPs. Previously, HAPs were regulated by the National Emission Standards for Hazardous Air Pollutants (NESHAPs) under Section 112 of the Act. All of the NESHAPs standards are incorporated into the HAPs program. The NESHAPs include such chemicals as beryllium, mercury, asbestos, vinyl chloride, benzene, Radon 222 from underground uranium mines, thermonuclide emissions from Department of Energy facilities, thermonuclide emissions from all metal phosphorus facilities, Radon 222 emissions from licensed uranium mill tailings, arsenic emissions from glass manufacturing plants, arsenic emissions from primary copper smelters, and fugitive emissions sources from equipment leaks.

Specific pollutants that are regulated are:

   Asbestos

   Benzene

   Beryllium

   Coke Oven Emissions

   Inorganic Arsenic

   Mercury

   Radionuclides

   Vinyl Chloride

TABLE 1

NSPS SUBPARTS THAT ARE SUBJECT TO SPECIFIC CEMS
AND RECORDKEEPING AND REPORTING REQUIREMENTS

Subpart Ca   Municipal Waste Combustors

Subpart D   Fossil Fueled Fired Steam Generators

Subpart Da   Electric Utility Steam Generating Units

Subpart Db   Industrial Commercial Institutional Steam Generating Units

Subpart Dc   Small Industrial Commercial Institutional Steam Generating Units

Subpart E   Incinerators

Subpart Ea   Municipal Waste Combustors

Subpart F   Portland Cement Plants

Subpart G   Nitric Acid Plants

Subpart H   Sulfuric Acid Plants

Subpart J   Petroleum Refineries

Subpart K   Storage Vessels for Petroleum Liquids, June 11, 1973 – May 19, 1978

Subpart Ka   Storage Vessels for Petroleum Liquids, May 18, 1978 – July 23, 1984

Subpart Kb   Volatile Organic Liquid Storage Vessels (including Petroleum Liquids) after July 23, 1984

Subpart N   Primary Emissions from Basic Oxygen Process Furnaces, Construction Commenced after June 11, 1973

Subpart Na   Secondary Emissions from Basic Oxygen Process Steel Making Facilities, Construction Commenced after January 20, 1983

Subpart O   Sewage Treatment Plants

Subpart P   Primary Copper Smelters

Subpart Q   Primary Zinc Smelters

Subpart R   Primary Lead Smelters

Subpart S   Primary Limited Reduction Plants

Subpart T   Phosphate Fertilizer Industry: Wet Process Phosphoric Acid Plants

Subpart U   Phosphate Fertilizer Industry: Super Phosphoric Acid Plants

14

TABLE 1

(CONTINUED)

Subpart V   Phosphate Fertilizer Industry: Diammonium Phosphate Plants

Subpart W   Phosphate Fertilizer Industry: Triple Super Phosphate Plants

Subpart X   Phosphate Fertilizer Industry: Granular Triple Superphosphate Storage Facilities

Subpart Y   Coal Preparation Plants

Subpart Z   Ferroalloy Production Facilities

Subpart AA   Steel Plants: Electric Arc Furnaces Constructed after October 21, 1974 and on or before August 17, 1983

Subpart AAa   Steel Plants: Electric Arc Furnaces in Argon Oxygen Decarbonization Vessels Constructed after August 7, 1983.

Subpart BB   Performance for Kraft Pulp Mills

Subpart CC   Glass Manufacturing Plants

Subpart EE   Surface Coating of Metal Furniture

Subpart GG   Stationary Gas Turbines

Subpart HH   Lime Manufacturing Plants

Subpart KK   Lead-Acid Battery Manufacturing Plants

Subpart LL   Metallic Mineral Processing Plants

Subpart MM   Automobile Light Duty Trucks Surface Coating Operations

Subpart NN   Phosphate Rock Plants

Subpart PP   Ammonium Sulfate Manufacture

Subpart QQ   Graphics Arts Industry: Publication Rotogravure Printing

Subpart RR   Pressure Sensitive Tape and Label Surface Coating Operations

Subpart SS   Industrial Surface Coating: Large Appliances

Subpart TT   Metal Coil Surface Coating

Subpart UU   Asphalt Processing and Asphalt Roofing Manufacture

Subpart VV   Equipment Leaks of VOC in the Synthetic Organic Chemical Manufacturing Industry

Subpart WW   Beverage Can Surface Coating Industry

Subpart XX   Bulk Gasoline Terminals

Subpart AAA   New Residential Wood Heaters (Manufacturers)

Subpart BBB   Rubber Tire Manufacturing Industry

TABLE 1

(CONTINUED)

Subpart DDD   VOC Emissions from Polymer Manufacturing Industry

Subpart FFF   Flexible Vinyl and Urethane Coating and Printing

Subpart GGG   Equipment Leaks of VOC in Petroleum Refineries

Subpart HHH   Synthetic Fiber Production Facilities

Subpart III   VOC Emissions from SOCMI Air Oxidation Unit Processes

Subpart JJJ   Petroleum Dry Cleaners

Subpart KKK   Equipment Leaks of VOC from Onshore Natural Gas Processing Plants

Subpart LLL   Onshore Natural Gas Processing: SO_2 Emission

Subpart NNN   VOC Emissions from SOCMI Distillation Operations

Subpart OOO   Non-Metallic Mineral Processing Plants

Subpart PPP   Wool Fiberglass Insulation Manufacturing Plants

Subpart QQQ   Petroleum Refinery Wastewater Systems

Subpart SSS   Magnetic Tape Coating Facilities

Subpart TTT   Industrial Surface Coating of Plastic Parts for Business Machines

Subpart VVV   Polymeric Coating of Supporting Substrates Facilities

Title III of the CAAA lists 189 chemicals that will be regulated. The new regulations will require that Maximum Achievable Control Technology (MACT) be applied by source category of manufacturing operation or process. There will be additional, as yet unspecified, monitoring, recordkeeping and reporting requirements for industry categories required to meet MACT.

Previously promulgated standards are found in the Code of Federal Regulations, Title 40, Part 61 (40CFR61). The Code of Federal Regulations is published each July, with any NSPS promulgated since the previous July included. 40CFR61 sets out the requirements and general provisions as they apply to the owner/operator of any stationary source which contains an affected facility. Any facility where construction or modification began after the date of proposal in the Code of Federal Regulations will be subject to the standard listed. NESHAPs promulgated after July will appear in the Federal Register (FR); potentially affected facilities must review the FR for HAPs revisions.

Most of the actual compliance and enforcement for HAPs has been delegated to the state agencies at the present time, while the EPA has reserved some authority.

There is a general provision under 40CFR61.14, "Monitoring Requirements", which deals with the installation and operation of Monitoring Systems (MS). Any owner/operator that is required to have an MS must meet specific reporting requirements. Other reporting requirements are found under the individual HAPs categories.

For purposes of discussion, we will deal with the reporting requirements of currently regulated pollutants. Since there are very few uranium producers, users of beryllium, and coke oven operators, we will not discuss those areas. The first MACT regulation proposals are being prepared by EPA, but none are in effect as yet.

Mercury is a regulated pollutant and is subject to monitoring and reporting requirements for various processes. These include mercury processing, chloroalkali plants, alkali metal hydroxide facilities and dry sewer sludge incineration facilities. Reporting is required for both continuous emission monitoring and other related indirect emission monitoring. Indirect emission monitoring refers to monitoring of pH alkali, pH of liquid scrubbers, liquid flow rates and exit gas temperatures. Vinyl chloride reporting and recordkeeping requirements

17

deal with both continuous emission releases and emergency releases and leaks. The leak monitoring requirements are very similar to those required for leaks in the refinery industry.

Metal phosphorus plants under Subpart K have monitoring and recordkeeping requirements on the control devices, such as installation date, calibrations, etc. It also requires information on continuous emission monitoring systems including monitoring of primary and secondary current and voltage in the electric fields that go to the electric furnaces that produce the phosphorus.

Subpart M of HAP standards deals with asbestos. Any owner/operator must maintain certain information on their control equipment and disposal of collected asbestos. This applies to sources that produce and actually use the asbestos in a manufacturing operation. For firms dealing with asbestos removal or disposal in demolition or renovation situations, there is a different set of reporting requirements that must be met, and these are subject to a separate Act, the Asbestos Hazard Emergency Response Act (AHERA). Those particular asbestos regulations and requirements should be reviewed.

Under Subpart N, inorganic arsenic emissions from glass manufacturing plants are subject to monitoring reporting requirements that include requirements for continuous emission monitors and other recordkeeping. The recordkeeping requirements are very specific as to what records must be maintained on production and control equipment operation. Likewise, Subpart O has monitoring requirements for arsenic emissions from primary copper smelters.

Subpart J of the HAP standards deal with fugitive emission leaks from benzene. The LDAR program applies to the benzene standards. The owner/operator must maintain records from leaks from pumps, compressors, relief valves, etc. for a period of two (2) years.

The Leak Detection and Repair (LDAR) program that was proposed in the March 6, 1991 Federal Register for chemical plants requires extensive recordkeeping and reporting provisions. The proposed rule will apply to any of the 453 processes that make or use the organic compounds listed in the proposed regulation. This proposed regulation requires the tracking of all valves, flanges, pumps, seals and open ended valves in a facility determined to be subject to the regulation. A leak detection and maintenance record must be maintained on each and every piece of equipment. This recordkeeping, due to the shear quantity and complexity of records, will require a computer-based data system for the recordkeeping and reporting. At this time, EPA has not issued any guidelines for standard report format for the LDAR program.

An example of the type of information that must be maintained is that each piece of equipment subject to regulation as a Vaporous Hazardous Air Pollutant (VHAP) must be identified by logging the location and description of the equipment. An initial report must be filed with EPA (or the delegated state agency) that describes the equipment, and every six months thereafter a report of each piece of equipment summarizing the results of monitoring, performance tests, changes to the process unit, changes in monitoring frequency, and monitoring alternatives. Records must be maintained on maintenance activities and repairs on each and every piece of equipment.

3.0 PSD and NSR

Prevention of Significant Deterioration (PSD) and New Source Review (NSR) are specific requirements of Part C of the Clean Air Act that deal with sources installed in areas classified as attainment for ambient air quality.

PSD is a federal program that has been delegated to most state agencies, but is still under the purview of the U.S. EPA. New Source Review is a new program that is administered by state agencies. The requirements by which facilities are subject to NSR vary from state to state. This is a program that is reviewed but not administered by EPA, and deals with sources that are smaller than those subject to PSD.

Monitoring and recordkeeping for PSD can begin prior to the actual construction of a facility. For many facilities in certain areas of the country, there are PSD ambient air monitoring requirements. These requirements may include monitoring for ambient air quality as well as for meteorological data. In the case where meteorological data is not available for a period of two years and at close enough proximity to the facility, the proposed facility must monitor ambient air quality data, and this data must meet certain criteria requirements specified in the EPA Guidelines. Likewise, where existing ambient air quality data is not available, one year of ambient air quality data for the regulated pollutant or pollutants in question must be obtained and must meet certain requirements. An example of this would be monitoring for NO_x or SO_2 in an area where there is no monitoring data, and the facility is going to be a major combustion source of those pollutants.

New Source Review pre-construction monitoring requirements can vary from state to state. Typically, states tend to be more lenient with NSR than with PSD, because NSR deals with smaller sized facilities which tend to have less impact on ambient air quality.

3.1 Permit Requirements

PSD and NSR permits are required under the CAA. These permitting requirements can go beyond the current recordkeeping and reporting requirements that may otherwise apply under the CAA. It is not uncommon for a state or the U.S. EPA to include monitoring or reporting requirements above and beyond the minimum required for such a facility under NSPS. For instance, a facility that is going to combust sewage sludge has certain monitoring requirements on the scrubber. The agency may put additional requirements above and beyond simply recording the pressure drop on that scrubber, such as requiring liquid flow measurements on the scrubber or temperature monitoring on the incinerator.

Likewise, a state agency under NSR can put additional permit requirements on sources. The agency typically selects regulatory requirements that would be required of an NSPS facility, even though the facility in question is not subject to NSPS or PSD regulations. For instance, an agency might require continuous emission monitoring or some other type of direct or indirect monitoring such as pH on the scrubber liquor or continuous emissions monitoring requirements on a combustion source for opacity, NO_x, CO, or oxygen.

4.0 COMPLIANCE ORDERS

Compliance orders issued by the EPA or a state agency typically have recordkeeping and recording requirements. These are negotiable items, and may be dictated by the state or EPA. Typically, these are negotiated with the company after a notice of violation (NOV) or non-compliance has been issued, but before an administrative or judicial order may be issued. The conditions that are part of the administrative or judicial order are typically negotiated so that the

20

reporting and recordkeeping requirements tend to be burdensome on the source. One issue to raise in the situation where there are excessive reporting requirements is whether the agency imposing the reporting requirements has the staff or the resources to evaluate the information being submitted. This is a point that should be made if the agency is requiring all records for continuous emission monitoring on a combustion source to be submitted for pollutants such as oxygen, CO, CO_2, NO_x, SO_2 and opacity. Are they indeed going to evaluate all the data the source is submitting? Are they putting undue requirements on that source?

4.1 Direct Monitoring

Direct monitoring is where monitoring occurs for a specific pollutant or diluent. Specific pollutants that are monitored are typically regulated pollutants, for instance, oxides of sulfur, oxides of nitrogen, carbon monoxide, and opacity. These are regulated limits that are measured. Diluents that are related to the emissions in a combustion source are CO_2 and O_2. All of these are direct monitoring; in other words the monitoring that takes place relates directly to emission limits.

4.2 Indirect Monitoring

Indirect monitoring, also called parametric monitoring, will be expanded under the CAAA of 1990. The May 10, 1991 Federal Register proposal for operating permit programs emphasizes the need for monitoring, but not always add-on continuous monitoring. EPA recognizes that a facility may be able to track emissions posed on operating conditions and other indirect measures as opposed to adding new instruments such as continuous emission monitors, especially for some organic chemical processes. Some examples of these are temperature monitoring (reporting and recordkeeping requirements on certain incinerators to be sure that the proper combustion temperatures are maintained); measurement of scrubber liquor where hypochlorite or a caustic scrubber is used; pressure drop across a scrubber; records on electrostatic precipitator performance; maintenance records or records of voltage or current drops, sparks per minute, etc.

4.3 <u>Reporting</u>

The compliance order may have a variety of reporting requirements to the agencies. The simplest of these would be typically where the instruments, either directly or indirectly, indicate there was a violation that occurred, and the duration, date, time, corrective action taken, etc. must be reported to the agency. Some agencies may actually request the reporting be done of all operations or monitoring. This again may be the issue of whether or not the agency has the capacity or manpower to actually evaluate such lengthy reports. Recordkeeping typically would be required above and beyond the malfunction stage, so that the agency could verify upon an audit or inspection that indeed the owner/operator was keeping adequate records. These records would back up what was stated as far as the violation is concerned; that type of recordkeeping is typically required in a compliance order.

5.0 <u>PERMIT REQUIREMENTS</u>

Permits issued by a state or local agency are authorized under the Clean Air Act, may become part of the State Implementation Plan, and any permit requirements can be federally enforceable. If a state agency has made specific permit requirements a part of their state implementation plan, these can be required and enforced as discussed in Section 4.

5.1 <u>Negotiation</u>

As was discussed earlier, permit conditions as with conditions under compliance orders are negotiable, or open to discussion with the state agency. In some cases, negotiations may be a give and take affair, with the facility giving up certain other points on the permit process, such as hours of operation or emission limits. It is up to the compliance source to determine how they can work with the permit conditions. Quite often there is an economic trade-off, when monitoring might be more expensive than limiting hours of operation. In most cases, unless they are explicit in the regulations, permit requirements are a negotiable item with the agencies.

Chapter 3

REPORTING AND RECORDKEEPING REQUIREMENTS UNDER THE COMPREHENSIVE ENVIRONMENTAL RESPONSE, COMPENSATION, AND LIABILITY ACT OF 1980

THEODORE W. FIRETOG
Environmental Counsel
Jaspan, Ginsberg, Schlesinger, Silverman & Hoffman

I. INTRODUCTION

The Comprehensive Environmental Response, Compensation, and Liability Act of 1980, commonly referred to as "Superfund" or "CERCLA," was passed by Congress and signed into law on December 11, 1980.[1] The primary purpose of CERCLA is to provide the funding and authority by which the federal government can effectively respond to the uncontrolled release of hazardous substances from any vessel or facility and to provide the mechanism for cleaning up the hundreds of inactive hazardous waste disposal sites around the country. CERCLA accomplishes its goal not through the use of extensive regulations but by imposing strict cleanup and emergency reporting requirements on a broad class of responsible parties.

The emergency notification requirements of CERCLA are contained in Section 103(a) of the statute. These requirements will be described in Part II of this Chapter. Other reporting requirements of Section 103, as well as those that may be required by specific administrative orders issued pursuant to Section 104 of CERCLA, will be discussed in Part III.

---

[1] 42 U.S.C. § 9601 *et seq*.

II. EMERGENCY NOTIFICATION REQUIREMENTS (SECTION 103(a))

Although CERCLA does not require any type of periodic reporting as may be common, for example, under the Clean Air and Clean Water Acts[2], it does contain certain important emergency notification requirements under Section 103 of the statute.

Specifically, Section 103(a) of CERCLA requires certain persons to immediately notify the National Response Center[3] [at 800-424-8802 (or at 202-267-2675 in the Washington D.C. area)] of an unpermitted release from a vessel or an offshore or an onshore facility into the environment of a hazardous substance in a quantity equal to or greater than the reportable quantity for that substance. The National Response Center, in turn, will then notify all appropriate agencies, as well as the Governor, of any affected state.[4]

Essentially, there are four elements of CERCLA's emergency notification requirements:

1. Certain Persons or Parties

2. Release

3. Hazardous Substance

4. Reportable Quantity

---

[2] 42 U.S.C. § 7401 *et seq.*; 33 U.S.C. § 1251 *et seq.*

[3] The National Response Center was established under the Clean Water Act, and is administered by the United States Coast Guard. *See* 33 U.S.C. § 1321(j).

[4] 42 U.S.C. § 9603(a).

Although the elements of the emergency notifications requirements are conceptually rather simple, in practice, the application of those requirements to a particular situation are not always clear. Who, for example, are the certain persons that must decide if a reportable release has occurred and, therefore, be reported? On what information must that person base his/her/its decision whether or not to notify the National Response Center? How does that person calculate the reportable quantity of the released hazardous substance if the release is intermittent, or the hazardous substance is mixed with unknown wastes? Is circumstantial evidence that a release occurred (*e.g.*, an increase in the level of contaminants in an on-site ground-water monitoring well) sufficient to trigger the notification requirements of CERCLA, or is there a duty to investigate the circumstances of the suspected release? How do the emergency notification requirements under CERCLA affect and interact with the reporting requirements contained in other federal and state statutes and regulations?

In practice, therefore, it becomes sometimes difficult to apply the four basic elements of the emergency notification requirements of Section 103(a) of CERCLA to an actual release. A greater understanding of each element is helpful for understanding how CERCLA's notification requirements may apply to such gray areas.

II.1 Persons Subject to Emergency Notification

The first element of the notification requirements of Section 103(a) focuses on the persons or parties who are required to report a release of a hazardous substance. Under CERCLA, the notification requirements apply to any <u>person</u> in <u>charge</u> of a vessel or facility.[5]

Section 101(21) of CERCLA defines "person" broadly to include an individual, firm, corporation, association, partnership, consortium, joint venture, commercial entity, and governmental body. However, the phrase "person in charge" is not defined in CERCLA or its regulations. Presumably, it refers to, and is more inclusive of, those persons who may be considered "owners" or "operators" pursuant to the liability provisions of Section 107 of the Act.[6]

Indeed, CERCLA case law indicates that the "person in charge" is a person who is in a responsible position to detect, prevent, and abate a release of hazardous substances, and includes low-level supervisory employees, regardless of whether others also exercised control.[7] Therefore, to a certain extent, the question of who is the person in charge of a vessel or facility will be determined on a case-by-case basis. Factors such as the management structure of the facility and the internal reporting procedures of the company may be relevant for making that determination.[8] It is important to remember, however, that there can be more than one person who has the responsibility to make the necessary notification under Section

---

[5]The term "person in charge" is also used in the Clean Water Act (33 U.S.C. § 1321(b)(5)). In contrast, the term "owner or operator" is used in the emergency release notification requirements of Section 304 of the Emergency Planning and Community Right-To-Know Act of 1986 (Title III of the Superfund Amendments and Reauthorization Act of 1986 ("SARA")), hereinafter referred to as "SARA Title III (EPCRA)," 42 U.S.C. §§ 11001-11050.

[6]*See* 42 U.S.C. §§ 9607, 9601(20)(a).

[7]*See* <u>U.S. v. Carr</u>, 880 F.2d 1550 (2nd Cir. 1989).

[8]The U.S. Environmental Protection Agency ("EPA") also has decided to answer the question of who is to be considered a "person in charge" on a case-by-case basis. *See* 50 Fed. Reg. 13456, 13460-61 (Apr. 4, 1985).

103(a). For example, the owner and operator of the facility, as well as the upper management and lower supervisory personnel of the facility may all be responsible (and therefore liable) for complying with CERCLA's notification requirements.

The responsibility of the "person in charge" to comply with the emergency notification requirements of CERCLA arises when that person receives actual knowledge of a release of a hazardous substance (assuming that the other criteria for notification have been satisfied). "Knowledge" refers to the act (*i.e.*, the release) not to the specific requirements or applicability of Section 103(a).

II.2 Releases Requiring Notification

The second element of the emergency notification requirements of Section 103(a) of CERCLA is that there must be a release.

The term "release" is broadly defined in the CERCLA regulations to mean:

> any spilling, leaking, pumping, pouring, emitting, emptying, discharging, injecting, escaping, leaching, dumping, or disposing into the environment.[9]

Basically, the definition includes any way in which a hazardous substance can move from a vessel or facility into the environment.

Under CERCLA, "public vessels" are not exempt from the notification requirements (as they are under the Clean Water Act[10]), and the term

---

[9]40 C.F.R. § 302.3.

[10]*See* 33 U.S.C. §1321(a)(3).

"vessel" includes every description of watercraft or other artificial contrivance used, or capable of being used, for water transportation.[11]

CERCLA's definition of the term "facility" is equally broad, including not only traditional notions of what constitutes a facility (that is, a building, structure, installation, container, motor vehicle, aircraft, etc.) but also encompassing any site or area where a hazardous substance has been deposited, stored, disposed of, or placed, or otherwise comes to be located.[12] Only consumer products in consumer use and vessels are specifically excluded from the definition.

To be considered a release under CERCLA, the hazardous substance, therefore, must move or escape from a vessel or facility into the environment. The statute defines "environment" to include:

- waters of the United States (which include navigable waters, waters of the contiguous zone, ocean waters where the natural resources are under the exclusive management authority of the United States, surface waters, ground water, and drinking water supply);

- land surface or subsurface strata; and

- ambient air.[13]

---

[11]42 U.S.C. § 9601(28).

[12]42 U.S.C. § 9601(9). The term "facility" as used in Section 103 of CERCLA refers to both "onshore" and "offshore" facilities (*i.e.*, facilities located in, on, or under, any land or nonnavigable waters within the United States, as well as, any facilities located in, on, or under, any of the navigable waters or other waters subject to the jurisdiction of the United States).

[13]42 U.S.C. § 9601(8).

Indeed, the only area that apparently is not included in the definition of "environment" is the interior of buildings and other structures. Therefore, a release of a hazardous substance that is contained solely within the confines of a building or other structure would not be subject to the emergency notification requirements of Section 103(a) of CERCLA. If, however, the release escapes to any area outside the building or structure, such as the ambient air, then a reportable release may have occurred.[14]

II.2.1 Excluded Releases

The following do not constitute a "release," as that term is defined in CERCLA[15]:

1. any release which results in exposure to persons solely within a workplace, with respect to a claim which such persons may assert against the employer of such persons[16];

2. emissions from the engine exhausts of a motor vehicle, rolling stock, aircraft, vessel, or pipeline pumping station engine;

3. the release of source, by-product, or special nuclear material from a nuclear incident, as those terms are defined in the Atomic Energy Act of 1954 (42 U.S.C. § 2014 *et seq.*), if the release is subject to the financial protection requirements

---

[14]Note in contrast, that under Section 304 of SARA Title III (EPCRA), a release of a reportable quantity of a hazardous substance is required only if the release results in exposure to persons beyond the facility's boundary. 40 C.F.R. § 355.40(a)(2)(i).

[15]42 U.S.C. § 9601(22).

[16]The EPA interprets this exclusion as applying to a release that occurs in a totally enclosed facility and does not reach the ambient air, water, or soil. *See* 50 Fed. Reg. 13456 (Apr. 4, 1985).

established pursuant to Section 170 of that Act; and

5.   the normal application of fertilizer.

Therefore, any movement of a hazardous substance from a vessel or facility into the environment that falls within any of the four categories above would not constitute a release under the statute, and consequently, would not trigger the notification requirements under CERCLA. In such a case, however, notification or reporting requirements contained in other federal or state statutes may apply.[17]

II.2.2   Exempted Releases

Four major types of releases (which would otherwise be included in the statutory definition of "release") are exempt from the emergency notification requirements of Section 103(a) of CERCLA.[18] These include:

---

[17] For example the Occupational Safety and Health Act ("OSHA"), 29 U.S.C. § 651 *et seq.*, regulates worker exposure to hazardous substances in the workplace.

[18] In addition, four categories of releases of radionuclides are exempt (40 C.F.R. § 302.8):

(1)   Releases of those radionuclides that occur naturally in the soil from land holdings such as parks, golf courses, or other large tracts of land;

(2)   Releases of radionuclides occurring naturally from the disturbance of land for purposes other than mining, such as for agricultural or construction activities;

(3)   Releases of radionuclides from the dumping of coal and coal ash at utility and industrial facilities with coal-fired boilers; and

- Federally Permitted Releases[19];

- Releases Required to be Reported (or are Exempted) Under the Resource Conservation and Recovery Act, *as amended*, 42 U.S.C. § 6901 *et seq.*, ("RCRA")[20];

- Continuous Releases[21]; and

- The Application of a Registered Pesticide, or the Handling and Storage of Such a Pesticide by an Agricultural Producer[22].

II.2.2.1   Exempted Releases: Federally Permitted Releases

The term "federally permitted release" is defined in Section 101(10) of CERCLA to include:

- Any discharge in compliance with a NPDES permit issued pursuant to Section 402 of the Clean Water Act;

- Any discharge in compliance with a legally enforceable dredge or fill permit issued under Section 404 the Clean Water Act;

- Any release in compliance with a legally enforceable final permit issued under RCRA to a hazardous waste treatment, storage, or disposal facility;

---

(4)   Releases of radionuclides from coal and coal ash piles at utility and industrial facilities with coal-fired boilers.

[19]42 U.S.C. § 9603(a).

[20]42 U.S.C. § 9603(f)(1).

[21]42 U.S.C. § 9603(f)(2).

[22]42 U.S.C. § 9603(e).

- Any release in compliance with a legally enforceable ocean dumping permit issued under Section 102 or Section 103 of the Marine Protection, Research and Sanctuaries Act of 1972 (33 U.S.C. § 1401 *et seq.*);

- Any injection of fluids authorized under the underground injection control program established under the Safe Drinking Water Act (42 U.S.C. § 300(f) *et seq.*);

- Any emission into the air that is subject to a permit or control regulation in accordance with the Clean Air Act;

- Any injection of fluids or other materials authorized under state law in the connection with the production and recovery of crude oil and natural gas;

- The introduction of any pollutant into a publicly owned treatment works where the pollutant is specified in and in compliance with applicable pretreatment standards in accordance with Clean Water Act; and

- Any release of source, special nuclear, or byproduct material in compliance with a legally enforceable license, permit, regulation, or order issued pursuant to the Atomic Energy Act of 1954.

If the release, discharge, injection, introduction, or emission is not covered by, or violates the permitted conditions, a reportable release under CERCLA may have occurred. This could arise, for example, if the facility violates the terms of its permit either because:

1. The characteristics of the release (*e.g.,* the character or quantity of the hazardous substance

released) are not in compliance with the applicable permit limits or conditions; or

2.   The release occurs into a medium other than that covered and specified in the applicable permit.[23]

II.2.2.2   Exempted Releases: Releases Under RCRA

As noted above, releases that are in compliance with a final permit issued under RCRA do not have to be reported under the emergency notification requirements of CERCLA -- they are federally permitted releases.[24]   Moreover, any release of a hazardous substance which is required to be reported (or is specifically exempted) under RCRA and which has been already reported to the National Response Center is also exempt from the CERCLA's notification requirements.[25]

II.2.2.3   Exempted Releases: Continuous Releases

With respect to "continuous releases," Section 103(f) of CERCLA states that no notification is required if the release is "continuous" and "stable in quantity and rate"; and is:

---

[23]The EPA had proposed regulations interpreting the scope and types of hazardous substance releases that would be included under the "federally permitted release" exemption. *See* 53 Fed. Reg. 27268 (July 19, 1988). Thus far, however, no regulations have been adopted.

[24]That is, as long as the permit specifically identifies the hazardous substance and makes that substance subject to some sort of control. 42 U.S.C. § 9601(10)(E).

[25]42 U.S.C. § 9603(f)(1).

1.   From a facility that has provided the EPA) with notice under Section 103(c) of CERCLA[26]; or

2.   A release of which notification has been given under CERCLA Section 103(a) for a period sufficient to establish the continuity, quantity, and regularity of the release.

The regulations at 40 C.F.R. § 302.8 set forth the specific requirements for reporting continuous releases under Section 103(a), both with respect to the initial notification and future reporting obligations.

Under the regulations, a continuous release is defined as one that occurs without interruption or abatement or that is routine, anticipated, and intermittent and incidental to normal operations or treatment processes. A release that is "stable in quantity and rate" is defined as one that is predictable and regular in amount and rate of emission.[27]

To qualify as a continuous release under the regulations, there must be an initial telephone notification to the National Response Center once the continuity and stability of the release has been established.[28]

To comply with the initial telephone notification requirement of the regulation, the person in charge of the facility or vessel, must identify the

---

[26] Section 103(c) refers to a one-time notice provision wherein certain facilities must have notified the EPA of their existence. *See* Part III of this Chapter.

[27] 40 C.F.R. § 302.8(b).

[28] The continuity and stability of the release may be established by either:

   (1)   Using release data, engineering estimates, knowledge of operating procedures, or best professional judgment; or

   (2)   Reporting the release to the National Response Center for a period sufficient to establish the continuity and stability of the release. 40 C.F.R. § 302.8(d)(1) and (d)(2).

notification as an initial continuous release notification report and provide the following information to the National Response Center:

- The name and location of the facility or vessel; and

- The name(s) and identity(ies) of the hazardous substance(s) being released.[29]

An initial written notification must be made to the appropriate EPA Regional Office within 30 days of the initial telephone notification, and must include the following information:

- The name of the facility or vessel; the location, including the latitude and longitude; the case number assigned by the National Response Center or the EPA; the Dun and Bradstreet number of the facility, if available; the port of registration of the vessel; and the name and telephone number of the person in charge of the facility or vessel;

- The population density within a one-mile radius of the facility or vessel, described in terms of the following ranges: 0-50 persons, 51-100 persons, 101-500 persons, 501-1,000 persons, more than 1,000 persons;

- The identity and location of sensitive populations and ecosystems within a one-mile radius of the facility or vessel (e.g., elementary schools, hospitals, retirement communities, or wetlands); and

- For each hazardous substance release which is claimed to qualify as a continuous release:

  -- The name/identity of the hazardous substance; the Chemical Abstracts Service Registry Number for the substance (if available); and if the substance being released is a mixture, the

---

[29]40 C.F.R. § 302.8(d)(3).

components of the mixture and their approximate concentrations and quantities, by weight.

-- The upper and lower bounds of the normal range of the release (in pounds or kilograms) over the previous year.

-- The source(s) of the release (*e.g.*, valves, pump seals, storage tank vents, stacks), and if the release is from a stack, the stack height (in feet or meters).

-- The frequency of the release and the fraction of the release from each release source and the specific period over which it occurs.

-- A brief statement describing the basis for concluding that the release is continuous and stable in quantity and rate.

-- An estimate of the total annual amount that was released in the previous year (in pounds or kilograms).

-- The environmental medium(a) affected by the release:

    o   If surface water, the name of the surface water body.

    o   If a stream, the stream order or average flowrate (in cubic feet/second) and designated use.

    o   If a lake, the surface area (in acres) and average depth (in feet or meters).

    o   If on or under ground, the location of public water supply wells within two miles.

-- A signed statement that the hazardous substance release(s) described is(are) continuous and stable in quantity and rate and that all reported information is accurate and current to the best knowledge of the person in charge.[30]

---

[30] 40 C.F.R. § 302.8(e).

Within 30 days of the first anniversary date of the initial written notification, the person in charge of the facility or vessel must evaluate each reported hazardous substance release to verify and update the information that was previously submitted and submit a follow-up notification to the appropriate EPA Regional Office.[31]

Once the initial telephone notification, the initial written notification, and the follow-up notification are made,[32] the regulations do not require any further notification unless:

1.   There is a change in the composition or source of
     the release;

2.   There is a statistically significant increase in the
     quantity of the hazardous substance being
     released; or

3.   There is a change in any of the information
     previously submitted in the initial written
     notification or the follow-up notification.

If there is a change in the composition or source of the release, the release will be considered by the EPA as a new release. It, therefore, must be reported using the initial telephone notification and initial written notification procedures in order to continue to qualify as a continuous release. The initial telephone notification that reports the change in the composition or source of the release should be made as soon as there is a

---

[31]40 C.F.R. § 302.8(f).

[32]In lieu of an initial written report or a follow-up report, an owner or operator of a facility that is subject to the requirements of Section 313 of SARA Title III (EPCRA) may submit to the appropriate EPA Regional Office a copy of the Toxic Release Inventory form submitted under Section 313 the previous July 1. *See* the discussion in the Reporting and Recordkeeping Chapter on the Emergency Planning and Community Right-To-Know Act.

sufficient basis for asserting that the change is continuous and stable in quantity and rate.[33]

If there is a statistically significant increase in hazardous substance being released, notification must be made to the National Response Center as soon as the person in charge of the facility or vessel has knowledge of the increase. The notification must be identified as a statistically significant increase in a continuous release by the person in charge of the facility or vessel.[34] A statistically significant increase is defined as an increase in the quantity of the hazardous substance that is released which is above the upper bound of the reported normal range of the release, with the normal range being defined as all releases of a hazardous substance reported or occurring over any 24-hour period under the preceding year's normal operating conditions.[35]

Changes in any of the information previously submitted in the initial written notification or the follow-up notification (other than a change in the

---

[33]40 C.F.R. § 302.8(g)(1).

[34]40 C.F.R. § 302.8(h).

[35]Only releases that are both continuous and stable in quantity and rate may be included in the normal range. 40 C.F.R. § 302.8(b). If there is a change that results in a number of releases that exceed the upper bound of the normal range, the person in charge of a facility or vessel may modify the normal range by:

-- Reporting at lease one statistically significant increase notification and, at the same time, informing the National Response Center of the change in the normal range; and

-- Submitting, within 30 days of the telephone notification, written notification to the appropriate EPA Regional Office describing the new normal range, the reason for the change, and the basis for stating that the release in the increased amount is continuous and stable in quantity and rate. 40 C.F.R. § 302.8(g)(2).

source, composition, or quantity of the release) must be provided in writing to the appropriate EPA Regional Office within 30 days of a determination that the previously submitted information is no longer valid. The notification must include the reason for the change, and the basis for stating the release is continuous and stable under the changed conditions.[36]

Notification regarding any change in the composition or source of the release, change in the normal range of the release (or a statistically significant increase in the quantity of the hazardous substance being released), or a change in any of the information previously submitted in the initial written notification or in the follow-up notification must include the original case number assigned by the National Response Center or the EPA and a signed certification that the hazardous substance release(s) described is(are) continuous and stable in quantity and rate and that all reported information is accurate and current to the best knowledge of the person in charge.[37]

According to Section 103(f)(2)(B) of CERCLA, notification regarding continuous releases was to be submitted annually. The regulations, however, modified this provision to require, instead, an annual evaluation to determine if changes have occurred in the information already submitted in the initial written notification, the follow-up notification, or any previous change notification.[38]

The documentation that the person in charge may rely upon in making the continuous release notifications includes recent release data, engineering estimates, the operational history of the facility or vessel, or other relevant

---

[36]40 C.F.R. § 302.8(g)(3).

[37]40 C.F.R. § 302.8(g)(4).

[38]40 C.F.R. § 302.8(i).

information to support notification. All supporting documents, materials, and other information must be kept on file at the facility, or in the case of a vessel, at an office within the United States in either a port of call, a place of regular berthing, or the headquarters of the business operating the vessel. Supporting materials and other information in the initial written report, the follow-up report, and the annual evaluations must be kept on file for a period of one year and be made available to the EPA upon request.[39]

II.2.2.4   Exempted Releases: Pesticides

The final type of release that is exempt from the emergency notification requirements of Section 103(a) is the application of a registered pesticide, or the handling and storage of such a pesticide by an agricultural producer. The applicability of this exemption is interpreted by the EPA as being valid only in those instances where a pesticide is being used in

---

[39]40 C.F.R. § 302.8(k). Aside from continuous release notifications, there are no specific requirements concerning the content of emergency release notifications reported under Section 103(a) of CERCLA. It is suggested, however, that any such notifications contain, at a minimum the following information:

- --   The identity of the hazardous substance that was released.
- --   The amount released into the environment, and the media affected.
- --   The time and duration of the release.
- --   Any response action undertaken.
- --   A contact's name, job title, and telephone number.

Additional information may be required if the notification is being made pursuant to Section 304 of SARA Title III (EPCRA). *See* 40 C.F.R. § 355.40(b)(2). Also, aside from continuous release notifications, no written follow-up reports are required under Section 103 of CERCLA, nor are there any references to documenting the release or document retention. It is suggested, however, that a permanent record of the release and the notification be maintained by the facility.

accordance with its approved label directions.[40]   Consequently, any accidental spill of a pesticide would not fall within this exemption and must be reported (assuming that the other criteria for notification have been satisfied).

II.3 Hazardous Substance Requirement

The third element of the emergency notification requirements of Section 103(a) of CERCLA is that such notification only applies to hazardous substances.   The term "hazardous substances" is defined in CERCLA Section 101(14) to include the following:

- Any hazardous substance designated pursuant to Section 1321(b)(2)(A) of the Clean Water Act;

- Any hazardous waste identified or listed pursuant to section 3001 of RCRA;

- Any toxic pollutant listed under Section 307(a) of the Clean Water Act;

- Any hazardous air pollutant listed under Section 112 of the Clean Air Act;

- Any imminently hazardous chemical substances or mixtures regulated by the EPA under Section 7 of the Toxic Substances Control Act (15 U.S.C. § 2601 *et seq.*); and

- Any additional hazardous substance that the EPA may designate as such pursuant to Section 102 of CERCLA.

---

[40]50 Fed Reg. 13456, 13464 (Apr. 4, 1985).

The statutory definition of "hazardous substance," however, specifically excludes petroleum, including crude oil or any fraction thereof,[41] natural gas, natural gas liquids, liquefied natural gas, or synthetic gas usable for fuel (or mixtures of natural gas and such synthetic gas).

A composite list of hazardous substances is contained in 40 C.F.R. Part 302, at Table 302.4. The composite list consists of over 760 listed substances. Also included in Table 302.4 are RCRA listed hazardous wastes (including residues, sludges, and wastewater), toxicity contaminants (on which the characteristic of toxicity is based for those unlisted RCRA hazardous wastes that exhibit toxicity), and radionuclides.

Certain hazardous substances are not listed in Table 302.4. These "unlisted hazardous substances" include unlisted RCRA hazardous wastes that exhibit characteristics of ignitability, corrosivity, reactivity, or toxicity (although the contaminants on which toxicity may be based are listed).

There also may be instances where a substance, which is not a CERCLA hazardous substance, is released into the environment, but upon its release forms a listed or unlisted hazardous substance. In such cases, the reaction product may become a CERCLA hazardous substance subject to the emergency notification requirements of Section 103(a).

II.4 Reportable Quantities

The fourth and final element of the emergency notification requirements of Section 103(a) is the "Reportable Quantity" requirement. That is, an unpermitted release of a hazardous substance from a vessel or facility into the environment must be reported to the National Response

---

[41]Such fraction is excluded as long as it is not specifically listed or designated as a hazardous substance under any of the other statutes that are referenced in CERCLA's definition of a hazardous substance.

Center when any person in charge of the vessel or facility has received actual knowledge of such a release -- but only if the quantity of hazardous substance released equals or exceeds the Reportable Quantity for that substance.

Section 102(a) of CERCLA authorizes the EPA to issue regulations that, among other things, establish or revise for each regulated hazardous substance a Reportable Quantity.[42] A Reportable Quantity (or "RQ") may be defined as the quantity of a hazardous substance which, when released, falls within the reporting requirements of Section 103(a). Five such Reportable Quantities are used: 1, 10, 100, 1000, and 5,000 pounds.[43]

In determining whether the Reportable Quantity of a released hazardous substance has been reached, a period of 24 hours is used.

Table 302.4 in the regulations not only contains the composite list of hazardous substances subject to the reporting requirement, but also sets forth the Reportable Quantity for each substance.

Suppose, for example, there was an unpermitted release of 11 pounds of ammonium picrate into the environment from your facility. By referring to Table 302.4 of the regulations, you would be able to determine that the RQ for that substance is 10 pounds or 4.54 kilograms. Thus, if the release occurred during any 24 hour period, the reporting requirements of Section 103(a) of CERCLA would have been triggered.

---

[42]Unless and until EPA establishes a Reportable Quantity for a regulated hazardous substance, Section 102 specifies that the reportable quantity is to be that established for that substance under the Clean Water Act, or if none has been established, one pound.

[43]This applies to hazardous substances other than radionuclides. For radionuclides, different quantities may apply, and the RQs are given in the radiological unit of measure of curie.

Incidentally, Table 302.4 also contains additional useful information. Again referring to ammonium picrate, you can see that the table identifies its Chemical Abstracts Service Registry Number (CASRN) as 131748, and lists the common regulatory synonyms for the substance (other names by which the substance is identified in other statutes), which include Phenol, 2, 4, 6-trinito-, and ammonium salt. Also, because ammonium picrate is a listed waste under RCRA, the Table includes its RCRA waste number, P009.

Unlisted hazardous substances are not contained in Table 302.4. These substances include RCRA hazardous wastes which were so designated because they exhibit the characteristics of ignitability, corrosivity, reactivity, or toxicity. For those RCRA hazardous wastes that exhibit the characteristics of ignitability, corrosivity, or reactivity an RQ of 100 pounds has been established.

For RCRA hazardous wastes that are designated as such because they exhibit toxicity characteristics, the RQ for such wastes is that which is listed in Table 302.4 for the contaminant on which the toxicity characteristic is based. Remember, however, that the RQ applies to the waste itself, not merely to the toxic contaminant.

In the case of reaction products, the emergency notification requirements of Section 103(a) would be triggered if the regulated hazardous substance formed as a result of the release equals or exceeds the RQ listed in Table 302.4 for that substance.

Because a release often involves a mixture or solution of hazardous substances, the regulations under CERCLA provide the means to calculate the RQ of mixtures and solutions (including hazardous waste streams) and to determine when notification is required.[44] If the quantity of _all_ of the

---

[44]40 C.F.R. § 302.8(b).

hazardous constituents of the mixture or solution is known, notification is required when the RQ of any hazardous constituent released is reached. If the quantity of one or more of the hazardous constituents of the waste is unknown, notification is required when the total amount of the mixture or solution released equals or exceeds the RQ for the hazardous constituent with the lowest RQ.[45]

Finally, the RQ of solid particles of antimony, arsenic, beryllium, cadmium, chromium, copper, lead, nickel, selenium, silver, thallium, and zinc

---

[45]Releases of mixtures or solutions containing radionuclides are subject to the following notification requirements:

(1) If the identity and quantity (in curies) of each radionuclide in a released mixture or solution is known, the ratio between the quantity released (in curies) and the RQ for the radionuclide must be determined for each radionuclide. The only such releases for which the notification requirements apply are those in which the sum of the ratios for the radionuclides in the mixture or solution released is equal to or greater than one.

(2) If the identity of each radionuclide in a released mixture or solution is known but the quantity released (in curies) of one or more of radionuclides is unknown, the only such releases for which the notification requirements apply are those in which to total quantity (in curies) of the mixture or solution released is equal to or greater than the lowest RQ of any individual radionuclide in the mixture or solution.

(3) If the identity of one or more radionuclides in a released mixture or solution is unknown (or if the identity of a radionuclide released by itself is unknown), the only such releases for which the notification requirements apply are those in which the total quantity (in curies) released is equal to or greater than either on curie or the lowest RQ of any known individual radionuclide in the mixture or solution, whichever is lower. 40 C.F.R. § 302.8(b)(2).

does not include particles released whose mean diameter is larger than 100 micrometers (0.004 inches).[46]

II.5 Local Publication of Release Information

Section 111(g) of CERCLA requires the owner and operator of any vessel or facility from which a hazardous substance has been released to provide reasonable notice to potential injured parties by publication of such notice in local newspapers serving the affected area. This notice requirement remains in effect until EPA promulgates specific rules and regulations covering the scope and form of the required notice. The EPA has not issued any rules or regulations pertaining to this Section, probably because the purpose and intent of the requirement has been subsumed by the provisions of SARA Title III (EPCRA).

II.6 Penalties

Section 103(b) of CERCLA provides for criminal penalties which may be imposed on any person in charge of a facility who fails to notify the National Response Center pursuant to Section 103 of CERCLA of a release of a hazardous substance as soon as that person has knowledge of such a release or who submits any information in the notification which that person knows to be false or misleading. Such a person, upon conviction, may be fined (in accordance with Title 18 of the United States Code) up to $250,000 ($500,000 for a corporation) or imprisoned for up to 3 years (or not more than 5 years in the case of a second or subsequent conviction), or both. The information obtained from such notification, however, cannot be used by the government against the person providing such notice or

---

[46]40 C.F.R. § 302.8(d). The RQs for radionuclides apply to chemical compounds containing the radionuclides and elemental forms regardless of the diameter.

information in any criminal case, except in a prosecution for perjury or for giving a false statement.

Although the EPA has increased its criminal enforcement of all environmental statutes generally, by far, most violations of the emergency notification requirements of CERCLA are enforced through administrative actions. Section 109 of CERCLA provides for administrative civil penalties which may be imposed for violations of the statute, including those relating to CERCLA's emergency notification requirements. No element of intent or degree of culpability is required for the imposition of administrative penalties, although such factors may be considered by the Agency in determining the amount of the penalty ultimately assessed. There are two categories of administrative civil penalties which may be imposed for violations of the Section 103(a) of CERCLA:

- Class I Administrative Penalties of not more than $25,000 per violation.

- Class II Administrative Penalties of not more than $25,000 per day for each day during which the violation continues. (In the case of a second or subsequent violation, the amount of the Class II penalty may be increased to not more than $75,000 for each day during which the violation continues.)

A Class I administrative penalty can be imposed with minimal procedural formalities and without a hearing on the record. However, no penalty may be assessed unless the person accused of the violation is given notice and an opportunity for a hearing with respect to the violation. In determining the amount of the penalty, the EPA must take into account the nature, circumstances, extent and gravity of the violation and the violator's ability to pay, any prior history of such violations, the degree of culpability, and any economic benefit or savings which resulted from the violation and such other matters as justice may require.

Class II administrative penalties must be assessed and collected after notice and an opportunity for a hearing on the record in accordance with the procedures set forth in the Administrative Procedures Act, 5 U.S.C. § 554.

Violations of the emergency notification requirements of CERCLA may also be enforced through proceedings brought in United States district courts. Such judicial assessments of civil penalties carry the same penalties as Class II administrative actions.

III. OTHER CERCLA REPORTING REQUIREMENTS

In addition to the emergency notification requirements of Section 103(a) of CERCLA, Section 103 contains a one-time notice provision. Under Section 103(c), any person who owned or operated a facility at which hazardous substances were stored, treated or disposed of, and such a facility had not been issued a permit under, or had been accorded interim status under RCRA, must have notified the EPA by June 9, 1981, of the existence of the facility, specifying the amount and type of any hazardous substance to be found there, and any known, suspected, or likely releases of such substances. Pursuant to Section 103(d), records are to be kept on such facilities for a period of fifty years, beginning with December 11, 1980 or the date of establishment of such records (whichever is later).[47] Failure to conform with §103(d) can result in a Title 18 fine and/or up to 3 years in

---

[47] Furthermore, it is unlawful for any person knowingly to destroy, mutilate, erase, dispose of, conceal, or otherwise render unavailable or unreadable or falsify any such records. 42 U.S.C. § 9603(d)(2).

prison (or not more than 5 years in the case of a second or subsequent conviction).

Section 104 of CERCLA provides the authority by which the government may respond to the release or to the substantial threat of a release into the environment of any hazardous substance or of any pollutant or contaminant which may present an imminent and substantial danger to the public health or welfare. Pursuant to Sections 104(b) and 104(e)(1) the Administrator may undertake such investigations and other information gathering as he or she may deem necessary or appropriate to identify the existence and extent of the release or threat of release or the need for response actions. In exercising the Administrator's authority under these Sections, it is the EPA's position that the Administrator can issue specific compliance orders which would require the reporting of such information.

Chapter 4

THE EMERGENCY PLANNING AND
COMMUNITY RIGHT-TO-KNOW ACT

Wayne T. Halbleib

Counsel
Mays & Valentine
Richmond, Virginia

1.0   OVERVIEW

On October 17, 1986, the "Superfund Amendments and Reauthorization Act of 1986" ("SARA") was signed into law. One part of the SARA legislation is Title III, otherwise known as the "Emergency Planning and Community Right-To-Know Act of 1986" ("EPCRA"). EPCRA requires states to establish a process for developing local chemical emergency preparedness programs and to receive and disseminate information on hazardous chemicals present at facilities within local communities.

EPCRA has four major components: (1) emergency planning (Sections 301-303); (2) emergency release notification (Section 304); community right-to-know reporting (Sections 311-312); and toxic chemical release inventory reporting (Section 313). Each component has its own facility and chemical substance reporting requirements. The information submitted by facilities under these four reporting requirements allows States and local communities to develop a broad perspective of chemical hazards for the entire community as well as for individual facilities.

2.0   EMERGENCY PLANNING

2.1   Overview

Section 301 of EPCRA requires the Governor of each state to designate a State Emergency Response Commission ("SERC"). The SERC is required to designate emergency planning districts within each state to facilitate the preparation and implementation of the emergency plans required under Section 303. In addition, Section 301 requires the SERC to appoint a local emergency planning committee ("LEPC") in each of those districts.[1]

---

[1]*See,* 42 U.S.C.A. § 11001(a)-(c).

2.2   Covered Facilities and Substances

Section 302 of EPCRA requires any facility that produces, uses or stores any of the substances on the U.S. Environmental Protection Agency's ("EPA's") List of Extremely Hazardous Substances in quantities equal to or greater than the threshold planning quantity established for each substance to notify the SERC.[2] A list of the extremely hazardous substances and their threshold planning quantities is contained in the EPA's *Title III List of Lists*.[3]

If a facility is covered by Section 302, the owner or operator of the facility should have notified the SERC by May 17, 1987, that the facility is subject to the emergency planning requirements. After May 17, 1987, the owner or operator must notify the SERC and the LEPC, within 60 days, if an extremely hazardous substance ("EHS") becomes present at the facility in a quantity that equals or exceeds the established threshold planning quantity ("TPQ").[4]

A covered facility must designate a facility representative who will participate in the local emergency planning process as a facility emergency response coordinator. In addition, the facility owner or operator must submit additional information to the LEPC upon request and notify the LEPC of any changes occurring at the facility which may be relevant to emergency planning (e.g., change in person designated as facility emergency response coordinator; any material change in the inventory of EHSs maintained by the facility).[5]

EHSs that are solids are subject to two threshold planning quantities as shown on the *Title III List of Lists* (i.e., 500/10,000 pounds). The lower quantity applies only if the solid exists in powdered form and has a particle size less than 100 microns; or is handled in solution or in molten form; or meets the criteria for a National Fire Protection Association ("NFPA") rating of 2, 3 or 4 for reactivity. If the solid does not meet any of the above-mentioned criteria, it is subject to the upper (10,000 pound) threshold planning quantity.[6]

2.3   Comprehensive Emergency Response Plans

Each LEPC is responsible for reviewing the information submitted by facilities covered by the emergency planning requirements and developing a plan to respond to local hazardous chemical emergency releases.[7] The local emergency response plan must:[8]

1.   Identify all the facilities subject to the emergency planning requirements within the emergency planning district;

---

[2]*See*, 42 U.S.C.A. § 11002(b)-(c); 40 C.F.R. § 355.30.

[3]*See*, EPA's *Title III List of Lists*, Document No. EPA 560/4-92-011 or Appendix A or Appendix B to 40 C.F.R. Part 355 for a list of the extremely hazardous substances.

[4]*See*, 42 U.S.C.A. § 11002(c); 40 C.F.R. § 355.30(b).

[5]*See*, 42 U.S.C.A. § 11003(d); 40 C.F.R. § 355.30(c) and (d).

[6]*See*, 40 C.F.R. § 355.30(e)(2)(i).

[7]*See*, 42 U.S.C.A. § 11003.

[8]*See*, 42 U.S.C.A. § 11003(c).

2.   Identify all routes within the emergency planning district used to transport extremely hazardous substances;

3.   Identify all risk-related facilities near covered facilities, such as natural gas facilities, power stations/high transmission towers, or schools or hospitals, within the emergency planning district;

4.   Describe the methods and procedures that will be followed by emergency response personnel to respond to a chemical release within the emergency planning district;

5.   Designate the community emergency response coordinator and identify all the facility emergency response coordinators within the emergency planning district;

6.   Describe the emergency notification procedures to be used to notify the public of a chemical release and the evacuation plans to be implemented in the event a chemical emergency requires an evacuation;

7.   Specify the methods for determining whether a chemical release has occurred and the probable affected area and population;

8.   List all community and facility emergency equipment or facilities available and their location as well as the persons responsible for them; and

9.   Describe the training program used to train emergency response personnel for chemical emergencies and list a schedule for exercising the emergency response plan within the emergency planning district.

Although the primary responsibility for emergency planning rests with the LEPC, the SERC must review each local chemical emergency response plan. The SERC must review each plan to determine whether all required plan elements have been included. In addition, the SERC's review will include recommendations to the LEPC on revisions to the plan that may be necessary to ensure coordination of the plan with the emergency response plans of other emergency planning districts.[9]

3.0.   EMERGENCY RELEASE NOTIFICATION

3.1   Covered Releases

Under Section 304 of EPCRA, the owner or operator of a facility which either produces, uses or stores a hazardous chemical must immediately notify the SERC and the LEPC if there is a release of a listed hazardous substance that is not federally permitted and which exceeds the reportable quantity ("RQ") established for that substance and results in exposure to persons off-site.[10] Substances subject to this notification requirement include substances on the EPA's List of EHSs and hazardous substances

---

[9]*See*, 42 U.S.C.A. § 11003(e).

[10]*See*, 40 C.F.R. § 355.40(a).

subject to the emergency notification requirements under Section 103(a) of the Comprehensive Environmental Response, Compensation and Liability Act of 1980 ("CERCLA").[11]

3.2   Notification Requirements

The initial notification of a release can be made by telephone, radio or in person. The owner or operator of a covered facility must immediately notify the community emergency coordinator for the LEPC of any area likely to be affected by the release and the SERC of any State likely to be affected by the release.[12] In addition, when there is a reportable release of a CERCLA listed hazardous substance, notification must be given to the National Response Center ("NRC") in Washington, D.C. at 1-800-424-8802.[13] The notifications made under EPCRA are in addition to the notifications normally made to local emergency response or fire personnel.

3.3   Contents of Notice

The emergency notification must include, to the extent known at the time of the release, the following information:[14]

1.   Name of the chemical substance involved;

2.   Indication of whether it is an extremely hazardous substance;

3.   Estimate of the amount released into the environment;

4.   Time and duration of the release;

5.   Environmental media into which the release occurred;

6.   Known or anticipated acute or chronic health risks associated with the release and advice regarding medical attention necessary for exposed individuals;

7.   Proper precautions to be taken as a result of the release, including evacuation; and

8.   Name and telephone number of a person at the facility to be contacted for further information.

---

[11]*Ibid.*

[12]*See,* 40 C.F.R. § 355.40(b).

[13]*See,* 40 C.F.R. § 302.6(a).

[14]*See,* 40 C.F.R. § 355.40(b)(2).

3.4 Written Follow-up Emergency Notice

Section 304 further requires that the owner or operator of a covered facility provide a written follow-up emergency notice as soon as possible after the release.[15] The notice must be sent to the appropriate SERC(s) and the appropriate LEPC(s). The follow-up notice must include the following information:[16]

1. An update of the information included in the initial release notification;

2. Information on actions taken to respond to and contain the release;

3. Any known or anticipated acute or chronic health risks associated with the release; and

4. Where appropriate, advice regarding medical attention for exposed individuals.

The written follow-up notice must be sent to the appropriate SERC(s) and the appropriate LEPC(s).

3.5 Transportation-Related Releases

The owner or operator of a facility from which there is a transportation-related release can satisfy the emergency release notification requirements under Section 304 by providing the above-mentioned information required during the initial notification to the 911 operator, or in the absence of a 911 emergency telephone, providing such information to the operator.[17] A "transportation-related release" includes a release during transportation, or storage incident to transportation if the stored substance is moving under active shipping papers and has not reached the ultimate consignee.[18]

3.6 Continuous Release Reporting

Reporting requirements for "continuous" releases of hazardous substances under CERCLA were issued by the EPA on July 24, 1990. Under the final rule, which became effective on September 24, 1990, releases that qualify as "continuous" and that are "stable in quantity and rate" are subject to reduced reporting under CERCLA § 103(f)(2).[19]

---

[15]*See,* 42 U.S.C.A. § 11004(c); 40 C.F.R. § 355.40(b)(3).

[16]*Ibid.*

[17]*See,* 42 U.S.C.A. § 11004(b)(1); 40 C.F.R. § 355.40(b)(4)(ii).

[18]*See,* 40 C.F.R. § 355.40(b)(4)(ii).

[19]*See,* 55 Fed.Reg. 30185 (July 24, 1990); 40 C.F.R. § 302.8.

The final rule defines "continuous" broadly to include a "release that occurs without interruption or abatement or that is routine, anticipated, and intermittent and incidental to normal operations or treatment processes." The definition of "stable in quantity and rate" includes a "release that is predictable and regular in amount and rate of emission."[20]

3.7 Continuous Release Notification

The new rule requires a minimum of one telephone call to the NRC under CERCLA § 103(a) and to the appropriate SERC(s) and LEPC(s) under EPCRA § 304. In addition, within 30 days of the initial telephone notification, an initial written notification must be made to the appropriate EPA Regional Office, the appropriate SERC(s), and the appropriate LEPC(s).

3.8 Initial Telephone Notification

To satisfy the initial telephone notification requirement, the person in charge of a facility or vessel must identify the release in the telephone call to the NRC, the appropriate SERC(s), and the appropriate LEPC(s) as a report under CERCLA § 103(f)(2) of a continuous release above the RQ.[21] The following information must be provided for each release:[22]

1. The name and location of the facility or vessel; and

2. The name(s) and identity(ies) of the hazardous substance(s) being released.

3.9 Initial Written Report

The initial written report must include the following information:[23]

1. The name of the facility or vessel; the location, including the longitude and latitude; the case number assigned by the NRC or the EPA; the Dun & Bradstreet number of the facility, if available; the port of registration of the vessel; the name and telephone number of the person in charge of the facility or vessel.

2. The population density within a one-mile radius of the facility or vessel, described in terms of the following ranges: 0-50 persons; 51-100 persons; 101-500 persons; 501-1,000 persons; more than 1,000 persons.

3. The identity and location of sensitive populations and ecosystems within a one-mile radius of the facility or vessel (e.g. elementary schools, hospitals, retirement communities, or wetlands).

---

[20]*See,* 40 C.F.R. § 302.8(b).

[21]*See,* 40 C.F.R. § 302.8(d)(3).

[22]*See,* 40 C.F.R. § 302.8(d)(3)(i)-(ii).

[23]*See,* 40 C.F.R. § 302.8(e)(1).

4.   The name/identity of the hazardous substance; the Chemical Abstracts Service ("CAS") Registry Number for the substance, if available. If the substance being released is a mixture, the components of the mixture and their approximate concentrations and quantities by weight.

5.   The upper and lower bounds of the normal range of the release (in pounds or kilograms) over the previous year.

6.   The source(s) of the release (e.g., valves, pump seals, storage tank vents, stacks). If the source is a stack, the stack height (in feet or meters).

7.   The frequency of the release and the fraction of the release from each release source and the specific period over which it occurs.

8.   A brief statement describing the basis for stating that the release is continuous and stable in quantity and rate.

9.   An estimate of the total annual amount of the hazardous substance that was released in the previous year (in pounds or kilograms).

10.   The environmental media affected by the release:

a.   If surface water, the name of the surface water body.

b.   If a stream, the stream order or average flowrate (in cubic feet/second) and designated use.

c.   If a lake, the surface area (in acres) and average depth (in feet or meters).

d.   If on or under ground, the location of public water supply wells within two miles.

11.   A signed statement that the hazardous substance release(s) described is(are) continuous and stable in quantity and rate and that all reported information is accurate and current to the best knowledge of the person in charge.

3.10   Follow-up Notification

Within 30 days of the first anniversary date of the initial written notification, the person in charge must evaluate the reported releases and submit a one-time follow-up report to the appropriate EPA Regional Office. The purpose of this report is to verify or update the information submitted in the initial written report.[24]

---

[24]*See,* 40 C.F.R. § 302.8(f).

3.11   Annual Evaluation of Continuous Releases

After the submission of the follow-up report, the person in charge must reevaluate annually each reported hazardous substance release within 30 days of the anniversary date of the initial written notification to determine whether there have been changes in the release that require modification of the information previously submitted.[25] Each annual evaluation must be documented, but no annual report or notification of the annual evaluation is required. Notification subsequent to the written follow-up report must be made to the appropriate EPA Regional Office only if there is a change in any of the information submitted previously.[26]

3.12   Change in the Composition or Source of the Release

If there is a change in the composition or source(s) of the release, the release is considered a "new" release. To qualify a "new" release for reduced reporting under CERCLA § 103(f)(2), both the initial telephone notification and the initial written notification must be made. The initial telephone notification should be made as soon as there is a sufficient basis for asserting that the "new" release is continuous and stable in quantity and rate.[27]

3.13   Notification of a Statistically Significant Increase

A "statistically significant increase" must be reported immediately by telephone to the NRC, the appropriate SERC(s) and the appropriate LEPC(s). A statistically significant increase in a release is defined as "an increase in the quantity of the hazardous substance released above the upper bound of the reported normal range of the release."[28] The normal range is defined to include all releases of a hazardous substance reported or occurring during any 24-hour period under normal operating conditions during the previous year.[29]

Because such a release is considered episodic, it must be reported under CERCLA § 103(a) and EPCRA § 304(b). The release must be identified by the person in charge as a statistically significant increase in a continuous release. The written follow-up emergency notice required under § 304 of EPCRA must also be made to the appropriate SERC(s) and LEPC(s) after the initial telephone notification of a statistically significant increase.[30]

---

[25]*See*, 40 C.F.R. § 302.8(i).

[26]*See*, 40 C.F.R. § 302.8(g).

[27]*See*, 40 C.F.R. § 302.8(g)(1).

[28]*See*, 40 C.F.R. § 302.8(b).

[29]*Ibid.*

[30]*See*, 40 C.F.R. § 355.40(b).

3.14   Changes in Other Reported Information

If there is a change in any information submitted in the initial written notification or the follow-up notification other than a change in the source, composition, or quantity of the release, the person in charge of the facility or vessel must provide written notification of the change to the appropriate EPA Regional Office within 30 days of determining that the information submitted previously is no longer valid.[31]

3.15   Use of the EPCRA Section 313 Form

In lieu of an initial written report or a follow-up report on a continuous release, owners or operators of facilities subject to the EPCRA Section 313 reporting requirements can submit to the appropriate EPA Regional Office, a copy of the relevant Toxic Chemical Release Inventory Reporting Form submitted to EPA the previous July 1st. If this option is selected, however, facility owners or operators must submit the following additional information:[32]

1. The population density within a one-mile radius of the facility or vessel, described in terms of the following ranges: 0-50 persons; 51-100 persons; 101-500 persons; 501-1,000 persons; more than 1,000 persons;

2. The identity and location of sensitive populations and ecosystems within a one-mile radius of the facility or vessel (e.g., elementary schools, hospitals, retirement communities, or wetlands);

3. The upper and lower bounds of the normal range of the release (in pounds or kilograms) over the previous year;

4. The frequency of the release and the fraction of the release from each release source and the specific period over which it occurs;

5. A brief statement describing the basis for stating that the release is continuous and stable in quantity and rate; and

6. A signed statement that the hazardous substance release(s) is(are) continuous and stable in quantity and rate and that all reported information is accurate and current to the best knowledge of the person in charge.

The person in charge can rely on recent release data, engineering estimates, the operating history of the facility or vessel, or other relevant information, including best professional judgment, to support notification. All supporting documents, materials, and other information shall be kept on file at the facility, or in the case of a vessel, at an office within the United States in either a port of call, a place of regular berthing, or the headquarters of the business operating the vessel. Supporting materials must be kept on file for one year. These materials must be made available to the EPA upon request.[33]

---

[31]*See*, 40 C.F.R. § 302.8(g)(3).

[32]*See*, 40 C.F.R. § 302.8(j).

[33]*See*, 40 C.F.R. § 302.8(k).

4.0   COMMUNITY RIGHT-TO-KNOW REPORTING

There are two community right-to-know reporting requirements contained within Sections 311 and 312 of EPCRA. Facilities covered under Section 311 are covered also under Section 312.

4.1   MSDS/List of Hazardous Chemicals

4.1.1   Overview

Section 311 requires the owner/operator of a facility which must prepare or have available material safety data sheets ("MSDSs") under the Occupational Safety and Health Administration's ("OSHA's") Hazard Communication Standard regulations to submit either copies of its MSDSs or a list of hazardous chemicals to the SERC, the LEPC and the local fire department ("LFD") with jurisdiction over the facility.[34] Most SERCs either require or encourage owners or operators of covered facilities to submit a "list" of hazardous chemicals grouped by health and physical hazard categories as defined by EPA in lieu of submitting the MSDS on each hazardous chemical.

4.1.2   Submission of a List of Hazardous Chemicals

If the facility owner or operator elects to submit a list of hazardous chemicals, the list must include the chemical or common name of each substance and it must identify the applicable hazard categories. The hazard categories are as follows:

1.   *Immediate (acute) health hazard* (which includes the OSHA health hazard categories: "highly toxic," "toxic," "corrosive," "irritant," and "sensitizer");

2.   *Delayed (chronic) health hazard* (which includes the OSHA-defined "carcinogen");

3.   *Fire hazard* (which includes the OSHA physical hazard categories: "combustible liquid," "flammable," "oxidizer," and "pyrophoric");

4.   *Sudden release of pressure hazard* (which includes the OSHA physical hazard categories: "compressed gas," and "explosive"); and

5.   *Reactive hazard* (which includes the OSHA physical hazard categories: "organic peroxide," "unstable reactive," and "water reactive").[35]

If the facility elects to submit a list, it must submit a copy of the MSDS for any chemical on the list upon the request of the SERC or the LEPC within 30 days of the receipt of such request.[36] EPA has established minimum threshold quantities for reporting hazardous chemicals present at a facility. The threshold levels are as follows:

---

[34]*See, also,* 40 C.F.R. § 370.21.

[35]*See,* 40 C.F.R. § 370.2.

[36]*See,* 40 C.F.R. § 370.21(d).

1.   "Hazardous chemicals" present in amounts equal to or greater than 10,000 pounds; and

2.   "Extremely hazardous substances" present in amounts equal to or greater than 500 pounds or the threshold planning quantity established for the substance, whichever is lower.

4.1.3   Reporting Requirements

The owners or operators of facilities subject to the reporting requirements under Section 311 had until October 17, 1990 to submit the required information. The owners or operators of new facilities (i.e., those opening after October 17, 1990) that are covered by the OSHA regulations must submit MSDSs or a list of MSDS chemicals within three months after they first become subject to the OSHA regulations.[37]

The owner or operator of a covered facility must provide within three months either MSDSs or a revised list of MSDS chemicals when new hazardous chemicals become present at a facility in quantities at or above the established threshold levels after the deadline.[38] The owner or operator of a covered facility must provide a revised MSDS within three months after discovery of significant new information concerning the hazardous chemical.[39]

4.1.4   Mixture Reporting

The vast majority of chemicals subject to reporting under Section 311 will be mixtures. The owner or operator of a covered facility has two options with respect to reporting hazardous mixtures. The first option is to provide the required information on the mixture itself. The second option is to provide the required information on each component in the mixture which is a hazardous chemical.[40]

The above-mentioned threshold levels apply to the *total quantity* of either the hazardous mixture, or each hazardous component that is present, at the facility at any time during the preceding calendar year. A hazardous component of a mixture which is present in an amount greater than 1% of the mixture (or 0.1% if carcinogenic) must be included when calculating the total quantity of the chemical subject to reporting.

The regulations require the owner or operator of a covered facility to *aggregate* (i.e., total) each extremely hazardous substance, whether it is present as a mixture component, or in its pure form, to determine whether the reporting threshold for an extremely hazardous substance has been met.[41] Aggregation of hazardous chemicals that are not extremely hazardous substances present in mixtures and in their pure form is not required, but may be done if a facility is reporting all hazardous chemicals in mixtures by component.

---

[37]*See,* 55 Fed. Reg. 30646 (July 26, 1990); 40 C.F.R § 370.20(b)(1).

[38]*See,* 40 C.F.R. § 370.21(c)(2).

[39]*See,* 40 C.F.R. § 370.21(c)(1).

[40]*See,* 40 C.F.R. § 370.28(a).

[41]*See,* 55 Fed. Reg. 30646 (July 26, 1990); 40 C.F.R § 370.28(c)(1).

Once the determination is made that an extremely hazardous substance must be reported, the owner or operator of the facility has the option of reporting the extremely hazardous substance separately, as a component of one or several different mixtures, or reporting the mixture(s) as a whole.[42]

4.2 Tier One/Tier Two Reporting

4.2.1 Overview

Section 312 requires the owner or operator of a covered facility to submit an emergency and hazardous chemical inventory form to the VERC, the LEPC and the LFD. The hazardous chemicals covered by Section 312 are the same chemicals for which facilities are required to submit MSDSs or a list of MSDS chemicals under Section 311. In addition, the threshold levels established for reporting under Section 312 are the same as those established for reporting under Section 311.[43]

4.2.2 Reporting Requirements

The inventory form incorporates a two-tier approach. Under Tier One, the owner or operator of a covered facility must submit for each health and physical hazard category the following aggregate information:

1. An estimate (in ranges) of the maximum amount of hazardous chemicals for each category present at the facility at any time during the preceding calendar year;

2. An estimate (in ranges) of the average daily amount of hazardous chemicals in each category; and

3. The general location of hazardous chemicals in each category.

Tier One information must be submitted on or before March 1st of the first year after a covered facility becomes subject to the reporting. The owner or operator of a covered facility is required to submit the Tier One information every year on or before March 1st.[44]

The public may also request additional information on specific facilities from the SERC or the LEPC. In addition, upon the request of the SERC, the LEPC or the LFD, the facility must provide for each substance covered by the request the following information:

1. The chemical name or the common name of the chemical and the CAS registry number as provided on the MSDS;

2. An indication of whether the hazardous chemical is an extremely hazardous substance;

---

[42]*See,* 40 C.F.R. § 370.28(c)(2).

[43]*See,* 40 C.F.R. § 370.20(b).

[44]*See,* 40 C.F.R. § 370.20(b)(2).

3.   An indication of whether the hazardous chemical is present at the facility in its pure state or in a mixture and whether it is a solid, liquid or gas;

4.   The applicable health and physical hazard categories;

5.   An estimate (in ranges) of the maximum amount of the hazardous chemical present at the facility at any time during the preceding calendar year;

6.   An estimate (in ranges) of the average daily amount of the hazardous chemical present at the facility during the preceding calendar year;

7.   The number of days the hazardous chemical was found on-site at the facility;

8.   A brief description of the manner of storage of the hazardous chemical at the facility;

9.   A brief description of the precise location of the hazardous chemical at the facility; and

10.   An indication of whether the owner or operator of the facility elects to withhold location information on a specific hazardous chemical from disclosure to the public.

This information is usually submitted as a Tier Two report. A covered facility may submit a Tier Two report to the SERC, the LEPC and the LFD in lieu of the Tier One report. EPA published a uniform format for the inventory forms on July 26, 1990.[45] The Tier Two report is preferred by most SERCs, LEPCs, and LFDs because of the chemical specific information it contains.

If the owner or operator of a covered facility elects to withhold location information on a specific chemical from disclosure to the public, the facility owner or operator must complete a separate Tier Two Confidential Location Information Sheet. When the Tier Two submissions are made, the Tier Two Confidential Location Information Sheet(s) must be attached to the Tier Two Inventory Form. The information contained on the Tier Two Confidential Location Information Sheet(s) is not subject to public disclosure.

5.0 TOXIC CHEMICAL RELEASE INVENTORY REPORTING

5.1. Overview

Section 313 of EPCRA requires the owners or operators of certain manufacturing facilities to submit annual reports on the amounts of listed "toxic chemicals" their facilities release into the environment, either routinely or as a result of an accident. The owners or operators of facilities subject to this reporting requirement must report releases to the air, water and land as well as discharges to publicly owned treatment works ("POTWs") and transfers to off-site locations for proper treatment, storage, or disposal. The initial reports were required to be submitted to EPA and a designated State official on or before July 1, 1988, and annually thereafter on July 1st, reflecting releases during each preceding calendar year.

---

[45]*See*, 55 Fed. Reg. 30632 (July 26, 1990); 40 C.F.R. §§ 370.40 and 370.41.

5.2 Reporting Requirements

The Section 313 reporting requirement applies to owners and operators of facilities that are in Standard Industrial Classification ("SIC") Codes 20 through 39; that have ten or more full-time employees; and that manufacture, import, process or otherwise use a listed toxic chemical in excess of established threshold quantities.[46]

A "full-time employee", for purposes of Section 313 reporting, is defined as 2,000 hours per year of full-time equivalent employment. This definition is dependent *only* upon the number of hours worked by all employees at the facility during the calendar year and *not* the number of persons working. A facility must calculate the number of full-time employees by totaling the hours worked during the calendar year by all employees, including contract employees, and dividing that total by 2,000 hours.[47] If the total number of hours worked by *all* employees is 20,000 hours or more, the facility meets the ten employee threshold.

Section 313 requires that reports be filed by the owners or operators of "facilities" which are defined as "all buildings, equipment, structures, and other stationary items which are located on a single site or on contiguous or adjacent sites and which are owned or operated by the same person." The SIC code system, however, classifies business "establishments," which are defined as "distinct and separate economic activities [that] are performed at a single physical location." Many facilities may include multiple establishments that have different primary SIC codes. Such facilities should calculate the *value* of the products produced or shipped from each establishment within the facility and determine whether the facility meets the SIC code criteria by using the following rules:

1. If the total value of the products shipped from or produced at establishments with primary SIC codes between 20 and 39 is greater than 50 percent of the value of the entire facility's products and services, the entire facility meets the SIC code criteria; and

2. If any one establishment with a primary SIC code between 20 and 39 produces or ships products whose value exceeds the value of products and services produced or shipped by any other establishment within the facility, the facility meets the SIC code criteria.[48]

The term "manufacture" means to produce, prepare, compound, or import a listed toxic chemical. The term "manufacture" also includes coincidental production of a toxic chemical (e.g., as a by-product or impurity) as a result of the manufacture, processing, use, or treatment of other chemical substances.[49] In the case of coincidental production of an *impurity* (i.e., a chemical that remains in the product that is distributed in commerce), the *de minimis* limitation applies. Thus, if a listed toxic chemical is present as an impurity in a concentration of 1 percent (0.1% if the listed toxic chemical is a carcinogen) or less, the

---

[46]*See*, 40 C.F.R. § 372.65(a) for a list of the chemicals subject to reporting under Section 313. In a proposed rule issued on January 12, 1994, EPA proposed the addition of 313 additional chemicals to the list of toxic chemicals subject to reporting under Section 313. EPA intends to evaluate the comments on its proposal and issue a final rule by November 30, 1994. *See*, 59 *Fed. Reg.* 1788, January 12, 1994.

[47]*See*, 40 C.F.R. § 372.3.

[48]*See*, 40 C.F.R. § 372.22.

[49]*See*, 40 C.F.R. § 372.3.

quantity of that chemical need not be considered for purposes of determining whether a reporting threshold has been met.[50]

The *de minimis* limitation does *not* apply to the coincidental production of a by-product (e.g., a chemical that is separated from a process stream and further processed or disposed). Certain listed toxic chemicals may be manufactured as a result of wastewater treatment or other treatment processes. For example, neutralization of nitric acid wastewater with ammonia can result in the coincidental manufacture of ammonium nitrate solution as a by-product. Thus, if the ammonium nitrate solution is produced in a quantity that exceeds the applicable threshold, the facility must report for ammonium nitrate solution.

The term "import" is defined as causing the listed toxic chemical to be imported into the customs territory of the United States.[51] When a facility orders a listed toxic chemical (or a mixture containing the chemical) from a foreign supplier, then the facility has imported the chemical when that shipment arrives at the facility directly from a source outside of the United States.

The term "process" means the preparation of a listed toxic chemical, after its manufacture, for distribution in commerce. Processing is usually the intentional incorporation of a toxic chemical into a product. Processing includes preparation of the chemical in the same physical state or chemical form as that received by the facility, or preparation that produces a change in physical state or chemical form. The term also applies to the processing of a mixture or other trade name product that contains a listed toxic chemical as one component.[52]

The term "process" would include use of the listed toxic chemical as (1) a reactant; (2) a formulation component; or (3) a component of an article distributed for trade, industrial or consumer use. The term "process" also would include the repackaging of a listed toxic chemical for distribution in commerce in a different form, state, or quantity.

The term "otherwise use" encompasses any use of a listed toxic chemical at a facility that is not covered under the definitions of "manufacture" or "process."[53] A chemical that is otherwise used by a facility is *not* intentionally incorporated into a product distributed in commerce. The term "otherwise use" would include use of the listed toxic chemical as (1) a cleaner; (2) a degreaser; (3) a fuel; (4) a lubricant; (5) a chemical used for treating waste; (6) a chemical processing aid (e.g., process solvents, catalysts, inhibitors, initiators, reaction terminators, and solution buffers); or (7) as a manufacturing aid (e.g., process lubricants, metalworking fluids, coolants, refrigerants, and hydraulic fluids).

5.3 Exemptions

Certain uses of listed toxic chemicals are specifically exempted: (1) use as a structural component of the facility; (2) use in routine janitorial or facility grounds maintenance, provided the product is similar in type or concentration to consumer products; (3) personal uses by employees or other persons at the facility of foods, drugs, cosmetics, or other personal items containing listed toxic chemicals; (4) use of products containing toxic chemicals for the purpose of maintaining motor vehicles operated by the facility; and (5)

---

[50]*See,* 40 C.F.R. § 372.38.

[51]*See,* 40 C.F.R. § 372.3.

[52]*See,* 40 C.F.R. § 372.3.

[53]*See,* 40 C.F.R. § 372.3.

use of listed toxic chemicals contained in intake water (used for processing or non-contact cooling) or in intake air (used either as compressed air or for combustion).[54]

The owner or operator of a covered facility does not have to factor into threshold or release determinations the quantities of a listed toxic chemical contained in an "article" when that article is processed or otherwise used at the facility. An "article" is defined as a manufactured item (1) which is formed to a specific shape or design during manufacture; (2) which has end use functions dependent in whole or in part upon its shape or design during end use; and (3) which does not release a toxic chemical under normal conditions of processing or use of that item at the facility or establishments.[55]

If the processing or otherwise use of similar articles results in a total release of less than 0.5 pound of a listed toxic chemical in a calendar year to any environmental media, EPA will allow this release quantity to be rounded to zero and the manufactured items remain exempt as articles. EPA requires the owners or operators of covered facilities to round off and report all estimates to the nearest whole number. The 0.5 pound limit does not apply to each individual article, but applies to the sum of all releases from processing or the otherwise use of like articles.

The article exemption applies to the normal processing or otherwise use of an article. It does not apply to the manufacture of an article. Listed toxic chemicals that are incorporated into articles produced at a facility must be factored into threshold and release determinations.[56] For example, if a facility services a transformer containing PCBs by replacing the PCBs, the PCBs added during the reporting year must be counted in making the threshold and release calculations.

The article exemption is not applicable when the processing or otherwise use of an item generates fumes, dust, filings, or grindings. The listed toxic chemicals in the item must be counted toward the appropriate threshold determination, and the fumes, dust, filings, and grindings reported as releases or wastes. In addition, scrap pieces of a manufactured item that are recognizable as an article do not constitute a release.

5.4   Threshold Levels

Section 313 reporting is required if established threshold quantities are exceeded. Separate threshold quantities apply to the amount of the listed toxic chemical that is manufactured, imported, processed or otherwise used.[57]

The owner or operator of a facility that "otherwise used" any of the listed toxic chemicals in amounts equal to or in excess of 10,000 pounds in a calendar year is required to submit a toxic chemical release form on each listed chemical by July 1 of the following year. Such reporting began with the 1987 calendar year. Similarly, owners or operators of facilities that manufacture, import or process any of the listed toxic chemicals in amounts equal to or in excess of 25,000 pounds in a calendar year are required to report by July 1 of the following year.[58]

---

[54]*See*, 40 C.F.R. § 372.38.

[55]*See*, 40 C.F.R. § 372.3.

[56]*See*, 40 C.F.R. § 372.3.

[57]*See*, 42 U.S.C.A. § 11023(f).

[58]*See*, 40 C.F.R. § 372.25.

5.5 Mixture Reporting

Listed toxic chemicals in mixtures and in trade name products must be factored into threshold and release determinations. If the owner or operator of a facility imported, processed, or otherwise used mixtures or trade name products during the preceding calendar year, the owner or operator is required to use the best information available at the facility to determine whether the components of a mixture are above the *de minimis* concentration. If the owner or operator knows that a mixture or trade name product contains a listed toxic chemical, the owner or operator must combine the amount of the listed chemical in the mixture or trade name product with the other amounts of the same chemical imported, processed or otherwise used at the facility for threshold and release determinations.[59]

If the owner or operator of a facility knows that a mixture contains a listed toxic chemical but no concentration information is provided by the supplier, then the facility does not have to consider the amount of the listed toxic chemical present in that mixture for purposes of threshold and release determinations.[60]

If the owner or operator of a facility only knows the lower bound concentration of a listed toxic chemical present in a mixture, the owner or operator should first subtract out the percentages of any other known components of the mixture to determine a reasonable "maximum" for the listed chemical. The owner or operator should assume the "maximum" is 100% if no other information is available. The owner or operator must then use the midpoint of the known "minimum" (the lower bound concentration) and the reasonable "maximum" for threshold determinations. The owner or operator should use an average of the low and high concentration numbers for threshold determinations if only a range of concentrations is available for a listed toxic chemical present in a mixture.

A listed toxic chemical does not have to be considered if it is present in a mixture at a concentration below the *de minimis* level.[61] If a mixture contains more than one member of a listed chemical category, the *de minimis* level applies to the aggregate concentration of all such members and not to each individually. In making threshold determinations, the *de minimis* limitation applies to the following:

1. A listed toxic chemical in a mixture or trade name product received by the facility; and

2. A listed toxic chemical manufactured during a process where the chemical remains in a mixture or trade name product distributed by the facility.

The *de minimis* limitation does *not* apply to a listed toxic chemical manufactured at the facility that does not remain in a product distributed by the facility. A threshold determination must be made on the annual quantity of the listed chemical manufactured regardless of the concentration. For example, quantities of formaldehyde produced as a result of waste treatment must be applied toward the threshold for "manufacture" of this chemical, notwithstanding the concentration of this chemical in the wastestream.

---

[59]*See,* 40 C.F.R. § 372.30(b)(3)(i).

[60]*See,* 40 C.F.R. § 372.30(b)(3)(iii).

[61]*See,* 40 C.F.R. § 372.38(a).

5.6   Supplier Notification Requirement

EPA requires some suppliers of mixtures and trade name products containing one or more of the listed toxic chemicals to notify their customers. This requirement has been in effect since January 1, 1989. The supplier notification requirement applies to facilities in SIC codes 20 through 39 that manufacture, import, or process a listed toxic chemical which is *sold or otherwise distributed* in a mixture or trade name product containing the listed chemical to either a facility that must report under Section 313 or a facility that in turn sells the same mixture or trade name product to a firm in SIC codes 20 through 39.[62]

Supplier notification is required if a waste mixture containing a listed toxic chemical is sold to a recycling or recovery facility. If, however, the waste mixture containing a listed toxic chemical is sent off-site as a waste for treatment or disposal, no supplier notification is required.

The supplier notification must include the following information:

1.   A statement that the mixture or trade name product contains a listed toxic chemical(s) subject to the reporting requirements of Section 313 and 40 C.F.R. Part 372;

2.   The name of each listed toxic chemical(s) and its applicable CAS registry number; and

3.   The percentage, by weight, of each listed toxic chemical(s) contained in the mixture or trade name product.[63]

The required notification must be provided at least *annually* in writing. Acceptable forms of notice are a letter, product labeling, and product literature distributed to customers. The owners and operators of facilities that are required to prepare and distribute a MSDS for the mixture under the OSHA Hazard Communication Standard must either attach their supplier notification to the MSDS or modify their MSDS to include the required information. Suppliers subject to the notification requirement must make it clear to their customers that any copies or redistribution of the MSDS must include the Section 313 notice.[64]

Suppliers must notify each customer receiving a mixture or trade name product containing a listed toxic chemical with the *first shipment of each calendar year*. Once customers have been furnished with a MSDS containing the Section 313 information, a supplier may refer to the MSDS by a written letter in subsequent years if the MSDS is current.[65]

Whenever a supplier's products contain newly listed toxic chemicals, the supplier must notify customers with the *first shipment made during the next calendar year* following EPA's final decision to add the chemical to the list.[66] Suppliers must send a *new notice* to their customers *within 30 days* when they discover that their previous notification did not properly identify the listed toxic chemical(s) in the mixture

---

[62]*See,* 40 C.F.R. § 372.45.

[63]*See,* 40 C.F.R. § 372.45(b).

[64]*See,* 40 C.F.R. § 372.45(c)(5).

[65]*See,* 40 C.F.R. § 372.45(c)(1).

[66]*See,* 40 C.F.R. § 372.45(c)(2).

or correctly indicate their percentage by weight. Suppliers must identify in the new notice the prior shipments of the mixture or product in that calendar year to which the new notification applies.[67]

Suppliers must send a *revised notice* to their customers when they change a mixture or trade name product by adding, removing, or changing the percentage by weight of a listed chemical. The revised notice must be sent with the *first shipment* of the changed mixture or trade name product to the customer.[68]

Supplier notification is *not* required for a "pure" listed toxic chemical unless a trade name is used. Supplier notification is also *not* required if the mixture or trade name product does not contain a listed toxic chemical in an amount greater than the applicable *de minimis* level established for that chemical. Likewise, supplier notification is *not* required if the mixture or trade name product is an "article"; food, drug, cosmetic, alcoholic beverage, tobacco, or a tobacco product packaged for distribution to the general public; or a "consumer product" as defined in the Consumer Product Safety Act packaged for distribution to the general public.[69]

If a supplier considers the specific identity of a listed toxic chemical in a mixture or trade name product to be a trade secret, the notice must contain a generic chemical name that is descriptive of the structure of that chemical (i.e., halogenated aromatic).[70] Similarly, if a supplier considers the specific percent by weight composition of a toxic chemical in the mixture or trade name product to be a trade secret under the Restatement of Torts, the notice must contain a statement that the listed chemical is present at a concentration that does not exceed a specified upper bound concentration value. The upper bound value chosen must be no larger than necessary to adequately protect the trade secret.[71]

Suppliers are required to retain for *three years* records of the following:

1. Copies of the notifications sent to customers;

2. All supporting materials and documentation used to determine whether a notice was required;

3. All supporting materials and documentation used to develop the notice;

4. All supporting materials and documentation which explain why a specific chemical identity is considered a trade secret and why the generic chemical name provided in the notification is appropriate; and

5. All supporting materials and documentation which explain why a specific concentration is considered a trade secret and the basis for the upper bound concentration limit.[72]

---

[67]*See,* 40 C.F.R. § 372.45(c)(4).

[68]*See,* 40 C.F.R. § 372.45(c)(3).

[69]*See,* 40 C.F.R. § 372.45(d).

[70]*See,* 40 C.F.R. § 372.45(e).

[71]*See,* 40 C.F.R. § 372.45(f).

[72]*See,* 40 C.F.R. § 372.10(b).

5.7   Reporting Form

Facilities covered by the Section 313 reporting requirements must use the Toxic Chemical Release Inventory Reporting Form ("Form R") to report the following information:

1.   The name, location and principal business activities at the facility;

2.   Off-site locations to which any waste that contains the listed chemical is transferred;

3.   Whether the listed chemical is manufactured, imported, processed, or otherwise used and the general use categories of the chemical;

4.   An estimate (in ranges) of the maximum amounts of the listed chemical present at the facility at any time during the preceding year;

5.   The quantity of the listed chemical entering each environmental medium-- air, water and land--annually;

6.   Waste treatment and disposal methods and the efficiency of such methods for each waste stream;

7.   Information on source reduction and recycling or pollution prevention; and

8.   A certification by a senior management official that the report is complete and accurate.

5.8   Mandatory Pollution Prevention Reporting On EPA Form R

The Pollution Prevention Act of 1990, passed in October 1990 as part of the Budget Reconciliation Act of 1990, requires the owners or operators of facilities that must report under Section 313 to provide information on source reduction and recycling activities with each annual toxic chemical release inventory report beginning with the 1991 calendar year.

The pollution prevention report on each chemical reported includes the following information:

1.   Amount entering the wastestreams before recycling, treatment, or disposal and the percentage change from the previous year;

2.   Amount recycled, the percentage change from the previous year, and the recycling process used;

3.   Amount treated on-site or off-site and the percentage change from the previous year;

4.   Estimate of the amount that will be reported as entering any wastestream prior to recycling, treatment, or disposal for the next two years;

5.   Estimate of the amount that will be reported as recycled for the next two years;

6. Specific source reduction practices used by the facility (e.g., equipment, technology, process, or procedure modifications; reformulation or redesign of products; substitution of raw materials; improvement in management, training, inventory control, or materials handling;

7. Techniques used to identify source reduction opportunities (e.g., employee recommendations, external and internal audits, participative team management, and material balance audits);

8. Ratio of production in the reporting year to production in the preceding year; and

9. Amount released because of accidents or other one-time events (e.g., catastrophic event or remedial action) not associated with production processes.

The pollution prevention data will facilitate a comparison between production levels and the amount of waste generated. The inclusion of this data in the Toxics Release Inventory will allow citizen groups, State and local governments, and EPA to see for the first time whether waste reduction is occurring at the source.

5.9 Recordkeeping Requirements

The owner or operator of a facility covered by the Section 313 reporting requirements (excluding the supplier notification requirements) must retain the following records:

1. A copy of each toxic chemical release inventory report;

2. All supporting materials and documentation used to make the compliance determination that the facility or establishments within the facility is a covered facility;

3. Documentation supporting any determination that a claimed allowable exemption applies;

4. Data supporting the determination of whether a reporting threshold applies for each reported chemical;

5. Documentation supporting the calculations of the quantity of each reported chemical released to the environment or transferred to an off-site location;

6. Documentation supporting the activities and use classifications and quantity on site reported for each reported chemical, including the date of manufacture, processing, or use;

7. Documentation supporting the basis of estimate used in developing any release or off-site transfer estimates for each reported chemical;

8. Receipts or manifests associated with the transfer of each reported chemical in waste to off-site locations; and

9.   Documentation supporting reported waste treatment methods, estimates of treatment efficiencies, ranges of influent concentration to such treatment, the sequential nature of treatment steps, if applicable, and the actual operating data, if applicable, to support the waste treatment efficiency estimate for each reported chemical.[73]

The records must be maintained at the facility for three years from the date each report was submitted and they must be readily available for inspection by EPA officials.[74]

In view of the data requirements mandated by the Pollution Prevention Act of 1990, EPA has proposed that several new records be maintained under Section 313.[75] Those records include the following:

1.   Documentation supporting the estimates of the amounts of the chemical entering any wastestream, recycled on-site, sent off-site for recycling or treatment, and entering any wastestream as a result of remedial actions, catastrophic, or one-time events;

2.   Documentation supporting the estimates for the previous year and the first and second years following the reporting year of the amounts of the chemical entering any wastestream or otherwise released to the environment, recycled on-site, and recycled off-site;

3.   Documentation supporting the estimates for the previous year of the amounts of the chemical entering treatment on-site and sent off-site for treatment;

4.   Documentation supporting the validity of the method used to estimate the amount that would have been generated in waste if source reduction had not been implemented, and the calculation of the estimate of that quantity, including index of production or activity level in the reporting year to the prior year level;

5.   Documentation supporting the determination of whether changes in accounting practices, estimation methods, or point of measurement occurred in the reporting year versus the previous year;

6.   Documentation supporting the type of recycling process used on-site and off-site;

7.   Documentation of the implementation of source reduction and recycling activities, including receipts for new capital equipment; and

8.   Documentation demonstrating how the production ratio or activity index was calculated.

---

[73]*See*, 40 C.F.R. § 372.10(a).

[74]*See*, 40 C.F.R. § 372.10(c).

[75]*See*, 56 Fed. Reg. 48475 (September 25, 1991).

6.0   FEDERAL COMPLIANCE WITH RIGHT-TO-KNOW LAWS AND POLLUTION PREVENTION REQUIREMENTS

6.1   Overview

On August 3, 1994, President Clinton signed Executive Order 12856 requiring federal facilities that manufacture, process, or otherwise use listed toxic chemicals to comply with the reporting requirements under EPCRA. The Order sets a goal for all federal agencies to reduce toxic releases and off-site transfers of listed Section 313 toxic chemicals by 50% by 1999. The Order also calls for changes in the procurement of hazardous substances and requires federal facilities to work with neighboring communities to develop local emergency response plans.[76]

6.2   Planning Requirements

The Order requires each federal agency to develop a written pollution prevention strategy for the entire agency. Each agency's pollution prevention policy statement must designate the principal responsibilities for development, implementation, and evaluation of the strategy. The policy statement also must designate an individual responsible for coordinating the agency's pollution prevention efforts. The written strategy must be submitted to the EPA Adminstrator by August 3, 1994.[77]

The Order required each federal agency to provide the EPA Administrator with a preliminary list of facilities that potentially meet the reporting requirements under EPCRA. The list was required to be submitted by December 31, 1993.[78]

6.3   TRI Reduction Goals

The Order directs each federal agency to develop voluntary goals to reduce total releases and off-site transfers of listed Section 313 toxic chemicals by 50% by 1999. The Order further directs each federal agency head to ensure that each of the agency's covered facilities develops a written pollution prevention plan by December 31, 1995.[79]

Under the Order, each federal agency may choose to expand their toxic chemical reduction goals to achieve a 50% reduction for all toxic pollutants by 1999. Baseline for measuring reductions will be either 1993 or 1994, depending on when federal agency first began Section 313 reporting.[80]

6.4   Acquisition and Procurement of Goods and Services Goals

The Order requires all federal agencies to establish a plan and goals for eliminating or reducing the unnecessary acquisition of products containing extremely hazardous substances or toxic chemicals.

---

[76]*See,* Executive Order 12856, 58 *Fed. Reg.* 41981 (August 6, 1993).

[77]*See, Ibid.,* Section 3-301.

[78]*See, Ibid.,* Section 5-501.

[79]*See, Ibid.,* Section 3-302(d).

[80]*See, Ibid.,* Section 3-302(b) and (c).

Moreover, the Order directs each federal agency to establish a plan and goals for voluntarily reducing its own manufacturing, processing, and use of products containing extremely hazardous substances or toxic chemicals.[81]

The Order further requires the Department of Defense ("DOD") and the General Services Administration ("GSA"), and other agencies, as appropriate, to review their specifications and standards and identify opportunities to eliminate or reduce acquisition and procurement of extremely hazardous substances or toxic chemicals. Such review and identification must be completed by August 3, 1995. By 1999, DOD, GSA and other affected agencies must make all appropriate revisions to their specifications and standards.[82]

Any revisions to the Federal Acquisition Regulation that are necessary to implement the Order must be made by August 3, 1995.[83]

The Order encourages federal agencies to develop and test innovative pollution prevention technologies at their facilities to promote the development of strong markets for such technologies. The Order further encourages partnerships between industry, federal agencies, government laboratories, academia, and others to assess and deploy innovative environmental technologies for domestic use and markets abroad.[84]

6.5 EPCRA Reporting Requirements

Under the Order, all federal facilities meeting the EPCRA definition of "facility"[85] and exceeding the thresholds for manufacture, use or processing of toxic chemicals must report under Section 313, as amended by the Pollution Prevention Act of 1990. Such reporting applies even if the facilities do not fall within SIC Codes 20-39.[86] Section 313 requirements became effective at such facilities no later than January 1, 1994. The first reports are due July 1, 1995.[87]

---

[81]*See, Ibid.*, Section 3-303(a).

[82]*See, Ibid.*, Section 3-303(b).

[83]*See, Ibid.*, Section 3-303(c).

[84]*See, Ibid.*, Section 3-303(d).

[85]EPCRA defines the term "facility" as follows: "all buildings, equipment, structures, and other stationary items which are located on a single site or on contiguous or adjacent sites and which are owned or operated by the same person (or by any person which controls, is controlled by, or under common control with, such person). For purposes of Section 304 (i.e., emergency release notification), the term includes motor vehicles, rolling stock, and aircraft. *See*, 42 U.S.C.A. § 11049(4).

[86]The Order does not apply to federal agency facilities outside the customs territory of the United States, such as the United States diplomatic and consular missions abroad. *See, supra.*, Executive Order 12856, Section 1-102.

[87]*See, supra.*, Executive Order 12856, Section 3-304(a)-(c).

All federal facilities are subject also to the other EPCRA requirements (i.e., Sections 302-312). The compliance dates are as follows:[88]

* March 3, 1994 - Submit Emergency Planning Notification under Section 302.

* August 3, 1994 - Submit information for the preparation of Comprehensive Emergency Response Plans under Section 303.

* August 3, 1994 - Submit MSDSs under Section 311.

* March 1, 1995 - Submit Tier I/Tier II Inventory Form for 1994 under Section 312.

* January 1, 1994 - Effective date for Emergency Notification of Releases of Extremely Hazardous Substances under Section 304 that occur on or after January 1, 1994.

The Order does not apply to Government-owned/Contractor-operated facilities ("GOCOs") not within SIC Codes 20-39 since they are not currently covered by Section 313. However, overall agency reports must take into account such activities. Future contract revisions will require GOCOs not within SIC Codes 20-39 to provide their agencies with the information necessary for TRI reporting.[89]

7.0   TRADE SECRETS

7.1   Overview

Only the specific chemical identity of a covered chemical can be claimed as a trade secret in submissions to EPA, the SERC, the LEPC, or the LFD required under Sections 303, 311, 312, and 313. EPCRA provides no trade secret protection for Section 304 submissions. When claiming confidentiality, the owner or operator of a covered facility must submit all other required information, including a generic name for the chemical whose identity is claimed as a trade secret, on the MSDS (or list of MSDS chemicals) and the Tier Two report.[90]

7.2   Substantiation Required

Substantiation for the claim must be provided to EPA, in both sanitized and unsanitized form, at the same time the Section 303, 311, 312 or 313 submission is made to the SERC, the LEPC or the LFD. The substantiation must include the following information:

1.   Specific measures taken to safeguard the confidentiality of the chemical identity claimed as a trade secret and whether these measures will continue in the future;

---

[88]*See, Ibid.*, Section 3-305(a)-(d).

[89]*See, Ibid.*, Sections 1-103 and 1-104.

[90]*See,* 42 U.S.C.A. § 11042(a); 40 C.F.R. § 350.5.

2. Whether the chemical identity claimed as a trade secret has been disclosed to any other person (other than a member of a LEPC, officer or employee of the U.S. or a State or local government, or an employee) who is not bound by a confidentiality agreement to refrain from disclosing this trade secret information to others;

3. All local, State and Federal government entities to which the specific chemical identity claimed as a trade secret has been disclosed;

4. Indication of whether a confidentiality claim for the chemical identity was asserted at the time of disclosure to the local, State and Federal government entities and whether the government entity denied that claim;

5. The specific use of the chemical claimed as a trade secret, including the product or process in which it is used;

6. Whether the company's or the facility's identity has been linked to the specific chemical identity claimed as a trade secret in a patent, or in publications or other information sources available to the public or competitors;

7. Explanation of how competitors could deduce the use of the chemical claimed as a trade secret from disclosure of the chemical identity together with other information on the SARA Title III submission;

8. Explanation of why the use of the chemical claimed as a trade secret would be valuable information to competitors;

9. Indication of the nature of the harm to the company's competitive position that would likely result from disclosure of the specific chemical identity and why such harm would be substantial;

10. The extent to which the chemical claimed as a trade secret is available to the public or competitors in products, articles, or environmental releases; and

11. Whether the chemical claimed as a trade secret is in pure form or is mixed with other substances.[91]

7.3   Trade Secret Disclosure

All information for which a trade secrecy claim is not ultimately upheld is available to the public on request with one exception. Under Section 324, the SERC, the LEPC, and the LFD are required to withhold information regarding the location within a facility of any specific chemical contained in a Tier Two report if requested to do so by the owner or operator of a facility submitting the report.

---

[91]*See*, 40 C.F.R. § 350.7(a).

Information concerning the specific chemical identity of a substance must be provided to health professionals upon request in the following situations:

1. The information is needed by a health professional for the purpose of diagnosis or treatment;

2. The information is needed by a health professional working for a local government to assess exposure; conduct sampling, periodic medical surveillance, or studies on the health effects of exposure; or provide medical treatment to exposed individuals or population groups; or

3. The information is needed by doctors or nurses in order to treat exposed individuals in a medical emergency.

The owner or operator of a covered facility is required to furnish the specific chemical identity in the first two situations described above only if the request for the information is <u>in writing</u> and is accompanied by a *written confidentiality agreement*. In a medical emergency, however, no written statement of need or written confidentiality agreement is required as a precondition to disclosure. The owner or operator of a covered facility may require a written statement of need and written confidentiality agreement as soon as circumstances permit.[92]

8.0   PUBLIC AVAILABILITY OF EPCRA INFORMATION

The information submitted by facilities under Sections 304 311, 312 and 313 must generally be made available to the public by the SERC and the LEPCs during normal working hours.[93] Each SERC must have established written guidelines on receiving and processing requests for information under EPCRA.[94]

As a general policy, the SERCs and LEPCs will make the fullest possible disclosure of records to the public consistent with the provisions of EPCRA and their State Freedom of Information Act. All SERC and LEPC records are available to the public unless they are specifically exempt from the disclosure requirements.

9.0   ENFORCEMENT AUTHORITIES AND PENALTIES

9.1   Overview

EPCRA contains a complex set of administrative, civil and criminal penalties for violations of its various provisions. Sections 325 and 326 authorize the EPA, the SERCs, the LEPCs, and citizens to take legal action against owners or operators of facilities who fail to comply with the law.

---

[92]*See,* 40 C.F.R. § 350.40.

[93]*See,* 42 U.S.C.A. § 11044(a).

[94]*See,* 42 U.S.C.A. § 11001(a).

The enforcement authorities vary for each requirement in EPCRA. In some instances, federal authority is primarily administrative, in other instances it is judicial. For some requirements, but not all, there is express authority for State and local suits. Similarly, for some requirements, but not all, there are citizen suits.

Congress intended that the implementation of EPCRA be mainly a State and local function with the notable exception of Section 313 pertaining to toxic chemical release inventory reporting. The EPCRA enforcement authorities are summarized below.

9.2   Violations of Sections 302 and 303

Section 325 of EPCRA authorizes the Administrator of the EPA to order the owner or operator of a covered facility to comply with Sections 302 and 303. The local U.S. district court has jurisdiction to enforce the order and impose a penalty.[95]

Under Section 326, the SERC and the LEPC can bring a civil action against the owner or operator of a covered facility for failing to report that the facility is covered by the emergency planning requirements.[96] The SERC and the LEPC can bring a civil action against the owner or operator of a covered facility for failing to notify the LEPC of a facility representative who will participate in the emergency planning process or for failing to provide information promptly upon request by the LEPC.[97] The local U.S. district court has the authority to impose civil penalties provided by EPCRA in such suits.[98]

Violations of Sections 302 and 303 subject the violator to civil penalties of up to $25,000 per day for each day the violation or failure to comply with the order continues.[99]

9.3   Violations of Section 304

The CERCLA Section 109 and EPCRA Section 325 enforcement provisions for emergency notification are very similar. Both establish administrative penalties and the authority to bring actions judicially to assess penalties for failing to notify the proper authorities at the time of an emergency release of a listed hazardous substance subject to reporting.[100]

CERCLA and EPCRA both provide criminal fines for knowingly failing to provide notice of a reportable release or providing false or misleading information.[101] Section 326(a) of EPCRA authorizes any citizen to file a civil action in the local U.S. district court for failure to submit a written follow-up report

---

[95]*See*, 42 U.S.C.A. § 11045(a).

[96]*See*, 42 U.S.C.A. § 11046(a)(2)(A).

[97]*See*, 42 U.S.C.A. § 11046(a)(2)(B).

[98]*See*, 42 U.S.C.A. § 11046(b)(1).

[99]*See*, 42 U.S.C.A. § 11045(a).

[100]*See*, 42 U.S.C.A. § 9609 and 42 U.S.C.A. § 11045.

[101]*See*, 42 U.S.C.A. § 9603(b) and 42 U.S.C.A. § 11045(b)(4).

of a release required to be reported to the SERC and the LEPC under Section 304(c).[102] The SERC and the LEPC may bring a civil action under the citizen suit provisions for Section 304 violations.[103]

Under Section 325 of EPCRA and CERCLA Section 109, a Class I administrative penalty of up to $25,000 per violation and a Class II administrative penalty of up to $25,000 per day for each day during which the violation continues may be assessed for each violation of Section 304.[104] This penalty also may be assessed judicially.[105]

In the case of a second or subsequent violation of Section 304, civil penalties of up to $75,000 per day for each day during which the violation continues may be assessed.[106] Both penalties also may be assessed judicially.[107]

Any person who knowingly and willfully fails to provide notice in accordance with EPCRA Section 304 can, upon conviction, be fined up to $25,000 or imprisoned for up to two years, or both.[108] In the case of a second or subsequent conviction, the violator is subject to a fine of up to $50,000 or imprisonment for up to five years, or both.[109]

9.4   Violations of Sections 311-313

Under Section 325 of EPCRA, the Administrator of the EPA can assess civil penalties for violations of Sections 311, 312, and 313 through the issuance of administrative orders or bring actions to enforce compliance and assess penalties in the local U.S. district court.[110]

Under Section 326 of EPCRA, the SERC and the LEPC can bring civil actions for failing to submit MSDSs or Tier One/Tier Two Inventory Reports under Sections 311 and 312.[111] Under the citizen suit provisions of Section 326, the SERC and the LEPC can bring a civil action for failing to submit toxic chemical release inventory reports under Section 313.[112]

---

[102]*See,* 42 U.S.C.A. § 11046(a)(1)(A)(i).

[103]*See,* 42 U.S.C.A. § 11049(7) and 42 U.S.C.A. § 11046(a). The term "person" used in Section 326 of EPCRA is defined to include, among others, "any ... State, municipality, commission, political subdivision of a State, or interstate body."

[104]*See,* 42 U.S.C.A. § 11045(b)(1) and (2); and 42 U.S.C.A. § 9609(a) and (b).

[105]*See,* 42 U.S.C.A. § 11045(b)(3) and 42 U.S.C.A. § 9609(c).

[106]*See,* 42 U.S.C.A. § 11045(b)(2) and 42 U.S.C.A. § 9609(b).

[107]*See,* 42 U.S.C.A. § 11045(b)(3) and 42 U.S.C.A. § 9609(c).

[108]*See,* 42 U.S.C.A. § 11045(b)(4).

[109]*Ibid.*

[110]*See,* 42 U.S.C.A. § 11045(c).

[111]*See,* 42 U.S.C.A. § 11046(a)(2).

[112]*See,* 42 U.S.C.A. § 11046(a)(1)(A)(iv).

Section 326 gives citizens the authority to bring a civil action against an owner or operator of a covered facility for violations of Sections 311, 312, and 313.[113] The local U.S. district court has the authority to enforce the reporting requirements and to impose any civil penalty provided for violation of the requirements.[114]

A violation of Section 311 subjects the violator to a civil penalty of up to $10,000 per day for each such violation.[115] Each day a violation continues constitutes a separate violation.[116]

A violation of Sections 312 or 313 subjects the violator to a civil penalty of up to $25,000 per day for each such violation.[117] Each day a violation continues constitutes a separate violation.[118]

10.0   CONCLUSION

Compliance with EPCRA presents a continuing challenge to those facilities subject to its planning and reporting requirements. Facilities subject to the emergency planning provisions should participate actively in the local planning process as a matter of good community relations and to provide the technical expertise needed by the LEPCs. Facilities subject to the reporting requirements need clearly written and rigorously implemented compliance plans and information management programs to avoid enforcement actions for noncompliance.

---

[113]*See,* 42 U.S.C.A. § 11046(a)(1).

[114]*See,* 42 U.S.C.A. § 11046(c).

[115]*See,* 42 U.S.C.A. § 11045(c)(2).

[116]*See,* 42 U.S.C.A. § 11045(c)(3).

[117]*See,* 42 U.S.C.A. § 11045(c)(1).

[118]*See,* 42 U.S.C.A. § 11045(c)(3).

Chapter 5

THE TOXIC SUBSTANCES CONTROL ACT

Wayne T. Halbleib

Counsel
Mays & Valentine
Richmond, Virginia

I.   INTRODUCTION

The Toxic Substances Control Act ("TSCA" or the "Act") was enacted on October 11, 1976.[1] The Act was designed to ensure that adequate data would be made available to the Administrator of the U.S. Environmental Protection Agency ("EPA") on the adverse health and environmental effects of chemical substances and mixtures.

While most environmental laws regulate wastes, emissions, pollutants, or by-products, TSCA regulates how commercial chemicals can be used. Under Section 4, EPA can require testing of chemical substances and mixtures for possible adverse health and environmental effects.   Section 5 requires each manufacturer or importer of a new chemical substance to submit a notice to EPA at least 90 days prior to the manufacture or importation of the substance.

Under Section 6, EPA can regulate the manufacturing, processing, distribution in commerce, use and disposal of chemical substances and mixtures through bans, labeling, public notification of risk, and product recalls. Section 8 authorizes EPA to gather existing information about chemical substances and mixtures from manufacturers, processors, and, in some cases, distributors.

II.   TESTING REQUIREMENTS

Section 4(a) of TSCA authorizes the EPA Administrator to issue a rule requiring a chemical substance[2] or mixture to be tested where certain findings can be made.[3] Such findings include:

---

[1]*See,* 15 U.S.C.A. § 2601 *et seq.*, Pub. L. No. 94-469.

[2]The term "chemical substance" means any organic or inorganic substance of a particular molecular identity, including (i) any combination of such substances occurring in whole or in part as a result of a

First, that the manufacture, distribution, processing, use, or disposal of the chemical substance or mixture may present an unreasonable risk of injury to health or the environment, or the substance or mixture is or will be produced in substantial quantities and either (i) enters or may reasonably be anticipated to enter the environment in substantial quantities, or (ii) there is or may be significant or substantial human exposure.

Second, there is insufficient data and experience to reasonably predict the effects of the chemical substance or mixture on health or the environment.

Third, testing is necessary to develop the data.

Substances and mixtures subject to testing under TSCA are listed in 40 C.F.R. Part 799.[4] The good laboratory practice standards for conducting studies relating to health and environmental effects and chemical fate testing are in 40 C.F.R. Part 792. The health and environmental effects and chemical fate testing guidelines are set forth in 40 C.F.R. Parts 795-798.

III. PREMANUFACTURE NOTICES

A. Persons Subject to Premanufacture Notices

Section 5(a) of TSCA requires any manufacturer or importer of a "new chemical substance" to submit a premanufacture notice or "PMN" to EPA at least 90 days prior to such manufacture or importation.[5] A person who intends to manufacture or import a chemical substance that does not appear on the published *TSCA Chemical Substance Inventory* can request EPA to determine whether the substance in question is included in EPA's Master Inventory File.[6] EPA will provide an answer only if the person who submits the inquiry is able to demonstrate a "bona fide intent" to manufacture or import the substance for a commercial purpose.

---

chemical reaction or occurring in nature, and (ii) any element or uncombined radical. The term does not include (i) pesticides when manufactured, processed, or distributed in commerce for use as a pesticide; (ii) tobacco or tobacco products; (iii) source materials, special nuclear materials and by-products as defined in the Atomic Energy Act; and (iv) foods, food additives, drugs, cosmetics, and devices when manufactured, processed or distributed in commerce as such. 15 U.S.C.A. §2602(2).

[3]*See*, 15 U.S.C.A. § 2603(a).

[4]In a final rule issued July 27, 1993, EPA required manufacturers and processors of 10 chemical substances to conduct testing for neurotoxcity. The ten substances are: acetone; n-amyl acetate; 1-butanol; n-butyl acetate; diethyl ether; 2-ethoxyethanol; ethyl acetate; isobutyl alcohol; methyl isobutyl ketone; and tetrahydrofuran. The rule requires cognitive function and screening level tests for neurotoxicity.

[5]A "new chemical substance" is defined as any chemical substance which is not included on the *TSCA Chemical Substance Inventory*. *See*, 40 C.F.R. § 720.3(v).

[6]The *TSCA Chemical Substance Inventory: 1985 Edition and the 1990 Supplement* together list 68,000 chemical substances. The chemical identity of almost 5500 of these chemical substances is considered confidential. Each of these substances has been assigned a generic name.

To demonstrate a "bona fide intent" to manufacture or import a new chemical substance, the person who proposes to manufacture or import the substance must submit to EPA the following information:

* The specific chemical identity of the substance.

* A signed statement that the person intends to manufacture or import the substance for commercial purposes.

* A description of the research and development activities conducted up to the time of submission.

* The purpose for which the person will manufacture or import the substance.

* An elemental analysis.

* Either an X-ray diffraction pattern (for inorganic substances), a mass spectrum (for most other substances), or an infrared spectrum of the substance.[7]

EPA will answer an inquiry on whether a substance is on the confidential Inventory within 30 days after receipt of a complete submission. If the substance is on the Inventory, the requestor is not required to submit a premanufacture notice and may commence manufacture or importation immediately. If the substance is not on the Inventory, the requestor must determine whether the substance is excluded from regulation under TSCA or whether it is exempt from the premanufacture notification requirements under TSCA § 5(h). If the substance is neither excluded or exempted, the requestor must comply with the PMN requirements before beginning the manufacture or importation of the substance.

B.   Substances Excluded From Notification

Certain substances are not subject to the premanufacture notification requirements. These substances include substances manufactured solely for use as pesticides, food, food additives, drugs, or cosmetics; tobacco and tobacco products; nuclear source materials; firearms and ammunition; mixtures, impurities; by-products which have no commercial use; non-isolated intermediates; and new chemical substances manufactured solely for export.[8]

---

[7]*See,* 40 C.F.R. § 720.25(b)(2).

[8]*See,* 40 C.F.R. § 720.30.

C.   Activities Exempted From Notification

1.   Research and Development Exemption

Small quantities of new chemical substances used solely for research and development ("R&D")[9] under the direct supervision of a technically qualified individual[10] are exempt from the premanufacture notification requirements.[11] Unlike other exemptions under TSCA § 5(h), the manufacturer or importer does not have to apply for the R&D exemption. Persons who engage in R&D for a manufacturer or importer or obtain an R&D substance from a manufacturer or importer, however, must be notified of any health risk which may be associated with the substance.[12] R&D conducted entirely in a laboratory[13] under prudent laboratory practices for handling chemical substances of unknown toxicity is exempt from the requirement for risk evaluation and notification.[14]

A manufacturer or importer can fulfill its obligation to notify the above-mentioned persons of any health risk which may be associated with the substance through several different methods. Such methods include (1) a container labeling system; (2) conspicuous placement of notices in areas where exposure may occur; (3) written notification to each person potentially exposed; or (4) any other method of notification which adequately informs persons of the health risk(s).[15]

Manufacturers and importers of R&D substances must retain records pertaining to (1) the information reviewed and evaluated to determine the need to make any notification of risk; (2) the nature and method of risk notification, including copies of any labels or written notices used; (3) prudent laboratory practices used instead of risk evaluation and notification; and (4) the identity and amount of the substance distributed and the names and addresses of any recipient of the substance.[16] In addition,

---

[9]R&D includes synthesis of new chemical substances or analysis, experimentation, or research on new or existing chemical substances, including product development activities. R&D may include tests of the physical, chemical, production, and performance characteristics of a substance.

[10]"Technically qualified individual" means a person or persons (1) who, because of education, training, or experience, or a combination of these factors, is capable of understanding the health and environmental risks associated with the chemical substance which is used under his or her supervision, (2) who is responsible for enforcing appropriate methods of conducting scientific experimentation, analysis, or chemical research to minimize such risks, and (3) who is responsible for the safety assessments and clearances related to the procurement, storage, use and disposal of the chemical substance as may be appropriate or required within the scope of conducting a research and development activity. 40 C.F.R. § 720.3(ee).

[11]*See*, 40 C.F.R. § 720.36.

[12]*See*, 40 C.F.R. § 720.36(a)(2).

[13]For purposes of the R&D exemption, a "laboratory" is defined as a contained research facility where relatively small quantities of chemical substances are used on a non-production basis, and where activities involve the use of containers for reactions, transfers, and other handling of substances designed to be easily manipulated by a single individual. 40 C.F.R. § 720.36(b)(2).

[14]*See*, 40 C.F.R. § 720.36(b)(2).

[15]*See*, 40 C.F.R. § 720.36(c)(1).

[16]*See*, 40 C.F.R. § 720.78(b)(1).

manufacturers and importers of an R&D substance in a quantity greater than 100 kilograms per year must retain records on the substance's identity, production volume, and disposition of the substance.[17] These records must be retained for five years after they are developed.[18]

2. Test Market Exemption

A manufacturer or importer that wants to determine the marketability of a new chemical substance may apply for a test market exemption ("TME") under TSCA § 5(h)(1). Test-marketing involves the distribution of a predetermined limited amount of the substance, or of a mixture or article containing the substance, to a specified number of customers to explore market acceptability before general distribution.

TME applications must be responded to within 45 days.[19] Applicants are not required but are encouraged to use the PMN form for a TME application. EPA will grant the exemption if the person demonstrates that the substance will not present any unreasonable risk of injury to health or the environment during the test-marketing activities.[20] TME applications must contain the following information:

*   All existing data regarding the health and environmental effects of the chemical substance, including physical/chemical properties.

*   The maximum quantity of the substance which will be manufactured or imported for test marketing.

*   The maximum number of persons who will be furnished the substance during test marketing.

*   The maximum number of persons who may be exposed to the substance as a result of test marketing, including information on duration and routes of exposure.

*   A description of the test-marketing activity, including its length and how it can be distinguished from full-scale commercial production and research and development.[21]

Manufacturers and importers operating under a TME must retain documentation of information in the application and documentation of compliance with any restrictions imposed by EPA when the application was granted. This information must be maintained for five years from the final date of manufacture or import under the exemption.[22]

---

[17]*See,* 40 C.F.R. § 720.78(b)(2).

[18]*See,* 40 C.F.R. § 720.78(b)(3).

[19]*See,* 40 C.F.R. § 720.38(d).

[20]*See,* 40 C.F.R. § 720.38(a).

[21]*See,* 40 C.F.R. § 720.38(b)(1)-(5).

[22]*See,* 40 C.F.R. § 720.78(c).

3. TSCA § 5(h)(4) Exemptions

Under TSCA § 5(h)(4), a manufacturer or importer may apply to EPA for an exemption from some or all of the premanufacture notification requirements. EPA will grant an exemption from the full PMN requirements if it makes an affirmative finding that the manufacture, processing, distribution in commerce, use or disposal of the new chemical substance will not present an unreasonable risk to health or the environment. Unlike the test marketing exemption, EPA can grant a §5(h)(4) exemption only by rule. EPA has issued two § 5(h)(4) exemptions, namely, the low volume exemption and the polymer exemption.

3a. Low Volume Exemption

A manufacturer or importer who intends to manufacture or import a new chemical substance in quantities of 1,000 kilograms or less per year can apply for a low volume exemption ("LVE").[23] Only one exemption is available for each chemical substance regardless of the number of potential manufacturers. Low volume exempt substances are not added to the TSCA Inventory, however, EPA maintains a separate inventory of LVEs granted.

Applicants for a LVE must submit to EPA a notice of intent to manufacture at least 21 days before beginning manufacture of the substance. LVE applicants are not required to use the PMN form. The notice must include the following: (1) the name and address of the manufacturer and the name and telephone number of a technical contact; (2) indication that the manufacturer is seeking a LVE; (3) the chemical identity and any anticipated impurities; (4) a description of its use (e.g., spray adhesive in the manufacture of laminates); (5) the site of its manufacture; (6) all test data in the possession or control of the applicant; (7) information on exposure controls, if desired; (8) a sanitized copy of the notice whenever any information on the notice is claimed as confidential; and (9) a certification that the substance will be manufactured or imported for commercial purposes in compliance with the LVE requirements.[24]

EPA will grant the LVE if it determines that the substance will not present an unreasonable risk of injury to health or the environment. If EPA determines, however, that the substance or a "reasonably anticipated metabolite or environmental transformation product of it" may cause either serious chronic or acute health effects or significant environmental effects, the LVE application will be denied.[25]

Each manufacturer and importer of a new chemical substance who is granted a LVE must maintain records of the annual production volume of the new substance and documentation of information in the exemption notice and compliance with the terms of the exemption. Such records must be retained for five years from the date of their preparation.[26]

---

[23]*See,* 40 C.F.R. § 723.50(a).

[24]*See,* 40 C.F.R. § 723.50(e).

[25]*See,* 40 C.F.R. § 723.50(d)(1)-(3).

[26]*See,* 40 C.F.R. § 723.50(o).

3b.   Polymer Exemption

A manufacturer or importer of a new polymer that (1) is a polyester made solely from a specified list of reactants or (2) has a number-average molecular weight greater than 1,000, may submit a notice under the polymer exemption.[27] This exemption is available for those classes of polymers which are not chemically active or bioavailable.

Applicants for the polymer exemption must complete applicable portions of the PMN form and submit it to EPA at least 21 days prior to the date of manufacture. The applicant must submit the following information: (1) name and address of the manufacturer and the name and telephone number of a technical contact; (2) type of polymer exemption; (3) site of manufacture; (4) chemical identity; (5) the number-average molecular weight; (6) maximum weight percent of each residual monomer and/or reactant; (7) impurity information; (8) maximum annual production volume; (9) a description of each use of the polymer; and (10) test data on the polymer in the possession or control of the manufacturer.[28]

EPA will grant the exemption if it determines that the substance will not present an unreasonable risk of injury. Unlike the other exemptions, substances subject to the polymer exemption are added to the TSCA Inventory and a Notice of Commencement ("NOC") must be submitted when commercial production commences.

Manufacturers who obtain a polymer exemption must retain certain records for five years from the date of commencement of manufacture. Records must be retained on the following information: (1) production volume for the first three years of manufacture; (2) date on which manufacture commenced; (3) data to demonstrate that the new polymer is not specifically excluded from the exemption; and (4) data to demonstrate that the polymer meets the exemption criteria.[29]

D.   Types of Premanufacture Notices

If a new chemical substance does not qualify for one of the above-mentioned exemptions, the manufacturer or importer must file a PMN. EPA published a revised PMN form and Instructions Manual in January 1991 to assist submitters preparing a PMN.

The revised PMN form is designed to allow the submitter to use the form for the submission of either: (1) a full PMN; (2) a consolidated PMN; (3) a significant new use; (4) a intermediate PMN;[30] (5) a test marketing exemption; (6) a low volume exemption; or (7) a polymer exemption.[31]

---

[27]*See*, 40 C.F.R. § 723.250(e).

[28]*See*, 40 C.F.R. § 723.250(f)(2).

[29]*See*, 40 C.F.R. § 723.250(r).

[30]The intermediate PMN is for a chemical substance which is an intermediate (i.e., a chemical substance that is consumed, in whole or in part, in chemical reactions used for the intentional manufacture of another chemical substance) used in the production of a final product for which a separate notice is submitted simultaneously. *See*, 40 C.F.R. § 700.43.

[31]*See*, EPA Form 7710-25 (Rev. 1-91).

Manufacturers of two or more structurally similar new substances should contact EPA's Prenotice Coordinator, Chemical Control Division, Office of Toxic Substances, to obtain prior approval to submit a single consolidated notice. A consolidated notice is suitable for chemical substances of similar structure with the same or similar uses and which share similar test data and other information. A consolidated notice is not suitable, however, for a series of intermediates and a final product because they do not share common uses, test data, and other information.[32]

E.   Contents of a PMN

The PMN form requires information on (1) the manufacturer's or importer's identity; (2) the common or trade name, the chemical identity, and the molecular structure of each chemical substance; (3) the proposed uses of the substance; (4) reasonable estimates of the total amount to be manufactured or processed; (5) a description of the by-products resulting from the manufacture, processing, use, or disposal of the substance; (6) reasonable estimates of the number of individuals who will be exposed to the substance in their place of employment and the duration of the exposure; (7) the manner or method of its disposal; (8) any test data in the possession or control of the submitter related to the effect of any manufacture, processing, distribution, use or disposal of the substance on health and the environment; and (9) a description of any other data concerning the health and environmental effects of the substance that is reasonably ascertainable to the submitter.[33]

A new section has been added on the revised PMN form for submitters to report on comparative risks, pollution prevention and recycling practices planned by the submitter concerning activities surrounding the manufacturing, processing, use, and disposal of the new chemical substances. This information will assist EPA in assessing the relative risks/benefits of a new chemical substance in comparison to substances already on the market.[34]

Documentation of the information submitted in a PMN must be retained for five years from the date of commencement of manufacture or importation.[35]

F.   Notice of Commencement of Manufacture or Import

Under TSCA § 5(a), EPA must review the PMN within ninety days. EPA may extend the review period for an additional ninety days under § 5(c) if it has "good cause." If EPA has not taken any action to regulate the new chemical substance during the review period, the submitter may begin commercial manufacture or importation immediately upon expiration of the review period. Within 30 calendar days of such manufacture or importation, the manufacturer or importer must file a Notice of Commencement of Manufacture or Import ("NOC").[36]

---

[32]*See, Instructions Manual for Premanufacture Notification of New Chemical Substances*, EPA Document 7710-25(l), (1991), p. 16.

[33]*See*, 40 C.F.R. §§ 720.45 and 720.50.

[34]*See*, EPA Form 7710-25 (Rev. 1-91), p. 11.

[35]*See*, 40 C.F.R. § 720.78(a).

[36]*See*, 40 C.F.R. § 720.102(b).

The NOC must contain the following information: (1) the specific chemical identity of the new chemical substance; (2) the premanufacture notice number; and (3) the date when manufacture or import began. A manufacturer or importer who claims the chemical identity confidential in the NOC, and wants the identity of the new substance to be listed on the confidential Inventory, must reassert and substantiate the claim in the NOC. Otherwise, EPA will list the specific chemical identity on the public Inventory.[37]

G.   Confidentiality Claims in a NOC

A manufacturer can substantiate the claim of confidentiality asserted in the NOC by (1) providing a generic chemical name; (2) allowing EPA to disclose to a person with a bona fide intent to manufacture or import the chemical substance that the substance is included on the confidential Inventory; (3) furnishing to EPA, upon request, an elemental analysis and either an X-ray diffraction pattern (for inorganic substances), a mass spectrum (for most other substances), or an infrared spectrum of the particular chemical substance; and (4) by answering a series of questions pertaining to the submitter's efforts to protect confidentiality, the harmful effects to the submitter's competitive position in the event of disclosure, the extent of disclosure to others, whether any federal agency or court has made any pertinent confidentiality determinations, and the purpose for which the substance is manufactured or imported.[38]

H.   Significant New Use of a Chemical Substance

The PMN requirements apply not only to new chemical substances but to significant new uses of existing chemicals. TSCA § 5(a)(2) allows EPA to determine by rule that a use is a "significant new use." The criteria which EPA must consider for a significant new use determination include (1) the projected production volume of the substance; (2) the form and duration of both human and environmental exposure to the substance; and (3) the anticipated hazards associated with the manufacture, processing, distribution, and disposal of the substance.

Once EPA issues a significant new use rule ("SNUR") for a chemical substance, no person may manufacture or process that chemical substance for those new uses unless the person submits a significant new use notice at least ninety days before the activity begins.[39] The PMN form must be used for any notice that is submitted in accordance with a significant new use rule. The chemical substances for which significant new use rules have been issued by EPA are listed in 40 C.F.R. Part 721, Subpart E.[40]

---

[37]*See*, 40 C.F.R. § 720.102(c).

[38]*See*, 40 C.F.R. § 720.85(b)(3).

[39]*See*, 40 C.F.R. § 721.25(a).

[40]On September 23, 1992, EPA issued a final SNUR for 63 chemical substances which were the subject of PMNs and which were subject to TSCA § 5(e) consent orders issued by EPA. *See*, 57 Fed.Reg. 44050 (September 23, 1992).

IV. REGULATION OF HAZARDOUS CHEMICAL SUBSTANCES

A. Scope of EPA's Regulatory Authority

Whenever EPA finds there is a reasonable basis to conclude that the manufacture, processing, distribution in commerce, use, or disposal of a chemical substance or mixture, or any combination of such activities, presents or will present an unreasonable risk of injury to health or the environment, EPA must issue a rule under Section 6(a) of TSCA to protect against such risk.[41] EPA's regulatory authority under Section 6(a) is substantially broad.

Section 6(a) authorizes EPA to take one or more of the following actions: (1) prohibit the manufacture, processing, or distribution of the substance or mixture; (2) restrict the amount manufactured, processed or distributed; (3) prohibit or restrict certain uses or concentrations; (4) require labeling, adequate warnings and instructions regarding use, distribution or disposal; (5) require recordkeeping or testing; (6) prohibit or regulate any manner or method of commercial use; (7) prohibit or regulate any manner or method of disposal; (8) require public notification of risk; and (9) require product recalls (i.e., replace or repurchase).

In addition, if EPA finds there is a reasonable basis to conclude that a manufacturer or processor is manufacturing or processing a chemical substance or mixture in a manner which unintentionally presents or will cause it to present an unreasonable risk of injury to health or the environment, EPA can by order require the manufacturer or processor to submit a description of the relevant quality control procedures used.[42] Moreover, if the EPA determines that a chemical substance or mixture subject to a proposed rule under Section 6 is likely to result in an unreasonable risk of serious or widespread injury to health or the environment before the effective date of the rule, EPA must make the proposed rule effective upon publication in the Federal Register.[43]

B. Regulation of Polychlorinated Biphenyls

Section 6(e) of TSCA prohibits the manufacture, processing, distribution in commerce, and use of polychlorinated biphenyls ("PCBs") except (1) in a totally enclosed manner; or (2) for activities that will not present an unreasonable risk of injury to health or the environment as determined by EPA; and (3) for activities that will not result in an unreasonable risk of injury to health or the environment and for which good faith efforts have been made to develop a chemical substitute for the PCB as determined by EPA in response to a petition. Moreover, Section 6(e) authorized EPA to issue rules which (1) designate the methods for disposing of PCBs; (2) require PCBs to be marked with clear and adequate warnings; and (3) establish instructions for the processing, distribution in commerce, use, or disposal of PCBs.[44]

---

[41]*See*, 15 U.S.C.A. § 2605(a).

[42]*See*, 15 U.S.C.A. § 2605(b).

[43]*See*, 15 U.S.C.A. § 2605(d).

[44]*See*, 15 U.S.C.A. § 2605(e).

C. PCB Transformers

EPA's regulations permit the use of most electrical equipment containing PCBs for the remainder of the useful life of the equipment. As a condition of use, however, EPA has imposed specific marking, storage, disposal, reporting, recordkeeping, and spill cleanup requirements. For example, PCBs at any concentration may be used in transformers (other than in railroad locomotives) and may be used for servicing such transformers for the remainder of their useful lives subject to certain use conditions. Those conditions include:

*   Prohibition on the use and storage for reuse of PCB Transformers (i.e., transformers that contain 500 ppm PCBs or greater) that pose an exposure risk to food or feed on or after October 1, 1985.

*   Prohibition on the use of network PCB Transformers with higher secondary voltages (480 volts and above, including 480/277 volt systems) in or near commercial buildings on or after October 1, 1990.

*   Prohibition on the installation of PCB Transformers in or near commercial buildings after having been placed into storage for reuse or removed from another location on or after October 1, 1985.

*   Installation of electrical protection to avoid transformer ruptures caused by high current faults on all radial PCB Transformers in use in or near commercial buildings and all lower secondary voltage network PCB Transformers (below 480 volts) not located in sidewalk vaults in or near commercial buildings no later than October 1, 1990.

*   Removal of all lower secondary voltage network PCB Transformers (below 480 volts) located in sidewalk vaults in use near commercial buildings no later than October 1, 1993.

*   Installation of electrical protection to avoid transformer ruptures caused by sustained high and low current faults on all radial PCB Transformers with higher secondary voltages (480 volts and above, including 480/277 volt systems) in use in or near commercial buildings no later than October 1, 1990.

*   Registration of all PCB Transformers (including PCB Transformers in storage for reuse) with fire response personnel with primary jurisdiction no later than December 1, 1985.

*   Registration of all PCB Transformers located in commercial buildings with the building owner no later than December 1, 1985.

*   Registration of all PCB Transformers located near commercial buildings with the owners of all buildings located within 30 meters of the PCB Transformer(s) no later than December 1, 1985.

* Prohibition on storing combustible materials within a PCB Transformer enclosure or within five meters of an enclosure or a PCB Transformer on or after December 1, 1985.

* Visual inspection of each PCB Transformer in use or stored for reuse must be conducted at least once every three months.

* Repair or replacement of a PCB Transformer which is found to have a leak. Cleanup must be initiated within 48 hours of discovery of the leak.

* Notification immediately to the National Response Center (1-800-424-8802) whenever a PCB Transformer is involved in a fire-related incident.

* Containment and control of any potential releases of PCBs into water by the owner of the PCB Transformer whenever there is a fire-related incident.

* Retention of inspection and maintenance records for at least three years after disposing of the PCB Transformer.[45]

The owner of a PCB Transformer must furnish the appropriate fire response personnel with the following information: (1) the physical location of the transformer(s); (2) the principal constituent of the dielectric fluid in the transformer(s) (e.g., PCBs, mineral oil, or silicone oil); and (3) the name and telephone number of the person to contact in the event of a fire involving the equipment.[46]

The owner of a PCB Transformer in use in or near commercial buildings must furnish the appropriate building owners with the following information: (1) the specific location of the PCB Transformer(s); (2) the principal constituent of the dielectric fluid in the transformer(s); and (3) the type of transformer installation (e.g., 208/120 volt network, 280/120 volt radial, 208 volt radial, 480 volt network, 480/277 volt network, 480 volt radial, 480/277 volt radial).[47]

The owner of a PCB Transformer involved in a fire-related incident resulting in the release of PCBs must furnish the National Response Center in Washington, D.C., with the following information: (1) the type of PCB Transformer installation involved (e.g., high or low secondary voltage network transformer, high or low secondary voltage simple radial system, expanded radial system, primary selective system, primary loop system, or secondary selective system or other system); and (2) the readily ascertainable cause of the incident (e.g., high current fault in the primary or secondary voltage system or low current fault in the secondary voltage system).[48]

The owner of a PCB Transformer must maintain the following information in the inspection and maintenance records for each PCB Transformer: (1) its location; (2) the date of each visual inspection and the date that a leak was discovered; (3) the name of the person conducting the inspection; (4) the location of any leak; (5) an estimate of the amount of dielectric fluid released from any leak; (6) the date of any

---

[45]*See*, 40 C.F.R. § 761.30(a).

[46]*See*, 40 C.F.R. § 761.30(a)(1)(vi).

[47]*See*, 40 C.F.R. § 761.30(a)(1)(vii).

[48]*See*, 40 C.F.R. § 761.30(a)(1)(xi).

cleanup, containment, repair, or replacement; (7) a description of any cleanup, containment, or repair performed; and (8) the results of any containment and daily inspection required for uncorrected active leaks.[49]

D.   PCB Spill Cleanup Policy

EPA has established a PCB Spill Cleanup Policy which applies to spills of materials containing PCBs at concentrations of 50 parts per million (ppm) or greater. The policy applies to spills which occur after May 4, 1987.[50] It creates numerical cleanup standards and uniform reporting requirements for such spills.

The cleanup standards and spill reporting requirements established in the policy do not preempt the standards or requirements imposed under other Federal acts. Where more than one standard applies, the stricter standard must be met.[51] Likewise, the spill reporting requirements are in addition to applicable reporting requirements under the Clean Water Act or the Comprehensive Environmental Response, Compensation and Liability Act ("CERCLA"), as amended by the Superfund Amendments and Reauthorization Act ("SARA").[52]

Spills contaminating surface waters, sewers, drinking water supplies, animal grazing lands, or vegetable gardens must be reported by the responsible party (i.e., owner or operator of the facility or equipment) to the appropriate EPA regional office (Pesticides and Toxic Substances Branch) within 24 hours after discovery.[53]

Spills of more than 10 pounds of PCBs by weight contaminating areas other than surface waters, sewers, drinking water supplies, animal grazing lands, or vegetable gardens, must be reported by the responsible party to the appropriate EPA regional office within 24 hours after discovery. Notification to EPA is not required for PCB spills of 10 pounds or less contaminating areas other than surface waters, sewers, drinking water supplies, animal grazing lands, or vegetable gardens.[54]

Cleanups of PCB spills must be documented with records of decontamination. The records must be maintained for 5 years from the date of the spill. Different decontamination levels are required depending upon spill location, potential exposure to residual PCBs remaining after cleanup, concentration of PCBs initially spilled, and the nature and size of the population potentially exposed. The types of records maintained on the PCB spill will depend on whether the cleanup involves less than 1 pound of PCBs by weight or involves 1 pound or more of PCBs by weight.

---

[49]*See*, 40 C.F.R. § 761.30(a)(1)(xii).

[50]*See*, 40 C.F.R. Part 761, Subpart G.

[51]*See*, 40 C.F.R. § 761.120(e).

[52]*See*, 40 C.F.R. § 761.125(a)(1).

[53]*See*, 40 C.F.R. § 761.125(a)(1)(i) and (ii).

[54]*See*, 40 C.F.R. § 761.125(a)(1)(iii) and (iv).

If the cleanup involves less than 1 pound of PCBs by weight (i.e., less than 270 gallons of untested mineral oil), the following records must be maintained:

*   Identification of the source of the spill (e.g., type of equipment).

*   Estimated or actual date and time of the spill occurrence.

*   Date and time cleanup was completed.

*   Brief description of the spill location.

*   Precleanup sampling data used to establish the spill boundaries where there are insufficient visible traces but other evidence of a spill.

*   Brief description of the sampling methodology used to establish the spill boundaries.

*   Brief description of the solid surfaces cleaned and the double wash/rinse method used.

*   Approximate depth of soil excavation and the amount of soil removed.

*   Certification statement signed by the responsible party stating that the cleanup requirements have been met and that the information contained in the record is true to the best of his/her knowledge.[55]

If the cleanup involves 1 pound or more of PCBs by weight (i.e., 270 gallons or more of untested mineral oil), the following records must be maintained:

*   Identification of the source of the spill.

*   Estimated or actual date and time of the spill occurrence.

*   Date and time cleanup was completed.

*   Brief description of the spill location (e.g., outdoor electrical substation, other restricted access location, or nonrestricted access area) and the nature of the nature of the material contaminated.

*   Precleanup sampling data used to establish the spill boundaries where there are insufficient visible traces but other evidence of a spill.

*   Brief description of the sampling methodology used to establish the spill boundaries.

*   Brief description of the solid surfaces cleaned.

---

[55]*See,* 40 C.F.R. § 761.125(b)(3).

* Approximate depth of soil excavation and the amount of soil removed.

* Postcleanup verification sampling data.

* Brief description of the sampling methodology and analytical technique used for the postcleanup sampling.[56]

E.   PCB Waste Disposal Records and Reports

All commercial storers, transporters, and disposers of PCB waste engaged in PCB waste handling activities on or before February 5, 1990 were required to notify EPA of their PCB waste activities by April 4, 1990. Notification must be made by filing a "Notification of PCB Waste Activity Form" (EPA Form 7710-53) with EPA.[57]

All commercial storers, transporters, and disposers of PCB waste who first engage in PCB waste handling activities after February 5, 1990 are required to notify EPA of their PCB waste activities by filing the Notification of PCB Waste Activity Form with EPA before engaging in PCB waste handling activities.[58]

Generators of PCB waste who use, own, service, or process PCBs or PCB Items must notify EPA of their PCB waste activities only if they own or operate facilities which (1) are used for the storage of PCBs and PCB Items designated for disposal, or (2) use storage containers for liquid PCBs which are larger than the shipping containers required by the U.S. Department of Transportation for the transportation of liquid PCBs.[59] Such generators are required to submit a separate notification to EPA for each storage facility. Upon receipt of the notification, EPA will assign a unique EPA identification number to each facility.

The following information must be reported to EPA on the Notification of PCB Waste Activity Form:

* Name of the facility and the name of the owner or operator.

* EPA identification number, if any, previously issued to the facility.

* Mailing address of the facility.

* Location of the facility.

* Facility contact and telephone number.

---

[56]*See*, 40 C.F.R. § 761.125(c)(5).

[57]*See*, 40 C.F.R. § 761.205(a)(1).

[58]*See*, 40 C.F.R. § 761.205(a)(2).

[59]*See*, 40 C.F.R. § 761.205(c)(2). Any container used for the storage of liquid PCBs should comply with the Shipping Container Specification of the DOT, 49 C.F.R. § 178.80 (Specification 5 container without removable head); 49 C.F.R. § 178.82 (Specification 5B container without removable head); 49 C.F.R. § 178.102 (Specification 6D overpack with Specification 2S(§ 178.35) or 2SL(§ 178.35a) polyethylene containers); or 49 C.F.R. § 178.116 (Specification 17E container).

* Type of PCB waste activity engaged in at the facility.

* Signature of the signer of the certification statement, typed or printed name, official title of the signer, and date signed.[60]

Generators who send their PCB waste to a commercial off-site storage or disposal facility must prepare a Uniform Hazardous Waste Manifest (EPA Form 8700-22), and if necessary, a continuation sheet. The generator of PCB waste must (1) sign the manifest certification, (2) obtain the handwritten signature of the initial transporter and date of acceptance on the manifest, (3) retain one copy for its records, and (4) give the remaining copies of the manifest to the transporter.[61]

Generators of PCB waste must keep a copy of each manifest signed by the commercial storer or disposer for at least 3 years from the date the PCB waste was accepted by the initial transporter. Similarly, the owner or operator of a PCB commercial storage or disposal facility must keep a copy of each signed manifest for at least 3 years from the date the facility received the off-site shipment of PCB waste.[62]

The owner or operator of a PCB commercial disposal facility must prepare a Certificate of Disposal for each shipment of manifested PCB waste accepted by the facility for disposal. The Certificate of Disposal must be sent to the generator of the PCB waste within 30 days of the date that the PCB waste was disposed of by the facility. A disposal facility must retain a copy of the Certificate of Disposal for at least 3 years after the facility is no longer used for disposal. A generator must retain a copy of the Certificate of Disposal for at least 3 years after the generator ceases using or storing PCBs and PCB Items.[63]

Generators of PCB waste must prepare an annual document log and maintain it at the facility for a minimum of three years after the facility ceases to use or store PCBs or PCB items. The log must include:

* The name, address and EPA ID number of the facility, and the calendar year covered;

* The unique manifest number of every manifest generated by the facility during the year;

* for bulk PCB waste (e.g., in a tank or truck), the

　　a.　weight of the waste in kilograms

　　b.　first date it was removed from service for disposal

　　c.　date it was placed into transport for off-site storage or disposal; and

---

[60]*See*, 40 C.F.R. § 761.205(a)(4).

[61]*See*, 40 C.F.R. §§ 761.207(a) and 761.208(a)(1).

[62]*See*, 40 C.F.R. § 761.209(a) and (c).

[63]*See*, 40 C.F.R. § 761.218.

     d.   date of disposal, if known.

*   the serial number (or other means) to identify each PCB Article (i.e., transformer, capacitor, electric motor), weight in kilograms of the PCB waste in each article, and the

     a.   date is was removed from service for disposal;

     b.   date it was placed in transport for off-site storage or disposal; and

     c.   date of disposal, if known.

*   a unique number identifying each PCB Container or PCB Article Container, plus:

     a.   a description of the contents;

     b.   the total weight in kilograms of the material in each container;

     c.   the first date material or an article placed in each PCB Container was removed from service for disposal;

     d.   the date each container was placed in transport for off-site storage or disposal;

     e.   the date of disposal, if known;

     f.   the total number by specific type of PCB Articles;

     g.   the total weight in kilograms of PCBs in PCB Articles; and

     h.   the total number of PCB Article Containers;

     i.   the total weight in kilograms of the PCB Article Containers;

     j.   the total number of PCB Containers;

     k.   the total weight in kilograms of the PCB Containers;

     l.   the total weight in kilograms of bulk PCB waste that was placed into storage for disposal or disposed of during the calendar year.

     m.   the total number of PCB transformers and the total weight in kilograms of PCBs in the transformers remaining in service at the end of the calendar year;

     n.   the total number of large high or low voltage PCB capacitors remaining in service at the end of the calendar year.

o.   the total weight in kilograms of any PCBs and PCB Items in PCB Containers remaining in service at the end of the calendar year.

p.   a record of each telephone call or other contact made with each designated commercial storer or disposer to confirm receipt of PCB waste transported by an independent transporter.[64]

V.   INFORMATION GATHERING

A.   Preliminary Assessment Information Rule

Section 8 of TSCA authorizes EPA to require chemical manufacturers, importers and processors to maintain records and to report certain information. EPA uses the information gathered under Section 8(a) to set priorities for testing under Section 4 and regulatory action under Section 6. The Agency has used its authority under Section 8(a) to issue rules which apply to specific chemicals. One of these rules is the Preliminary Assessment Information Rule ("PAIR").

Under the PAIR, manufacturers and importers must report on each listed chemical substance which is manufactured or imported for commercial purposes during the reporting period established for that substance. The chemical substances subject to reporting under the PAIR are listed in 40 C.F.R. § 712.30.[65] Processors are exempt from reporting under the PAIR. The PAIR form ("Manufacturer's Report-Preliminary Assessment Information," EPA Form No. 7710-35) requires the following information:

*   Certification of the technical accuracy and confidentiality of the data reported.

*   Physical location of the plant site, its mailing address, and its Dunn & Bradstreet number.

*   Name of a technical contact person familiar with the information submitted.

*   Chemical identity of the substance.

*   Amount of the chemical substance manufactured or imported.

*   Amount of the chemical substance routinely lost during manufacturing operations.

*   Description of the amount processed in enclosed, controlled release, or open process operations.

---

[64]*See*, 40 C.F.R. § 761.180(a).

[65]*See*, 40 C.F.R. § 712.30(d) through (w).

* Number of workers involved in each process operation.

* Quantity of the substance prepared for distribution for industrial and consumer products.

* Quantity of the substance for export.

* Quantity of the substance consumed as a reactant.

* Quantity of the substance for which customer uses are unknown.[66]

Chemical substances can be added under the PAIR after (1) a notice of a proposed amendment appears in the Federal Register, (2) a 30 day public comment period, (3) consideration of the comments received, and (4) issuance of final amendment by the EPA. Substances identified by the Interagency Testing Committee, established under Section 4(e) of TSCA, for priority testing by the EPA, are also added 30 days after EPA publishes in the Federal Register a rule amendment listing these substances.[67]

Certain manufacturers and importers are exempt from the PAIR reporting requirements. Exemptions have been provided for the following activities:

* Manufacture or importation of the chemical substance during the reporting period solely for the purpose of research and development.

* Manufacture or importation of less than 500 kilograms (1100 pounds) of the chemical substance at a single plant site during the reporting period.

* Manufacture or importation of the chemical substance during the reporting period as: (i) a by-product that was not used or sold; (ii) a non-isolated intermediate; or (iii) an impurity.[68]

Small manufacturers and importers of a chemical substance manufactured at a particular plant site are exempt from PAIR reporting if two conditions can be met. First, total annual sales of all sites owned or controlled by the domestic or foreign parent company must be below $30 million for the reporting period. Second, total production of the listed substance must be below 45,400 kilograms (100,000 pounds) at the plant site for the reporting period.[69]

---

[66]*See*, 40 C.F.R. § 712.28.

[67]*See*, 40 C.F.R. § 712.30(b) and (c). In a final rule issued February 9, 1994, EPA added 34 chemical substances to the PAIR. *See*, 59 *Fed. Reg.* 5959 (February 9, 1994).

[68]*See*, 40 C.F.R. § 712.25(a), (b) and (d).

[69]*See*, 40 C.F.R. § 712.25(c).

B.   **Comprehensive Assessment Information Rule**

On December 22, 1988, EPA issued a second rule for gathering information on chemical substances under Section 8(a) of TSCA. This rule is the Comprehensive Assessment Information Rule ("CAIR").[70] The CAIR establishes uniform reporting and recordkeeping requirements for those substances subject to reporting.

There are three basic differences between the PAIR and the CAIR. First, only manufacturers and importers are subject to the PAIR, whereas processors are potentially covered by the CAIR. Second, the CAIR reporting form is longer and more detailed than the PAIR form. Each question on the PAIR form requires an answer. CAIR respondents, however, are required to answer only the questions designated for each chemical substance. Third, while most substances on the PAIR list are added without notice and public comment (i.e., when the Interagency Testing Committee designates or recommends that EPA require testing under Section 4 of TSCA), EPA can amend the list of substances subject to the CAIR only by notice and public comment rulemaking.

Under the CAIR, manufacturers, importers, or processors of a listed chemical substance are potentially subject to CAIR reporting requirements. Many activities that are typically considered manufacturing or processing are exempt from the CAIR. For example, the CAIR exempts (1) the processing or importing of a CAIR listed substance solely as part of an article, (2) the manufacture of a CAIR listed substance solely as a non-isolated intermediate, and (3) the manufacture, import, or processing of small quantities of a CAIR listed substance solely for research and development.[71] In addition, the CAIR exempts small manufacturers, importers and processors.[72] Finally, a repackager of a CAIR listed substance is exempt from the CAIR reporting and recordkeeping requirements if it does not engage in any other processing activities.[73]

The CAIR rule lists only 19 chemical substances subject to reporting.[74] The time period during which the reportable activity must have occurred to trigger the reporting requirements is February 8, 1987 to February 5, 1989. Respondents were required to report only on activities that occurred during their latest reporting year (i.e., fiscal or calendar year) which fell within the CAIR coverage period.[75] Respondents had 90 days after the effective date of February 6, 1989 to make a timely submission.[76]

---

[70]*See*, 40 C.F.R. Part 704, Subparts C and D.

[71]*See*, 40 C.F.R. § 704.210.

[72]Under the CAIR, a manufacturer, importer, or processor is considered "small" if it manufactures, imports or processes less than 45,400 kilograms (100,000 pounds) of the listed substance annually and has total annual sales of less than $40 million. In addition, a manufacturer, importer or processor is considered "small" if its total annual sales are less than $4 million, regardless of the quantity of the listed chemical produced, importer or processed. The above-mentioned sales figures include those of its parent company as well.

[73]A "repackager" is a person who buys a CAIR listed substance, removes the substance from the container in which it was bought, and transfers the substance, as is, to another container for sale.

[74]*See*, 40 C.F.R. § 704.225(a).

[75]*See*, 40 C.F.R. § 704.214(d).

[76]*See*, 40 C.F.R. § 704.223(a).

Respondents must answer all questions in Section 1 of the CAIR Reporting Form (EPA Form 7710-52). Additional questions selected for each listed chemical substance are specified in the chemical substance matrix set forth at 40 C.F.R. § 704.225. One CAIR Reporting Form must be submitted for each site at which a listed substance is manufactured, imported, or processed. If a person is engaged in more than one activity (i.e., manufacturing and processing of the listed substance) at the same site, that person is only required to report on the activity or activities specified for the substance.[77]

The CAIR Reporting Form consists of 10 sections.[78] Each section contains specific questions which pertain to the subject matter found in that particular section. The sections cover the following categories of information:

* General Manufacturer, Importer, and Processor Information.

* Manufacturer, Importer, and Processor Volume, and Use.

* Processor Raw Material Identification.

* Physical/Chemical Properties.

* Environmental Fate Data.

* Economic and Financial Information.

* Manufacture and Process Information.

* Residual Treatment, Generation, Characterization, Transportation,and Management.

* Worker Exposure.

* Environmental Release.

Respondents must assert and substantiate all claims of confidentiality at the time the CAIR form is submitted. Failure to provide substantiation of a confidentiality claim at the time of submission results in a waiver of the claim. Respondents who assert a confidentiality claim on submitted information must submit both their complete CAIR form and a second copy which contains only information not claimed as confidential. In addition, respondents must substantiate their confidential business information ("CBI") claims by completing the pertinent portions of the CBI substantiation form found in Appendix II of the CAIR form.[79]

Respondents must maintain a copy of each CAIR report submitted to EPA, supporting materials and documentation sufficient to verify or reconstruct each report, and a copy of all notices sent to and all return receipts received from their customers to whom they distributed a listed substance under a trade name. These records must be retained for three years from the date they were prepared.[80]

---

[77]*See*, 40 C.F.R. § 704.212.

[78]*See*, 40 C.F.R. § 704.207.

[79]*See*, 40 C.F.R. § 704.219.

[80]*See*, 40 C.F.R. § 704.11.

C.   Inventory Update Rule

TSCA Section 8(b) requires EPA to identify, compile, update, and publish a list of chemical substances manufactured, imported or processed for commercial purposes in the United States. This list is known as the TSCA Chemical Substance Inventory. The Inventory contains a total of 68,000 chemical substances.[81]

Update reporting is required for those persons who manufacture or import 10,000 pounds or more of any listed chemical substance at any single site during their latest complete corporate fiscal year prior to August 25, 1990, or before August 25th every four years thereafter.[82] Current data on production volume and plant site must be provided. Small manufacturers and manufacturers or importers of chemical substances used solely for research and development are exempt from these requirements.[83] In addition, persons who import the substance as part of an article, or manufacture the substance as an impurity, a by-product, a nonisolated intermediate, or in a manner incidental to its end use, are exempt from these reporting requirements.

All TSCA Inventory update information must be submitted during the applicable reporting period. The first recurring reporting period was from August 25, 1990 to December 23, 1990. Subsequent recurring reporting periods are from August 25th to December 23rd every four years thereafter.[84] The update information may be submitted in writing or on computer tape. Written submissions must be on EPA Form No. 7740-8 entitled "Partial Updating of TSCA Inventory Database Production and Site Report."[85] Manufacturers and importers subject to these reporting requirements must retain relevant records for 4 years from the effective date of the reporting period.[86] Moreover, volume records must be maintained for 4 years on those substances that are manufactured or imported in amounts less than 10,000 pounds annually as evidence to support a decision not to report.

D.   Records of Significant Adverse Reactions

Section 8(c) of TSCA requires manufacturers, processors, and distributors to maintain records of "significant adverse reactions to health or the environment" alleged to have been caused by a chemical substance or mixture. A "significant adverse reaction" is a reaction that may indicate a substantial impairment of normal activities, or long-lasting or irreversible damage to health or the environment.[87]

---

[81]*See*, 55 Fed. Reg. 33959 (1990).

[82]*See*, 40 C.F.R. § 710.28(b).

[83]*See*, 40 C.F.R. §§ 710.29 and 710.30.

[84]*See*, 40 C.F.R. § 710.33(b).

[85]*See*, 40 C.F.R. § 710.32(a) and (b).

[86]*See*, 40 C.F.R. § 710.37.

[87]*See*, 40 C.F.R. § 717.3(i).

Manufacturers of chemical substances covered by TSCA are subject to the recordkeeping requirements established in Section 8(c) of TSCA.[88] Manufacturers involved solely in mining and other extractive operations, e.g., mineral ores, petroleum, natural gas, non-metallic minerals, coal, etc., however, are exempt from these recordkeeping requirements.[89] Processors who process chemical substances to produce mixtures (e.g., formulators) or who repackage chemical substances or mixtures are subject to these recordkeeping requirements.[90] EPA, however, has exempted retailers and sole distributors engaged solely in the distribution of chemical substances from the provisions of Section 8(c).[91]

Allegations of significant adverse reactions to human health that must be recorded include, but are not limited to, the following:

* Long-lasting or irreversible damage, such as cancer or birth defects.

* Partial or incomplete impairment of bodily functions, such as reproductive disorders, neurological disorders or blood disorders.

* Impairment of normal activities experienced by all or most of the persons exposed at one time.

* Impairment of normal activities which is experienced each time an individual is exposed.

* Human health effect that is significantly more toxic than previously described in the scientific literature or the material safety data sheet ("MSDS").

* Human health effect that shows a toxic effect after a significantly shorter exposure period or lower exposure level than previously described in the scientific literature or the MSDS.

* Human health effect that shows a toxic effect by an exposure route different from that previously described in the scientific literature or the MSDS.[92]

Allegations of significant adverse reactions to the environment that must be recorded, even if restricted to a plant or disposal site, include, but are not limited to, the following:

* Gradual or sudden changes in the composition of animal or plant life, including fungal or microbial organisms, in an area.

* Abnormal number of deaths of organisms (e.g., fish kills).

---

[88]*See,* 40 C.F.R. § 717.5(a).

[89]*See,* 40 C.F.R. § 717.7(a).

[90]*See,* 40 C.F.R. § 717.5(b).

[91]*See,* 40 C.F.R. § 717.7(c) and (d).

[92]*See,* 40 C.F.R. § 717.12(a) and (b).

* Reduction of the reproductive success or the vigor of a species.

* Reduction in agricultural productivity whether crops or livestock.

* Alterations in the behavior or distribution of a species.

* Long lasting or irreversible contamination of the groundwater, surface water and soil.[93]

Firms subject to the Section 8(c) recordkeeping requirements are not required to record a significant adverse reaction to the environment if the alleged cause can be directly attributed to an accidental spill or other accidental discharge, an emission exceeding permitted limits, or other incident of environmental contamination that has been reported to the federal government.[94]

An "allegation" is defined by EPA as "a statement, made without formal proof or regard for evidence, that a chemical substance or mixture has caused a significant adverse reaction to health or the environment."[95] Allegations may be submitted either orally or in writing. If the allegation is submitted orally, the firm must transcribe the allegation into written form, or it must inform the alleger that the allegation may be subject to TSCA Section 8(c) regulations and request that the alleger submit the allegation in writing and sign it.[96]

No evidence or proof, such as a medical doctor's report, is required for an allegation to be recordable. An allegation must state the alleged cause of the significant adverse reaction by identifying one or more of the following:

* The specific substance which allegedly caused the significant adverse reaction.

* A mixture that contains the specific substance.

* An article that contains the specific substance.

* A company process or operation in which the substance is involved.

* An effluent, emission, or other discharge from a site where the substance is manufactured, processed or distributed.[97]

Allegations meeting the criteria mentioned above that are received on or after November 21, 1983 are subject to the recordkeeping requirements under TSCA Section 8(c). Allegations may be made to a firm from any source, including an employee of the firm, individual consumer, a neighbor of the firm's

---

[93]*See*, 40 C.F.R. § 717.12(c).

[94]*See*, 40 C.F.R. § 717.12(d).

[95]*See*, 40 C.F.R. § 717.3(a).

[96]*See*, 40 C.F.R. § 717.10(b)(1).

[97]*See*, 40 C.F.R. § 717.10(b)(2).

plant, another firm on behalf of its employees or an organization on behalf of its members.[98] In addition, a lawsuit or legal proceedings, including pre-trial discovery documents, which meet the criteria under TSCA Section 8(c), can constitute an allegation.

EPA does not require allegations of significant adverse reactions to be recorded on a specific form. Records of such allegations must be kept at the firm's headquarters or at any other appropriate location central to the firm's chemical operations.[99] In addition to the original allegation, the firm's records must consist of an abstract of the allegation containing the following information:

* Name and address of the plant site which received the allegation.

* Date the allegation was received at that site.

* Name of the implicated substance, mixture, article, company process or operation, or site discharge.

* Description of the alleger (e.g., "company employee," "individual consumer," "plant neighbor"). If the allegation involves a health effect, the sex and year of birth of the individual should be recorded.

* Description of the alleged health effect(s). The description must relate how the effect(s) became known and the route of exposure, if explained in the allegation.

* Description of the nature of the alleged environmental effect(s), identifying the affected plant and/or animal species, or contaminated portion of the physical environment.[100]

In addition, a firm's records should include (1) the results of any self-initiated investigation related to an allegation, and (2) copies of any required records or reports relating to the allegation (e.g., OSHA records).[101] The firm's records must be retrievable by the alleged cause of the significant adverse reaction, such as (1) specific chemical identity; (2) a mixture; (3) an article; (4) a company process or operation; or (5) a site emission, effluent or other discharge.[102]

Records of significant adverse reactions to the health of employees must be retained for 30 years from the date such reactions were first reported. Thus, an employee health related allegation of a significant adverse reaction, arising from any employment related exposure, must be retained for 30 years even if the allegation was submitted by an organization on behalf of the employee. All other records of significant adverse reactions must be maintained for 5 years from the date such reactions were first reported. If a firm ceases to do business, the successor firm must receive and maintain the TSCA Section

---

[98]*See*, 40 C.F.R. § 717.10(a) and (c).

[99]*See*, 40 C.F.R. § 717.15(a).

[100]*See*, 40 C.F.R. § 717.15(b).

[101]*See*, 40 C.F.R. § 717.15(b)(3) and (4).

[102]*See*, 40 C.F.R. § 717.15(c).

8(c) records. If there is no successor to receive and maintain the records for the prescribed period, the records must be forwarded to EPA.[103]

TSCA Section 8(c) records are subject to inspection by EPA. In addition, EPA can require submission of the Section 8(c) records upon letter request or notice in the Federal Register.[104]

E.   Health and Safety Data Reporting Rule

Section 8(d) of TSCA authorizes EPA to require manufacturers, processors, or distributors of any chemical substance or mixture to submit lists and copies of unpublished health and safety studies conducted by, known to, or reasonably ascertainable by such persons. EPA uses the information obtained from these studies to make regulatory decisions under Sections 4, 5 and 6 of TSCA.

Under the TSCA Section 8(d) final rule, submission of copies of unpublished health and safety studies is required on those chemical substances or mixtures listed at 40 C.F.R. § 716.120. Substances and mixtures designated or listed by the Interagency Testing Committee are automatically added to the list and other substances and mixtures can be added by notice and public comment rulemaking.[105]

Manufacturers, importers, or processors of any of the specifically listed substances or mixtures and persons who manufactured, imported, or processed any of the listed substances or mixtures within the ten years preceding the effective date of the listing are subject to the Section 8(d) final rule. In addition, persons who propose to manufacture, import or process any of the listed substances or mixtures on or after the effective date of the listing and persons who proposed to manufacture, import or process any of the listed substances or mixtures within the ten years preceding the effective date of the listing are subject to the Section 8(d) reporting requirement.[106]

Health and safety study submissions must be postmarked on or before the 60th day after the effective date of the listing, or within 60 days of proposing to manufacture, import, or process a listed substance or mixture if the proposal is made after the effective date of the listing. Copies of any additional studies that are ongoing must be submitted within 30 days of their completion. In addition, EPA must be informed within 30 days of any study on a listed substance or mixture which is initiated by or for such manufacturer, importer, or processor after the initial 60 day reporting period.[107] These reporting requirements can continue for 10 years after the effective date of the listing or until the substance or mixture is removed from the list.[108]

The term "health and safety study" has been defined by EPA to mean "any study of any effect of a chemical substance or mixture on health or the environment or on both, including underlying data and epidemiological studies, studies of occupational exposure to a chemical substance or mixture, toxicological,

---

[103]*See*, 40 C.F.R. § 717.15(d) and (e).

[104]*See*, 40 C.F.R. § 717.17(a) and (b).

[105]*See*, 40 C.F.R. § 716.1(a). In a final rule issued February 9, 1994, EPA added 28 chemical substances to the Health and Safety Data Reporting Rule. *See*, 59 *Fed. Reg.* 5960 (February 9, 1994).

[106]*See*, 40 C.F.R. § 716.5.

[107]*See*, 40 C.F.R. § 716.60.

[108]*See*, 40 C.F.R. § 716.65(a).

clinical, and ecological or other studies of a chemical substance or mixture, and any test performed under TSCA."[109] EPA interprets this definition broadly so that other information relating to the effects of a chemical substance or mixture on health or the environment is included. The following types of tests are examples of health and safety studies within the meaning of the definition:

* Long and short-term tests of mutagenicity, carcinogenicity, or teratogenicity; data on behavioral disorders; dermatoxicity; pharmacological effects; mammalian absorption, distribution, metabolism, and excretion; cumulative, additive, and synergistic effects; and acute, subchronic, and chronic effects.

* Tests for ecological or other environmental effects on invertebrates, fish, or other animals, and plants, including, acute and chronic toxicity tests, critical life-stage tests, behavioral tests, algal growth tests, seed germination tests, plant growth or damage tests, microbial function tests, bioconcentration or bioaccumulation tests, and model ecosystem (microcosm) studies.

* Assessments of human and environmental exposure, including workplace exposure, and impacts of a particular chemical substance or mixture on the environment, including surveys, tests, and studies of biological, photochemical, and chemical degradation; structure/activity relationships; air, water, and soil transport; biomagnification and bioconcentration; and chemical and physical properties.

* Monitoring data, when they have been aggregated and analyzed to measure the exposure of humans or the environment to a chemical substance or mixture.[110]

Studies of chemical and physical properties mentioned above are reportable if performed for the purpose of determining the environmental or biological fate of a substance, and only if they investigated one or more of the following ten properties:

* Water solubility.

* Adsorption/desorption on soil.

* Vapor pressure.

* Octanol/water partition coefficient.

* Density/relative density (specific gravity).

* Particle size distribution for insoluble solids.

* Dissociation constant.

---

[109]*See*, 40 C.F.R. § 716.3.

[110]*See*, 40 C.F.R. § 716.3.

* Degradation by photochemical mechanisms-aquatic and atmospheric.

* Degradation by chemical mechanisms-hydrolytic, reductive, and oxidative.

* Degradation by biological mechanisms-aerobic and anaerobic.[111]

EPA has exempted certain types of studies from the copy and list submission requirements set forth in the Section 8(d) rule. The exemptions are as follows:

* Studies which have been published in the scientific literature.

* Studies previously submitted to the EPA's Office of Toxic Substances,[112] including, Section 8(e) submissions (to be discussed *infra.*); studies submitted during Section 4 proceedings; and studies submitted with premanufacture notices or significant new use notices.

* Studies previously submitted to a federal agency, other than EPA's Office of Toxic Substances, are exempt only from the copy submission requirements. Lists of such studies, however, must be furnished.

* Studies conducted or initiated by or for another person subject to TSCA Section 8(d).

* Studies of chemical substances which are not on the TSCA Inventory. This exemption applies only to those substances within categories listed under 40 C.F.R. § 716.120(c).

* Certain acute and primary toxicity studies. This exemption applies only when the substance tested was a mixture known to contain a listed substance or mixture. The following studies performed on mammals do not have to be submitted: (1) acute oral toxicity studies; (2) acute dermal toxicity studies; (3) acute inhalation toxicity studies; (4) primary eye irritation studies; (5) primary dermal irritation studies; and (6) dermal sensitization studies.

* Studies not involving one of the ten physical/chemical properties mentioned above. Studies involving any of the ten physical/chemical properties mentioned above are subject to reporting.

* Monitoring data collected more than five years before the substance or mixture was added to the TSCA Section 8(d) list.

---

[111]*See*, 40 C.F.R. § 716.50.

[112]EPA's Office of Toxic Substances ("OTS") has been renamed the Office of Pollution Prevention and Toxics ("OPPT").

* Studies of listed substances or mixtures manufactured or processed only as impurities.

* Studies of listed substances or mixtures previously submitted by trade associations within sixty days of listing by the EPA .

* Studies on plant growth or damage from ureaformaldehyde resins when applied as a fertilizer.[113]

Persons subject to reporting under TSCA Section 8(d) must submit copies of any nonexempt health and safety studies in their possession on the listed substances or mixtures to EPA. Submissions must be identified either on the face of the study or otherwise by the appropriate chemical name and Chemical Abstract Service Registry ("CAS") number, if any, and must be accompanied with a cover letter. The cover letter must contain the name, job title, address, and telephone number of the submitter, and the name and address of the manufacturing or processing firm on whose behalf the submission is made. In addition, the cover letter must identify any known impurity or additive which was present in the substance or mixture studied unless its presence is noted in the study.[114]

Persons subject to reporting under TSCA Section 8(d) also must submit lists of ongoing health and safety studies being conducted by or initiated for them. Each entry on the list must include the following information: (1) the beginning date of the study; (2) the purpose of the study; (3) the types of data to be collected; (4) the anticipated date of completion; and (5) the name and address of the laboratory conducting the study.[115]

In addition, persons subject to reporting under TSCA Section 8(d) must submit a list of unpublished health and safety studies known to them but for which they do not have copies. Moreover, the name and address of any person known to them to possess a copy of the unpublished study must accompany each such entry on the list.[116]

A list of unpublished health and safety studies which were sent to any federal agency without any claims of confidentiality also must be submitted by persons subject to the TSCA Section 8(d) requirements. Each entry on such list must include the following information: (1) the title of the study; (2) name and address of the person to whom the study was sent; and (3) the month and year in which the study was submitted.[117]

Each list submission must be identified by the appropriate chemical name and CAS number, if any, and must be accompanied by a cover letter. The cover letter must contain the name, job title, address and telephone number of the submitter, and the name and address of the manufacturing or processing firm on whose behalf the submission is made.[118]

---

[113]*See*, 40 C.F.R. § 716.20.

[114]*See*, 40 C.F.R. § 716.30.

[115]*See*, 40 C.F.R. § 716.35(a)(1) and (2).

[116]*See*, 40 C.F.R. § 716.35(a)(3).

[117]*See*, 40 C.F.R. § 716.35(a)(4).

[118]*See*, 40 C.F.R. § 716.35(b).

F.   Substantial Risk Notification

Section 8(e) of TSCA requires "any person who manufactures, [imports], processes, or distributes in commerce a chemical substance or mixture and who obtains information which reasonably supports the conclusion that such substance or mixture presents a substantial risk of injury to health or the environment" to immediately inform the EPA Administrator of such information unless that person has actual knowledge that the Administrator has been adequately informed of such information.[119] This section was enacted by Congress to ensure that information which indicates substantial risk receives prompt attention by EPA.

Substantial risk information which is reportable to EPA under Section 8(e) is "new information that reasonably supports a conclusion that a chemical substance or mixture presents a substantial risk of injury to health or the environment." The term "new information" refers to information (including preliminary data) which EPA has not been adequately informed. Such information most typically does not establish conclusively that a substantial risk of injury to health or the environment exists.[120]

Two factors must be considered in deciding whether information is "substantial risk" information. First, the seriousness of the adverse effect, and second, the fact or probability of the effect's occurrence. This criteria should be weighed differently depending upon the seriousness of the effect or the extent of the exposure, i.e., the more serious the effect, the less heavily one should weigh actual or potential exposure, and vice versa. For example, in cases where serious effects such as birth defects or cancer (as evidenced by benign and/or malignant tumors) are observed, the mere fact that the implicated substance is in commerce or in the R&D stage constitutes sufficient evidence of exposure to submit new toxicity data.[121]

Persons subject to TSCA's Section 8(e) reporting requirement should focus primarily on whether the toxicity or exposure information offers reasonable support for a conclusion of substantial risk on the basis of the above-mentioned criteria, but should not focus at all on whether the information is conclusive regarding the risk. A decision to report information under Section 8(e) should not involve exhaustive health and/or environmental risk assessments or any evaluation of the economic or social benefits of the uses of the substance.[122]

Persons who manufacture, process, or distribute in commerce a chemical substance or mixture for commercial purposes are subject to TSCA's Section 8(e) reporting requirements.[123] There are no exemptions for small businesses, small production or importation volumes, or commercial activities such as manufacture for export only or research and development. However, a person who obtains substantial risk information about a substance or mixture that the person did at one time manufacture, import, process or distribute in commerce, is not required to submit the information under Section 8(e) if that person no longer is engaged in such activity.

---

[119]*See,* 15 U.S.C.A. § 2607(e).

[120]*See,* 56 Fed. Reg. 4128 (1991).

[121]*See, Ibid.*

[122]*See, Ibid.*

[123]*See, Statement of Interpretation and Enforcement Policy on Notification of Substantial Risk,* 43 Fed. Reg. 11110, 11111 (1978) ("EPA's TSCA Section 8(e) Policy Statement").

EPA's TSCA Section 8(e) Policy Statement provides that within business entities, the president, chief executive officer, and any other officers responsible and having authority for the organization's Section 8(e) obligations must ensure that the organization reports any substantial risk information to EPA within 15 working days after the organization obtains it. The business entity is considered to have obtained the Section 8(e) information when any officer or employee "capable of appreciating the significance of that information" obtains it.[124]

Individual officers and employees can discharge their individual Section 8(e) responsibilities once they notify a designated supervisor or official in full about the pertinent information, provided the business entity has established, internally publicized and affirmatively implemented procedures governing such notices. EPA's TSCA Section 8(e) Policy Statement specifies that such procedures, at a minimum, must:

(1)   specify the information that must be reported;

(2)   indicate how the reports are to be prepared and submitted internally;

(3)   note the Federal civil and criminal penalties for failure to report substantial risk information; and

(4)   provide a mechanism for the timely notification of officers and employees who submitted reports about the disposition of those reports. Such written notification should inform the reporting officer or employee as to whether the information was submitted to EPA, and if not, inform the officer or employee of their protected right under TSCA Section 23 to report the information directly to EPA.[125]

The above-mentioned procedures are designed to ensure prompt and appropriate processing and consideration of pertinent information by persons subject to Section 8(e). EPA maintains that despite the establishment of such procedures, those officers and employees who are responsible for actual management of the organization's Section 8(e) reporting obligations retain personal civil and/or criminal liability for ensuring that substantial risk information is submitted to EPA. In the absence of such established internal procedures, all employees and officers capable of appreciating the significance of substantial risk information retain their individual responsibilities and liabilities for ensuring that such information is reported to EPA.[126]

Except for those chemical substances specifically excluded by definition from TSCA jurisdiction,[127] Section 8(e) applies to all chemical substances and mixtures including, but not limited to, the following:

*   Research and development chemical substances and mixtures (including those intended for use as pesticides prior to application for an Experimental Use Permit ("EUP") or a registration under the Federal Insecticide, Fungicide and Rodenticide Act ("FIFRA").

*   Laboratory reagents used for detecting or measuring a component.

---

[124]*See, Ibid.*

[125]*See, Ibid.*

[126]*See, Ibid.*

[127]*See, Footnote 2.*

* Low volume chemicals.

* Polymers.

* Chemicals that are manufactured solely for export.

* Intermediates including nonisolated intermediates as well as pesticide intermediates.

* Catalysts.

* By-products.

* Impurities.[128]

TSCA Section 8(e) reportable information can be found in a variety of sources including draft, interim or final written reports (i.e., study reports, letters, telegrams, telex reports) or verbal reports (received at meetings or by phone) that involve observations (including preliminary observations) from, controlled or uncontrolled:

(1) human or animal studies/events (including but not limited to studies/events that involve high dose levels or non-routine routes of exposure); or

(2) environmental events/studies (including but not limited to aquatic toxicity studies, bioaccumulation studies, and chemical monitoring studies.[129]

Under EPA's TSCA Section 8(e) Policy Statement, a person is considered to have complied with the TSCA Section 8(e) reporting obligation if the information is received at EPA Headquarters in writing within 15 working days after the person obtained the information. Relevant or significant supplemental data obtained after an initial Section 8(e) submission should also be reported in writing to EPA immediately (i.e., within 15 working days).[130]

A Section 8(e) submission must be transmitted in a manner that allows EPA to verify receipt of the submission (e.g., certified or registered mail). The submission must state clearly that it is being submitted in accordance with Section 8 of TSCA. In addition, the submission must contain the following information:

* Name, job title, address, telephone number, and signature of the person reporting the information.

* Name and address of the establishment with which the reporting person is affiliated.

* Name of the chemical substance or mixture (including, the CAS No., if known).

---

[128]*See, TSCA Section 8(e) Reporting Guide*, Office of Toxic Substances, U.S. Environmental Protection Agency (1991), p. 5.

[129]*See,* EPA's *TSCA Section 8(e) Policy Statement*, 43 Fed. Reg. 11110, 11112 (1978).

[130]*See, Ibid.*, p. 11113.

* Summary describing the nature of the adverse effects and the extent of the risk involved.

* Source of any available supporting technical data.[131]

Information that qualifies for Section 8(e) reporting does not need to be submitted if the information meets one or more of the following criteria:

* Is contained in an EPA study or report.

* Is published in the scientific literature and referenced by the following abstract services: (1) Agricola, (2) Biological Abstracts, (3) Chemical Abstracts, (4) Dissertation Abstracts, (5) Index Medicus, (6) National Technical Information Service.

* Is obtained from major U.S. news publications (e.g., newspapers or news magazines with national circulation) or nationally broadcast U.S. radio and/or television news reports.

* Has been submitted already in writing to EPA pursuant to mandatory reporting requirements under TSCA or any other authority administered by EPA.

* Is contained in a formal publication/report or a formal statement made available to the general public by another federal agency.

* Is corroborative (in terms of, for example, route of exposure, dose, species, time to onset, severity, species, strain, etc.) of a well established adverse effect already documented in the scientific literature.

* Is contained in a notification of spills under Section 311(b)(5) of the Clean Water Act.

* Is information for which the EPA Administrator has waived compliance with TSCA in general or Section 8(e) specifically upon a request and determination by the President of the United States that such a waiver is required in the interest of the national defense.[132]

Notwithstanding these exemptions from the Section 8(e) reporting requirements, information that newly identifies a serious toxic effect at a lower dose level or confirms a serious effect that was previously only suspected, is not considered by EPA to be corroborative and should be reported under Section 8(e).[133]

---

[131]*See, Ibid.*

[132]*See, TSCA Section 8(e) Reporting Guide,* Office of Toxic Substances, U.S. Environmental Protection Agency, (1991), p. 6; and *TSCA Section 8(e) Policy Statement,* 43 Fed. Reg. 11110, 11112 (1978).

[133]*See, TSCA Section 8(e) Reporting Guide,* Office of Toxic Substances, U.S. Environmental Protection Agency (1991), p. 8.

TSCA's Section 8(e) Policy Statement also requires immediate reporting of "Emergency Incidents of Environmental Contamination" ("EIEC"). An EIEC is an environmental contamination (accidental or intentional in nature) involving a chemical known to be a serious human or environmental toxicant and which because of the extent, pattern and amount of the contamination (1) seriously threatens humans with cancer, birth defects, mutation, death or serious or prolonged incapacitation (e.g., neurotoxicologic effects, serious reproductive system effects), or (2) seriously threatens non-human organisms with large-scale or ecologically significant population destruction.[134]

An EIEC must be reported immediately (i.e., as soon as is reasonably possible) by telephone to the appropriate EPA Regional Office in whose jurisdiction the EIEC occurred or was discovered. The current 24-hour phone numbers for EPA's 10 Regional Offices are as follows:

Region I (Maine, Rhode Island, Connecticut, Vermont, Massachusetts, New Hampshire), (617) 223-7265.

Region II (New York, New Jersey, Puerto Rico, Virgin Islands), (201) 548-8730.

Region III (Pennsylvania, West Virginia, Virginia, Maryland, Delaware, District of Columbia), (215) 597-9898.

Region IV (Kentucky, Tennessee, North Carolina, South Carolina, Georgia, Alabama, Mississippi, Florida), (404) 347-4062.

Region V (Wisconsin, Illinois, Indiana, Michigan, Ohio, Minnesota), (312) 353-2318.

Region VI (New Mexico, Texas, Oklahoma, Arkansas, Louisiana), (214) 655-2222.

Region VII (Nebraska, Iowa, Missouri, Kansas), (913) 236-3778.

Region VIII (Colorado, Utah, Wyoming, Montana, North Dakota, South Dakota), (303) 293-1788.

Region IX (California, Nevada, Arizona, Hawaii, Guam), (415) 744-2000.

Region X (Washington, Oregon, Idaho, Alaska), (206) 442-1263.

The initial telephone report of an EIEC must provide the time and location of the incident and as much of the following information as is possible at the time:

*	That it is being submitted in accordance with TSCA Section 8(e).

*	Name, job title, address, and telephone number of the person reporting and the name and address of the facility.

*	Name of the chemical substance or mixture.

*	Summary of the nature and extent of the risk involved and the adverse effects of the contamination.

---

[134]*See, TSCA's Section 8(e) Policy Statement*, 43 Fed.Reg. 11110, 11113 (1978). On June 20, 1991, EPA announced that it was suspending the applicability of Part V(c) ("emergency incidents of environmental contamination") of the *TSCA Section 8(e) Policy Statement*. Persons are still responsible under TSCA Section 8(e) to report information that reasonably supports a conclusion of substantial risk of injury to the environment. *See,* 56 Fed.Reg. 28458, 28459 (1991).

    *   Source of any supporting technical data on the contamination.[135]

If a person reporting an EIEC cannot reach the appropriate EPA Regional Office by telephone, the person reporting should immediately call the National Response Center in Washington, D.C. at (800) 424-8802 or (202) 426-2675. The caller should provide all known information requested by the officer on duty. Under these circumstances, EPA will consider the caller to have satisfied the initial Section 8(e) notification requirement.[136]

In addition, a written follow-up report must also be sent to EPA Headquarters within 15 working days of the date on which the telephone report was made. The written report must be transmitted in a manner that permits EPA to verify receipt of the submission (e.g., certified or registered mail). It must contain the following information:

    *   That it is being submitted in accordance with TSCA Section 8(e).

    *   Name, job title, address, telephone number and signature of the person reporting and the name and address of the facility.

    *   Name of the chemical substance or mixture (including, if known, the CAS No.).

    *   Summary of the nature and extent of the risk involved and the adverse effects of the contamination.

    *   Source of any supporting technical data on the contamination.[137]

TSCA Section 8(e) submissions, including written follow-up reports for an EIEC must be transmitted to EPA at the following address:

> Document Processing Center (TS-790)
> Attn: Section 8(e) Coordinator
> Office of Pollution Prevention and Toxics
> U.S. Environmental Protection Agency
> 401 M Street, S.W.
> Washington, D.C. 20460

It is important to note that all information reported under specific TSCA requirements is subject to the disclosure of data provisions of Section 14 of TSCA and EPA's regulations on confidentiality of business information (40 C.F.R. Part 2). Any person who submits confidential business information ("CBI") to EPA under Section 8(e) must submit two copies of such data. The first copy should be complete, with all CBI marked carefully and clearly by boxing, circling or underlining. Each page containing CBI should be stamped "CONFIDENTIAL". The other copy should have all of the confidential information removed. This "sanitized" version is required for EPA's public files. Any person who submits CBI to EPA under Section

---

[135]*See, TSCA Section 8(e) Policy Statement*, 43 Fed.Reg. 11110, 11113 (1978).

[136]*See, TSCA Section 8(e) Reporting Guide*, Office of Toxic Substances, U.S. Environmental Protection Agency, (1991), pp.12-13.

[137]*See, TSCA Section 8(e) Policy Statement*, 43 Fed.Reg. 11110, 11113 (1978).

8(e) of TSCA must provide a detailed written substantiation for all TSCA CBI claims. *See*, EPA Document entitled *Support Information for Confidentiality Claims*, which is attached as Appendix I.

On February 1, 1991, EPA announced the opportunity for persons to register for the TSCA Section 8(e) Compliance Audit Program ("CAP"). The CAP was a one-time voluntary compliance audit program developed to obtain outstanding TSCA Section 8(e) data and foster compliance with the statutory obligations of Section 8(e).[138] On June 20, 1991, EPA announced that the registration deadline/audit commencement date had been extended until July 1, 1991.[139] Persons interested in participating in the CAP were required to sign and return a CAP Agreement to EPA by certified mail-return receipt requested no later than July 1, 1991. A copy of the CAP Agreement is attached as Appendix II.

VI.   IMPORT REQUIREMENTS

Section 13 of TSCA requires the Secretary of the Treasury to refuse the entry into the U.S. Customs territory of any chemical substance, mixture, or article containing a chemical substance or mixture offered for such entry if: (1) if fails to comply with any rule in effect under TSCA; or (2) it is offered for entry in violation of either (i) Section 5 or 6, (ii) a rule or order under Section 5 or 6, or (iii) an order issued in a civil action brought under Section 5 or 7.[140]

A final Customs rule under Section 13 was issued on August 1, 1983.[141] EPA issued a policy statement on December 13, 1983 to explain how it will interpret and implement its responsibilities under the Customs rule.[142] Under the Customs rule, an importer of a chemical shipment must certify at the port of entry for shipments entering commerce in the U.S. that either: (1) the shipment is subject to TSCA and complies with all applicable rules and orders thereunder; or (2) it is not subject to TSCA.[143] An importer, or an authorized agent, can fulfill this requirement by signing, at the time of Customs clearance, one of the following brief statements which can be typed, stamped, preprinted on the invoice or otherwise included in the entry documentation:

POSITIVE CERTIFICATION

"I certify that all chemical substances in this shipment comply with all applicable rules or orders under TSCA and that I am not offering a chemical substance for entry in violation of TSCA or any applicable rule or order thereunder."

---

[138]*See*, 56 Fed. Reg. 4128 (1991).

[139]*See*, 56 Fed. Reg. 28458 (1991).

[140]*See*, 15 U.S.C.A. § 2612(a).

[141]*See*, 19 C.F.R. §§ 12.118 through 12.127, and 127.28.

[142]*See*, 40 C.F.R. Part 707.

[143]*See*, 19 C.F.R. § 12.121(a).

NEGATIVE CERTIFICATION

"I certify that all chemicals in this shipment are not subject to TSCA."[144]

The importer must use one of the above-mentioned statements. No other language can be substituted. The certification may be signed by means of an authorized facsimile signature.[145] The importer (or agent, i.e., the Customs broker) must keep a copy of this certification along with other Customs entry documentation for five years from the date of entry of the shipment.[146]

An importer can use a single or "blanket" certification to cover several shipments of the same chemical made over a one-year period if the certification has been authorized by the appropriate District Director of U.S. Customs and a statement to that effect is included on the commercial invoice or entry document.[147] A blanket certification must be made on the letterhead of the importer and signed by an authorized person.[148]

The format to be used for blanket certifications and the format for the required statement which references the blanket certification are attached as Appendices III, IV, V and VI.

VII.   EXPORT REQUIREMENTS

Section 12(a) of TSCA provides a qualified exemption from certain TSCA requirements for any chemical substance, mixture or articles containing a chemical substance or mixture which are manufactured, processed or distributed solely for export from the United States. Section 12(a), however, does not exempt such chemical exports from the reporting and recordkeeping requirements of Section 8.[149] Moreover, such chemical exports must bear a stamp or label stating that the substance, mixture, or article is intended for export to qualify for the exemption.[150]

Section 12(b) of TSCA requires a chemical exporter to notify EPA before making a shipment to a foreign country of any substance or mixture for which (1) test data is required under Section 4 or 5(b), (2) an order has been issued under Section 5, (3) a rule has been proposed or issued under Section 5 or 6, or (4) an action is pending or relief has been granted under Section 5 or 7. Upon such notification, EPA must notify the government of the importing nation of such test data, rule, order, action, or relief.[151]

---

[144]*See*, 19 C.F.R. § 12.121(a).

[145]*See*, 19 C.F.R. § 12.121(c).

[146]*See*, 19 C.F.R. § 162.1c.

[147]*See*, *Toxic Substances Control Act: A Guide for Chemical Importers/Exporters*, Office of Toxic Substances, U.S. Environmental Protection Agency (1991), p. 20.

[148]*See*, *Ibid.*, p. 21.

[149]*See*, 15 U.S.C. § 2611(a).

[150]*See*, 15 U.S.C. § 2611(a)(1)(B).

[151]*See*, 15 U.S.C. § 2611(b)(1) and (2).

EPA issued its Export Notification Rule on December 16, 1980. Under this rule, an exporter must submit for each regulated substance or mixture a written notice for the first export or intended export to a foreign country in a calendar year. The notice must be postmarked within seven days of forming the intent to export[152] or on the date of export, whichever is earlier. If the notice is prompted by the issuance of a proposed rule, the exporter has thirty days after publication of the rule to submit the notice to EPA.[153]

In a final rule published on July 27, 1993, EPA amended its Export Notification Rule for those chemicals subject to test rules under Section 4 of TSCA. Under the rule, exporters are required to submit a one-time notice to EPA for export of a Section 4 chemical substance or mixture to a foreign country instead of an annual notice. The rule became effective on January 1, 1994. Any export notice that is submitted prior to January 1, 1994, however, will satisfy the one-time reporting requirement established in the new rule.[154]

No notice of export is required for articles containing a chemical substance or mixture unless EPA specifically requires such notice in individual Section 5, 6, or 7 actions.[155] PCB articles,[156] however, are not exempt from the export notification requirements.[157]

The written export notice to EPA must include the following information:

* Name of the chemical substance or mixture that appears in the Section 4, 5, 6, or 7 action.

* Name and address of the exporter.

* Name of the importing country (countries).

* Date of export or intended export.

* Section (4, 5, 6, or 7) of TSCA under which EPA has taken action.[158]

---

[152]Intent to export a regulated substance or mixture "must be based on a definite contractual obligation, or an equivalent intra-company agreement, to export the regulated chemical. *See*, 40 C.F.R. § 707.65(a)(3).

[153]*See*, 40 C.F.R. § 707.65.

[154]*See*, 58 *Fed. Reg.* 40238 (July 27, 1993) and 59 *Fed. Reg.* 2999 (January 20, 1994).

[155]*See*, 40 C.F.R. § 707.60(b).

[156]The term "PCB Article" means any manufactured article, other than a PCB Container, that contains PCBs and whose surface(s) has been in direct contact with PCBs. The term includes capacitors, transformers, electric motors, pumps, pipes and any other manufactured item (1) which is formed to a specific shape or design during manufacture, (2) which has end use functions dependent in whole or in part upon its shape or design during end use, and (3) which has either no change of chemical composition during its end use or only those changes of composition which have no commercial purpose separate from that of the PCB Article. *See*, 40 C.F.R. § 761.3.

[157]*See*, 40 C.F.R. § 707.60(b).

[158]*See*, 40 C.F.R. § 707.67.

VIII. PENALTIES FOR NONCOMPLIANCE

The failure or refusal by any person to comply with the reporting and recordkeeping requirements under TSCA is a violation of the Act. Penalties for violations can be imposed under Section 16 of TSCA. Section 16 authorizes both civil and criminal penalties for reporting and recordkeeping violations under the Act. Under Section 16(a), EPA can assess a civil penalty in the amount of $25,000 for each reporting and recordkeeping violation. Moreover, each day a violation continues constitutes a separate violation. In addition, under Section 16(b), any person who knowingly or willfully violates a reporting or recordkeeping requirement is subject, upon conviction, to a criminal fine in the amount of $25,000 for each day of violation and imprisonment for up to one year.[159]

---

[159]*See*, 15 U.S.C.A. § 2615(a) and (b).

APPENDIX I

Support Information for Confidentiality Claims

Information submitted under specific reporting requirements of the Toxic Substances Control Act (TSCA) or in support of TSCA is subject to the provisions of Section 14 of TSCA and to EPA's Regulations on the Confidentiality of Business Information (see 40 CFR Part 2). You must comply with the following procedures to assert a claim of confidentiality for the information solicited in the attached letter. Failure to follow these procedures fully at the time you submit the information to EPA will be interpreted by the Agency as a waiver of your claim of confidentiality.

Asserting a Claim

Information claimed as confidential must be clearly marked by boxing, circling or underlining. All pages containing such information should also be stamped **"CONFIDENTIAL"**. Care should be taken to ensure that these markings do not obscure the submission's text.

Sanitized Copy

Two copies must be submitted of any documents containing information claimed as confidential. One copy should be complete, with the information being claimed as confidential marked in the manner described in the preceding paragraph. The other copy should have all of the information claimed as confidential excised. This version will be placed in EPA's Public Files.

Substantiating Claims of Confidentiality

Detailed written responses to the following questions must be provided at the time you submit information for any portion of the information you claim as confidential. Your responses should be as specific as possible, with examples as appropriate, and should provide substantiation arguments for all types of information (e.g., sales or production/importation volumes, chemical identity, company identity) you claim as confidential.

1. For what period of time do you assert this claim of confidentiality? If a claim is to extend until a certain event or point in time, please indicate that event or time period. Explain why the information should remain confidential until such event or time.

2. Have there been any confidentiality determinations made by EPA, other Federal agencies, or courts in connection with this information? If so, please enclose copies.

3. Has any of the information that you are claiming as confidential been disclosed to individuals outside your company? Will it be disclosed to such persons in the future? If so, what restrictions, if any, apply to use or further disclosure of the information?

4. Briefly describe any physical or procedural restrictions within your company relating to the use and storage of the information you are claiming as confidential. What other steps, if any, have you taken to prevent undesired disclosure of the information during its use or when an employee leaves your company?

5. Does the information claimed as confidential appear or is it referred to in any of items listed below:

   - advertising or promotional materials for the chemical or the end product containing it;

119

- safety data sheets or other similar materials for the chemical or the end product containing it;

- professional or trade publications; or

- any other media available to the public or to your competitors.

If you answered yes to any of the above questions, you must indicate where the information appears and explain why it should nonetheless be treated as confidential.

6. Would disclosure of this information be likely to result in substantial harm to your competitive position? If so, you must specifically describe the alleged harmful effects and indicate why they should be considered to be substantial. Also, you must describe how disclosure of the information would cause the harm.

7. If the information in question is "health and safety data" pursuant to 40 CFR Part 2.306(3)(i), do you assert that disclosure of the information you are claiming as confidential would reveal:

    a) confidential process information;

    b) confidential proportions of a mixture; or

    c) information unrelated to the effects of the substance on human health or the environment?

If your answer to any of the above questions is yes, you must explain how such information would be revealed.

APPENDIX II

UNITED STATES ENVIRONMENTAL PROTECTION AGENCY
OFFICE OF PESTICIDES AND TOXIC SUBSTANCES

REGISTRATION AND AGREEMENT FOR TSCA SECTION 8(e)
COMPLIANCE AUDIT PROGRAM

The United States Environmental Protection Agency ("EPA") and the Regulatee, the Parties herein, wishing to register for and enter into this Agreement for a Toxic Substances Control Act ("TSCA") Section 8(e) Compliance Audit Program ("CAP Agreement") and having consented to the terms of this CAP Agreement do therefore agree to fully comply with the terms of this CAP Agreement.

I. Registration Requirements

A.   The Regulatee agrees to conduct a TSCA Section 8(e) Compliance Audit Program to determine its compliance status with TSCA section 8(e).

B.   To register for the TSCA Section 8(e) Compliance Audit Program, the Regulatee must, no later than July 1, 1991, sign and return this CAP Agreement by certified mail-return receipt requested to:

Michael F. Wood, Director
Compliance Division (EN-342)
Office of Compliance Monitoring
Environmental Protection Agency
401 M St., SW.
Washington, DC 20460

C.   After EPA receives this signed CAP Agreement from the Regulatee, EPA will sign this CAP Agreement and enter the following identification number (_____) to the copy of this CAP Agreement which will be returned to the Regulatee. The Final Report and all other documents submitted pursuant to Unit II.C of this CAP Agreement must display the identification number established by this paragraph.

D.   The TSCA Section 8(e) Compliance Audit Program shall commence no later than July 1, 1991.

E.   The TSCA Section 8(e) Compliance Audit Program shall terminate on February 28, 1992, and all submissions under this TSCA Section 8(e) Compliance Audit Program must be delivered to EPA no later than February 28, 1992. The Regulatee may petition EPA in writing at the address specified in Unit I.B of this CAP Agreement for an extension of the February 28, 1992, termination date. Extension requests must be received by EPA no later than November 29, 1991, and must contain an adequate justification for the extension.

II. Terms of Agreement

EPA and the Regulatee mutually initiated this TSCA Section 8(e) Compliance Audit Program in response to February, April, and June 1991, Federal Register notices announcing the opportunity to participate in the TSCA Section 8(e) Compliance Audit Program. As part of this CAP Agreement, EPA and the Regulatee agree to the following:

A. General Provisions

1.   This CAP Agreement and the Consent Agreement and Consent Order in this matter shall be a complete settlement of all civil and administrative claims and causes of action which arose or could have arisen under TSCA section 8(e) in connection with any study or report listed or submitted pursuant to the terms of this CAP Agreement. Pursuant to TSCA, EPA will consider ability to pay/effect on ability to continue to do business claims during the course of development of the Consent Agreement and Consent Order in this matter. The Regulatee will be responsible for submitting adequate documentation of such claims to EPA at the time of submission of the Final Report required by this CAP Agreement.

2.   For purposes of this CAP Agreement and any subsequent proceeding, without trial or any adjudication of the facts, the Regulatee admits that EPA has jurisdiction over the subject matter of the terms of this CAP Agreement and any study or report listed or submitted pursuant to this CAP Agreement.

3.   The Regulatee waives its right to request a judicial or administrative hearing, under TSCA section 16(a)(2)(A) or other provisions of law, on any issue of law or fact that has arisen or may arise regarding the application of TSCA Section 8(e) to any study or report listed or submitted pursuant to Unit II.B.1 of this CAP Agreement.

4.   The Regulatee neither admits nor denies that the listing or submission of studies or reports by the Regulatee under this TSCA Section 8(e) Compliance Audit Program and pursuant to the terms of this CAP Agreement constitutes admission of a violation of TSCA Sections 8(e) and 15(3)(B), but agrees to pay a stipulated civil penalty for each study or report in accordance with Units II.B.2 and 3 of this CAP Agreement. Any study or report submitted under TSCA section 8(e) prior to the date of commencement of the TSCA Section 8(e) Compliance Audit Program is not subject to the terms of this CAP Agreement or the TSCA Section 8(e) Compliance Audit Program.

5.   EPA reserves its rights under TSCA section 16 to take appropriate enforcement action if EPA determines later that the Regulatee was required to submit under TSCA section 8(e) a study or report determined by the Regulatee to be not reportable and therefore not listed or submitted under the TSCA Section 8(e) Compliance Audit Program. In such event, the terms of the EPA TSCA Sections 8, 12, and 13 Enforcement Response Policy will apply to such proceeding.

6.   EPA reserves its rights to challenge the categorization of studies or reports submitted or listed under this TSCA Section 8(e) Compliance Audit Program pursuant to the requirements of Units II.B.2.a and b and II.B.3 of this CAP Agreement.

7.   EPA agrees that any listing or submission made pursuant to the terms of this CAP Agreement and the TSCA Section 8(e) Compliance Audit Program will be viewed by EPA as one "prior such violation" under TSCA section 16(a)(2)(B) for future violations of TSCA section 8(e) only.

8.   The Final Report submitted pursuant to Unit II.C.4 of this CAP Agreement shall be the controlling document for purposes of determining what was listed or submitted under the TSCA Section 8(e) Compliance Audit Program and this CAP Agreement.

9.   Any listing or submission made by the Regulatee to EPA that does not meet all of the requirements of the TSCA Section 8(e) Compliance Audit Program and this CAP Agreement is subject to the EPA TSCA Sections 8, 12, and 13 Enforcement Response Policy.

B. TSCA Section 8(e) Compliance Audit Program and Civil Penalties

1.   In conducting the TSCA Section 8(e) Compliance Audit Program, the Regulatee shall follow the statutory language of TSCA section 8(e) and EPA's guidance on section 8(e) in the March 16,

1978, "Statement of Interpretation and Enforcement Policy; Notification of Substantial Risk" (43 FR 11110) ("TSCA Section 8(e) Policy Statement"), with the exception of Parts V(b)(1) and V(c) of the TSCA Section 8(e) Policy Statement, to determine whether the reviewed study or report is:[1]

    a.   <u>Not reportable under TSCA Section 8(e)</u>: The Regulatee will not list or submit the study or report.

    b.   <u>Reportable under TSCA Section 8(e)</u>: The Regulatee will submit the study or report.

    c.   <u>Data that would have been reportable under TSCA section 8(e) when initially obtained by the Regulatee, and that subsequent to the section 8(e) reporting deadline (and before June 18, 1991), were (i) submitted in writing to and received by EPA pursuant to a mandatory reporting requirement of TSCA or another statute administered by EPA, or (ii) received by the Office of Toxic Substances (OTS) on a "For Your Information" ("FYI") basis and included in the formal OTS "FYI" filing system</u>: The Regulatee will list the study or report pursuant to Unit II.B.3 of this CAP Agreement. Only information that meets the requirements of Unit II.B.1.c is eligible for this listing provision.

Upon Registration for the TSCA Section 8(e) Compliance Audit Program, the Regulatee will receive a copy of the TSCA Section 8(e) Policy Statement, the publication numbers of publicly available and previously published volumes of Section 8(e) "Status Reports" available through the National Technical Information Service, copies of Question and Answer documents developed in response to specific questions involving section 8(e), a document entitled "Substantiating Claims of Confidentiality," and a TSCA section 8(e) reporting guide.

    2.   The Regulatee agrees to pay the following stipulated civil penalties for all studies or reports submitted under this TSCA Section 8(e) Compliance Audit Program as TSCA section 8(e) data:

    a. $15,000 per study for any submitted study or report involving effects in humans.

    b. $6,000 per study for any other submitted study or report submitted as TSCA section 8(e) data.

    3.   The following provisions shall govern the list required to be submitted under Unit II.B.1.c of this CAP Agreement:

    a.   For each study or report listed, the listing must comply with the requirements of Unit II.C of this CAP Agreement, must describe the date of the submission and (i) the mandatory reporting requirement of TSCA or another EPA-administered statute under which the study or report was submitted, or (ii) the Office of Toxic Substances "FYI" filing system number for the submission. Within 360 days after submission of the list, EPA may request the Regulatee to submit any of the listed information in order to determine if the Regulatee correctly listed rather than submitted the study or report.

    b.   The Regulatee agrees to pay the following stipulated civil penalty for information listed under this audit as data that would have been reportable under TSCA Section 8(e) when initially obtained by the Regulatee, and that subsequent to the section 8(e) reporting

---

[1]   In determining whether the kind of information or studies referenced in Parts V(b)(1) and V(c) of the TSCA Section 8(e) Policy Statement (i.e., widespread and previously unsuspected distribution in environmental media and emergency incidents of environmental contamination) should be submitted under the TSCA Section 8(e) Compliance Audit Program, the Regulatee should make a reasonable judgement whether such information meets the statutory standards of TSCA section 8(e) instead of relying on the guidance in Parts V(b)(1) and V(c) of the TSCA Section 8(e) Policy Statement.

deadline as specified in Part IV of the TSCA Section 8(e) Policy Statement (and before June 18, 1991), were (i) submitted in writing to and received by EPA pursuant to a mandatory reporting requirement under TSCA or another statute administered by EPA, or (ii) received by the Office of Toxic Substances (OTS) on an "FYI" basis and included in the formal OTS "FYI" filing system: $5,000 per study or report.

As a matter of policy under this TSCA Section 8(e) Compliance Audit Program, EPA agrees to a $1,000,000 cap on the total civil penalty for the Regulatee.

4.   The Regulatee shall be exempt from any additional late and/or nonreporting TSCA section 8(e) civil liability which arose or could have arisen for any study or report submitted or listed under this TSCA Section 8(e) Compliance Audit Program.

5.   Upon termination of the TSCA Section 8(e) Compliance Audit Program, the Regulatee shall provide EPA with a Final Report certifying that the TSCA Section 8(e) Compliance Audit Program has been completed. Such Final Report shall be signed and certified by the appropriate corporate official with authority to settle claims on behalf of the Regulatee. Such Final Report shall also comply with the requirements of Unit II.C.4 of this CAP Agreement.

6.   Following termination of the audit, EPA will present the Regulatee with a Consent Agreement and Consent Order summarizing the results of the TSCA Section 8(e) Compliance Audit Program and specifying the terms of payment of stipulated civil penalties. The Regulatee will have 30 calendar days from its receipt of an executed copy of the Consent Order to pay any stipulated civil penalties.

C. Information Submission and Final Report

1.   All studies or reports listed or submitted to EPA by the Regulatee under the terms of this CAP Agreement shall be identified pursuant to the categories established in Units II.B.2.a and b and II.B.3 of this CAP Agreement, and shall be sent to the following address:

Document Processing Center (TS-790)
Office of Toxic Substances
Environmental Protection Agency
401 M St., SW.
Washington, DC 20460
Attn: Section 8(e) Coordinator (CAP Agreement)

2.   The Regulatee shall submit one original and two full copies of all cover letters, studies, reports, lists, substantiations of confidentiality claims, and, as appropriate, sanitized copies of cover letters, studies, reports, lists, or substantiations of confidentiality claims.

3.   In accordance with Part IX of the TSCA Section 8(e) Policy Statement, each study or report listed or submitted to EPA by the Regulatee under the terms of this CAP Agreement shall be accompanied by a separate cover letter containing the following information:

a.   Company name, address and telephone number.

b.   The signature and printed name, title and telephone number of the person listing or submitting the study or report.

c.   A clear statement that the document, identified on the cover letter by the identification number established by Unit I.C of this CAP Agreement, is being submitted or listed pursuant to the TSCA Section 8(e) Compliance Audit Program and this CAP Agreement.

d.   The exact identity of each tested chemical or mixture or component of a tested mixture including the CAS Registry Number, if known.

e.   The title of the listed or accompanying study or report.

f.   A full summary of the reportable adverse effect(s) or exposure(s) observed in the listed or accompanying study or report. In addition, the cover letter should identify by EPA Document Control Number any previous TSCA section 8(e) submission(s) or premanufacture notification(s) (PMN(s)) submitted by the Regulatee on the subject chemical substance(s) or mixture or component(s) of such mixture.

4.   Each study or report listed or submitted to EPA by the Regulatee under the terms of this CAP Agreement shall be listed in a Final Report. Such Final Report shall list each listed or submitted study or report by title pursuant to the categories established in Units II.B.2.a and b and II.B.3 of this CAP Agreement, and shall display the identification number established by Unit I.C of this CAP Agreement. Such Final Report shall certify that the TSCA Section 8(e) Compliance Audit has been completed and include the following statement: "I certify that the information contained in or accompanying this Final Report is true, accurate, and complete. As to any identified portion(s) of this Final Report for which I cannot personally verify its truth and accuracy, I certify as the company official having supervisory responsibility for the person(s) who, acting under my direct instructions, made the verification, that this information is true, accurate, and complete." The Final Report will be the controlling document as to what was or was not submitted under the terms of this CAP Agreement and shall be sent to the address specified in Unit I.B of this CAP Agreement.

D. Other Matters

1.   Nothing in this CAP Agreement shall relieve the Regulatee from complying with all applicable TSCA regulations or other applicable environmental statutes.

2.   This CAP Agreement shall be binding upon the Parties and in full effect pursuant to the requirements specified in Unit I. of this CAP Agreement.

3.   The Regulatee's obligations under this CAP Agreement shall end when the Final Report required by Unit II.C.4 of this CAP Agreement has been submitted to EPA and stipulated civil penalties paid.

4.   Failure to comply with the terms of this CAP Agreement permits EPA to proceed under TSCA section 16 to impose the civil penalties allowable under the existing EPA TSCA Sections 8, 12, and 13 Enforcement Response Policy for any study or report listed or submitted pursuant to Unit II.C of this CAP Agreement.

5.   All of the terms and conditions of this CAP Agreement together comprise one agreement, and each of the terms and conditions is in consideration for all of the other terms and conditions. In the event that this CAP Agreement (or one or more of its terms and conditions) is held invalid, or is not executed by all of the signatory parties in identical form, then the entire CAP Agreement shall be null and void.

6.   The Regulatee may assert claims of confidentiality under TSCA section 14 for submissions under this CAP Agreement. The Regulatee must, at the time of submission, provide substantiation for all information claimed as confidential. The Regulatee agrees that the failure to assert a claim of confidentiality for studies, reports, or information submitted under the terms of this CAP Agreement shall be interpreted by EPA as a waiver by the Regulatee of the right to assert a claim of confidentiality.

7.   Submissions containing information claimed as TSCA Confidential Business Information (TSCA CBI) shall contain cover sheets bearing the typed or stamped legend "company confidential,"

"proprietary," or "trade secret." Information contained in the submission which is claimed as TSCA CBI must be clearly marked by boxing, circling, or underlining the specific text so claimed. All pages containing such information shall also be marked "CONFIDENTIAL." Care should be taken to ensure that these markings do not obscure the text of the submission. Submissions directed to EPA in this manner should be sent by certified mail-return receipt requested or in any other way which will permit verification by the Regulatee of its receipt by EPA.

8.   If the Regulatee chooses to assert a confidentiality claim, the Regulatee shall provide two sets of each such submission: one set shall have the TSCA CBI material marked in the manner contemplated under 40 CFR 2.203(b) and Unit II.D.7 of this CAP Agreement; the second set shall have the TSCA CBI material excised. The Regulatee is advised that the second, "sanitized" set will be available for public review without further notice to the Regulatee and therefore care should be exercised in the creation of this set. Each sanitized and unsanitized submission must comply with Unit II.C.2 of this CAP Agreement and thus will consist of one original and two copies.

9.   The Regulatee is advised to review carefully the confidentiality claim procedures at 40 CFR 2.201. Specific information concerning TSCA section 8(e) confidentiality claims is contained at Part X of the TSCA Section 8(e) Policy Statement.

10.   The Regulatee agrees that if the specific chemical identity is claimed as confidential in a submission, a generic non-confidential chemical identity will be included on the sanitized version of the submission. Guidance for developing appropriate generic chemical identities may be obtained by consulting the TSCA Chemical Substance Inventory: 1985 Edition, or by contacting the Office of Toxic Substances' Chemical Inventory Section at (202) 382-3527.

11.   The Regulatee agrees that confidentiality claims will be honored by EPA only if each claim is accompanied by responses to the questions in the document provided with this CAP Agreement entitled "Substantiating Claims of Confidentiality." The Regulatee shall provide an original and two copies of these responses in accordance with Unit II.C.2 of this CAP Agreement. The Regulatee shall also, in the event the Regulatee desires information in these responses to be considered TSCA CBI, provide a sanitized original and two copies in accordance with Unit II.C.2 and Unit II.D.8 of this CAP Agreement.

12.   The Regulatee agrees that failure to adhere to each requirement pertaining to TSCA CBI may result in forfeiture of the CBI protection for the submission and its subsequent availability in its entirety for public review.

WE AGREE TO THIS:

For EPA: For Regulatee:

_____   _____

Michael F. Wood,
Director, Compliance Division
Office of Compliance Monitoring

_____   _____

Michael J. Walker,
Associate Enforcement Counsel
    for Pesticides and Toxic Substances

APPENDIX III

POSITIVE CERTIFICATION

TO: District Director
        U.S. Customs Service
        _____, _____
          (City)   (State)

CERTIFICATE

The undersigned, as an authorized officer or agent of _(Importer)_ , hereby certifies that all chemical substances in all shipments of product(s) listed herein and imported from suppliers listed below, namely:

PRODUCTS
(list name and HTS item number)

SUPPLIERS
(list name and address)

comply with all applicable rules or orders under TSCA, and _(Importer)_ , is not offering a chemical substance for entry in violation of TSCA or any applicable rule or order thereunder.

Dated this _____ day of _____, 19___.

                _____
                    (Authorized Signature)

                _____
                         (Title)

HTS - Harmonized Tariff Schedule of the U.S.

TSCA

APPENDIX IV

<u>NEGATIVE CERTIFICATION</u>

TO: District Director
        U.S. Customs Service
        _____, _____
          (City)   (State)

CERTIFICATE

The undersigned, as an authorized officer or agent of _(Importer)_ , hereby certifies that all chemical substances in all shipments of product(s) listed herein and imported from suppliers listed below, namely:

<u>PRODUCTS</u>
(list names and HTS item number)

<u>SUPPLIERS</u>
(list names and address)

are not subject to TSCA.

Dated this _____ day of _____, 19___ .

_____
(Authorized Signature)

_____
(Title)

HTS - Harmonized Tariff schedule of the U.S.

APPENDIX V

FORM OF STATEMENT

ON COMMERCIAL INVOICE

ON ENTRY DOCUMENT
(COMPLYING PRODUCTS)

"Importation of the products described above are subject to certificate on file with the District Director in respect of compliance with TSCA executed by __(Importer)__, on _____, 19__, the terms of which, including the fact of its execution are incorporated herein by this reference."

APPENDIX VI

FORM OF STATEMENT

ON COMMERCIAL INVOICE

ON ENTRY DOCUMENT
(PRODUCTS NOT SUBJECT TO TSCA)

"Importation of the products described above are subject to certificate on file with the District Director indicating that they are not subject to TSCA executed by ___(Importer)___, on _____, 19__, the terms of which, including the fact of execution are incorporated herein by this reference".

Chapter 6

**COMPANY DOCUMENT RETENTION
AND DESTRUCTION POLICIES**

John C. Knoepfler
Attorney
Robins, Kaplan, Miller & Ciresi
Minneapolis, Minnesota

I. <u>INTRODUCTION AND OVERVIEW</u>.

It is a rare business enterprise today that is not directly and significantly affected by one or more reporting and recordkeeping requirements imposed under the various environmental statutes and regulations discussed in these materials (e.g. the Clean Air Act, Clean Water Act, Toxic Substances Control Act, RCRA, CERCLA, SARA Title III, OSHA, etc.). These recordkeeping requirements are detailed, complex, overlapping in content, and increasingly expensive to satisfy. If ignored or overlooked, significant civil or criminal penalties can be sought, and at least at the federal level, enforcement activities continue to rise with respect to recordkeeping and reporting violations.

Despite the tremendous increase in the number of records that today's businesses are required to maintain, and

the significant adverse consequences if proper recordkeeping
is not conducted, many major businesses do not have any formal
document retention and destruction policies or programs. It
is not uncommon to find important environmental records, such
as hazardous waste manifests or monitoring and test results,
tucked away and forgotten in the back of a desk drawer.
Document retention is disorganized. Document destruction is
an _ad hoc_ process prompted by such events as the need for more
filing space, the departure of an employee, or the
reorganization of a department.

The intent of this article is to go beyond the various
environmental regulatory requirements mandating the retention
of documents, and discuss why a well designed and well operated
document retention and destruction policy is beneficial, what
objectives such a policy and program should have, and how such
a program might be structured.

II.   **THE NEED FOR A RECORDS MANAGEMENT PROGRAM**.

A company's need for a formal document and retention
program can be weighed against several basic economic facts:
1) filing space costs money; 2) time spent searching for
records costs money; and 3) defending against and paying the
fines and penalties for not having required records costs
considerable money.

Company management often perceives a records management
program as requiring a significant cash investment with little

or no return. In fact, a well designed and well maintained program can provide a substantial cost savings. While a records management program is not a "profit center," it can dramatically reduce current expenditures for space, filing equipment, employee time and interaction with regulators.

Some of the savings that may be realized through an effective records management program include:

- A reduction in the volume of records on prime floor space.

- A reduction in the prime floor space required to accommodate the records equipment.

- A reduction in the number of file cabinets and records equipment.

- Controlling and designating records and information that are required for compliance with mandated government regulated guidelines.

- Faster record and information retrieval and handling tasks.

- Eliminating the number and volume of duplicate records.

- Providing control mechanisms for vital records protection.[1]

As a starting point, a good records maintenance program ensures that records space is used efficiently. Many records retained to meet legal requirements have no inherent value and are not used or referred to in day-to-day activities. Such

---

[1] F. Dires, <u>The Bankruptcy of Records Retention Schedules</u>, 24 Records Management Quarterly 3, 3 (April, 1992).

"inactive" records can be screened and removed to less expensive storage areas. For "record intensive" businesses, records management specialists estimate that records storage costs can be cut by more than a third through an effective records management program.[2]

As an offset to records maintenance costs, considerable personnel hours will not be wasted in searching for documents that have been haphazardly maintained. On average, a single misfiled record has been estimated to cost a company at least $80 in clerical time searching for the record.[3] Any company that has ever tried to respond to the document requests of the EPA or other regulatory agencies knows that countless hours can often be spent looking for records generated years before.

As already mentioned, if documents cannot be located to respond to the requests of regulatory agencies, heavy monetary penalties may possibly be assessed and criminal action may be considered.[4] Even if requested records are ultimately located, the inability to produce records promptly can damage

---

[2] Stevens, <u>Making Records Retention Decisions: Practical and Theoretical Considerations</u>, 22 Records Management Q. 3, 4 (1988).

[3] S. Diamond, <u>Records Management</u>, 3-4 (1983).

[4] As merely one example, consider the Occupational Health and Safety Administration's (OSHA) proposed $2,059,000 fine in 1987 against Iowa Beef Packers. The case involved what OSHA described as the worst case of recordkeeping the agency had ever seen in matters of worker health and safety. Slyke, <u>Records Management and the Law</u>, 23 Records Management Q. 26 (1989).

the company's image with regulatory staff and create the impression that the company is being uncooperative or is not seriously concerned with environmental and safety matters.

As an additional matter, regulations governing record retention are rarely models of clarity. Where recordkeeping requirements are ambiguous or vague, an established pattern of document retention and destruction, pursuant to company policy, can serve as effective evidence of a company's good faith in attempting to conform to the law. This is particularly true where the time period for maintaining records is unclear.

An effective records retention program may reduce the company's legal exposure and costs of responding to discovery during the course of litigation. Managing records in compliance with established retention policies and destroying documents that have no ongoing value in accordance with those policies will allow the organization to respond to document requests more efficiently. With an effective and well-managed document retention program, the busines will be in a much better position to assert that certain records have been destroyed as part of the business' normal operations, rather than as a result of litigation or governmental investigations.[5]

In addition, any experienced litigator can tell his or her pet "horror story" about a devastating rough draft or marked-up copy of a document that mystifyingly appeared in the

---

[5] Dires, _supra_ note 1, at 6.

back of a file drawer to hinder their client's cause. These types of legal risks will be reduced where a records management program is routinely reviewing records for destruction or storage and ensuring that only necessary copies are maintained and subsequently destroyed.

Finally, a good records management program can play an important role in sound environmental risk management. Again, environmental records and recordkeeping requirements will be reviewed on a regular basis. This will enhance any opportunity for early identification and correction of potential environmental risks, and early detection of any gaps in records.

III. POTENTIAL DISADVANTAGES IN RECORDS MANAGEMENT.

While the advantages of a formal records management program are significant, disadvantages do exist. Depending on the amount of records involved and the size and structure of the organization, the creation of a formal document management program can have burdensome start-up costs. As already noted, however, these costs should largely be offset over time.

Another disadvantage is that by maximizing the destruction of records, a company increases the chance that it will later be unable to affirmatively prove certain facts. This situation is frequently seen in "Superfund" cases where companies have been identified as potentially responsible parties (PRPs) for the cleanup of a hazardous waste site based on alleged disposal activities that occurred years or even decades before. The evidence against the particular company may be slight. Nevertheless, without being able to negate the allegations through invoices, waste manifests or other documents, the company may face the unpleasant choice of helping to fund a cleanup remedy for which it doesn't believe it is responsible, or paying the often expensive costs of protracted litigation with the EPA or other PRPs.

Finally, there are a whole host of problems that arise when the document management program that exists on paper isn't followed in practice. Incomplete compliance with the program raises the inference of poor organization. Even more damaging are the inferences that can be made if the destruction of documents is not in compliance with the policies (presumably inadvertently). Destruction may appear suspicious with no formal document program in effect or if the formal program is not followed. The company then might be open to the charge by other parties in litigation or the government that the company's retention program is a sham, and that the destruction was in bad faith.[6]

, it appears doubly so if the program exists but isn't complied with.

---

[6] R. Bianchi, <u>Document Retention in the Twilight Zone: The Perils of Policies Unpolices</u>, 16, 17 (January 1993).

Finally, the existence of the document management program may itself be discoverable in litigation and require the additional expenditure of time documenting how it was complied with or explaining away items of noncompliance that might otherwise have had no significance.

These advantages and disadvantages will balance out differently for each company. For larger and more document intensive organizations, however, the advantages would seem to far outweigh the disadvantages. Certainly, documents may be lost that might prove to be of use at a later date, but more often than not, the company that retains most of its paper will end up generating expenses well out of proportion to whatever value the records might have over time. In addition, the retained document may just as often be detrimental. In litigation, or in responding to regulators, each document found must be copied, stamped, summarized and analyzed, sometimes repeatedly, and, quite possibly, without the benefit of the now deceased or missing author. Much of this is needless expense that can be avoided by a well designed and well run document policy and program.

IV.   **UNIFORM PRESERVATION OF PRIVATE BUSINESS RECORDS ACT.**

Although many environmental regulations provide specific time periods for the retention of records, there are numerous statutes affecting businesses which require the keeping of records, yet specify no time period whatsoever. To deal with this problem, some few states have enacted laws allowing for the destruction of required records after a specified period unless there is a clearly expressed statutory requirement for longer retention. An example is the Uniform Preservation of Private Business Records Act, 14 U.L.A. 203 (1954). Section 2, the key provision of the Act, states:

> Unless a specific period is designated by law for their preservation, business records which persons of the laws of this state are required to keep or preserve may be destroyed after the expiration of three years from the making of such records without constituting an offense under such laws. [This section does not apply to minute books of corporations nor to records of sales or other transactions involving weapons, poisons or other dangerous articles or substances capable of use in the commission of crimes.]

To date, the Uniform Act has been adopted only in the states of Illinois, New Hampshire and Oklahoma.[7] Although the Act would have no effect on any overriding <u>federal</u> document retention requirements, it does provide limited relief from ambiguous state statutory requirements which mandate the creation and retention of records yet are silent as to the retention period.

V. DESIGNING A DOCUMENT RETENTION AND DESTRUCTION POLICY.

The Appendix to this section of the materials contains a "sample" Document Retention and Destruction Policy. It is offered more as an example for consideration, rather than an

---

[7]   Ill. Ann. Stat. ch. 116, ¶¶ 59 - 64 (Smith-Hurd); N.H. Rev. Stat. Ann. §§ 337-A:1 - 337-A:6; 67 Okl. Stat. Ann. §§ 251 - 256.

ideal policy. Each business must tailor its own document policy and program to fit its particular size, structure and document requirements. Larger companies may even have more than one program, such that each division, subsidiary or profit center has its own document system. A program might even be designed to deal solely with environmental documents.

The first step is to analyze the company's need for information, including an examination of corporate structure and goals. Areas to be reviewed include:

- The company's mission and goal statements.

- The company's "information strategy and use patterns.

- The company's information systems, including the methods used to store, retrieve and disseminate data.

- A physical inventory of the company's records and documents.

- The internal and external requirements on the information.[8]

One of the most complex tasks in designing a records management program is developing a written retention schedule or timetable governing the disposition of records.[9] Initially, this requires an analysis of the statutes and regulations applicable to the corporation and each of its divisions and

---

[8]   Dires, <u>supra</u> note 1, at 7.

[9]   Sherman, <u>Record Retention Schedules: You Start With an Inventory</u>, 105 The Office 98 (1987).

subsidiaries.[10]   Simultaneously, the company must conduct a records inventory to systematically collect information about the types of records currently existing within the organization. Such an inventory must also provide sufficient information to permit an evaluation of the function and use of each category of record.[11] This will require department personnel to physically go through existing documents and perform a written inventory. In the alternative, records management specialists can be retained to conduct or coordinate this process.

Ideally, a comprehensive records program should include the following requirements:[12]

(1)   all records are retained for at least the minimum period stated in applicable statutes and regulations;

(2)   records affecting company obligations are retained for the period required to ensure their availability when needed;

(3)   records are maintained to substantiate compliance with relevant laws;

(4)   document destruction occurs pursuant to a standard policy that has been developed for business reasons, thereby avoiding the accusation that document destruction has occurred for improper motives;

---

[10]   Murray, <u>Legal Considerations in Records Management</u>, 12 Records Management Quarterly 25 (1978).

[11]   Sherman, <u>supra</u> note 4, at 98.

[12]   Fedders and Guttenplan, <u>Document Retention and Destruction: Practical, Legal and Ethical Considerations</u>, 56 Notre Dame Law. 7, 14 (1980).

(5)   a mechanism exists to halt the destruction of specified records following (a) service of legal process for the production of records, (b) notice of a government inquiry, or (c) identification of a specific claim, investigation, or lawsuit;

(6)   "vital records" are identified and protected, i.e. records essential for the continuity of operations or the restoration of the company's legal and financial status following a disaster;

(7)   the confidentiality and security of records is maintained; and

(8)   employees are provided with written policy and procedures, informed of their responsibilities, and trained concerning the use of procedures.

Once the company's policy is defined, its documents identified, and a retention schedule established, consideration must be given to an appropriate storage and retrieval system. In the present age of rapidly advancing automation and technology, an effective storage and retrieval system may require specialized training and consultation. Microfilm and microfiche systems, computerized information storage and data base techniques, automated "tickler" systems for document review, and various types of specialized advice in forms management, file management and office layout may come into play in designing a major records management program.[13]

Once a program is working, one of the more difficult matters to ensure compliance with is the suspension of the program in the event of a regulatory investigation, lawsuit, subpoena of records, or similar event. It is essential that

---

[13]   *Id.* at 15.

a document program have a mechanism for suspending destruction procedures that can respond on short notice.[14] More importantly, affected employees must be made aware that requested documents will be produced and cannot be destroyed. Attention should also be paid to immediately securing records, particularly in situations where specific employees might be motivated to destroy documents for their own purposes.

As a final matter, the best conceived records management plan will most assuredly go astray without management's continuing support and the ongoing efforts and cooperation of employees. Support can be demonstrated, and cooperation fostered, through a comprehensive education plan at the time the document program is implemented.[15] In addition to simply instructing employees as to how the document program will work, an education plan should also (a) demonstrate the value of the program to employees and (b) generate an understanding that corporate records are not personal records.[16]

As to the latter point, one can think of numerous situations where employees maintain their own pet files of correspondence and other documents, sometimes even at home. Often these same employees operate under the assumption that

---

[14]   *Id*. at 18.

[15]   *Id*. at 19; Gammie, <u>Records Management Training -- Your Company Needs It</u>, 6 Records Management Q. 18 1972).

[16]   Fedders and Guttenplan, <u>supra</u> note 7, at 19.

these documents are their own property and are not discoverable. Employees must understand that such documents are subject to discovery and will be an immediate focus of attention by any experienced investigator or litigator.

The emphasis on records as corporate property can also serve as a vehicle for conveying the care that employees must take in any document they generate. As one commentator quite cogently emphasizes, "The key point to remember on the subject of document creation can be stated very simply: Every document created within a corporation has on it these additional words-- 'Copy enemy'."[17] Employees must consider the tone and wording of documents. Counsel should review documents of a sensitive nature, and employees should be sensitized to the need to identify and seek assistance as to documents subsequently discovered to contain errors or omissions such that an appropriate explanatory or corrective memo can be added to the file.

VI.   **CONCLUSION**.

The increasing number of environmental records that businesses are legally required to generate and maintain are actually only a small segment of a typical company's document inventory. A well designed and managed document retention and destruction program will help ensure that these legal

---

[17]   Greenberg, <u>Document Creation and Retention</u>, 57 Antitrust L.J. 201 (1988).

requirements are recognized and complied with, and that these documents are not lost in the larger shuffle of paper. Such a program can be an important factor in environmental risk management. In addition, a comprehensive document management program can help cut operating expenses and reduce liability exposure at a time of increasing regulatory vigilance and tight economic conditions.

Chapter 7

OSHA
INJURY AND ILLNESS RECORDKEEPING
AND REPORTING REQUIREMENTS

David G. Sarvadi
Martha E. Pellegrini*
Keller and Heckman
Washington, D.C.

INTRODUCTION

The Secretary of Labor, through the efforts of the Occupational Safety and Health Administration (OSHA or the Agency) develops statistical data on workplace illnesses and injuries. This information is used to prioritize enforcement goals and regulatory efforts. The following discussion explores OSHA's illness and injury recordkeeping regulations and examines recent case law interpreting these rules and OSHA's authority to require recordkeeping. It includes a discussion of the guidelines issued by OSHA "interpreting" the regulations, as well as the reasons for their significance at this particular time.

STATUTORY BASIS

Over twenty years ago, Congress concluded that the government needed injury and illness information to administer effectively the nation's workplace safety and health programs by ensuring that full and accurate information would be available to the government and employers. In enacting the Occupational Safety and Health Act (OSH Act), Congress included a provision requiring the Secretary of Labor to issue regulations "requiring employers to maintain accurate records of, and make periodic reports on, work-related deaths, injuries and illnesses..."[1] A second provision further ordered the Secretary to "develop and maintain an effective program of collection, compilation and analysis of occupational safety and health statistics."[2] As indicated by the statute's language on injury and illness reporting, Congress intended that the scope of injuries and illnesses covered by the Act should be quite broad, but recognized that some conditions are so trivial that no public health purpose would be served by recording them. In both of the statutory provisions noted above, Congress excluded "minor injuries requiring only first aid treatment and which do not involve medical treatment, loss of consciousness, restriction of work or motion, or transfer to another job."

Many private entities -- as well as OSHA -- interpret these words to mean that all illnesses need to be recorded, but that only some, albeit a large majority of, injuries qualify as recordable cases. It is not clear that Congress intended that all illnesses be recorded, however. The legislative history of the OSH Act clearly shows that Congress considered that injuries and illnesses involving "only a minimal loss of work time or perhaps none at all may not be of sufficient significance to the Government to require their being recorded..." Further, in authorizing the Secretary to compile statistics on workplace injuries and illnesses, Congress specifically limited the Secretary's authority to "all <u>disabling, serious, or significant</u> injuries and illnesses..." [emphasis added]. In directing the Secretary to establish standards, Congress clearly focused the Secretary's attention on those working conditions which threaten workers with material impairment of health or functional capacity.[5] As described below, case law also supports the notion that some "ailments," as well as some minor injuries, are not recordable.

HISTORICAL DEVELOPMENT OF THE CURRENT REGULATION

The original rule on injury and illness recordkeeping was adopted as 29 C.F.R. 1904 in July, 1971. Minor revisions were proposed in November of 1971 and were adopted in January 1972. These amendments, among other things, extended the permissible recording period from two days to six days, provided for summaries to be prepared for each "establishment," and required the log to be current within 45 days at establishments where the principal records are not kept. In July of 1972, the provisions related to employees not in fixed establishments were proposed; they were quickly adopted the following October. In 1977, the Agency adopted the Form 200, replacing the old Forms 100 and 102, and added the definitions now appearing on the back of the form. OSHA deemed a notice and comment period on the form change to be unnecessary and impractical because the amendments were "of a minor and technical and non-substantive nature."[6] The current definition of an occupational illness, located on the back of the form, was adopted as a "non-substantive" amendment at this time and has been the basis for many of OSHA's citations involving the definition of an illness.

In addition to the regulations, a series of publications from the Bureau of Labor Statistics (BLS) has provided guidance to employers in completing the forms. The most recent, published in April 1986, included answers to questions commonly asked by employers. Another publication, titled "100 Questions and Answers About OSHA" was first published in 1972, but also has some answers to questions about recordkeeping that are still valid. In addition, OSHA periodically responds to individual requests for interpretations on OSHA illness and injury recordkeeping issues. OSHA's letter responses frequently adopt the question and answer format of the recordkeeping guidance documents. These responses are obtainable from OSHA through a Freedom of Information Act (FOIA) request.

Over the last two years, two cases have strengthened OSHA's authority to issue and interpret its regulations. The most recent U.S. Supreme Court case, <u>Martin v. OSHRC</u>[7], held that courts must defer to the Secretary's interpretation of OSHA regulations so long as they are reasonable in the context of the statute and the regulations themselves. In <u>Dole v. United Steelworkers</u>[8], the Supreme Court addressed

148

the authority of the Office of Management and Budget (OMB) to influence OSHA's regulatory approach. Through OMB's responsibility for implementing the Paperwork Reduction Act and subsequent legislation, OMB must approve forms and data-gathering requirements of federal agencies. However, OMB's review authority was limited by the Steelworkers case to those requirements which relate to information required to be sent or made available to federal agencies. OMB has concluded that the BLS guidelines are "supplemental instructions" to the OSHA recordkeeping forms. As a result, the BLS guidelines are clearly within the scope of OMB's review authority as defined by the Steelworkers case, and OMB's conclusion lends support to OSHA's position that the guidelines are not subject to notice and comment because they are merely supplemental instructions.

In this context, the BLS guidelines take on increased importance. OSHA has attempted -- through its current enforcement initiative -- to give the guidelines binding effect. Employers fined hundreds of thousands of dollars for their failure to follow the BLS guidelines will find little comfort in the OMB-OSHA position that the guidelines are merely supplemental instructions. As discussed below, OSHA is continually expanding the definition of illness through its enforcement process, and is now well beyond the classical dictionary definition of "a sickness of body or mind, or ailment" to include minor deviations from normal responses without regard for the establishment of a specific medical diagnosis. An employer may challenge the underlying validity of an OSHA's standard or interpretation in the course of an enforcement proceeding. The fact that guidelines are not adopted as regulations through a formal rulemaking process reduces the inherent validity of guidelines as enforceable criteria. An employer could contend, pursuant to Martin v. OSHRC and its progeny, that the guidelines constitute an unreasonable interpretation of the rules, i.e. that the guidelines are not consistent with a fair reading of the plain language of the regulation or are inconsistent with the Agency's prior statements and policies. At this date, this argument is more likely to fail than succeed because the regulations and associated guidelines have been in effect for so long. Moreover, OSHA's position that the guidelines merely interpret the rules, supported by OMB's conclusion, reduces the argument to a challenge on the basis of a procedural defect: if the guidelines are a substantive as opposed to a procedural change in the Agency's position, they must be adopted through rulemaking under OSHA's enabling legislation.

RECORDKEEPING OBLIGATIONS

The recordkeeping regulations promulgated by the Department of Labor (DOL) impose three basic obligations on employers. First, employers must maintain a log and summary of recordable occupational injuries and illnesses for each business establishment using OSHA Form No. 200 or its equivalent. OSHA regulations define "establishment" as a "single physical location where business is conducted or where services or industrial operations are performed."[10] However, if distinctly separate activities are performed at a single physical location, each activity should be considered a separate establishment and OSHA records should be maintained separately.

Second, employers must prepare a supplementary, detailed record, the OSHA Form No. 101, <u>Supplementary Record of Occupational Injuries and Illnesses</u>, for each recordable occupational injury or illness.[11] The employer may keep the required information on other forms, such as workers compensation forms, Supervisor's First Report of Accident forms, or other insurance forms, so long as all the necessary information is present.

Third, from February 1 to at least March 1, employers must post an annual summary for each establishment which describes that facility's recordable occupational injuries and illnesses for the past calendar year.[12] Occasionally, OSHA may require an employer to complete and return a statistical survey form on annual occupational injuries and illnesses.

EXEMPTIONS

The standard generally applies to all employers to whom the OSH Act applies. However, the regulations provide exceptions for small employers and employers classified in certain "low hazard" industries. Small employers are those who have fewer than 11 employees at all times during a calendar year. They are required only to log all cases, to report fatalities and multiple hospitalizations and to complete the BLS statistical survey if requested.[13] Small employers do not have to complete the supplemental OSHA No. 101 form for each occupational injury or illness, nor do they have to compile and post an annual summary of recordable injuries and illnesses.

OSHA exempts employers in certain industries because they are considered low hazard industries.[14] Generally, the exempted industries include employers in certain retail trades, financial services, insurance, real estate, and other service-based industries. For employers whose establishments are mixed use, the predominant classification by the largest share of production, sales, or revenue controls the classification of the establishment. Payroll or employment may be used where the primary economic activity is not accurately measured by revenue indicators. The exempted industries include most but not all classifications in Standard Industrial Classification Codes 52-89.

RECORDABLE INJURIES AND ILLNESSES

As suggested by the statutory language described above, there are three classifications of injuries and illnesses that come within OSHA's recordkeeping obligations:

1)   Occupational fatalities, regardless of the time between the injury and death or the length of the illness;

2)   Occupational injuries and illnesses, other than fatalities, that result in lost workdays; and

3)   Non-fatal occupational injuries or illnesses that do not involve lost workdays but result in the transfer of the employee to another job or termination of employment, require medical treatment (other than first aid)[15], or involve loss of consciousness or restriction of work or motion. Also included in this last category are diagnosed occupational illnesses that are reported to the employer (but are properly not classified as fatalities or lost workday cases).

To help an employer decide whether a particular case needs to be recorded, OSHA suggests the following five-step analysis:

1)   Determine whether a case occurred (that is, whether there was a death, injury, or illness);

2)   Determine whether the case was work-related (whether it was caused, contributed to, or was aggravated by an event or exposure in the work environment);

3)   Decide whether the case is an injury or an illness;[16] and

4)   If the case is an illness, record it and check the appropriate illness category on the log; or

5)   If the case is an injury, decide if it is recordable based on a finding of medical treatment, loss of consciousness, restriction of work or motion, or transfer to another job.[17]

One serious problem is that the definition of the term "illnesses" on the back of the Form 200 appears to be over-inclusive when compared to the plain language of the regulation and to OSHA's statutory authority. The regulation defines non-fatal cases to include "any _diagnosed_ occupational illnesses..."[18] OSHA has made a concerted effort to have the legal definition of a recordable occupational illness interpreted to include any "abnormal condition or disorder," defined on the back of the form as an "atypical condition." An example given is that of an abnormal chest x-ray, which the agency considers recordable. BLS guidelines assert that "all occupational illnesses are recordable."[19] While several cases have rejected this argument, OSHA has recently been making in-roads with its interpretation.

151

1.   <u>Abnormal Conditions: Degree of Significance Required for Reporting</u>

Beginning in 1981, in the case of <u>Ohio Edison Co.</u>,[20] a citation for failure to record a skin rash that was presumed to be caused by exposure to creosote, a potent skin irritant, was vacated because the condition did not rise to the level of significance necessary to fall within the reporting requirement. In considering the issue, the Administrative Law Judge (ALJ) addressed the statutory basis for the recordkeeping requirement, and specifically rejected OSHA's contention that <u>all</u> illnesses be recorded.

In 1986, the Occupational Safety and Health Review Commission (OSHRC or Review Commission) held in <u>Amoco Chemical</u> that the employer need record only diagnosed occupationally-related illnesses. The Review Commission specifically rejected the Secretary's position that: 1) it was irrelevant what the employer called the condition or whether the condition was diagnosed as a particular illness, and 2) the Secretary need only show that employees experienced lost workdays or were placed on work restriction as a result of "work-related conditions".[21] Amoco had hired an outside physician to evaluate the company's employees. Several employees were identified by the physician as having abnormal pulmonary function tests which were consistent with asbestosis. No medical diagnosis of asbestosis was made by this physician.[22]

The Review Commission rejected OSHA's position that these "conditions" were recordable. The Commission distinguished between "conditions" which differ from expected norms, and "illnesses" which must be recorded. The Secretary's contention that OSHA only need prove that an employee was suffering from an "occupationally-related condition" was rejected. Following <u>Ohio Edison</u>,[23] the Commission held that a medical diagnosis of an illness was required before the illness need be recorded. In this case, an abnormal condition identified in a diagnostic test was not an illness.

Further discussion of Amoco's determination that the employees were not suffering from diagnosed illnesses turned on the basis of the judgment made by Amoco. The Commission concluded that there was "no clear indication of what kind of medical review the standard require[d]."[24] In the absence of clear regulatory guidance, the Review Commission held that the employer must make a reasonable judgment based on the information and expertise available to it.[25] The Commission stated that Amoco cannot be required to exercise the "same medical judgment as the best qualified experts in the nation."[26] OSHA had the burden of proving that the employer's decision was unreasonable.

More recently, OSHA persuaded the OSHRC of its position that an abnormal condition without frank symptomatology or a physician's diagnosis of disease caused by occupationally-related environmental factors may be an "illness" that an employer must record on the OSHA Form 200. In <u>Secretary of Labor v. Johnson Controls, Inc.</u>

152

(February 3, 1993), the Review Commission affirmed an ALJ decision which upheld a minor citation issued for the company's failure to record an employee's elevated blood lead level of the 65 μg/100 g of whole blood as an "illness" on its OSHA Form 200.

Johnson Controls initially recorded the elevated blood lead level of one of its employees as an illness on its 1988 OSHA Form 200. It later crossed out the employee's name after an occupational health nurse determined that the employee had never shown physiological changes evidencing occupational illness. OSHA issued a citation because the elevated blood lead level was not recorded as an illness. The main issue in the case was whether the meaning and scope of the term "illness" included measured blood lead levels over 50 μg/100 mg. Johnson Controls, relying on the earlier Review Commission decisions, argued that an illness does not arise until an abnormal condition, such as an elevated blood lead level, causes such additional physiological change that a physician would diagnose an illness. The Commission disagreed.

In upholding the Secretary's interpretation of "illnesses" to mean "any abnormal condition or disorder;. . .caused by exposure to environmental factors," the Review Commission looked to the OSH Act's legislative history for the intended interpretation of the term. The Commission stated that Congress recognized the need for "full and accurate information" as a precondition for a worthwhile occupational safety and health program, and the Secretary's definition "effectuates the intent of Congress that is implicit in the Act and explicit in the legislative history." The Commission distinguished its earlier decisions by noting that it did not have the opportunity to give full consideration to the meaning of the term "illness" in those cases.

The Johnson Controls decision indicates that OSHA may require employers to record certain other abnormal conditions identified in diagnostic tests which meet the referenced definition of "illness" on the OSHA Form 200 log and summary. While many new occupationally related conditions that would not normally be considered recordable may now need to be listed on the OSHA Form 200, Johnson Controls does not require employers to record all abnormal conditions identified in diagnostic tests. Unlike the abnormal pulmonary conditions in Amoco, elevated blood lead levels are specifically addressed in the 1986 guidance document that BLS (and now OSHA) published to tell employers what their recordkeeping duties are. In contrast, an abnormal pulmonary condition, which may be indicative of several different illnesses is not discussed in the document. For example, to diagnose asbestosis, an additional physiological change is required. Thus, Johnson Controls is consistent with the Martin case in that OSHA's reasonable interpretation of its regulations is controlling, and the requirement to record blood lead levels above 50 μg/100 mg simply has long been considered recordable by OSHA.

However, a better analysis of the decision and facts in the case is that OSHA, in the Recordkeeping Guidelines, interpreted the term "illness" to include specifically elevated blood levels, and that the Commission was merely deferring to OSHA's reasonable interpretation of its regulations. Because of the regulatory history of the blood lead recording requirement, and its consideration in the lead standard, it is not clear that this specific case can be generalized to adopt OSHA's broader definition of "illness," or that such a definition is reasonable in all cases of "abnormal conditions."

2. **Hearing Loss**

The BLS guidelines identify hearing loss as a recordable illness if it is determined to be work-related. One particularly difficult area of compliance concerns the 1983 amendments to the OSHA Noise Standard and the degree of change in hearing acuity measured in industrial hearing conservation programs which rises to the level of an "illness." Data submitted to the Agency in the rulemaking on noise indicated that there are significant problems in repeatability and precision of hearing testing in the typical industrial situation. The Carter administration, in its last gasp, issued a final rule which would have required the recording of a "Significant Threshold Shift" (STS)[27] if it were determined to be permanent on retest.

The rule was stayed and the record reopened, and the present rule adopted in 1983 deleted the recording requirement. In part, this was due to a change in the definition of STS, now called a "Standard Threshold Shift." The STS was originally defined by OSHA using the smallest change which could be reliably measured by the pure-tone audiometry prescribed by the rule. However, numerous comments in the record, and OSHA's own words in the Preamble to the rule, recognized that this measure of hearing loss is insufficient to diagnose occupationally induced hearing loss, and, moreover, changes as small as those identified as STS do not rise to the level of a material impairment of health.

OSHA unilaterally changed its policy in 1991, and began to cite employers for failure to record STS absent an affirmative medical determination that the condition was not work-related. This change began its life in a proposed draft compliance instruction that was circulated to Area Directors, among others. Some Area Directors began enforcing the interpretation as written while others hesitated. Industry was understandably confused, and in some cases, certain OSHA offices advanced the suggestion of spectacular fines for failure to record barely measurable changes in hearing that in many cases were neither work-related nor permanent to coerce companies into recording these cases. The unilateral nature of the policy change was contrary to current administrative law governing changes in agency interpretations. It was hard to see how OSHA could reconcile its action with the explicit statutory duty to "prescribe regulations requiring ...accurate records,"[28] particularly when its changing interpretations reduce the accuracy of year-to-year comparisons.

OSHA subsequently issued a letter clarifying present policy on recording hearing loss which instructs inspectors to cite employers for failure to record STS exceeding 25 dB when calculated according to the procedure specified in the current noise standard. Employers are "encouraged" to record STS between 10 and 25. The inappropriateness of such an approach is obvious. Either the case is recordable or not. In addition to an increase in the reported numbers of cases of hearing loss on the Form 200 in the face of significant efforts on the part of industry to control the condition through the use of hearing protection, a logical result of the "clarification" is increased liability for those employers that fail to "voluntarily" record at 10 dB.

If the standards of recordability are to change, it should be through notice and comment rulemaking, according to the terms of the OSH Act. In fact, OSHA is expected to initiate a formal rulemaking in the near future to attempt to make 10 dB the recordable level of hearing loss.

DETERMINATION OF WORK RELATEDNESS

As a general rule, injuries that occur <u>anywhere</u> on the employer's premises are considered work-related. Thus, an injury that occurs in a company bathroom or a hallway is an occupational injury. The major exceptions are injuries that occur on company recreational facilities and in company parking lots, which are not recordable unless the employees were engaged in some work-related activity. It is immaterial for recordkeeping purposes whether the employer or employee was at fault for the injury or illness or whether the injury or illness was preventable.

OSHA argues that the presumption of work-relatedness is necessary when cases occur on the employer's premises to keep the recording criteria simple. Nevertheless, the presumption is rebuttable and the case is not recordable if there is no relationship between the person's presence on the premises and his status as an employee. This is a point that is frequently overlooked. The basis for OSHA's position is to maintain simplicity in the system. But OSHA's authority is limited to responsibility for <u>work-related</u> cases.

Examples used in the BLS guidelines referring to horseplay and employees choking while eating lunch in a company cafeteria are considered recordable by OSHA. But employers must determine whether a case is work-related in other more obscure situations, such as when a condition manifests itself at the job site but is unrelated to the individual's status as an employee. It is hard to understand OSHA's position that injuries due to non-work related conditions should be reported in a system directed toward improving safety in the workplace simply because they occur on the premises. This is inconsistent with the Agency's approach that illnesses of equally obvious non-occupational origin are not recordable. OSHA has stated that it plans to consider revising its approach to cases that are not truly work-related as well as eliminating the distinction between illnesses and injuries in the upcoming rulemaking.

REPORTING OF FATALITY OR MULTIPLE HOSPITALIZATION ACCIDENTS

OSHA's revised final rule on "Reporting of Fatality or Multiple Hospitalization Accidents" became effective on May 2, 1994. The new rule requires that employers report work-related accidents which result in at least one worker fatality or the hospitalization of <u>three</u> or more employees to the OSHA within <u>8 hours</u> after becoming aware of the accident. Previously, employers had up to 48 hours to report fatalities to OSHA and were required to report hospitalizations only if five or more employees were involved in a work-related accident.

The new rule requires employers to report workplace fatalities or hospitalizations either: (1) in person to the nearest OSHA area office,[29] or (2) by telephone using OSHA's toll free central telephone number, 1-800-321-OSHA. The rule clarifies that an employee is considered "hospitalized" only when he or she is admitted to the hospital on an "in-patient" basis. Employees admitted for observation are considered "in-patient" hospitalizations under the rule, which changed prior practice under earlier case law.

If an employer does not immediately learn of a reportable incident, the reporting period begins when the employer actually obtains the information. An employer is obligated to report an incident if any agent or employee (<u>e.g.</u>, managers, supervisors, safety officers, receptionists, switchboard personnel) of the employer becomes aware of the incident. If an incident is not immediately reportable, but subsequently results within 30 days in the death of an employee or the in-patient hospitalization of three or more employees, the employer must report the fatalities/multiple hospitalization within 8 hours after learning of it.

In addition to this reporting, OSHA may require supplemental reports and, even more importantly, OSHA will investigate these incidents through on-site inspections. In some jurisdictions, any work-place fatality is automatically the subject of a criminal investigation. This approach changes the rules of the game to increase the potential liability of managers, supervisors, and other staff personnel, as well as that of the corporate employer. The OSH Act has criminal penalty provisions for willful violations resulting in an employee fatality, and the recordkeeping provisions are supported by a provision involving misdemeanor criminal penalties for knowingly making false statements. Moreover, state and local prosecutors are more actively seeking to apply general criminal codes to situations involving death or serious injury. Liability under state criminal statutes, unlike the OSH Act, is not limited to employers; fellow employees may be charged as well.

There is often a potential for an ethical conflict of interest between the position of the corporation and that of the individual employee. Attorneys must be wary of this potential, especially in investigations of accidents, because of the natural tendency on the part of many individuals to cooperate. Individual rights against self-incrimination are often forgotten or ignored. The efforts of certain officials to find and punish "someone" in publicized cases is often counter-productive, precisely because it leads to much less cooperation on the part of those closest to the incident. One of the long-standing tenets of accident investigation is to avoid looking only for someone to blame, and to focus on underlying causes over which individuals have some control. Certainly, any attorney advising a supervisor in a situation involving severe injuries or fatalities will consider whether the client should seek immunity from criminal prosecution before answering questions.

In light of these provisions, employers should be more circumspect about OSHA inspections investigating fatalities and catastrophes, and more cognizant about the potential for both corporate and individual criminal liability. While every OSHA inspection need not be treated as a criminal investigation, certainly fatality and accident investigations should, and OSHA requests for records should be reviewed by counsel in all cases. Employers also want to keep abreast of differences in enforcement policies and priorities at the state level.

RECORDKEEPING DOCUMENTS

To ensure uniform and complete recording of occupational injuries and illnesses, employers must maintain the OSHA Form 200, Log and Summary of Occupational Injuries and Illnesses, or an equivalent injury/illness summary on a calendar year basis. For each recordable occupational injury or illness, there must be a separate entry in the log which identifies the employee and briefly describes the injury or illness. The employer is required to record this information for recordable injuries and illnesses as soon as possible, but no later than six working days after learning that a recordable occupational injury or illness has occurred.

1.   "Maintaining" Versus "Retaining" Records

OSHA interprets its regulations governing the obligation to record an injury or illness as extending for the five-year period that the employer is required to retain its log. For example, an employer may discover some time after the fact that a former employee was injured or became ill due to a work-related event while still employed by the employer. If this discovery is made within the five-year record retention period, OSHA contends that the employer must generally record that injury or illness on the log for the year in which the case occurred, even though the involved employee may have not worked at the facility for several years.

However, the regulations state that the records which employers are required to keep must be "retained" for five years after the end of the reporting year.[30]   Some employers have been cited for failing to "maintain the log," i.e., update it after the close of the reporting year. It is not clear what purpose is served by updating what is essentially historical data. OSHA annually surveys employers to develop the statistical data reported in the annual survey of Occupational Injuries and Illnesses in the United States by Industry. These data are collected once a year by mail from selected employers. Until recently, any further use of the records kept by employers, aside from their own internal use, apparently has been limited to determining whether employers comply with the recordkeeping requirements during OSHA inspections. It would seem somewhat inconsistent with the statutory mandate to obtain information "with a minimum burden on employers"[31] to interpret the word "retain" in the manner in which OSHA presently enforces the rule. In Secretary of Labor v. General Dynamics Corp. Electric Boat Division Quonset Point Facility,[32] however, the Review Commission accepted OSHA's interpretation.

General Dynamics was cited for inaccurate and missing entries on the OSHA Form 200 and OSHA Form 101, as well as for the failure to prepare the OSHA Form 101 for certain injuries and illnesses. The injuries and illnesses at issue occurred in 1985 and 1986. OSHA discovered the violations during an inspection conducted in January of 1987 and the citations were issued in July of that year. OSHA argued that the citations were timely because it issued them within six months of when it first discovered or reasonably should have first discovered the violations. General Dynamics, on the other hand, claimed that it was cited only for identifiable, not continuing, errors and omissions in its recordkeeping entries, and that each alleged error and omission occurred more than six months before OSHA issued the citations. While the ALJ decided in favor of General Dynamics and held the citations were time-barred, his decision was reversed by the Review Commission.

The six-month statute of limitations invoked by General Dynamics is found in Section 9(c) of the OSH Act. The statute of limitations issue typically arises in the context of a citation issued more than six months after the date of the alleged illness and injury recordkeeping violation. OSHA most often argues that the five-year requirement mandates maintenance rather than mere retention, because OSHA is attempting to hold employers responsible for events which occurred years after the act of recording the case. While a purely technical legal argument regarding the statute of limitations may occasionally provide an advantage to employers, it is clear that intentional falsification of the records is risky business. The penalty provisions of § 17(g) of the Act make knowing false representation of any "statement, representation, or certification in any application, record, report, plan or other document filed or required to be maintained..." a misdemeanor.[33] Responsible employees are subject to criminal prosecution under OSHA's interpretations of these rules.

Upon review, the Review Commission held that the obligation to correct errors or omissions on an employer's OSHA Form 200 continues until the error or omission is either corrected by the employer, or discovered, or reasonably should have been discovered by the Secretary. This obligation is limited to the five-year retention period of 29 C.F.R. § 1904.6. The Review Commission stated that it has generally upheld OSHA's authority to issue a citation for an unsafe condition that a compliance officer first discovers during an inspection conducted more than six months after the unsafe condition's creation. The Commission concluded that the obligation to correct an error or omission in an employer's injury records continues until the error or omission is either corrected by the employer, or discovered or reasonably should have been discovered by the Secretary.

A concurring Review Commission opinion agreed that the Review Commission could not properly vacate a recordkeeping citation pursuant to § 9(c) of the OSH Act simply because it believed the Secretary "reasonably should have discovered the violation during a prior inspection." The concurring opinion noted that it is well-established that OSHA's failure to issue a citation following a prior inspection does not preclude the Agency from subsequently issuing a citation for the violation.

Interestingly, when there is a change in ownership in an establishment, OSHA interprets the retention requirement to relieve the new owner of the obligation to update the records. The regulations require the new owner to preserve the records of the prior owner, and to record cases only for that portion of the year of which he owns the establishment.

2.   Obligation to Post Annual Summary

An employer must post in each of its establishments a copy of the summary of the previous calendar year's recordable occupational injuries and illnesses for the establishment by February 1 of the following year. The summary must be presented on the right-hand portion of the OSHA Form 200. The summary is designed to remove personal identifiers and the specific description of the illness or injury. It must include the calendar year covered, the company's name, the facility's address, a signature certifying that the information contained on the annual report is correct, the title of the person signing, and the date of the certification. This summary must be posted throughout the month of February in a conspicuous place or places where notices to employees are customarily posted. If an employer has employees who do not regularly report or work at a single facility, the employer must mail or present a copy of the summary to those employees at the appointed time. The person signing the summary is specifically subject to enforcement sanctions for providing any false or misleading information.

3.   **Record Retention and Availability**

As mentioned above, the OSHA Form 200, the Supplementary Record (OSHA No. 101), and the annual summary must be retained by the employer for five years following the end of the year to which they relate. Upon request, employees, former employees, and their representatives must be provided access to the records for examination and copying in a reasonable manner and at reasonable times. The regulations require that mandated records also be provided to OSHA inspectors and representatives of the Secretary of the Department of Health and Human Services upon request. The legal debate continues over whether an employer can withhold data in the absence of an OSHA warrant or subpoena.

The 1991 case of Monfort of Colorado, Inc.[35] involved the issue of accessibility of these records to the specified persons. A former employee, at the time a union employee, requested copies of the OSHA Form 200 for the years 1982-1986, ostensibly to investigate a back and neck injury she allegedly incurred while working at the plant. The rule in question specifically includes former employees among those who are to be provided access to the records. Monfort argued that the rule violated the Fourth Amendment right against unreasonable search and seizure because it authorized the access without a warrant. The Review Commission held that when the Form 200 is posted, whatever reasonable expectation of privacy Monfort might have had in the information was lost, and lacking this element, the access requirement under the rule did not violate the Constitution.

Despite the legal debate over whether OSHA must possess a warrant or subpoena, many employers freely provide such information to OSHA inspectors. Depending on the circumstances, firms often conclude that it is more beneficial to be cooperative than confrontational, reasoning that an evaluation of injury and illness records might limit the scope of an inspection. This judgment may be based in part on the relative ease with which OSHA might obtain a warrant or subpoena. A recent study also showed that uncooperative employers on average received almost twice as many proposed penalties as cooperative employers. Nevertheless, OSHA citations are occasionally vacated when challenged on the grounds of employer objections to the lack of a warrant, and the employer's right to require a warrant is firmly established even for the most unobtrusive request by OSHA inspectors.

Upon obtaining a subpoena or warrant, OSHA can petition the courts for enforcement when employers will not cooperate. As a general rule, an OSHA subpoena will be enforced if it meets the following four criteria:

1)   the subpoena must be within OSHA's "authority";

2)   OSHA must satisfy "due process" in issuing the subpoena;

3)   the information OSHA seeks must be "relevant and material" to an Agency investigation; and

4)   the subpoena must not be "unduly burdensome."

These four criteria are generally broadly interpreted, allowing inspectors to receive vast information from employers.

In a recent court decision, the Fourth Circuit enforced an OSHA subpoena for the OSHA 200 logs for all of an employer's worksites, even though the specific complaint only involved one worksite. In <u>Reich v. National Engineering and Contract Company</u>,[36] OSHA investigated a media report of an incident in which an employee fell off a bridge at a West Virginia construction site while performing bridge renovation work. In the course of an on-site inspection, OSHA discovered that two employees had sustained serious falls at the site in two separate incidents. The Agency then requested the employer's OSHA 200 logs for all worksites outside of West Virginia, allegedly in an effort to determine whether accidents at the inspected site represented isolated incidents or evidence of an inadequate program on a corporate-wide basis.

The employer refused to voluntarily produce the requested 200 logs from its other sites, on the ground that the logs were not relevant and material to OSHA's accident investigation, in accordance with the third criteria listed above. OSHA petitioned a federal district court to enforce its subpoenas for those documents. The trial court ruled in favor of OSHA and the Fourth Circuit upheld the trial court's ruling.[37]

In dicta, the Fourth Circuit noted that the Fourth Amendment does not require OSHA to rely on the subpoena process when it seeks an employer's OSHA 200 logs during an on-site inspection. As authority for that statement, the court cited a decision establishing the right of an employee (not an OSHA compliance officer) to obtain the OSHA 200 for a single site without legal process. According to the court, OSHA may obtain the 200 forms "simply by requesting them" in the course of an on-site investigation. It should be noted that while an employee complaint to OSHA only allows OSHA a warrant for a limited on-site inspection, such a complaint-initiated warrant authorizes OSHA to review all of the required illness and injury records.[38]

At least within the Fourth Circuit, this dicta is likely to encourage OSHA to issue willful violations to employers who refuse to provide OSHA 200 logs to a compliance officer who requests them during the on-site inspection. Where OSHA elects to move more quickly, the court's suggestion that a subpoena for the logs would be enforced without a formal consideration of the four criteria noted above clearly invites OSHA to pursue future subpoenas on that basis.

Allowing OSHA the virtually unlimited investigatory powers suggested by the court would create an enormous potential for prosecutorial abuse and/or harassment by OSHA or an unhappy employee. Without "probable cause," OSHA could obtain the OSHA 200 logs for all of an employer's worksites on the basis of an alleged shortcoming in one area (e.g., fall protection) at one site. The Agency would be free to examine those forms and identify any number of additional issues (e.g., ergonomics, machine guarding) for further investigation at one or more sites.

The case apparently involved OSHA's issuance of a subpoena to a company without separate divisions or separately incorporated subsidiaries. Accordingly, it is not clear what entity or entities OSHA would name in a subpoena in that type of situation or whether a court would enforce a subpoena seeking the records for an entire corporate family based on multiple incidents at one facility. Moreover, although the case involved two construction companies at a temporary worksite, its rationale would seem applicable to fixed site manufacturing operations. The subpoena in this case was limited to the OSHA 200 logs but, under the court's rationale, it appears that the court would have enforced a broader subpoena seeking all of the other documents at the employer's sites bearing on the hazard in issue (in this case -- fall protection programs).

It is likely that, at least in the Fourth Circuit, a court would enforce a corporate-wide subpoena for OSHA 200 logs and other documents bearing on a particular health and safety issue in a manufacturing setting, at least under the following conditions:

1)   The site being inspected experienced multiple incidents demonstrating the failure of a particular safety program;

2)   The site does not appear to have taken adequate corrective action; and

3)   The other sites have some significant level of activities or hazards which are common to the inspected site.

In addition to its holding, National Engineering illustrates the determination of OSHA to push to the very limits -- not yet defined -- of its existing enforcement powers. Overall, the case demonstrates that employers must have a formal, effective system for handling OSHA inspections, including policies and procedures for addressing various types of multi-site document requests.

RECENT ENFORCEMENT ACTIVITY

Within recent years, OSHA has initiated aggressive and well-publicized programs of enforcing occupational injury and illness recordkeeping requirements. In the first year of its aggressive recordkeeping enforcement campaign (late 1986 through most of 1987), the Agency proposed more substantial fines for recordkeeping violations than it did in the previous six years combined. These efforts have continued through the present time.

OSHA generated headlines by issuing citations and proposing penalties of six figures or more against major corporate employers for recordkeeping violations. Ford Motor Company, Caterpillar Tractor, Yale-New Haven Hospital, Union Carbide, and John Morrell & Co. are among the many firms that faced proposed fines of hundreds of thousands of dollars for recordkeeping problems. Prior to the change in the OSHA penalty structure, the Agency assessed proposed penalties of this magnitude through its calculation of the maximum financial penalties under the OSH Act and applied those penalties to each perceived violation. It remains to be seen whether the Agency will calculate the penalties at the maximum permitted now that the ceilings have been raised (i.e., $70,000 for "willful" violations).[39] Enforcement efforts will likely continue to be highly visible.

Observers have linked OSHA's recordkeeping enforcement activities to several factors. First, the Agency came under increased legislative scrutiny throughout the late 1980's regarding its rule-making and compliance activities. Democratic control over both houses of Congress, combined with a perceived increase (an incorrect perception) in the rate of work place fatalities, enhanced pressure on OSHA after what was generally viewed as a relaxation of OSHA enforcement during earlier years. In addition, tragic events such as Bhopal, the ARCO refinery fire, the Phillips Petroleum and BASF explosions, and more recent disasters made both employees and the general public aware of the potential dangers that exist in the work place.

Employers entangled in citations, fines and litigation over recordkeeping practices angrily assert that emphasis on these "paperwork" obligations does not adequately reflect a firm's substantive safety and health practices. OSHA's method for assessing such violations is considered by industry as regulatory "overkill." Employers believe that illness and injury recordkeeping requirements clearly envision the exercise of judgment in classifying a recordable event. Moreover, the courts have repeatedly supported the view that such violations are not serious, holding that they are not directly related to safety and health of employees, where the employer is not impeding the inspection by OSHA. The severity of the case more often turns on the question of employers' bad faith or evidence of numerous prior violations.

A substantial proposed penalty for violations of the recordkeeping regulations occurred in the General Dynamics case mentioned above. OSHA alleged 122 willful violations of the recordkeeping regulations and proposed penalties totalling $615,000. The cited violations occurred in 1985 and 1986. Notably, OSHA began its inspection of the company in response to an employee complaint that the injury and illness logs were not available for employees to see and copy, as required by OSHA regulations. The complaint had further alleged that the logs were incomplete.

It seems as though OSHA can never win. Labor unions have contended that these efforts constituted headline-grabbing actions to deflect attention from inadequate standards, diminished inspection resources, and trivial penalties for noncompliance. In response, the Agency notes that the injury and illness recordkeeping requirements are pivotal in its overall enforcement scheme and that uncovering violations in this area effectively targets employers for more comprehensive inspections.

COMPREHENSIVE OSHA REFORM LEGISLATION

Legislation, known as the Comprehensive Occupational Safety and Health Reform Act (COSHRA), has been introduced in the House (H.R. 1280) and Senate (S. 575) which would seriously revise the OSH Act, if enacted. The Clinton Administration has endorsed the primary components of the Democratic sponsored versions of the bill, introduced by Rep. William D. Ford (D-Mich.), and by Senators Howard Metzenbaum (D-Ohio) and Edward Kennedy (D-Mass.). Several labor unions such as the AFL-CIO also support the legislation, but industry and Republican leaders are opposed to the plan.

Many of the provision of the bills simply codify present OSHA regulations. For example, illnesses discovered as a result of medical monitoring under a substance-specific standard, or medical conditions related to ergonomic stresses are already subject to the injury and illness recording regulations. And many of the provisions setting timetables for rulemaking on specific subjects have been outdated by recently promulgated standards. However, two specific provisions will affect employer's recordkeeping duties.

First, OSHA would be required to collect and make publicly available information that identifies:

1) industries, employers, processes, operations, and occupations that have a high rate of injury and illness;

2) factors that cause or contribute to injuries and illnesses; and

3) workers' compensation costs associated with the injuries and illnesses.

Presently, OSHA publishes statistics by industry and occupation. Although unclear, it appears that OSHA would be required to publish data indicating that a particular company or a particular process or operation within a company has a high injury or illness rate. Aside from the negative public reaction (literally interpreted, this could mean a public blacklisting), OSHA would be pressured to use this information in targeting its inspections and enforcement.

164

While such an approach may seem attractive at first blush, most people, as well as most safety and health experts, know that statistics rarely tell the whole story. Annual rates are subject to wide fluctuation that is often beyond the control of the employer. For small companies or locations, a few or even a single seriously disabling case can inflate the statistics currently published. Safety experts often say that the severity of injury from an accident is more the result of luck; it is the frequency of human behaviors that lead to injury which modern safety programs seek to change.[40] Due to the vagaries of fate, even companies with aggressive, effective occupational safety and health programs will occasionally be identified as a high risk employer. Because of this lack of differentiation, the proposed approach is too simplistic to be fair.

The second proposed change affecting recordkeeping duties relates to criminal penalties. COSHRA would increase the maximum jail time for knowingly making a false statement, representation or certification on the OSHA log from six months to one year, turning this criminal misdemeanor into a felony violation. Moreover, the bill's sponsors propose to adopt explicitly the Justice Department's interpretation of the 1984 Sentencing Reform Act, and increased OSHA maximum penalties, by referencing the U.S. code sections containing the standard fine structure. This would result in codification in the OSH Act of maximum fines of $250,000 for individuals and $500,000 for corporations for willful violations resulting in death. The potential prison term for this kind of violation would increase to ten years for a first time offense and twenty years for a second offense. For all other violations, maximum fines of $25,000 for individuals and $100,000 for corporations would become part of the OSH Act.

The legislation also creates a new crime for willful violations that result in "serious bodily injury." Presently, those willful violations that cause death may result in criminal prosecution. The definition of "serious bodily injury" is very broad, covering "protracted loss or impairment of the function of a bodily . . . organ." Is an injury or illness (such as a CTD) resulting in one week of restricted duty a "protracted loss?" The present language leaves much to interpretation, and the associated risk to the individual is obvious. The first conviction for this new violation could result in up to five years imprisonment for the individual, and subsequent convictions carry a ten year jail term. Managers and supervisors are specifically included under the definition of individuals who can be held liable for criminal violations under the Act.

The House Education and Labor Committee recently approved a substitute version of COSHRA. Representative Ford has stated that he expects to bring the measure to a vote in the House in 1994, even though it appears that Republicans and moderate Democrats alike are opposed to the plan.

Major changes made in the House committee which relate to recordkeeping and reporting requirements for illnesses and injuries include:

- requiring immediate abatement not only of every serious violation but also of every repeat or willful violation, even though they may not pose any significant health or safety hazard (the penalty for the failure to abate a violation could be imposed only when there is an "unreasonable" failure to abate).

- retaining the new crime for willful violations resulting in "serious bodily injury," but narrowing that definition slightly.

- clarifying that individual criminal liability would not extend to all managers and supervisors, but only those with the authority to prevent the violation that causes a death or serious bodily injury (the bill is unclear on whether any criminal conduct can be attributed to every manager or supervisor with that authority).

- adding a new civil penalty of up to $70,000 for any "written misrepresentation" made by an employer to OSHA regarding OSHA compliance ("knowing" written misrepresentations in documents required to be maintained for review by OSHA or filed with OSHA are already subject to criminal penalties).

In the Senate, Senators Nancy Kassenbaum (R-KS) and Orrin Hatch (R-UT) introduced a Republican alternative bill (S. 1950) which is substantially the same as the House Republican bill introduced by Representative Harris Fawell (R-IL). On March 22, the Senate Labor Committee held its final hearing on COSHRA. A vote has not been scheduled in the Senate Labor Committee at this writing.

PENDING RULEMAKINGS

For years, OSHA has been criticized for failure to develop an effective procedure for targeting employers for inspection. As part of its re-invention efforts, the Agency plans to implement a data collection program pursuant to existing regulations, and is also developing a proposal to revise the recordkeeping rules. According to officials, a proposed rule will be published in 1994, with publication of a final rule in 1995. The OSHA 200 and 101 forms will be revised, reducing the number of information columns on the log. The proposal is expected to eliminate the distinction between illness and injury on the OSHA 200 log, and may establish a set of criteria to determine what must be recorded. According to OSHA officials, the Agency is considering five categories for recordation: employee fatalities, loss of consciousness, medical treatment beyond first aid, "abnormal health conditions," and restricted work activity or job transfer. OSHA is also debating how to deal with certain types of workplace violence, such as when one family member injures another at the workplace for reasons wholly unrelated to work.

In addition, OSHA may propose to lift the recordkeeping exemption currently in place for employers with 10 or fewer employees. The Agency is considering whether the recordkeeping exemption should be based upon criteria other than the number of employees. To assist in interpretation of requirements, OSHA may create a guidebook. The proposal overall may or may not clarify the recordkeeping requirements, but it will certainly increase the administrative burden on employers.

The Agency is considering a plan to initiate collection of OSHA 200 logs pursuant to current authority. The program would ultimately require almost all medium and large-sized employers covered by OSHA to submit their illness and injury logs directly to OSHA. The plan would be phased in over two to three years, beginning in 1995. According to OSHA's Office of Statistics personnel, the filing requirement would initially be limited to those employers in the manufacturing and construction industries with 100 or more employees and selected other employers. OSHA estimates that approximately 30-40,000 employers will be affected. A year or so later, the requirement would expand to cover those employers in manufacturing, construction and some other industries with 50 or more employees. The program estimates that from 120,000 to 130,000 employers would be required to submit their logs by 1997.

Despite claims from opponents that OSHA cannot initiate the proposal without notice and comment rulemaking, some OSHA personnel believe 29 C.F.R. 1904.7 grants sufficient authority. OSHA's position means that employers could be directed to submit calendar year 1994 data to OSHA in early 1995, or possibly earlier as part of a pilot project. However, many outside the Agency do not share that view of the law and are amassing opposition to the proposal among business and government leaders.

To alleviate procedural hurdles, OSHA may specifically incorporate the framework for this data collection program in its recordkeeping proposal. OSHA could require on the revised 200 forms that particular employers must submit completed forms directly to OSHA. Some OSHA personnel believe OSHA will begin these pilot projects before the recordkeeping proposal is issued. Hence, the new recordkeeping rule would be issued about the time OSHA prepares to begin full-scale implementation of the OSHA 200 data collection program. The Agency contends that it has no experience with a data collection effort of this magnitude and should begin with one or more pilot projects of increasing size, leading up to full-scale implementation. In addition to legal challenges, implementation of even a pilot program will be subject to the availability of funding and OMB approval.

The site-specific OSHA 200 information would be used for inspection targeting and employer "behavior modification" -- with the twin goals of improving workplace health and safety programs, and reducing workplace injuries and illnesses. Apparently, OSHA headquarters personnel would: (1) review the data; (2) identify sites with one or more high injury and/or illness rates (e.g., LWDI) or apparent program deficiencies; and (3) direct the responsible Area Offices to inspect those sites.

According to OSHA, the company-specific OSHA 200 information would be entered into a computer data base and made available to the public through the Freedom of Information Act. OSHA personnel see this as having two beneficial effects. First, greater publicity would theoretically encourage more accurate reporting because the affected employees would be in a position to point out any obvious errors. Second, the potential for adverse publicity would motivate employers to establish and maintain good safety programs in order to achieve and maintain low injury and illness rates.

It is unclear whether OSHA plans to publish a list of what it considers to be "bad actors." Some OSHA personnel believe the Agency should rely on the media and the marketplace to use the information in much the same way that EPA's Toxic Release Inventory Database is used -- e.g., headlines purporting to name "The 10 Worst Injury and Illness Records." This apparently would be facilitated if not encouraged by the Agency, although the OSHA 200 data has a significant potential to be erroneous or grossly misleading. While EPA release data, such as the Toxic Release Inventory, are quantifiable measures subject to verification, OSHA 200 entries are not. An injury or illness is currently recordable on the OSHA 200 if, to any degree the work caused, contributed to, or aggravated the condition. Often, the causal link is nothing more than a suspicion or an unverifiable employee assertion. This is the rule even if the workplace contribution to the condition was as little as a fraction of 1% and the balance of the contribution was due to a pre-existing condition or factors totally unrelated to work. Due to the inherent unreliability of the information, publication could unfairly show conscientious employers in a bad light.

In light of these significant changes on the horizon, employers are encouraged to monitor developments in this area, to be prepared for a request to participate in a pilot project, and to file comments with OSHA or OMB on any OSHA data collection initiative and proposed recordkeeping rulemaking.

GUIDANCE FOR EMPLOYERS

Employers must recognize that any company may be investigated by OSHA for recordkeeping violations (as well as deficiencies in meeting substantive safety and health requirements) if an employee files a complaint. In addition, if the firm's records are reviewed by OSHA and numerous problems appear to be present, adverse publicity for the offending company is a virtual certainty. Moreover, during its enforcement emphasis on injury and illness recordkeeping, OSHA appears likely to assert that significant underreporting or failure to report constitutes a "willful" recordkeeping violation. Such a characterization implicates substantially greater financial liability in light of the increased OSHA penalty structure as well as public notoriety.

As we have seen, the most substantial guidance on the application of OSHA's regulations to particular work place injuries and illnesses is contained in Agency guidelines. However, some of the interpretations in the BLS guideline have been rejected by the courts as unreasonable, and others have become dated as technology and the law evolve. Nevertheless, OSHA's interpretations still carry significant weight, especially in light of <u>Martin v. OSHRC</u>.[42] As previously noted, the Supreme Court held that, between the Review Commission and OSHA, the interpretation offered by OSHA should be followed by the reviewing courts so long as it is reasonable. This decision lends increasing stature to "interpretative" guidelines and increases the burden on employers by requiring that they go beyond the regulations to both internal and external memoranda of the agency to determine what the regulations specifically require.

As highlighted in the preceding discussion, the improper classification of work place injuries and illnesses may create serious potential liability for employers under OSHA's rules. Human resources executives and corporate safety officials must ensure that the plant or operations managers who are responsible for determining recordable injuries and illnesses have a clear understanding of the applicable OSHA rules and interpretations, including specific training in the proper procedures for employees making the recording decisions. Given OSHA's current enforcement posture, some employers may believe it prudent to record incidents whose recordability may be questionable, even though this results in "inflated" injury rates. The alternative strategy -- narrowly reading the OSHA regulations and the BLS guidelines -- risks the possibility that OSHA will find the employer guilty of recordkeeping violations. However, the rules require "accurate" records, and over-reporting is equally culpable, although unlikely to be enforced by OSHA with the same vigor.[43] In addition to negative publicity, a citation for recordkeeping violations may have adverse effects on employee relations. Although employers must necessarily apply some measure of judgment in determining the recordability of an injury or illness, firms that appear to be less than vigilant with their injury and illness records may pay a price that is not measured in dollars alone.

* The assistance of Lawrence Halprin, David Berry, and Katherine Harman in updating this paper is gratefully acknowledged.

1. 29 U.S.C. § 657(c)(2) (Pub.L. 91-596, enacted Dec. 29, 1970).

2. 29 U.S.C. § 673(a).

3. Senate Report, p. 16. The House bill mandated reporting of all cases. However, the House receded in conference and the final bill exempted minor cases.

4. 29 U.S.C. § 673(a).

5.   29 U.S.C. § 655 (6)(b)(5).

6.   42 Fed. Reg. 65165 (1978).

7.   <u>Martin, Secretary of Labor v. Occupational Safety and Health Review Commission</u>, 111 S.Ct. 1171 (1991).

8.   <u>Dole, Secretary of Labor, et al. v. United Steelworkers of America, et al.</u>, 494 U.S. 26 (1990).

9.   29 C.F.R. § 1904.2(a).

10.   29 C.F.R. § 1904.12(g)(1).

11.   29 C.F.R. § 1904.4.

12.   29 C.F.R. § 1904.5.

13.   29 C.F.R. § 1904.15.

14.   29 C.F.R. § 1904.16.

15.   OSHA's regulations define "medical treatment" as treatment administered by a physician or by a registered health professional under the standing orders of a physician. Medical treatment does not include first-aid assistance, regardless of who provides this service. "First aid" is defined as any one-time treatment of minor scratches, cuts, burns, splinters, and comparable conditions which ordinarily do not require medical care, even though provided by a physician or other registered health professional. Follow-up visits for observation are also classified as first-aid assistance. 29 C.F.R. § 1904.12(d), (e).

16.   An "occupational illness" is any abnormal condition or disorder (other than one resulting from an occupational injury) caused by exposure to environmental factors associated with employment. It includes acute and chronic illnesses or diseases that may be caused by inhalation, absorption, ingestion, or direct contact. An "occupational injury" is any injury which results from a work accident or from an exposure involving a single incident in the work environment. <u>Log and Summary of Occupational Injuries and Illnesses</u>, OSHA No. 200.

17.   Bureau of Labor Statistics, <u>Recordkeeping Guidelines for Occupational Injuries and Illnesses</u>, p. 28 (U.S. Department of Labor 1986).

18.   29 C.F.R. § 1904.12(c)(3) (emphasis added).

170

19.	BLS Recordkeeping Guidelines, p. 38 (1986).

20.	1981 OSHD (CCH) ¶ 25, 272; 9 OSHC (BNA) 1450 (1981).

21.	Id. at 1852. An occupational illness is defined on the back of OSHA Form 200. See Endnote 16. However, this definition and, in particular, the reference to an "abnormal condition" was not adopted through rulemaking and conflict with Amoco Chemical. In adopting the present version of the Form 200 in 1978, OSHA stated: "[t]his revision combines, with certain technical changes, forms OSHA No. 100 and No. 102 into form OSHA No. 200 [emphasis added]." 42 Fed. Reg. 65165. No reference was made in the notice to the changes in definitions contained on the reverse of the form. The language of the definition of "illness" in 1904.12(c), was adopted in 1972 in the original recordkeeping rulemaking. See 36 Fed. Reg. 12614.

22.	A diagnosis of asbestosis was subsequently made by physicians retained by Amoco employees but was not provided to Amoco. Therefore, this diagnosis was not relevant to the recording issue.

23.	Ohio Edison, 9 OSHC 1450, OSHD ¶ 25,272 (1981). Ohio Edison did not record four cases of skin irritation resulting from exposure to creosote in which there was no medical treatment, no medical evaluation, no lost time, and no restriction of work activity.

24.	Amoco Chemical, 12 OSHC 1849, 1855; OSHD ¶27,621 (1986).

25.	Id. at 1855.

26.	Id.

27.	46 Fed. Reg. 4163 (1981).

28.	29 U.S.C. § 657(c)(1).

29.	See Appendix for a list of OSHA area offices and phone numbers.

30.	29 C.F.R. § 1904.6.

31.	29 U.S.C. § 657(d).

32.	1990 W.L. 122615 (O.S.H.R.C.), 1990 OSHD (CCH) ¶ 29,000.

33.	Indeed, OSHA reform legislation currently pending in Congress would upgrade this violation to a felony, punishable by up to one year in jail.

34.   29 C.F.R. § 1904.11.

35.   1991 OSHD (CCH) ¶ 29,246 (Rev. Comm'n 1991).

36.   13 F.3d 93 (4th Cir. 1993).

37.   <u>Id.</u>

38.   <u>Trinity Industries, Inc. v. Occupational Safety and Health Review Commission</u>, 16 F.3d 1455 (6th Cir. 1994).

39.   OSHA has approved increased penalty provisions for states which adhere to their own occupational safety and health plans. Twenty-three states have created penalties comparable to the recent substantial increases in federal penalties: Alaska, Arizona, California, Hawaii, Indiana, Iowa, Kentucky, Maryland, Michigan, Minnesota, Nevada, New Mexico, North Carolina, Oregon, Puerto Rico, South Carolina, Tennessee, Utah, Vermont, Virginia, Virgin Islands, Washington and Wyoming.

40.   Dan Petersen, *Safety Management, A Human Approach*, 2nd ed., Aloray, Inc., Goshen, NY, 1988.

41.   In the Omnibus Budget bill passed last fall, Congress increased OSHA's penalties by a factor of seven, with the largest potential fine for a single violation reaching $70,000.

42.   <u>Martin, Secretary of Labor v. Occupational Safety and Health Review Commission</u>, 111 S.Ct. 1171 (1991).

43.   <u>Secretary of Labor v. Con Agra Flour Milling Co.</u>, 1991 OSHD (CCH) ¶ 29267 (directed for review March 20, 1991) involved a citation for including benzene on the list required by the Hazard Communication standard when it was not specifically present in the workplace.

APPENDIX

**WHERE TO CALL TO REPORT AN ACCIDENT
RESULTING IN A FATALITY OR MULTIPLE HOSPITALIZATION**

Employers are required to report work-related accidents which result in at least one worker fatality or the hospitalization of three or more employees. To report such accidents, employers must contact the nearest OSHA office in person or by telephone, Below is a listing of the current telephone numbers for the area offices. The toll-free number is 1-800-321-OSHA.

STATE	CITY	PHONE NUMBER
Alabama	Birmingham	(205) 731-1534
	Mobile	(205) 441-6131
Alaska	Anchorage	(907) 271-5152
Arizona	Phoenix	(602) 640-2007
Arkansas	Little Rock	(501) 324-6292
California	Sacramento	(916) 978-5641
	San Diego	(619) 557-2909
	San Francisco	(415) 744-7120
		(415) 744-6670
Colorado	Denver	(303) 844-5285
		(303) 391-5858
	Englewood	(303) 843-4500
Connecticut	Bridgeport	(203) 579-5579
	Hartford	(203) 240-3152
Delaware	Wilmington	(302) 573-6115
District of Columbia	Washington	(202) 523-1452
Florida	Fort Lauderdale	(305) 424-0242
	Jacksonville	(904) 232-2895
	Tampa	(813) 626-1177
Georgia	Atlanta	(404) 347-3573
	Savannah	(912) 652-4393
	Smyrna	(404) 984-8700
	Tucker	(404) 493-6644
Hawaii	Honolulu	(808) 541-2685
Idaho	Boise	(208) 334-1867
Illinois	Calumet City	(708) 891-3800
	Chicago	(312) 353-2220
	Des Plaines	(708) 803-4800
	Fairview Heights	(618) 632-8612
	North Aurora	(708) 896-8700
	Peoria	(309) 671-7033
Indiana	Indianapolis	(317) 226-7290
Iowa	Des Moines	(515) 284-4794

STATE	CITY	PHONE NUMBER
Kansas	Overland Park	(913) 236-3220
	Wichita	(316) 269-6644
Kentucky	Frankfort	(502) 227-7024
Louisiana	Baton Rouge	(504) 389-0474
Maine	Augusta	(207) 622-8417
	Bangor	(207) 941-8177
Maryland	Baltimore	(410) 962-2840
Massachusetts	Boston	(617) 565-7164
	Braintree	(617) 565-6924
	Methuen	(617) 565-8110
	Springfield	(413) 785-0123
Michigan	Lansing	(517) 377-1892
Minnesota	Minneapolis	(612) 348-1994
Mississippi	Jackson	(601) 965-4606
Missouri	Kansas City	(816) 426-2756
		(816) 426-5861
	St. Louis	(314) 425-4249
Montana	Billings	(406) 657-6649
Nebraska	Omaha	(402) 221-3182
Nevada	Carson City	(702) 885-6963
New Hampshire	Concord	(603) 225-1629
New Jersey	Avenel	(908) 750-3270
	Hasbrouck Heights	(201) 288-1700
	Marlton	(609) 757-5181
	Parsippany	(201) 263-1003
New Mexico	Albuquerque	(505) 766-3411
New York	Albany	(518) 464-6742
	Bayside	(718) 279-9060
	Bowmansville	(716) 684-3891
	New York	(212) 264-9840
	New York	(212) 337-2378
	Syracuse	(315) 451-0808
	Tarrytown	(914) 682-6151
	Westbury	(516) 334-3344
North Carolina	Raleigh	(919) 856-4770
North Dakota	Bismarck	(701) 250-4521
Ohio	Cincinnati	(513) 841-4132
	Cleveland	(216) 522-3818
	Toledo	(419) 259-7542
Oklahoma	Oklahoma City	(405) 231-5351
Oregon	Portland	(503) 326-2251

STATE	CITY	PHONE NUMBER
Pennsylvania	Allentown	(215) 776-0592
	Erie	(814) 833-5758
	Harrisburg	(717) 782-3902
	Philadelphia	(215) 597-4955
	Philadelphia	(215) 596-1201
	Pittsburgh	(412) 644-2903
	Wilkes-Barre	(717) 826-6538
Puerto Rico	Hato Rey	(809) 766-5457
Rhode Island	Providence	(401) 528-4669
South Carolina	Columbia	(803) 765-5904
Tennessee	Nashville	(615) 781-5423
Texas	Austin	(512) 482-5783
	Corpus Christi	(512) 888-3257
	Dallas	(214) 320-2400
	Dallas	(214) 767-4731
	El Paso	(915) 534-7004
	Fort Worth	(817) 885-7025
	Houston	(713) 286-0583
	Houston	(713) 591-2438
	Lubbock	(806) 743-7681
Utah	Salt Lake City	(801) 524-5080
Virginia	Norfolk	(804) 441-3820
Washington	Bellevue	(206) 553-7520
	Eau Claire	(715) 832-9019
	Seattle	(206) 553-5930
West Virginia	Charleston	(304) 347-5937
Wisconsin	Appleton	(414) 734-4521
	Madison	(608) 264-5388
	Milwaukee	(414) 297-3315

Chapter 8

OCCUPATIONAL SAFETY AND HEALTH ADMINISTRATION

GENERAL RECORDKEEPING REQUIREMENTS
UNDER OSHA

David G. Sarvadi
Martha Pellegrini
Keller and Heckman
Washington, D.C.

INTRODUCTION

When Congress passed the Occupational Safety and Health Act, (OSH Act) it provided authority for the Secretary of Labor to promulgate rules regulating employer's conduct in operation of their businesses. Section 6 of the Act gave the Occupational Safety and Health Administration (OSHA) general rulemaking authority with specific procedural guidelines, and specifically authorized OSHA to include provisions requiring employers to maintain records for various purposes. We discuss below the basis for OSHA's authority, identify the kinds of records that must be kept, and review the retention period and the rules regarding access to the records by various parties.

WHY KEEP RECORDS

Recognizing that government must have information with which to be effective, Congress authorized OSHA to require employers to keep records. Specifically, the OSH Act provides that:

Each employer shall make, keep, and preserve, and make available to the Secretary... such records regarding his activities relating to this Act as the Secretary ... may prescribe....

The Secretary... shall prescribe regulations requiring employers to maintain accurate records of, and to make periodic reports on, work-related deaths, injuries and illnesses....

176

The Secretary... shall issue regulations requiring employers to maintain accurate records of employee exposures to potentially toxic materials or harmful physical agents....[1]

Another reason to keep records is the need to document the history of employee's work environment, recognizing that some kinds of work-related illnesses develop after exposure over long periods of time. At the time Congress enacted the OSH Act in 1970, little information was available to define on the basis of objective science "safe" working conditions.

A more basic reason for the requirement to keep records, which also explains the tendency of OSHA to increase these requirements continually, is that records allow the Agency to document the existence of violations to enforce its rules. It is not possible for OSHA inspectors to be present on the job site every day, or even to inspect each workplace each year. It thus falls to the inspector to ascertain the compliance status of the employer through other means. Principal among these means is the inspection of the records kept in the ordinary course of business. This is the classic approach of the government lawyer in searching the "paper trail" for evidence of wrongdoing.

Records of activities and programs are always a double-edged sword. On one hand, they document the reasonable and prudent actions of company officials and employees in conducting the business lawfully. They also often document the failure of company personnel to perform specific tasks, or of the corporate organization to respond adequately to problems. This tension between the utility of records and the risks inherent in keeping them has created a significant dilemma for many people. Nevertheless, most employers find that maintaining good records is, on balance, positive.

WHAT RECORDS MUST BE KEPT

OSHA-related records will generally fall into one of these four classes:

- Government Specified Records: These are records mandated by government at all levels. In many instances, they are the same as those described below which would otherwise be discarded quickly and be unavailable for governmental purposes because they lose their business utility as more current data develop. Government, on the other hand, wants the paper trail to remain, at least until the statute of limitations runs, in order to facilitate its functions.

---

[1] 29 U.S.C. 657 § (c)(1), (2), and (3).

●   <u>Company Communications</u>: These are the usual kinds of communications between individuals both within the organization and with those outside the organization. They document the steps the responsible manager takes to carry out company policies and activities.

●   <u>Written Policies and Procedures</u>: The third type of ordinary corporate records kept are written expressions of company policies, procedures and instructions. These document the specific actions that the company takes to implement both mandated and voluntary programs. In some case, the statutes or regulations require that a written program be developed; in others, it is simply good management practice to prepare such documents to consolidate the instructions to company personnel.

●   <u>Internal Reports</u>: The fourth type of record are those documents that describe the specific day-to-day activities of company employees in carrying out the mandates of company programs and policies. These include daily, weekday or monthly inspection reports, summary management reports, records of training and discipline and similar documents.

Throughout, the OSHA standards enumerate requirements for the preparation and maintenance of records. In other cases, record requirements are inferred from the performance-oriented nature of the standard. The discussion of the Hazard Communication Standard[2] which follows illustrates the variety and types of records required.

RECORDS ASSOCIATED WITH HAZARD COMMUNICATION

The HCS covers virtually all employers in the private sector in the U.S. with exception of the mining industry. The standard requires employers to address all hazardous chemicals to which employees may be exposed.[3] All employers are required to communicate to their employees information about hazardous substances which are known to be present a the worksite. This requirement applies regardless of whether the employer creates the exposure. The issue for all employers is whether they "know" that their employees are exposed.

---

[2]   29 C.F.R. 1910.1200, 1926.58, 1915.99, 1917.28, 1918.90, 1928.21

[3]   29 C.F.R. 1910.1200(b)

Chemical manufacturers and importers are required to perform hazard determinations on all chemicals they produce or import. If downstream employers, such as wholesalers and distributors, relabel products or in any other way choose not to rely on the manufacturer's determination of hazard, they too must perform the determination.

The HCS imposes a comprehensive duty on employers to develop written documents both explicitly and implicitly. In general, four types of records must be kept under the HCS. First, there is the written program. This must contain sections which address specific subjects listed in the standard.[4] Secondly, every employer must maintain a list of hazardous chemicals to which employees may be exposed. This list must include the products that are used listed by the names on the label and on Material Safety Data Sheets (MSDS), so that the user can find the appropriate MSDS from the name on the label or on the list. Consequently, it is not clear that the OSHA standard requires the inclusion of component chemical names on the list of hazardous chemicals. This is a common misconception.

The third kind of record that must be kept is the MSDS. The ostensible purpose of the MSDS is to provide information to employees about the hazardous chemicals to which they are exposed. However, OSHA attributes a secondary purpose to both the list of hazardous chemicals and the MSDS: to document the exposures of employees over time for use as a tool in conducting epidemiological studies. Thus, these two types of records are considered records of exposure which are subject to the record retention provisions of 1910.20(d)(1)(ii).

The last kind of record is implicitly required by the HCS, and that is the response of the employer to requests for copies of MSDSs or other information by medical specialists in an emergency. Under the standard, manufacturers may withhold chemical composition information from labels and MSDS, but must disclose the information when a bona fide request is received from a physician or other health care professional.[5] These requests must be in writing and must contain specific information, and the responses must be prepared accordingly. Of course, such correspondence inevitably creates a record of the transaction which then must be maintained.

---

[4]   29 C.F.R. 1910.1200 (e).

[5]   29 C.F.R. 1910.1200(i).

OSHA'S EXPLICIT REQUIREMENTS

OSHA sometimes is very explicit about what is expected. In the HCS, the definition of the written program elements is detailed in very simple language.

> Employers shall develop, implement, and maintain a written hazard communication program for their workplaces which at least describes how the criteria specified in paragraphs (f), (g), and (h) of this section. . . will be met. . . .[6]

However, to meet the standard of describing how these requirements are met requires an extensive written program. Simply paraphrasing the language of the standard is not sufficient.

Implicitly associated with the requirements of the standard (e.g., training and hazard communication) are records that may not be subject to any particular retention policy but which are necessary to document compliance activities. OSHA expects to see details such as responsible managers, descriptions, and procedures written out. In the OSHA Compliance Instruction (CPL) CPL 2-2.38C, Inspection Procedures for the Hazard Communication Standard, OSHA defines what it expects to see in a written Hazard Communication Program (HCP). It must contain the following elements:

(1)   A determination of whether or not the employer has addressed the issues in sufficient detail to ensure that a comprehensive approach to hazard communication has been developed.

(2)   In general, the written program should consider the following elements where applicable:

   (a)   Labels and Other Forms of Warning.

   i)   Designation of person(s) responsible for ensuring labeling of in-plant containers.

   ii)   Designation of person(s) responsible for ensuring labeling on shipped containers.

   iii)   Description of labeling system(s) used.

---

[6]   29 C.F.R. 1910.1200(e)(1).

iv)   Description of written alternatives to labeling of in-plant containers, where applicable.

v)   Procedures to review and update label information when necessary.

(b)   Material Safety Data Sheets.

    i)   Designation of person(s) responsible for obtaining/maintaining the MSDS.

    ii)   How such sheets are to be maintained (e.g., in notebooks in the work area(s), via a computer terminal, in a pick-up truck at the jobsite, via telefax) and how employees obtain access to them.

    iii)   Procedures to follow when the MSDS is not received at the time of the first shipment.

    iv)   For chemical manufacturers or importers, procedures for updating the MSDS when new and significant health information is found.

(c)   Training.

    i)   Designation of person(s) responsible for conducting training.

    ii)   Format of the program to be used (audiovisuals, classroom instruction, etc.).

    iii)   Elements of the training program -- compare to the elements required by the HCS (paragraph (h) of 1910.1200).

    iv)   Procedures to train new employees at the time of their initial assignment and to train employees when a new hazard is introduced into the workplace.

v)   Procedures to train employees of new hazards they may be exposed to when working on or near another employer's worksite (<u>i.e.</u>, hazards introduced by other employees).

vi)   Guidelines on training programs prepared by the Office of Training and Education entitled "Voluntary Training Guidelines" (49 Fed. Reg. 30290 (July 27, 1984)) can be used to provide general information on what constitutes a good training program.

(d)   <u>Additional Topics To Be Reviewed</u>

i)   Does a list of the hazardous chemicals exist and if so, is it compiled for each work area or for the entire worksite and kept in a central location?

ii)   Are methods the employer will use to inform employees of the hazards of <u>non-routine</u> tasks outlined?

iii)   Are employees informed of the hazards associated with chemicals contained in unlabeled pipes in their work areas?

iv)   Does the plan include the methods the employer will use at multi-employer worksites to inform other employers of any precautionary measures that need to be taken to protect their employees?

v)   For multi-employer workplaces, are the methods the employer will use to inform the other employer(s) of the labeling system used described?

vi)   Is the written program made available to employees and their designated representatives?

Thus, implementation of the written program necessitates the generation of additional records, such as historical records of program reviews, notes on hazard determinations, drafts of labels and material safety data sheets and training records. These records are almost always necessary to document that the program in fact is implemented. Only in the case of the employer who relies solely on its suppliers for MSDS and labels will there be no hazard determinations. And, unless an employer can demonstrate that employees are well trained by other means, records of training will be necessary.

Labels may also be considered records, although they are arguably not exposure records. Certainly, companies will want to keep records of what label statements were used and, in particular, the reasons for the choice of the statements. The standard requires that "appropriate hazard warnings"[7] be used on labels on all containers in the workplace. OSHA recognizes that appropriate labels need not include warnings about every toxic effect of every component in a product.[8] Therefore, where labels evolve as manufacturers learn more about their products, in terms of the inherent dangers and the usage characteristics of customer's operations, the "appropriate" warnings will change. It is important to document this evolution, both for OSHA as well as other legal purposes, and such records will thus become part of the ordinary business records system.

Recent technical amendments which were effective as of March 11, 1994, clarify certain aspects of HCS recordkeeping. New and more focused compliance documentation requirements are implicitly required with regard to such things as:

- The consideration of intermediate uses when determining whether chemical substance exposures will occur which present a hazard to employees.

- Demonstrating that employee use of a consumer product containing hazardous chemicals is of a duration and frequency that clearly falls within OSHA's consumer product exemption.

- Examination of not only the chemical hazards, but also the physical hazards (e.g., irritant effects), associated with nuisance dust as part of the hazard determination process.

- Labeling for specific target organ effects. OSHA clarified that the phrase "hazard warning" on container labels means that the label must make a reference to the specific bodily organ affected by a substance, also known as a "target organ effect." OSHA's requirement of target organ effects on

---

[7] 29 C.F.R. 1910.1200(f)(5)(ii).

[8] OSHA Compliance Instruction (CPL) CPL 2-2.38C, Inspection Procedures for the Hazard Communication Standard, p. A-20.

labels was upheld last fall by a federal court of appeals (Martin v. American Cyanamid 5.F.3d 140, (6th Cir. 1993)).

- The adequacy of alternative labeling systems to develop warning statements which enumerate the actual hazards of the chemical.

- Provisions for sufficient communication at multi-employer worksites in written hazard communication programs.

- A requirement that significant new information regarding the hazards of a chemical must be added to a label within three months of becoming aware of the new information. This is identical to the existing provision for updating MSDSs.

- Documenting employee re-training required by the HCS when a new hazard is brought into the workplace, not a new chemical. Thus, where there are many chemicals in the workplace, and they change frequently, OSHA determined that it would be more appropriate to train workers regarding all types of hazards, by categories, rather than addressing each individual substance.

- Generally improving the quality, uniformity, and current availability of MSDSs.

ORDINARY BUSINESS RECORDS UNDER THE HCS

It is not always obvious that records are being developed when managers perform their jobs. The process of requesting material safety data sheets generates additional records that OSHA inspectors wish to see. These documents are evidence of good faith in carrying out an employer's responsibilities under the HCS. In addition, they leave an audit trail for in-house verifications that compliance programs are effective.

Audits generate additional records that demonstrate both compliance and corporate commitment. These documents are not primary sources of compliance information, but rather document the internal feedback systems necessary for management to assure that company policies and programs are effectively implemented.

In developing records under the HCS, it becomes important to consider what information must be kept. With regard to hazard determinations, chemical manufacturers should document the decision-making process which they follow to prepare MSDS

Table 1
29 C.F.R. § 1910 Chemical Specific Standards

Section	Title	Section	Title
1001	Asbestos	1002	Coal Tar Pitch Volatiles
1003	4-Nitrobiphenyl	1004	alpha-Naphthylamine
1006	Methylchloromethyl ether	1007	3,3'-dichlorobenzidine
1008	bis-Chloromethyl ether	1009	beta-Naphthylamine
1010	Benzidine	1011	4-Aminodiphenyl
1012	Ethyleneimine	1013	beta-Propiolactone
1014	2-Acetylaminofluorene	1015	4-Dimethylaminoazobenzene
1016	N-Nitrosodimethylamine	1017	Vinyl Chloride
1018	Inorganic arsenic	1025	Lead
1027	Cadmium	1028	Benzene
1029	Coke Oven Emissions	1030	Bloodborne Pathogens
1043	Cotton Dust	1044	1,2-dibromo-3-chloropropane
1045	Acrylonitrile	1047	Ethylene Oxide
1048	Formaldehyde	1050	Methylenedianline

This list may not be complete.

(j)(3)(iv)	Information to Physicians
(j)(3)(v)	Written Medical Opinions
(l)(1)(ii)	Training Program
(l)(1)(iii)	Initial Training
(l)(1)(iv)	Annual Training
(l)(2)(i)	Employee Requests for Information
(l)(2)(ii)	DOL Requests for Information
(m)(2)(ii)	Sign Cleaning
(n)(1)	Exposure Monitoring Recordkeeping
(n)(2)	Medical Surveillance Recordkeeping
(n)(3)	Medical Removal Recordkeeping
(o)(2)(ii)(c)	Observation of Monitoring

That is, there are 29 provisions of the lead standard in which some form of record is implied or required. This is, of course, an enormous burden, but more importantly, it creates a significant problem for assuring compliance. Not only do the records have to

and labels. These records should reflect the specific sources of information considered, the issues related to selection of hazard warning statements, and considerations of normal use or foreseeable emergency.

The importance of these documents is that they establish both the employer's good faith efforts to evaluate the hazard as well as the rationale for selecting the particular content and wording of labels and MSDS. In an inspection, the compliance officer is at a distinct disadvantage because he does not have reference sources available. Where the procedures and decisions are adequately documented, he is not in a position to question them unless he is willing to spend a significant amount of time researching the issues. Moreover, the judgement of hazard is the employer's, which, of course, can be subject to review by OSHA, but the burden is then on OSHA to demonstrate that the employer's determination is incorrect.

OTHER OSHA STANDARDS

Other OSHA standards are equally broad. The chemical specific standards often include requirements for the development of specific exposure and medical records, administrative memoranda, reports, and certifications. Table 1 lists the chemical specific standards presently in effect.

The lead standard, for example, requires development of the following records:

(d)(2)	Initial Determination
(d)(4)	Initial Monitoring
(d)(5)	Negative Initial Determination Record
(d)(7)	Additional Monitoring
(e)(1)	Infeasible Engineering Controls
(e)(3)	Written Compliance Program
(e)(5)	Measurements of Mechanical Ventilation
(e)(6)	Job Rotation Schedules
(f)(1)	Written Respirator Program
(f)(2)	Respirator Selection
(f)(3)	Respirator Fit Testing
(g)(2)(vi)	Notice to laundries
(g)(2)(vii)	Laundry Container Labels
(j)(2)	Blood lead monitoring
(j)(2)(iii)	Employee Blood Lead Notifications
(j)(3)	Medical Examinations
(j)(3)(iii)(B)	Second Opinion Notifications

be kept, they must be maintained. This is interpreted by OSHA to mean that the information in the records must be updated when it changes.

Some of the OSHA standards which imply significant recordkeeping requirements do so because they require some kind of periodic inspection. For example, the standard on Portable Wood Ladders requires that

> Ladders shall be inspected frequently and those which have developed defects shall be withdrawn from service...."9/

This provision does not explicitly require any records. However, most employers would find them useful if an inspector found an employee using a ladder that had a defect.

The defense to such a citation would likely be the defense of "employee misconduct," that the employee failed to perform his job properly. The employer would have to show through contemporaneous records the existance of: (1) a policy; (2) of training the employee; (3) of conducting inspections regularly; and (4) of supervisors enforcing the requirement. The last element would likely be shown through evidence that employees had been disciplined for failure to perform the required acts. This illustrates that the rule could be interpreted to require that at least four types of records would have to be kept to demonstrate employer compliance with the inspection requirement. Of course, not all employers will have such records, and in fact, many do not keep them. Nevertheless, because the burden is on the employer to demonstrate compliance with the standard when the prima facie case is made in an OSHA complaint, records of such kinds of activities are always desirable.

Table 2 is a listing, by no means complete, of other OSHA standards that have either written program, training, or inspection requirements. Nearly every standard that is proposed by OSHA today has some provision for additional records. Table 3 lists those standards which are presently in development by OSHA which will likely have significant recordkeeping provisions included. We can anticipate that all future standards will be similarly designed to provide an adequate record for inspectors to use in evaluating compliance.

9/ 29 C.F.R. 1910.25(x).

Table 2

Current Requirements for Health and Safety Records in the Workplace

	Written Program	Specific Training	Routine Inspections	1910 Section
Portable Ladders	N	N	Y	25
Walking Working Surfaces	N	N	Y	21-32
Emergency Response	Y	Y	N	38
Powered Platforms for Building Maintenance	Y	Y	Y	66
Manlifts	N	Y	Y	68
Ventilation Systems	N	N	Y	94
Noise	N	Y	Y	95
Ionizing Radiation	N	Y	Y	96
Flammable/Combustible Liquids	N	N	N	106
Process Safety Management	Y	Y	Y	119
Hazardous Waste	Y	Y	N	120
Personal Protective Equipment	Y	Y	N	132
Respirators	Y	Y	Y	134
Confined Space Entry	Y	Y	Y?	146
Lockout/Tagout	Y	Y		147
Medical Services and First Aid	N	Y	Y	151
Fire Brigades	Y	Y	Y	156
Fire Extinguisher	Y	Y	Y	157
Sprinklers/Hoses Standpipes	Y?	Y?	Y	158
Employee Alarms	Y	Y	Y	165
Servicing Truck Tires	N	Y	N	177
Powered Industrial Trucks	N	Y	Y	178

Table 2
(continued)
Current Requirements for
Health and Safety Records
in the Workplace

	Written Program	Specific Training	Routine Inspections	1910 Section
Cranes	N	N	Y	178, 179
Derricks	N	Y	Y	181
Slings	N	N	Y	184
Machine Guarding	N	N	Y	217
Mechanical Power Presses	N	Y	Y	217
Portable Power Tools	N	N	Y?	241, 244
Welding	N	Y	N	252
Electrical Systems	N	Y	N	301-399
Bloodborne Pathogens	Y	Y	Y	1030
Hazard Communication	Y	Y	Y	1200
Laboratories (Non -production)	Y	Y	N	1450

Table 3

Anticipated Requirements for
Health and Safety Records
in the Workplace

	Written Program	Specific Training	Routine Inspections
Ergonomics	Y	Y	N
Motor Vehicle Occupant Safety	Y	Y	Y
Indoor Air Quality	Y	Y	Y

RETENTION OF AND ACCESS TO RECORDS

As demonstrated above, OSHA does not have a generic recordkeeping standard. There is a single provision that addresses retention periods and authorized access to medical records. The retention provision requires employers to maintain medical and exposure records for thirty (30) years,[10] and provide for the transfer of records to the National Institute for Occupational Safety and Health (NIOSH) in the event the employer intends to dispose of them or ceases to do business.[11] Medical records are defined to exempt health insurance claims records, first aid records of one-time treatment and subsequent observation of cases not involving medical treatment, and to records of employees employed for less than one year who are given the records on termination of employment. The exemption for first aid records applies essentially to those cases which would otherwise not be recordable on the OSHA Form 200.

This section also establishes the right of employees and their designated representatives to obtain access to and copies of medical and exposure records.[12] Employers may not charge for initial copies of records, and must provide access within fifteen working days of a request. Employee medical records are subject to a provision that can limit access by the employee if, in the opinion of an employer's physician, there is information regarding a terminal illness or psychiatric condition that could be detrimental to the employee's health. In such cases, the employer may provide the information to another physician of the employee's choosing after denying the employee access to the detrimental information in writing. Confidential information identifying persons who have provided information about the employee may be excised from the record provided to the employee.

A separate provision authorizes OSHA access to the records under the statute. Regulations found at 29 C.F.R. § 1913.10 define agency practice and procedure for gaining access. The rules, issued to satisfy privacy concerns, limit the types of requests that can be made, the agency personnel who may be granted authority to access the records, and the uses to which the records are put.

---

[10]   29 C.F.R. 1910.20(d).

[11]   29 C.F.R. 1910.20(h).

[12]   29 C.F.R. 1910.20(e).

CONCLUSION

Increasing numbers of OSHA standards require the completion and maintenance of records. The challenge for employers today is to envision what records are necessary to document compliance, assure that the records are being kept, and that they are accurate and updated regularly.

Chapter 9

AVAILABLE MICROCOMPUTER SYSTEMS FOR
ENVIRONMENTAL REPORTING AND RECORDKEEPING

June C. Bolstridge
President
GAIA Corporation
Silver Spring, Maryland

Ever-increasing environmental reporting requirements demand the kind of data aggregation, comparison to thresholds, and completion of reports that computers can easily perform. This paper provides an overview of environmental information management systems by describing the types of environmental tasks that computers are appropriate to address. An approach to developing and prioritizing system specifications is described which includes the development of an understanding of the cultural, economic, and time limitations involved.

Once a system has been selected or developed, the work has just begun, and this paper provides suggestions for installing and maintaining the system. A description of some of the approaches used for chemical inventories is provided to illustrate the variability in available environmental data management systems. Finally, an approach to disaster preparedness is described to protect the investment that has been made. A list of reference sources and resources for obtaining information on commercially available software is also provided.

The Need for Environmental Computer Systems

Environmental information management is changing extremely rapidly because it represents the overlap of two industries that are each involved in constant change. Environmental requirements and regulations are intensifying the frequency and complexity of environmental data collection and reporting. Computerized hardware and software capabilities and accessibility are also expanding at an extremely fast rate.

In addition, there is a marked increase in the data management expertise of regulatory agencies, environmental groups, and the general public. These organizations have become capable of advanced evaluations of environmental data reported by industry and are more demanding of the types and forms of information available. It is no longer an option whether computers will be used in environmental data management, but merely a question of the most appropriate tasks and the types of approaches that are to be used for the application of computers.

Understanding the Scope of Environmental Software

Environmental data management systems take many forms. Commercial environmental data systems are available to meet many types of needs. Some of these systems are little more than reference sources for information concerning the regulatory requirements or for information about the regulated chemicals. Others track regulatory deadlines, assist in the compilation of daily inventory records, compare data to the reporting thresholds, prepare the data in the format required for submission, and do everything except seal and stamp the envelope to the regulatory agency.

Software is currently available to assist with nearly all types of environmental data management, including:

Chemical and Waste Management

- Identification of regulated chemicals
- Maintenance of chemical inventories
- Management of Material Safety Data Sheets
- Reorder and shipping management
- Waste manifesting and tracking
- Disposal records

Regulatory Requirement Analysis and Documentation

- Calculation of thresholds
- Documentation of assumptions
- Preparation of Federal reports
- Preparation of State and Local reports
- Identification of reporting errors
- Referencing regulatory text
- Records of employee exposure
- Records of employee training

Emergency Response Planning and Analysis

- Identification of chemical storage areas
- Identification of sensitive populations
- Mapping of locations and evacuation routes
- Documentation of response equipment available
- Modeling of releases
- Preparation of Emergency Response Plans
- Decision making in emergency situations

Alternatives to purchasing commercially available software packages include assembling several commercial systems to meet the requirements, or developing a system internally.

In combining several commercial systems, the best of each system can be blended together to obtain capabilities that are not available from any individual system. Portions of the system can be phased in to obtain immediate benefits and delay some expenses. There are, however, also some disadvantages to assembling commercial systems, including the need for more evaluations and selections; dependency on multiple vendors; problems between systems may not be supported by any vendor; updates by one vendor may require complex and intricate revisions; more training may be required; and there will be less consistency in user's commands.

Developing a computerized environmental system in-house provides the most control over the capabilities of the system, including the ability to address local government and internal needs. System development can be performed in phases, based on needs and resources available. An internally developed system is guaranteed to be expendable and available, however this approach also has some strong disadvantages that are often overlooked. Internal development of any system requires a long-term commitment because of the development time required. Decisions concerning what data to include (and leave out) can become critical, as everyone identifies something else they want the system to do as development progresses. Finally, it can be difficult to motivate internal personnel to do not-for-profit work, and to keep management committed to system implementation and maintenance.

Considerations for Specifying Environmental Software

Few companies realize the investment required to evaluate software or developing system specifications. Such activities take time from other tasks, and because they can never be completed (new needs and systems are

constantly appearing) they can absorb endless amounts of
effort. It is important to realize that in selecting or
specifying software, an investment is being exchanged for
relatively intangible compensation. Effort of evaluating,
specifying, and implementing a computerized environmental
data management system is exchanged for the opportunity to
develop better environmental data, better understand the
data reported, improve regulatory compliance and thereby
reduce potential fines, better train employees, and be more
prepared to address future issues as they arise.

The success of any system depend on the existing
information management practices, computer equipment, and
computer capabilities of the personnel involved. Criteria
that can help you determine your current information and
computer status include:

1. What systems (paper or computerized) are in place
   and which ones contain data that will be needed to
   meet the environmental regulatory requirements?

2. What types of access are required to use the
   information and in what form will the data be most
   useful?

3. What computer knowledge will be required to use the
   system, maintain the system, and troubleshoot the
   system?

4. How well do you and other facility personnel
   understand what computers can and cannot do?

5. Are facility personnel biased against computer use?
   What can be done to avoid implementation problems?

Choosing the 'BEST' System

One of the most common questions is: "What is the
'best' computer system to manage our environmental data?"
However, obtaining the best environmental data management
system much more like choosing a pair of shoes than a
refrigerator -- a proper fit is extremely important, since
environmental computer systems are built to meet the needs
of a particular set of users. The normal purchasing
criteria of cost and system capabilities have to be
replaced with a careful assessment of the organization that
is purchasing the system, and the goals to be met.

The most important part of choosing a software system,
is to examine your needs, put them into the context of your
operations, and describe those needs clearly and
succinctly. This examination of needs will translate into
the criteria for use in development or purchase of the

195

system. The criteria can be ranked by importance and be classed as immediate needs versus those that can be delayed until additional resources are available. In developing the selection or development criteria, consider the following questions:

1. What timeframe is required for an effective system to be in place?

2. What regulatory reports must be created and what requirements must be met by the system?

3. What internal needs and requirements should also be addressed by the system?

4. How quickly are regulatory and internal needs expected to intensify (e.g., tightening thresholds; increased chemical use; added data management)?

5. What trade-offs will be required in terms of time required to put the system into place and the time savings resulting from the system use for the first year and for subsequent years?

Even if your organization has chosen to develop a software system internally, reviewing the products of commercial vendors that have been developed to address similar needs can help to refine your specifications. (See the list of sources at the end of this paper to identify environmental software vendors.) In addition, you may find that a commercial vendor has a system that will meet most of your needs for a fraction of the cost of developing the system in-house. This initial market survey should be used to identify 8 to 12 systems within the price range identified which appear to meet the minimum criteria.

Vendors should then be contacted to assure that their systems remain available, and to request demonstration diskettes and brochures or other literature concerning the software capabilities. Select at least 5 vendors who appear to be reasonably accessible, willing to assist you, and competent. Selecting a vendor is as important as selecting a software package.

Review the materials provided by the vendors to determine the strengths and weaknesses of each system. Review the market one last time to assure yourself that nothing new has appeared that should be included in your review.

Then, evaluate each system that appears to be of interest based on the detailed criteria that you have established. Assess the systems' philosophy and scope to assure that it is something that you can work with. Based on this evaluation, select 2 to 4 for final review and evaluation.

Finally, complete the internal selection process based on all of the information available. Request trial copies of the software or sample user's manuals to better understand the structure and user interface of the software. Contact other users of the software to determine what they consider the major weaknesses of the systems. Make the purchase decision and document your review process to justify the selection to your management. Documentation of the review will also be critical if the purchase is delayed or must be reviewed by someone else in your organization.

Life After the System Specification

Investing in implementation and use are extremely important to system success since value is obtained only if a system is used and maintained. Most companies have at least one bookshelf filled with software packages that were purchased but have never been used. A long-term commitment to the system, including the allocation of resources for its use and continued maintenance, should be established prior to the system's purchase or development.

Installation costs and the long-term investment required to maintain and operate the full working system will include:

- Assembling the required data;
- Validating and entering data;
- Training new personnel;
- Purchasing or developing software updates; and
- Correcting and amending the data.

Variability of Environmental Information Systems

Although it might first appear that environmental information systems should be readily compared, at least within a category, systems that are described as similar by vendors can have widely different capabilities. Inventory systems will be described to illustrate such differences, however similar variability will be found in systems for other environmental uses.

As a minimum an inventory consists of data on chemical identity, amounts present, and locations. Some types of inventories must include information on the form of the chemical (e.g., granular solid, liquid), the purity (e.g., mixture, pure form), storage conditions (e.g., temperature, pressure), and storage types (e.g., bulk tank). Inventory systems may be used as the basis of other compliance activities by comparing chemical amounts to the thresholds for reporting under various regulations. Computer systems may differ greatly in their ability to identify the components of chemical mixtures based on synonyms, to address trade secret materials, and handle exemptions for minimal concentrations, forms, or uses of the chemical at the facility. Inventory data may be used in the development of purchase requisitions or to schedule the re-order of materials, and therefore only address mixtures rather than the components. Inventories may be applied to identify substitute chemicals, reduce waste through scheduling use, identify the content of storage areas, or identify the chemical hazards to include in worker or emergency responder training programs. Because of these widely differing uses of inventory data, certain inventories may only record total purchases for the year, while other inventories may identify the amount of the chemical or material that is present on-site at any time.

Disaster Preparedness Planning

Any interruption to the use of an environmental computer system can result in regulatory non-compliance and fines. Disasters that destroy computer systems can't be prevented, but their effects can be reduced by careful planning. The goal of disaster preparedness planning is to protect any essential information to allow the business to continue to operate. A suggested approach to disaster preparedness planning includes allocating resources to:

1.   Identify essential data, equipment, and programs based on: cost; reproducibility; frequency of use; consequences of unavailability; data volume; and confidential status.

2.   Identify the types of potential disasters, and identify methods to minimize their effects, such as:

  • Smoke, fire, or flood destroying equipment and data; minimize effects by off-site backups

  • Equipment failure, producing minor to total data loss; minimize effects through backups

  • Power surges, spikes brownouts, producing minor to total data loss; minimize effects through backups

  • Employee loss producing down time, errors; minimize effects by training a minimum of 3 users

  • Employee error producing corrupted data, inaccuracy; minimize effects through backups

- Software bugs producing down time, inaccuracy, data loss; minimize effects through backups and validate to original

- Viruses producing minor to total loss; minimize effects through backups and validate to original

- Sabotage producing minor to total loss; minimize effects by strict security and backups

3. Manage the system in a way that plans for disaster in everyday operations by producing reserve copies of data that are current and properly stored.

4. Develop complete procedures for reconstructing the entire system, including: equipment sources; load procedures; default values; quirks that were once solved; and sources of information.

5. Test the plan when the system or the personnel involved change. An untested or out-of-date plan has no value.

Conclusions

Computer systems are essential to the management of environmental data because of the increasing requirements for data collection and reporting. However, computer systems are tools that must be chosen and applied carefully to achieve effective results. Criteria for the selection or development of environmental software must take into account the tasks to be performed, as well as the culture and limitations of the organization involved. Options for applying computers to environmental data management include: purchase of a single commercially available system; assembly of several commercially available systems to perform different functions; and in-house development. Each of these options provide opportunities and disadvantages which should be considered. Implementing and maintaining a computer system is labor intensive and includes training users and keeping the system up-to-date. Disaster preparedness planning can help to reduce the adverse effects of an interruption to accessing the system and therefore help to protect the investment.

Publications and Journals on Environmental Computer Systems:

Air and Waste Management Association Journal
Microcomputer Software Reviews, monthly feature article
1 Gateway Center, 3rd Floor
Pittsburgh, PA 15222
(412) 232-3444
$14.50 a copy; major credit card orders may be faxed to (412) 232-3450

American Chemical Society
Journal of Chemical Information and Computer Sciences
CHEMputer Buyer's Guide
Louis Gonzalez, Author
1155 16th Street, N.W.
Washington, D.C. 20036
(800) 227-5558

Donley Technology
Environmental Software Report
Environmental Software Directory
Ms. Elizabeth Donley, Publisher
Box 335, Garrisonville, VA 22463
(703) 659-1954

Pollution Engineering Magazine
January Issue: "Environmental Software Review"
Cahners Publishing
P.O. Box 7610
Highlands Ranch, CO 80126
(800) 662-7776

World Information Systems
Hazardous Materials Intelligence Report
George Stubbs, Editor
P.O. Box 535, Harvard Square Station
Cambridge, MA 02238
(617) 491-5100

Chapter 10

RESOURCE CONSERVATION AND RECOVERY ACT (RCRA)

John Knoepfler
Richard Bale
ROBINS, KAPLAN, MILLER & CIRESI
2800 LaSalle Plaza
800 LaSalle Ave.
Minneapolis, Minnesota 55402

Introduction.

The Resource Conservation and Recovery Act ("RCRA"), 42 U.S.C. §§ 6901 et seq., establishes a comprehensive scheme of reporting and recordkeeping to serve RCRA's goal of tracking the nation's hazardous wastes. RCRA and the regulations of the Environmental Protection Agency ("EPA") require all persons that generate, store, transport or dispose of hazardous waste to maintain detailed records and plans and to provide periodic reports on these activities.

Many state agencies have been delegated the authority to administer the RCRA program in their states. These state programs may vary in some respects from the EPA's RCRA regulations, but they must be at least as stringent as the federal program. In these states, the state rather than the EPA is primarily responsible for the enforcement of the reporting and recordkeeping requirements. The EPA and state agencies have the authority to assess severe penalties for violations of the RCRA regulations. Compliance with the RCRA regulations, although time consuming and sometimes expensive, is crucial in order to minimize the risk of enforcement actions by EPA or the state.

Identification of Hazardous Waste.

Every person that produces a solid waste must determine whether the material is a hazardous waste within the meaning of the RCRA regulations. A solid waste is a hazardous waste if either: (a) it is specifically listed by EPA as a hazardous waste or (b) the waste exhibits any one or more of the following characteristics as defined by EPA: ignitability, corrosivity, reactivity or toxicity, unless the waste is specifically excluded.

If the waste is considered a hazardous waste, the person that produces the waste is considered a generator for purposes of RCRA and must comply with the standards applicable to generators of hazardous waste. See RCRA § 3002(a)(6), 42 U.S.C. § 6922. RCRA's reporting and recordkeeping requirements also apply to those that transport hazardous wastes and those that treat, store, or dispose of hazardous wastes.

Parties that transport hazardous wastes must comply with the requirements in 40 C.F.R. Part 263, which is a duplication of the regulations promulgated by the United States Department of Transportation pursuant to the Hazardous Materials Transportation Act. Facilities that treat, store, or dispose of hazardous wastes ("TSD facilities") must comply with the RCRA requirements and regulations for TSD facilities. See 40 U.S.C. § 6924-25 and 40 C.F.R. Parts 264 and 265.

Certain types of solid waste are excluded from regulation as hazardous waste. For example, excluded wastes include household waste, some solid wastes generated by growing crops and raising animals, mining overburden returned to the mine site, ash waste produced from the combustion of fossil fuels, and wastes from oil and gas exploration. See 40 C.F.R. § 261.4. A generator may also petition EPA to delist a waste that it generates which otherwise would be included as a listed waste.

The analysis of waste to determine whether it falls within the RCRA regulations can be difficult, time consuming and expensive. The RCRA regulations are extraordinarily complicated and their interpretation is the subject of a significant amount of litigation. A hazardous waste generator must use caution in selecting competent professionals to perform the testing and provide adequate documentation.

Waste Generation Notices.

Once a person has determined that they are a generator of hazardous waste, they must apply to the EPA for a EPA Identification number. This EPA Identification number will be used to identify the generator on all reports and documentation that are required by EPA.

The generator must notify the EPA of the location and description of the waste generating activities. The generator also must identify the types of hazardous wastes produced by the waste codes set forth in EPA's RCRA regulations.

This notification must be filed within 90 days of the generation of a RCRA hazardous waste. Also, EPA may amend its regulations in a way that changes formerly non-hazardous waste to hazardous waste. The person generating these new hazardous wastes must also file the notification form within 90 days of the effective date of the change in the regulations.

RCRA Requirements for Generators.

Any person that produces hazardous waste is considered a generator for purposes of RCRA. RCRA requires the EPA to promulgate regulations requiring generators to prepare and maintain records in the following four major categories.

1. Generators must record the quantities and constituents of the hazardous wastes they produce and the disposition of these wastes.

2. Generators must provide accurate and complete information to transporters and TSD facilities on the chemical composition of the hazardous wastes produced by the generator.

3. Generators are responsible for tracking the fate of all hazardous wastes they produce by using a hazardous waste manifest to ensure that all hazardous wastes shipped to a permitted TSD Facility arrive at their intended destination.

4. Generators must periodically report to the EPA or responsible state agency on the type and quantity of hazardous wastes generated and the disposition of these wastes.

5. Generators must report on their efforts to reduce the generation of hazardous wastes and the results of these efforts.

See RCRA § 3002(a), 42 U.S.C. 6922.

Hazardous Waste Manifest.

The hazardous waste manifest is the most important document in the RCRA hazardous waste management program. A manifest must accompany each shipment of hazardous wastes from the generator to the final disposal location. The manifest must contain information on the source of the waste and its intended destination. The generator of the hazardous waste is responsible for filling out the information required by the manifest.

The generator must sign the manifest certification that the information in the manifest is complete and accurate. The certification also requires the generator to attest that the hazardous waste has been properly packaged and labeled and is suitable for transportation pursuant to the applicable regulations.

Upon transferring the hazardous waste to the transporter, the generator must obtain the signature of the transporter on the manifest and retain a copy.

The generator must designate on the manifest the TSD facility to which the hazardous waste is to be shipped. The manifest also must indicate whether the waste should be sent to an alternate facility or returned to the generator in the event that the designated facility is unable to receive the waste. 40 C.F.R. § 262.20(a)-(d).

A generator of between 100 kilograms and 1,000 kilograms of hazardous waste a month does not have to fill out a manifest for a shipment of hazardous wastes to a recycling facility provided there is a written agreement specifying the type and quantity of wastes to be reclaimed and transportation is accomplished in vehicles owned by the recycling facility.

The generator must use the manifest form required by the state to which the hazardous wastes are being sent for treatment and disposal. If the state to which the hazardous wastes are being sent does not require a particular manifest form, the generator must use the form specified by the state in which the wastes are generated. If neither state requires a particular manifest form, the generator must use the form required by the EPA.

The manifest must be prepared with sufficient copies for the generator, each transporter that handles the waste, the TSD facility that receives the waste, and a return copy for notification to the generator that the wastes have been received by the TSD Facility.

Before turning the waste over to the transporter, the generator must sign the manifest certification <u>by hand</u> and obtain the handwritten signature of the transporter that picks up the waste. The generator must deliver the remaining copies of the manifest to the transporter. The transporter must ensure that the waste is accompanied by the manifest throughout its journey to the TSD Facility.

For bulk shipments of hazardous waste by water, the generator must send three dated and signed copies of the manifest to the TSD Facility. Where the hazardous wastes are shipped by rail, the generator must send at least three copies of the dated and signed manifest to the first non-rail transporter or the TSD Facility if transported solely by rail.

A generator must not treat, store, dispose of, transport, or offer for transportation a hazardous waste without having received an EPA identification number. A generator also must not offer hazardous waste to a transporter or send the hazardous waste to a TSD Facility if the transporter or TSD Facility has not received an EPA identification number.

Exception Reporting.

RCRA requires that a generator who has not received a completed copy of the manifest with a handwritten signature from the TSD facility within 35 days of the shipment of the hazardous wastes to contact the transporter or the TSD Facility to determine the status of the shipment. If the generator cannot locate the shipment of hazardous wastes, or if the generator does not receive a signed and completed copy of the manifest within 45 days of the shipment, the generator must send an Exception Report to the EPA.

The Exception Report must include a legible copy of the manifest and a letter explaining the generator's efforts to find the hazardous waste shipment.

A small quantity generator, defined as a generator of between 100 kilograms to 1,000 kilograms per month, has 60 days to receive a signed, completed copy of the manifest before it is required to file an Exception Report.

These exception reports must be retained for at least three years.

Land Ban Reporting

RCRA regulations prohibit the disposal of hazardous wastes in landfills and other land-based disposal facilities unless the waste has been treated in accordance with EPA requirements or is exempted from the "Land Ban" regulations. The Land Ban regulations contain several recordkeeping and reporting requirements applicable to generators.

EPA has specified various treatment methods depending on the type of hazardous waste to be disposed of on land. Generators are responsible for knowing these various treatment methods for each type of hazardous waste produced. Generators must provide accurate notification to the treatment facility and the land disposal facility of the required treatment methods for each shipment of hazardous wastes, or must specify the land ban exemption that applies to the waste.

The generator must send a notice specifying the treatment method and required by EPA with each shipment of hazardous wastes. For most wastes, this notice may specify the proper treatment standards by simply referencing the section of the Code of Federal Regulations that contains those standards. Some types of wastes require the actual treatment process to be stated on the notice. The wastes that require a full statement of the treatment process are identified in 40 C.F.R. § 268.7(a)(1). The notice must identify any applicable disposal prohibition levels that apply to that waste. The notice must contain the proper waste code, and the supporting data from a waste analysis used to determine the proper waste code. The notice also must display the generators' EPA Identification number and the manifest number for that shipment. 40 C.F.R. § 268.7(a)(1).

The generator may determine that its hazardous waste meets the applicable treatment standards even before being sent to a treatment facility. In this case, the generator must prepare a Certification document that states that the waste may be land disposed without treatment. The Certification must include a signed statement that provides that the generator "certifies under penalty of law" that the waste has been examined and found to meet the treatment standards in 40 C.F.R. Part 268 Subpart D and all applicable prohibitions in 40 C.F.R. 268.32 or RCRA § 3004(d). This Certification document must contain the proper waste code and supporting waste analysis data, treatment standards and disposal prohibitions, and manifest number. These Certifications must be retained for at least five years.

If the waste is a type that is subject to an exemption from the land ban regulations, the generator must state the exemption in the notice to the disposal facility that receives the waste. 40 C.F.R. § 268.7(a)(3).

Small quantity generators are relieved from these notification requirements where they are sending wastes to a treatment facility under a tolling agreement. In these cases, the small quantity generator is only required to send the notice to the treatment facility with the initial shipment of wastes. 40 C.F.R. § 268.7(a)(10).

Reports Required For Waste Storage.

EPA requires several reports to be prepared as a requirement for a generator to store hazardous wastes on site for up to 90 days without obtaining a permit or achieving interim status. In addition to certain storage requirements, the generator that stores hazardous wastes on site must prepare the following reports:

1. A report describing the procedures that will be followed to ensure that all wastes are removed from waste containment and collection systems once every 90 days.

2. A report documenting the quantity of waste removed from containment and collection systems and the date and time of the removal.

3. A report describing the procedures to ensure that waste placed in a containment building remains in the building for no more than 90 days (or a report that documents actual removal every 90 days).

4.   A report describing the waste generation and management practices for a facility that places waste in a containment building, and which demonstrates that they are consistent with the 90-day storage limitation (or a report that documents actual removal every 90 days).

See 40 C.F.R. § 262.34.

Inspection Reports

RCRA requires a generator to inspect hazardous waste tanks and other container storage areas. These inspections should be documented in reports that are retained on-site by the generator. The inspection reports should provide a full description of the scope of the inspection and the observations of the inspector.   The generator also should prepare an inspection plan to govern the periodic review of the tanks and other hazardous waste storage containers. The inspection plan should establish a reasonable schedule for these inspections and set out in detail the scope of the inspection of each unit.

Facility Training Records

A generator must provide training to its employees in the proper management and handling of hazardous wastes. This training also should focus on employee safety and emergency response. Employees should be thoroughly familiar with the generator's Contingency Plan in the event of hazardous waste release and must have ready access to telephone numbers for local emergency services and company supervisors.

The generator must establish a system to document the contents of this training program and the participation of those employees that take part in the training. The hazardous waste training program records should include the name and title of the employees that take part and a description of the training provided to each employee. The description of the training should be detailed to show the information and training techniques that were employed. This information should be retained to demonstrate compliance with facility training requirements.

Biennial Report.

A generator who ships any hazardous waste off-site to a TSD facility must file a biennial report with the EPA by March 1 of each even numbered year. Many states with delegated authority to administer the RCRA program require annual reports. The report must contain the EPA identification numbers of the generator as well as all transporters and TSD facilities that handled the generator's hazardous waste.

The report must describe the type of hazardous waste generated during the reporting period, the quantity of each type of hazardous waste generated, and details regarding the shipments and destination of the hazardous wastes.

The report also must contain a description of the efforts taken during the year to reduce the volume and toxicity of the hazardous wastes generated, and a description of the actual changes in the volume and toxicity of the hazardous wastes that were generated during the reporting period.

Waste Minimization Reporting

Generators are required to report on their efforts to reduce the volume and toxicity of their hazardous wastes. A generators' annual report must detail the efforts that generator has taken to minimize its hazardous wastes during the past year. The generator must also document the results of these efforts. This information can be obtained from a review of annual reports and a comparison of the information on the quantity and toxicity of the hazardous wastes produced in past years with the current year.

Generators also must certify on each hazardous waste shipment manifest that they have determined the best practical or affordable method of reducing the volume of waste produced. This statement is called a waste minimization certification, and must be signed by the generator each time it ships hazardous waste for treatment and disposal. The statement reads as follows:

> If I am a large quantity generator, I certify that I have a program in place to reduce the volume and toxicity of waste generated to the degree I have determined to be economically practicable and that I have selected the practicable method of treatment, storage, or disposal currently available to me which minimizes the present and future threat to human health and the environment; OR, if I am a small quantity generator, I have made a good faith effort to minimize my waste generation and to select the best waste management method that is available to me and that I can afford.

The best method of satisfying the regulatory obligations to reduce the volume and toxicity of hazardous wastes is to prepare a waste minimization plan. This plan can provide guidance to employees in seeking new and cost-effective methods of waste minimization. This plan also provides documentation in support of the manifest certification and the annual report.

Chapter 11

ENVIRONMENTAL AUDITS:
How to Evaluate Your Reporting and Recordkeeping Requirements

Lawrence B. Cahill
Senior Program Manager
ERM, Inc.
Exton, PA

Environmental audits have become a common technique used by U.S. industry to assure management that its facilities are operating consistent with all applicable rules and regulations. In addition, many companies in industry are also auditing waste transporters, non-company owned disposal sites where residuals are sent, and potential acquisitions. In the U.S., environmental audits have been endorsed by the U.S. Environmental Protection Agency in its July 1986 Environmental Auditing Policy Statement (51FR25004, July 9, 1986).

While audits have been conducted routinely among many Fortune 500 companies since the early 1980's, recent trends indicate that increasing public pressure will be brought to bare to assure that companies are consistently and independently assessing compliance. For example:

- Legislation is being proposed in the U.S. Congress calling for mandatory, third-party audits under the Clean Water Act and the Resource Conservation and Recovery Act.

- The Valdez Principles, sponsored by the Coalition of Environmentally Responsible Economies (CERES) and other "green" institutional investors, call for completion and disclosure of annual facility audits. The CERES-led group brought 56 resolutions before company shareholder groups, including these at General Motors and DuPont, at annual meetings in the Spring of 1991, but failed to win a majority at any meeting. CERES intends to intensify its efforts in 1992.

- In 1991, the Department of Justice (DOJ) issued a policy directive stating that DOJ will use "enforcement discretion" where companies report compliance problems identified through self-audits. Moreover, as reported by DOJ and EPA, penalties can be reduced by as much as (and possibly more than) 50% where disclosure is made **and** the firm has a sound audit program.

- Environmental audits are a logical component of a program designed to respond to the Chemical Manufacturers' Association Responsible Care initiatives **and** Total Quality Management Principles.

213

- There is a recent grass-roots movement in the U.S. to have companies "certify" their environmental performance in annual reports.

Thus, it appears that major, visible companies will find that a corporate audit program will be routinely expected by shareholders, regulatory and enforcement agencies, trade associations and the public at large.

With some exceptions, the scope of an audit or compliance review is fairly standard and typically involves a review against Federal and state requirements associated with:

- The Clean Air Act (CAA)

- The Clean Water Act (CWA)

- The Safe Drinking Water Act (SDWA)

- The Hazardous and Solid Waste Amendments of 1984 (RCRA/HSWA)

- The Superfund Amendments and Reauthorization Act of 1986 (CERCLA/SARA)

- The Federal Insecticide, Fungicide and Rodenticide Act (FIFRA)

- The Toxic Substances Control Act (TSCA), including regulation of PCBs

- The Occupational Safety and Health Act (OSHA), emphasizing hazardous materials management

One also evaluates compliance against corporate standards, local rules (e.g., sewer ordinances, noise), and best management practices. Consistent with good risk management and stated objectives, the scope of environmental compliance reviews will be designed to:

- Assess compliance with applicable Federal, state and local air, water, and waste regulations.

- Assess the potential for future liabilities that might arise from present practices.

- Identify and assess where future regulatory trends might affect existing and future compliance.

- Determine what actions might be required to bring the facility into compliance if any noncompliance issues are identified.

The inherent nature of the audit ensures not only that the above objectives are met, but that the audit will also provide a trigger mechanism to determine where additional analysis is required. That is, if significant issues or areas of noncompliance are identified (such as the potential for groundwater contamination), the company typically would conduct a more detailed analysis under an independent program, as required.

Many companies and regulated entities prefer a review that addresses not only detailed compliance issues but management systems as well. The general approach discussed below is reflective of this two-pronged objective.

1.0 MANAGEMENT SYSTEMS REVIEW

Many organizations are conducting reviews of not only facility compliance but their overall environmental management systems as well. This philosophy is appropriate during a time when U.S. EPA's enforcement posture is "aggressive". (See Figure 1 on the following page.) Further, it is generally more important to determine if a given site has implemented systems to manage compliance effectively in the long-term than to assess whether every hazardous waste drum has the appropriate label. Examples of the kinds of systems that might be review candidates are[1]:

- **Emergency response.** This is one of the key systems, often required of facilities under the Clean Water Act (CWA), the Resource Conservation and Recovery Act (RCRA), the Superfund Amendments and Reauthorization Act (SARA) and the Occupational Safety and Health Act (OSHA), most recently under the Hazardous Waste Site Operations and Emergency Response rules effective March 1990. A good emergency response planning review would assure the existence of contingency and preparedness plans, assurance of their successful execution should there be an incident (e.g., periodic drills) and the existence of proper internal reporting procedures, should there be an incident.

- **Training.** Full and complete environmental training assures that staff are aware of requirements and will do the right thing both day-in and day-out and in emergency situations. RCRA requires annual generator training and OSHA's Hazard Communication Program requires one-time and update training of all staff handling hazardous chemicals. The challenge for most facility managers is to assure that regulatory training requirements are met and that all site staff are environmentally aware and astute.

---

[1]Some of the discussion that follows is adapted from *Environmental Audits*, 6th Edition, published by Government Institutes, Inc. and written by the author of this paper.

FIGURE 1

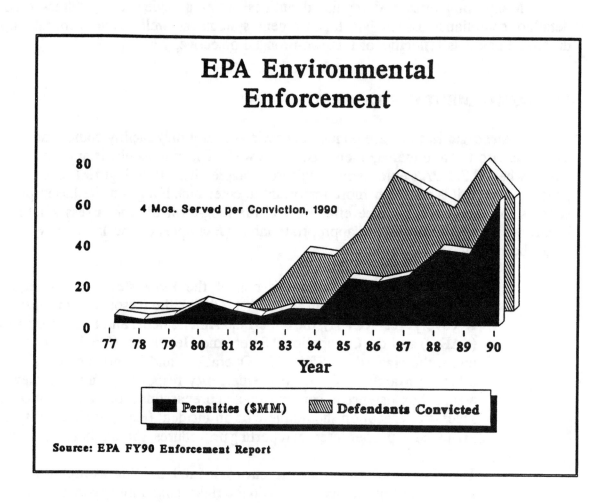

- **Regulation Tracking.** Whether this is accomplished at the corporate or plant level, there should be a system to track the development of federal, state, and local regulations and any changes in corporate policies and procedures.

- **Auditing.** Most firms of any size do now have an environmental audit program. This program should help to assure compliance at the facility and is therefore an integral part of the environmental management system.

- **Special Purpose Audits.** Due to the doctrine of joint and several liability, most companies have expanded their compliance audit program to include one or more of the following: waste disposal contractors, acquisitions and divestitures, out-sourcing contractors (i.e., job shops), and on-site contractors and vendors. Many of these audits are the responsibility of site staff and should result in written reports and decisions on liability exposure.

- **Communications.** There should be clear and facile communications between environmental staff and other organizations such as purchasing, research and development, facilities planning, corporate planning, production and personnel. Each of these organizational units can have adverse impacts on environmental performance where planning, hiring, purchasing and acquisitions are made without appropriate input.

- **Management Support.** There should be clear evidence that management supports good environmental performance. A written environmental policy that is distributed to all staff would be one example. Plant managers with environmental standards as part of their overall performance standards would be another. All staff should not only understand the productive mission of the operation but the environmental mission as well.

- **Management Responsibilities.** Although not all sites require the assignment of full-time environmental coordinators, each facility should have staff responsible for those areas applicable to the site. Staff should have the needed responsibilities and authorities. Further, there should be one or more designated staff on each of the shifts operating at a given site.

- **Records Retention.** Managing the mountain of paper required by regulatory programs is a considerable challenge. Sites should have well-organized files with retention consistent with standards or corporate policy, whichever is more stringent.

- **Regulatory Inspections.** How a facility handles an agency inspection is an important part of its overall efforts. Mishandling the visit up-front can alienate an inspector and result in an aggressive approach. And inspectors will find **something** if they stay long enough or look hard enough.

From the above discussion, the reader can appreciate why a focus on management systems helps an independent auditor determine whether an operation is being run in a way to minimize environmental liabilities. At best, a detailed compliance audit alone only gives you a snap-shot of operations and not necessarily a sense of comfort that, long-term, appropriate management systems are in place.

2.0 COMPLIANCE AUDIT

Environmental audits are typically conducted in three phases, as outlined below: preaudit activities, on-site activities, and post-audit activities. The following section highlights certain key techniques (e.g., statistically sampling large populations), that would be especially important in completing an audit.

2.1 Phase I - Preaudit Activities

There are several key activities that should be completed before the team arrives on-site. They include:

2.1.1 Meet to discuss and decide upon audit procedures

It is crucial that a planning meeting be held to discuss key program issues. These include:

- Audit scope
- Specific audit schedule
- Confidentiality measures
- Reporting protocols
- Safety and security requirements
- Corporate policies and procedures

Thus, each audit program should be initiated with a meeting or conference call between the corporate staff, legal counsel (if desired), and the audit team. This assures that all parties have a common understanding of both the process and the product.

2.1.2 Submit previsit questionnaire to the facility

The purpose of the previsit questionnaire is two-fold. It enables the audit team to become familiar with the general environmentally-related activities and operations before they arrive on-site. Second, it serves as a timely alert to the facility manager so that he may better prepare himself and his staff for the audit. On short-turnaround assignments the questionnaire can be replaced by the submission of background reports on the facility (e.g., Emergency Response Plans) to the auditors and a phone interview with facility management.

2.1.3 Review relevant regulations

There are numerous regulatory requirements that are administered by Federal, state, and local authorities. As shown in Figure 2, U.S. EPA is now responsible for over 10,000 pages of regulations, with plans to issue another almost 300 sets of regulations in the next year. Each level of government will have a major influence on some areas and have little or no effect at all on other compliance areas. Before the audit, the pertinent Federal and state environmental regulations should be reviewed. The U.S. Army Corps of Engineers Computer-Aided Environmental Legislative Data System (CELDS), which contains on-line abstracts of all 50 states environmental regulations, is especially helpful in this effort. CELDS is operated and maintained for the Army by the University of Illinois.

2.1.4 Contact Federal, state and local regulators

As a supplementary option, using blind phone calls, the team can determine important regulatory trends and obtain information from regulatory agencies. No calls to regulatory agencies should be made without prior clearance from site staff.

2.1.5 Define assessment scope and team responsibilities

Most initial assessments are multimedia in scope (i.e., air, water, and waste). However, it is not always necessary that all compliance areas be reviewed during the site visit, if it is felt that time would be better spent concentrating on a few compliance areas that represent a higher exposure.

2.1.6 Develop detailed site agenda

The agenda allows the facility manager to alert key facility staff when they will be required to talk with the audit team and, generally, the nature of the audit topics. When management, key supervisors, and other significant personnel are prepared for the team, the audit results are generally more complete and more useful. The agenda is typically transmitted by phone or fax to the facility contact prior to the visit.

2.1.7 Review audit protocols

Protocols or checklists are used during the audit to enable compliance status of the facility to be evaluated in an organized, rational manner. Many companies now have existing protocols covering all major compliance programs. Checklists should cover the following areas:

- Hazardous Waste Management
- Wastewater Discharges
- Air Emissions
- Underground Injection/Groundwater Protection

FIGURE 2

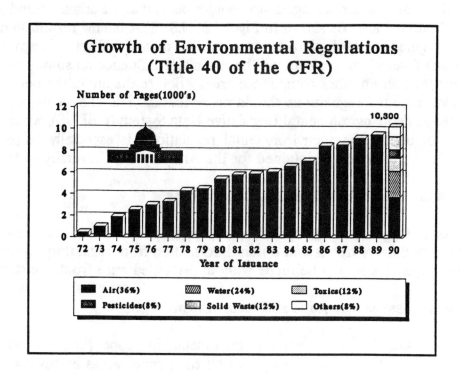

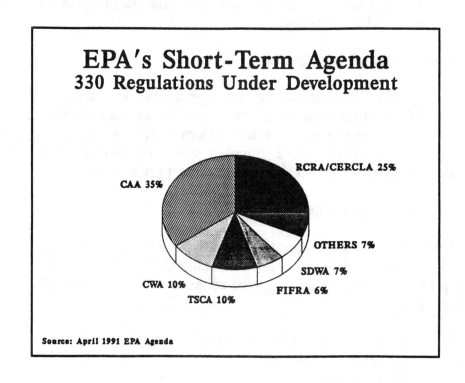

- Toxic Substances Compliance
- Solid Waste
- Spill Response/Contingency Plans
- Occupational Safety and Environmental Health
- Drinking Water
- PCBs
- Hazardous Materials Management
- Nuisances

Federal and state regulatory requirements, good management practices, and company policies are typically addressed in the protocols. One of the biggest challenges for most companies is keeping the protocols up-to-date. This is only done through perseverance and a commitment of resources.

2.2 Phase II - On-Site Activities

On-site activities during an environmental audit are of four principle types, as discussed below.

2.2.1 Records/documentation review

Normally, records should be reviewed just before conducting interviews and inspecting facilities. Table 1 provides a listing of the more relevant records typically found at a site.

One of the most important things to remember concerning review of documentation is that many compliance requirements are contained within the records. For example, a wastewater permit may have numerous conditions on Best Management Practices (BMP's) listed in the permit. The team will need to scan these documents looking specifically for applicable terms, conditions or requirements.

2.2.2 Interviews with facility staff

Proper interviewing during an environmental audit is perhaps the single most important aspect of the audit process. A skilled interviewer will be sensitive to the individual's nervousness and possible defensiveness yet obtain responses enabling him to evaluate past and current operating practices. Interview candidates will include site management, site environmental management, and unit operators and supervisors. Auditors should be prepared to verify statements made by site staff through a review of records or physical observation. This "verification" step is used routinely in auditing and site staff should be made aware that it is not meant to be a challenge to the veracity of their statements.

TABLE 1
Environmental Compliance Audit Program
Documents to Review

General

General correspondence file
Notices of violation
Consent orders
Agency inspection reports
Corporate environmental policies

Boiler Operations

Boiler operating permits
Opacity records
Sulfur content for fuel oil
Daily boiler records
Stack emission test records
Boiler operation inspection
   records
Fuel use reports

Process Air Emissions

Stack/vent operating certificates
Source emission inventory
Records on petroleum storage
facilities and vapor control
   systems
Permits

Hazardous Waste Generation

Hazardous waste manifests
Biennial/annual reports
Manifest exception reports
Waste analysis test results
Contingency plans
Inspection records
Medical waste records
Training records
Waste minimization plan
Treatment/disposal Permit
Superfund involvement

Pesticide Use

Application Permits
List of Certified Applicators
Training records for applicators
List of restricted use pesticides
Spill plan for storage area
Pesticide waste disposal records
Records of pesticide applications
Annual reports
Medical tests for applicators

Drinking Water

Records on water system repairs,
maintenance, changes
Permits
Analytical records

Oil Operations

Spill Plan
Oil discharge reports/notifications
Oil storage systems inspection records
Waste oil disposal records
Recycled oil disposal records
Underground storage tank records

Land Use

Deed restrictions
Wetlands
Reclamation requirements
Closure requirements
Post-closure care requirements

TABLE 1
Environmental Compliance Audit Program
Documents to Review
(Continued)

Wastewater Discharges

Discharge Permit
Sludge disposal permit
Sewer ordinance
Discharge monitoring reports
Exception reports
Laboratory certifications
Off-site disposal records
Operator training certifications
Stormwater management records
Septic tank maintenance records

PCB's

Annual PCB Reports
PCB disposal records/manifests
PCB inspection records
PCB spill reports/notifications
Testing records of PCB equipment

Hazardous Materials

Hazardous Materials spill
  plan
Hazard Communications
  program plan
Hazard Communications
  training records
MSDS's
Community Right-
  to-Know Reports
Spill/incident reporting

Health and Safety

Medical Monitoring Records
Exposure Monitoring Records
Health & Safety Procedures
Health & Safety Training
  Records
Employee Accident/Injury
  Records

2.2.3 Physical inspection of facilities

There are many facilities, operations, and pieces of equipment, that will be inspected during the audit. Physical inspections may include areas concerned with well operations, organic air emissions, hazardous waste generation, drinking water, fuels and oil management, wastewater treatment and discharge, sludge disposal, PCBs, and hazardous materials management.

The field work will usually result in the identification of a variety of findings. Some of the more typical are found in Table 2.

2.2.4 Sampling Techniques

Auditors must be thorough in their field investigations. This is true whether the investigation is a review of paperwork or a physical inspection of the plant equipment. However, this does not mean that the auditor must review each of several thousand hazardous waste manifests or several hundred emission sources, for example, to meet the thoroughness objective.

Statistical sampling is a common technique used during environmental audits when a large universe of items needs to be reviewed. This could include manifests, PCB transformers and capacitors, stormwater outfalls on a large site, and permitted air emission sources. In these cases, auditors can use sampling techniques to determine whether there is evidence of a compliance problem.

Sampling theory can provide a means to identifying the number of items to be reviewed to be fairly confident the results are representative. That is, when a confidence interval of a given width is desired for an unknown proportion, p (in this case the proportion of sources that are in compliance), the sample size, n, required can be obtained using a formula given by Inman and Conover.[2] However, the formula applies to an infinite population. A correction for finite population is given by Cochran.[3] The finite population correction is close to unity when the sampling fraction n/N remains low (approximately 5% or less). Combining the two formulae gives:

$$n = (4z[\alpha/2]^2pqN)/(w^2N - w^2 + 4z[\alpha/2]^2pq)$$

---

[2]Inman, R.L. and Conover, W.J., *A Modern Approach to Statistics,* John Wiley and Sons, New York, NY.

[3]Cochran, W.G., *Sampling Techniques,* Second Edition, John Wiley and Sons, New York, NY.

TABLE 2
Frequently Encountered Problems on
Environmental Audits

WATER

► Process discharges to the storm sewer.
► Inoperative or poorly maintained sampling equipment.
► No effluent flow-measurement device.
► Process-area diking broken or nonexistent.
► Storm/floor drains in liquid bulk-transfer areas.
► Oil-water separators improperly installed.
► No laboratory quality-control/quality assurance program.
► Runoff from storage piles going to the storm sewer.
► Improper permit reporting.
► Outdated or poorly written Spill Control Plan.

AIR

► Vents and exhausts not registered.
► Lack of data on registered or unregistered emission points.
► Lack of Air Pollution Episode Alert Plan.
► "Guesstimates" on performance of control equipment.
► Improper worker protection industry environment.
► Neighborhood compliant file incomplete and/or lacking resolution of compliant.
► Dust from plant operations on roof and pavement.

SOLID WASTE

► Sloppy housekeeping.
► Careless drum or container handling (leaks and/or dents).
► Mixing process waste with office trash.
► Unreported in-plant dumpsites.
► Poor recordkeeping.
► Incomplete analysis of hazardous wastes being sent off-site.
► Incomplete files on past disposal practices.
► Unlabeled drums.
► Leaking containers.
► Untested/leaking underground storage tanks.
► No land disposal restriction notifications or certifications.

SAFETY AND HEALTH

► Insufficient railings.
► Open gates on second floors.
► No written respirator program.
► Insufficient hazard communication labelling.
► Outdated material safety data sheets.
► No target organ information on labels.
► Inconsistent use of personnel safety equipment (e.g., safety glasses, hard hats).
► Poor maintenance/inaccessibility of safety equipment (e.g., eye washes, showers, fire extinguishers).
► Slippery floors.

Source: From McLaren/Hart Experience and Russell, D.L. "Managing Your Environmental Audit", Chemical Engineering, June 24, 1985.

Where,

n is the required number of sources in the sample

$z[\alpha/2]$ is the $(1-\alpha/2)$ quantile from the standard normal probability function; that is:

Confidence Level	α	$1-\alpha/2$	$z[\alpha/2]$
95%	0.05	0.975	1.96
90%	0.10	0.950	1.65
85%	0.15	0.925	1.44
80%	0.20	0.900	1.28
75%	0.25	0.875	1.15

p is the proportion of interest (proportion of sources in compliance); when p is unknown it is set equal to 0.5 to give the most conservative possible value of n

q is (1-p)

N is the total population being sampled

w is 2α

Table 3 and Figure 3 which are based on the above equation, can be used to select a sample size where this approach is necessary. For example, if the site contains 250 air emission sources and the auditor does not have the time to inspect each one, a sample of the sources could be inspected. If the auditor believes that the physical inspection is "extremely important in terms of verifying compliance with applicable requirements," then column A would be chosen. This implies that 61%, or 152, or the emission sources should be inspected. If, on the other hand, the auditor believes that the physical inspection will "provide additional information to substantiate compliance or non-compliance and/or is of considerable importance to the corporation in terms of potential or actual impacts associated with non-compliance," then Column B would be selected. In that case, only 21%, or 52, emission sources would have to be inspected. The auditor, therefore, must use some judgement in deciding the relative importance of the inspection in determining compliance.

There is often a tendency to increase the sample size when problems are noted during the inspection. If, during the sampling, non-compliance situations are identified, the recommended approach for auditors is to continue with the sampling scheme as originally proposed. Remember that the fundamental purpose of environmental audits is to verify the existence of appropriate site-level compliance management systems. If a sampling scheme

TABLE 3
Selecting a Sample Size
on Environmental Audits

Population Size	Suggested Minimum Sample Size		
	A	B	C
10	98%	88%	72%
25	94%	74%	49%
50	89%	58%	32%
100	80%	41%	19%
250	61%	21%	8%
500	43%	12%	4%
1000	28%	6%	2%
2000	16%	3%	1%

A - Suggested minimum sample size for a population(s) being reviewed which is considered to be extremely important in terms of verifying compliance with applicable requirements, and/or is of critical concern to the corporation in terms of potential or actual impacts associated with non-compliance. A confidence interval of 95% is assumed.

B - Suggested minimum sample size for a population(s) being reviewed that will provide additional information to substantiate compliance or non-compliance and/or is of considerable importance to the corporation in terms of potential or actual impacts associated with non-compliance. A confidence interval of 90% is assumed.

C - Suggested minimum sample size for a population(s) being reviewed that will provide ancillary information in terms of verifying overall compliance with a requirement. A confidence interval of 85% is assumed.

FIGURE 3

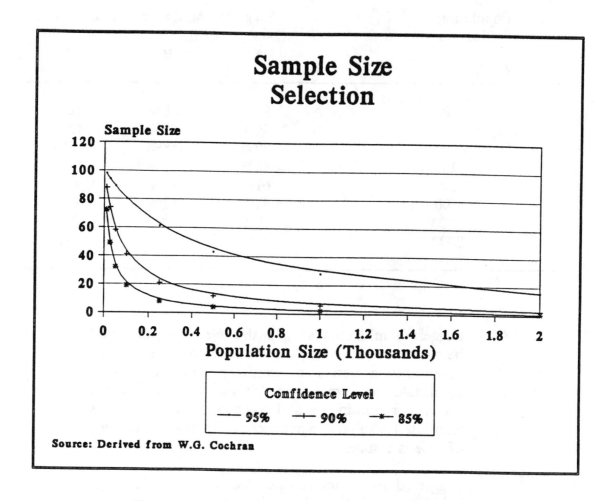

Source: Derived from W.G. Cochran

has identified a number of non-compliance problems, then the reviewer has determined that there is a problem of consequence requiring action by site staff. It is not typically necessary to further verify this problem by inspecting the entire universe of sources.

Where sampling schemes are used, it is critical that the audit team **document** in the audit report the approach taken. This will prevent misunderstandings later on if, by chance, a non-compliance problem is identified by a third party after the audit has been completed for a source that was supposedly covered by the audit, but was not physically inspected by the audit team.

2.3 Phase III - Post-audit Activities

After the field work has been completed, there are two principal post-audit activities that should occur to complete the audit process.

2.3.1 Conduct debriefing

The debriefing serves two useful purposes. First, it provides an opportunity to review the team's findings in an informal manner before anything is written down in a report. Second, it provides the audit team with an opportunity to identify additional data or information it needs to complete its analysis. Both site and headquarters staff are usually debriefed before developing the audit report.

2.3.2 Develop audit reports

The audit report is the document or product in which the findings of the audit team are presented with respect to the compliance status of the facility. Audit teams typically develop both draft and final reports, unless instructed not to do so. More frequently now, audit teams are carrying portable computers and providing typed, draft reports to facility staff prior to departure.

The reports typically include a brief description of the facility, a discussion of the audit process, an executive summary, and descriptions of regulatory compliance and liability exposure findings in each of the areas investigated (e.g., hazardous waste).

Teams often prioritize the findings by the extent of liability posed and the resource requirements needed to remedy the situation. Each finding can be placed in one of four categories:

- Compliance Findings
  - High Priority
  - Low Priority

- Liability Exposure Findings
  - High Priority
  - Low Priority

Recommendations or corrective actions are either included in the report or developed as a separate document. The identification and documentation of corrective actions are more often than not the responsibility of the site staff. A proposed outline for the report is listed below:

Management Systems

> Overview
> Organization
> Communications
> Training
> Regulatory Tracking
> Records Management/Retention
> Regulatory Agency Inspections
> Environmental Audits
> Emergency Response
> Management Support

Compliance Areas

> Air Quality
> Water Quality
> Drinking Water/Groundwater
> Fuel/Oil Operations
> Pesticides
> PCB's
> Hazardous Materials
> Solid and Hazardous Wastes
> Reclamation

One of the most crucial components of an effective environmental audit program is also one of the most commonly observed weaknesses: follow-up. That is, how does company management assure itself that the compliance deficiencies identified through the audit are, in fact, corrected expeditiously? It is often not prudent to wait for the next scheduled audit, which may occur two years later. If may also not be prudent to simply assume site management will execute its responsibilities as defined in the Corrective Action Plan. As a consequence, many companies have developed formal tracking systems where corporate environmental staff are required to formally monitor and report on progress made by site management. Without this final "closure" exercise some would say a company may be better off without an environmental audit program. Full commitment is essential in order to identify problems and eliminate liabilities.

Chapter 12

CLEAN WATER ACT*

I. Introduction:

    The primary statute governing water pollution control is
the Federal Water Pollution Control Act, often called the Clean
Water Act (CWA). 33 U.S.C. §§ 1251-1376. The CWA regulates
the discharge of pollutants to waters of the United States
through a permit system. Under the CWA, the world of water
pollution control is divided into two spheres: direct
dischargers and indirect dischargers. Direct dischargers are
those who discharge pollutants directly to waters of the United
States. Indirect dischargers are those who discharge
pollutants to Publicly Owned Treatment Works (POTWs), which in
turn directly discharge pollutants to waters of the United
States. 40 C.F.R. § 122.2.

    Different permitting systems govern direct and indirect
dischargers, leading to different reporting and recordkeeping
requirements for each class of dischargers. Direct
dischargers, including POTWs, are regulated through a permit
program called the National Pollution Discharge Elimination
System (NPDES). In essence, the CWA prohibits the addition of
pollutants from a point source to waters of the United States
except as authorized by an NPDES permit. 33 U.S.C. §§ 1311(a)
and 1342. The NPDES permit specifies effluent limitations
applicable to the permit holder, as well as monitoring,
reporting and recordkeeping requirements. In contrast,
industrial facilities that are indirect dischargers to a POTW
are not regulated by NPDES permits, but rather by both national
pretreatment standards and local pretreatment programs designed
to ensure that the POTW does not violate its NPDES permit.
There are two sources of national pretreatment standards. The
first source is EPA's General Pretreatment Program, found at 40
C.F.R. Part 403, which contains NPDES permit-like prohibitions,
conditions and similar requirements that are directly

---

*/ This chapter is based on the original manuscript which was
    authored by Lisa I. Cooper with assistance from Neal J. Cabral.
    Chapter updated by Theodore W. Firetog.

applicable to all indirect dischargers. 40 C.F.R. § 403.6. The second source is so-called national categorical standards found at 40 C.F.R. Parts 405-471, which impose effluent limitations directly on specific types of industries (e.g. 40 C.F.R. Part 405 contains national categorical standards applicable to industries in the Iron and Steel Manufacturing Category). The second potential source of regulation for indirect discharges are local limits. All POTWs with a design flow of 5 million gallons daily must develop a local pretreatment program. 40 C.F.R. § 403.8(a). Local pretreatment programs must include authority for the POTW to control, through permits or other means, industrial discharges. These so called local limits will include, as appropriate, effluent limitations, monitoring and reporting requirements to ensure that industrial discharges to the POTW will not cause the POTW to violate its NPDES permit. Thus, indirect dischargers must also comply with local POTW regulations. These regulations are often incorporated into a local sewer use ordinance, although more and more POTWs are actually issuing individual permits to their industrial dischargers, and must, in accordance with recent EPA regulations, issue permits to all "significant" industrial dischargers. 40 C.F.R. § 403.8(f). Once established, local limits constitute enforceable pretreatment standards for purposes of the CWA.

One type of discharge that causes some confusion is discharges of stormwater. A brief discussion of stormwater reporting and recordkeeping issues is included in the following section on direct dischargers. By way of introduction, one critical point to remember about stormwter discharges is that there are no indirect stormwater discharges. Stormwater can be discharged in three ways: (1) directly to waters of the United States; (2) into a combined sewer system (a combined sewer system is a sewer system that leads to a POTW, and does not segregate out stormwater discharges); or (3) a municipal separate storm sewer system (a sewer system that contains only stormwater flows). Dischargers that discharge stormwater directly to waters of the United States must file a stormwater NPDES permit application. Dischargers that discharge to combined sewer systems, which exist

United States must file a stormwater NPDES permit application. primarily in older cities, do <u>not</u> need to file a stormwater permit application, since these discharges are excluded from the NPDES program as indirect discharges to a POTW. In contrast, however, most cities have separate sewers from stormwater only, called "municipal separate storm sewers" which do not go to a POTW. Dischargers of stormwater to a municipal separate sewer system are considered direct dischargers of stormwater, and <u>must</u> file an NPDES stormwater permit application. This is because discharges to municipal storm sewer systems, while seemingly indirect discharges, do not go to POTWs and hence are not indirect discharges excluded from the NPDES program.

One final layer of complexity under the CWA involves the federal-state relationship. EPA is the primary administrator of the CWA and will receive NPDES applications and issue permits in non-delegated states. Under the CWA, EPA may delegate to the states the authority to implement the CWA programs. 33 U.S.C. § 1342(b). To do this states usually create a state agency equivalent of EPA, and adopts EPA's CWA regulations or their equivalents. EPA will then approve the state programs and the state will be the primary CWA regulating entity. This means CWA permit applications must be sent to the state, and the state, not EPA, will issue the NPDES permits. States must obtain separate approval for the NPDES program and the pretreatment program. Currently, 39 states have approved state NPDES programs and 27 has approved pretreatment programs. However, and this is critical, state programs only need be at least as stringent as EPA's program, but can be more stringent. This will often lead to differences between EPA's CWA program, and a state's program. A common example is the definition of "waters of the United States". Under the CWA, only discharges to "waters of the United States", which does not include groundwater, are covered. However, many states adopt their own definition of "waters of the State" for their CWA program, and this state definition will often include groundwater.

II. <u>Reporting Requirements for Direct (NPDES) Dischargers</u>:

A. <u>Permit Application Reporting and Recordkeeping</u>:

Applicants applying or reapplying for NPDES permits must report significant and sometimes sensitive information in their permit applications. Where EPA is the permitting authority, applicants must submit EPA Form 1 and EPA Form 2C (for existing process wastewater discharges) or EPA Form 2D (for new sources or discharges of process wastewater) or EPA Form 2F (for stormwater discharges).

1. Applicants must provide routine information about the facility, including information about other environmental permits. 40 C.F.R. § 122.21(f). States with delegated NPDES programs and multi-media permitting regulations or initiatives, may utilize this information to combine permits and tighten controls; e.g., renewing an air-related permit for the wastewater treatment plant and the plant's NPDES permit at the same time.

2. Applicants permitting existing manufacturing, commercial, mining and silvicultural discharges must provide quantitative data for the discharge of certain specified pollutants. 40 C.F.R. § 122.21(g). Similar requirements are specified for new sources and new discharges. 40 C.F.R. § 122.21(i).
a. All applicants must report quantitative data for the seven pollutants listed at 40 C.F.R. § 122.21(g)(7)(i)(A).

b. All applicants with processes in any of the 34 NPDES Primary Industry Categories listed in Appendix A of Part 122 must report quantitative data for the organic toxic pollutants, toxic metals, and other pollutants specified in Tables I and III of Appendix D to Part 122. 40 C.F.R. § 122.21(g)(7)(i)(A).

c. Each applicant must indicate "<u>whether it knows or has reason to believe</u>" that any of

(i) the conventional and nonconventional pollutants listed in Table IV of Appendix D to Part 122 are discharged. 40 C.F.R. § 122.21(g)(7)(iii)(A). To the extent an applicable effluent guideline limitation (a categorical standard) directly or indirectly limits a pollutant listed in the Table, quantitative data must be reported for that pollutant. For all other pollutants "expected" to be discharged, the applicant must <u>either</u> report quantitative data or describe the reasons the pollutant is expected to be discharged.

(ii) the toxic and other pollutants listed in Tables II and III of Appendix D to Part 122 are discharged. 40 C.F.R. § 122.21(g)(7)(iii)(B). For pollutants "expected" to be discharged in concentrations of 10 ppb or greater (except for 4 specified pollutants), quantitative data must be reported. For pollutants "expected" to be discharged in concentrations less than 10 ppb, the applicant must <u>either</u> report quantitative data or describe the reasons the pollutant is expected to be discharged. Method detection limits and practical quantification levels of applicable analytical methods must be considered by the applicant in this reporting.

(iii) the hazardous substances (and asbestos) listed in Table V of Appendix D to Part 122 are discharged. 40 C.F.R. § 122.21(g)(7)(iv). For pollutants expected to be discharged, the applicant must describe the reasons the pollutant is expected to be discharged and report any quantitative data it has for any pollutant. Note that unless these hazardous substance discharges are covered by an NPDES permit or condition, they may have to be reported under the CWA hazardous substances reporting requirements set forth in 40 C.F.R. Part 117.

(iv) 2,3,7,8-tetrachlorodibenzo-p-dioxin (TCDD) is discharged. 40 C.F.R. § 122.21(g)(7)(v). This requirement applies if the applicant "knows or has reason to believe" TCDD is being discharged, or if it uses or manufactures the TCDD-related substances specified in 40 C.F.R. § 122.21(g)(7)(v)(a).

(v) "An applicant is expected to 'know or have reason to believe' that a pollutant is present in an effluent based on an evaluation of the expected use, production, or storage of the pollutant, or on any previous analysis of the pollutant." 40 C.F.R. § 122.21(g)(7). The instructions for EPA's NPDES permit application Form 2C state "Base your determination that a pollutant is present in or absent from your discharge on your knowledge of your raw materials, maintenance chemicals, intermediate and final products and byproducts, and any previous analysis known to you of your effluent or similar effluent."

(vi) Consider whether any of the information requested and/or reported in the permit application is "trade secret" and take appropriate steps to protect this information from public availability. Assess whether the reporting of monitoring data from upstream internal discharges is required and if so will you have difficulty meeting upstream/internal monitoring points, if established by EPA. These considerations are also extremely important where the permittee expects to utilize the combined wastestream formula to set end-of-pipe effluent limits.

d. All applicants must provide a listing of every toxic pollutant used or manufactured. 40 C.F.R. § 122.21 (g)(9). The toxic pollutants are EPA's "priority pollutants" and are listed in Item V-C of Form 2c. This provision was upheld as a reasonable exercise of EPA's broad authority, conferred under Section 308 of the CWA, to require reporting of information from permittees. NRDC v. EPA, 822 F.2d 104, 118-121 (D.C. Cir. 1987).

   e. All applicants must identify any biological toxicity tests which the applicant "knows or has reason to believe" have been made within the last 3 years on any of the applicants discharges or on a receiving water in relation to a discharge. 40 C.F.R. § 122.21(g)(11); see also Form 2c. This requirement is not limited to tests conducted by the applicant; nor does it necessarily require that the results of the tests be turned over to the permitting authority. However, should the permitting authority request this information, section 308 of the CWA, 33 U.S.C. § 1318, gives EPA broad authority to require dischargers to produce information relevant to the permitting process. If you do not wish to hand over these test results, your best approach may be to convince EPA the tests are not representative of current conditions.

   f. EPA may request any other reasonable information including "additional quantitative data and bioassays to assess the relative toxicity of discharges to aquatic life and requirements to determine the cause of the toxicity." 40 C.F.R. § 122.21(g)(13).

   g. Many of EPA's categorical standards specify a preference for "mass" or "production-based" limitations, which are usually expressed in terms of an allowable mass of pollutant that can be discharged per unit of product produced. See 40 C.F.R. § 122.45(f). Permittees subject to categorical standards where production-based discharge limits are used must report applicable production units. 40 C.F.R. § 122.21(g)(5). Permit limits are to be based on a "reasonable measure of actual production", not plant design capacity. 40 C.F.R. § 122.45(b)(2). Actual levels of production must then be reported along with sampling results. 40 C.F.R. § 122.45(b)(2)(ii)(B)(3). Since a permittee's pemit limits for production-based standards will be a function of production levels, it is critical that appropriate production figures are reported in the application and that accommodations for anticipated fluctuations are reached. See 45 Fed. Reg. 38031 (1980) for EPA's views on establishing appropriate production levels. When reporting production data determine whether your production information is trade secret. If so, take appropriate steps to protect it. Also remember, if you don't appropriately account for anticipated production fluctuations, you may need to provide notice and/or submit a new NPDES application to the permitting authority during the NPDES permit term if you experience a significant increase in production.

h.   Records of all data used to complete permit applications must be maintained for at least 3 years from the date the application is signed, except for POTWs, which must keep data submitted under 40 C.F.R. § 122.21(d)(3)(ii) for at least 5 years. 40 C.F.R. § 122.21(p). Since the civil statute of limitations for violations of federal permits is 5 years, the permittee must assess whether to maintain records for that longer period of time. However, you should note that at least one court has concluded that there is no applicable statute of limitations for a delegated state action to enforce a state-issued NPDES permit. Student Public Interest Research Group, Inc. v. AT&T Bell Lab, 617 F. Supp 1190, 1203 (D.N.J. 1985).

3.   All quantitative data reported in the permit application must be sampled and analyzed in accordance with the analytical methods approved under 40 C.F.R. Part 136. 40 C.F.R. § 122.21(g)(7). When no analytical method is approved for a pollutant, the applicant may use "any suitable method", but must provide a description of the method. The permitting authority must approve use of these test methods. An applicant may also apply for approval of an alternate test method. 40 C.F.R. § 136.4.

4.   All permit reporting requirements should be assessed, and a permitting strategy developed. For example, where a permittee questions the validity of the data included in the application, utilize a footnote or a supplemental report to explain the result. This applies equally to numerical and biological data. Depending upon the regulatory climate and the permittee's enforcement posture, recognize that this information will be thoroughly reviewed by the regulatory authority and potentially a citizens group or the news media. Determine whether sensitive information should be reviewed with higher management and internal liasons with the news media.

5.   EPA has issued final stormwater permitting regulations. EPA's individual stormwater permit application, EPA Form 2F, is relatively similar to EPA's process wastewater application Form 2C. Many of the rules outlined above will also apply to stormwater permit applications. Some of the unique aspects of this new permit application are discussed below.

a.   Each applicant must provide a site map showing the topography of the facility, including drainage and discharge structures. 40 C.F.R. § 122.26(c)(1)(i)(A). This map must indicate potential areas of stormwater contamination including each past or present area used for the storage or disposal of such items as raw mateials, fuels, solvents, products, hazardous substances, SARA Title III chemicals and pesticides and fertilizers. Extra care should be taken in making these designations since "skeletons in the closet" that exist at every old manufacturing plant may be revealed. In this case, the applicant may want to consider alternative stormwater application routes, or expend extra resources to attempt to be excluded from stormwater permitting requirements.

b. Applicants must also estimate the area of impervious surfaces and total area drained by each stormwater outfall <u>and</u> provide a narrative description for the past three years of such activities as the method of storage, treatment or disposal of materials, fuels, solvents, hazardous substances and SARA Title III chemicals where the storage, treatment or disposal of such materials allowed exposure to stormwater. 40 C.F.R. § 122.26(c)(1)(i)(B). Again, extreme care should be exercised in completing this description to avoid unnecessary or potentially criminal admissions.

c. Applicants must certify that all outfalls that should contain stormwater only have been "tested or evaluated" for the presence of non-stormwater discharges which are not covered by an NPDES permit. 40 C.F.R. § 122.26(c)(1)(i)(B).

d. Applicants must provide any "existing information" regarding significant leaks or spills of toxic or hazardous pollutants at the facility within the past three years. 40 C.F.R. § 122.26(c)(1)(i)(B). When such spills are specified in the application, it is advisable that the applicant indicate whether and how such spills were reported to appropriate authorities under applicable reporting statutes and any existing CWA permit and, if not reported, why they did not need to be reported.

e. Applicants must also report quantitative data, under 40 C.F.R. § 122.26(c)(1)(i)(E)(1)-(6), for:

   (i)   any pollutant limited in an effluent guideline to which the facility is subject;

   (ii)   Any pollutant "listed" (not just limited) in the facility's NPDES permit for its process wastewater;

   (iii)   Oil and grease, pH, BOD_5, COD, TSS, total phosphorus, total kjeldah nitrogen, and nitrate plus nitrate nitrogen;

   (iv)   To the extent the applicant "knows or has reason to believe" that the toxic pollutants and hazardous substances described above in Sections II.A.2.c. (ii) and (iii) of this outline are discharged. If a particular pollutant is present anywhere on the facility site (including in fertilizers or pesticides) it is probably much more difficult for an applicant to "reasonably believe" that this pollutant is not picked up and discharged in stormwater runoff than it is in the case of process wastewater discharges.

    B.   <u>Reporting and Recordkeeping Requirements Under NPDES Permits</u>.

        Most reporting and recordkeeping requirements will be contained in a permittee's permit. Every permit condition must be complied with, and a violation of a permit reporting requirement is treated no differently under the CWA than a violation of a numerical permit effluent limitation. 40 C.F.R. § 122.41(a). Moreover, additional penalties relating to falsified or incorrect reports can apply. Monitoring information is usually reported to the permitting authority on forms called Discharge Monitoring Reports (DMRs).

    1.   <u>Routine Reporting of Monitoring Results</u>:

        a.   The permittee must maintain records of all monitoring information, including all calibration and maintenance records and all original strip chart recordings for continuous monitoring instrumentation, copies of all reports required by the permit, and records of all data used to complete the application, for 3 years from the date of the sample, measurement, report or application. 40 C.F.R. § 122.41(j)(2). The permittee must also provide copies of all records required to be kept by the permit, as well as any information EPA <u>may request</u> to determine whether "cause exists for modifying, revoking and reissuing, or terminating the permit or to determine compliance with the permit." 40 C.F.R. § 122.41(h). Again, permittees may want to consider retaining this information for at least five years.

        b.   Records of monitoring information must include the information (dates, places, time, persons involved, techniques etc.) specified at 40 C.F.R. § 122.41(j)(3). Not all this information will need to be reported on reporting forms, but this information must still be kept and available for inspection or reporting upon request.

        c.   Monitoring results required under NPDES permits must be conducted using test procedures approved under 40 C.F.R. Part 136, unless other test procedures have been specified in the permit. 40 C.F.R. § 122.41(j)(4). 40 C.F.R. § 122.44(h)(iv) requires that a test method be specified in the permit for pollutants for which no approved test method exists. Permittees may wish to negotiate, comment upon and contest an unsatisfactory test method since it is extremely difficult to contest the reliability of a test method in defense to a permit violation. Particular attention should be paid to test methods when limits are set at very low levels. See, Natural Resources Defense Council v. Outboard Marine Corp, 702 F.Supp. 690, 693 (N.D. Ill. 1988).

d. All applications, including DMRs, reports or information submitted to the permitting authority must be signed by a principal executive officer of the corporation or a duly authorized representative, and certified in accordance with 40 C.F.R. § 122.22. 40 C.F.R. § 122.41(k). The certification has been used to argue that it precludes a defense to a permit violation based on a sampling error. See Natural Resources Defense Council, Inc. v. Texaco Refining & Marketing, Inc., 719 F. Supp. 281, 288-89 (D. Del. 1989) (Defendant's DMR's are practically unassailable evidence of liability, despite claims of sampling error).

e. All permits must specify monitoring requirements including type, intervals, and frequency, and specifications for proper monitoring procedures and methods. 40 C.F.R. § 122.48. Unless otherwise indicated in the permit, monitoring results must be submitted on a Discharge Monitoring Report (DMR), and reported at the intervals specified in the permit. 40 C.F.R. § 122.41(1)(4). The DMR is the primary reporting document under the CWA, and implements the Act's self-policing mechanism. In effect, the permittee must report its own effluent limit violations to the permitting authority. Since DMRs are certified reports, they often in and of themselves establish the permittee's liability. Sierra Club v. Union Oil Co., 813 F.2d 1480, 1491-92 (9th Cir. 1987). Citizen groups also have access to these records and most CWA citizens suits are based on violations reported in DMRs. Therefore, the permittee must ensure the accuracy of the data reported on the DMR ie., make sure conversion or transposition errors are avoided and if a result seems flawed, discuss with the permitting authority the use of an asterisk and include the result and the explanation in the description following the asterisk. Make sure bypasses and upsets are also noted so appropriate defenses can be established in response to a citizen suit.

f. If a permittee monitors more frequently than required by the permit using a approved test method, these results must be included in the DMR. 40 C.F.R. § 122.41(1)(4)(ii). This can work to a permittees advantage in the case of "evening out" an aberrant result to determine compliance with effluent limits based on averages. See Student Public Interest Group v. AT&T Bell Lab., 617 F.Supp. 1190, 1204-05 (D.C. N.J. 1985). This technique should not be overlooked since violations of an average limitation will be alleged as 30 or 31 days times $25,000 per day. See Atlantic States Legal Foundation, Inc. v. Tyson Foods, Inc., 897 F.2d 1128, 1139 (11th Cir. 1990) (holding that a violation of a monthly average should be deemed to involve a violation for each of the days of that month). Calculations for all limits which require averaging of measurements must use an arithmetic mean. 40 C.F.R. § 122.41(1)(4)(iii).

g. 40 C.F.R. § 122.45(b)(2)(ii)(B) specifies notification requirements for changes in levels of production above the lowest production level contained in the permit for production-based limits. This notification is critical because in the absence of such notification, the permittee must comply with the limitations that correspond to the lowest level of production specified in the permit. 40 C.F.R. § 122.45(b)(2)(ii)(B)(2).

h. On April 2, 1992, EPA published a final rule with respect to reporting and recordkeeping requirements for storm-water permits. 57 Fed. Reg. 11394. The new regulations have been added to 40 CFR 122.44(i), revising subsection (2) and adding subsections 3-5. Generally the reporting and record-keeping requirements will be established on a case by case basis.

2. Events Triggering Non-Routine Reporting Requirements.

A number of non-routine events will trigger a requirement to report the occurrence to the permitting authority. Most of these requirements will be specified in the permit, others are in the regulations.

a. Twenty-four hour reporting. Any noncompliance "which may endanger health or the environment" must be reported orally within 24 hours from the time the permittee becomes aware of the circumstances. 40 C.F.R. § 122.41(1)(6)(i). A written report must be provided within 5 days and must describe the noncompliance, its cause and other circumstances and developments. As well, any unanticipated bypass which exceeds any applicable effluent limitation, any upset exceeding effluent limitations and any violation of a maximum daily discharge limitation for pollutants specified in the permit, pursuant to 40 C.F.R. § 122.4(g), as subject to 24 hour reporting must also be reported within 24 hours, as described above. 40 C.F.R. § 122.41(l)(6)(ii). Most permits will specify that violations of toxic pollutants and hazardous substances will require twenty-four hour reporting. Note that the availability of the unavoidable bypass defense and the upset defense are contingent upon providing the required notice and report, and the likelihood of establishing these affirmative defenses in a lawsuit depends on the permittee's adherence to pertinent recordkeeping and notice requirements. 40 C.F.R. §§ 122.41(m)(4)(i)(C); 122.41(n)(3)(iii).

  b. All instances of other non-compliance not reported in a DMR or 24 hour report must be reported at the time monitoring reports are submitted, in a non-compliance report, and must include the information required by the 24 hour notice reporting requirements. 40 C.F.R. § 122.41(l)(7).

  c. When the permittee becomes aware that it failed to submit any "relevant facts" in a permit application or submitted incorrect information in a permit application or in any report, it must promptly submit such facts or information. 40 C.F.R. § 122.41(l)(8).

  d. The permittee must notify EPA, under 40 C.F.R. § 122.41(l)(1) and (2), as soon as possible of any planned physical alterations or additions to the permitted facility when:

    (i) the alteration or addition may make the facility a "new source";

    (ii) the alteration or addition "could significantly change the nature or increase the quantity of pollutants discharged." This notification only applies to pollutants not limited in the permit or subject to notification levels under 40 C.F.R. § 122.42(a)(1).

    (iii) the alteration or addition results in a significant change in the permittee's sludge use or disposal practices.

  e. The permittee must give advance notice of any anticipated noncompliance; e.g. any planned changes in the permitted facility or activity which "may result in noncompliance with permit requirements". 40 C.F.R. § 122.41(l)(2).

f. Anticipated bypass. If the permittee knows in advance of the need for a bypass, it must submit prior notice, if possible at least 10 days before the date of the bypass. 40 C.F.R. § 122.41(m)(3).

g. Notification levels. 40 C.F.R. § 122.42(a) establishes a variety of "notification levels" applicable to all toxic pollutants not limited in the permit. All existing manufacturing, commercial, mining and silvicultural dischargers must notify EPA as soon as they "know or have reason to believe" that any activity has occurred or will occur that will result in the discharge of any toxic pollutant, not limited in the permit, above specified notification levels. 40 C.F.R. § 122.42(a). The notification levels are different depending on whether the discharge is of a routine frequent nature or a non-routine non-frequent nature.

III. Reporting Requirements for Indirect Discharges

Reporting and monitoring requirements applicable to many industrial dischargers to Publically Owned Treatment Works (POTWs) (indirect discharges) have increased dramatically. The regulations establish a number of reporting requirements directly applicable to POTWs and indirect dischargers. These are separate from reporting requirements POTWs may impose in individual permits or through local sewer use ordinances. You may soon see some of these requirements incorporated into you local sewer use codes. Most reports in this section go to the "Control Authority," which is the POTW or other local sewer entity if an approved pretreatment program exists, and is otherwise the State or EPA.

There are a bewildering array of types of indirect dischargers, with overlapping but often different reporting requirements applicable to each. These categories are defined below. An indirect discharger could be a significant industrial user, it could be subject to the Categorical Pretreatment Standards or it could be neither of these. All dischargers subject to Categorical Pretreatment Standards are significant industrial users, but not all significant industrial users are subject to Categorical Pretreatment Standards. There are also requirements that apply to all indirect dischargers, including significant industrial users and those subject to Categorical Pretreatment Standards.

A.   <u>Reporting Requirements for Industrial Users Subject to Categorical Pretreatment Standards</u>.

1.   A Significant Industrial User (SIU) is defined, in part, as:

a.   all industrial users subject to Categorical Pretreatment Standards.

2.   The POTW <u>must</u> now control SIUs through permits or other similar individual control mechanisms. 40 C.F.R. § 403.8(f)(1)(iii). The permits must include self-monitoring, sampling, reporting, notification and recordkeeping requirements, including identification of pollutants to be monitored, sampling frequency, type and location, based on applicable categorical pretreatment standards, local limits, state and local law.

3.   The POTW must specifically inspect and sample the effluent from each SIU at least once a year and evaluate at least once every two years whether the SIU needs a plan to control "slug" discharges (a slug discharge is generally a non-routine batch discharge or spill). 40 C.F.R. § 403.8(f)(2)(v). If a slug control program is needed, procedures must be developed for immediately notifying the POTW of slug discharges, with follow-up written notification within 5 days.

4.   Within 180 days of promulgation of a new Categorical Pretreatment Standard or an EPA determination of the applicability of a category to an indirect discharger or 90 days prior to commencement of discharge by a New Source, dischargers must submit a baseline monitoring report BMR. 40 C.F.R. § 403.12(b)(6). The BMR includes among other information:

a.   flow measurement information including non-regulated streams as necessary to use the Combined Wastestream Formula;

b.   for existing sources, identification of applicable Pretreatment Standards and sampling and analysis results of regulated pollutants from each regulated process as a daily maximum and a daily average performed in accordance with the techniques specified in 40 C.F.R. Part 136 or, if no method applies, through use of "validated analytical methods or any other applicable sampling and analytical procedures" and otherwise complying with all the requirements specified in 40 C.F.R. § 403.12(b)(4)-(5); new sources are to provide estimates; and

c. for existing dischargers only, a certification by a qualified professional indicating whether Pretreatment Standards are being met on a "consistent basis", and, if not, whether additional operation, maintenance or pretreatment is required for consistent compliance.

d. Once a BMR is completed, the permittee may need a compliance schedule and interim effluent limitations to be incorporated into its permit. You may also need to hire an engineering firm to complete the BMR. If enforcement is a possibility, consider having your attorney hire the engineering firm to protect the information provided. Discuss with higher management that capital investments may be necessary in order to meet new limitations. For categorical discharges, the limits in your local sewer use code will be superceded by the federal categorical limits, if more stringent and vice-versa.

5. Within 90 days of the final compliance date for Categorical Pretreatment Standards or, for New Sources, 90 days following commencement of discharge of wastewater to the POTW, the industrial user must submit all the information discussed in 4. a., b. and c. above in a 90-day compliance report. 40 C.F.R. § 403.12(d). Essentially, the 90-day compliance report must contain current monitoring results of the monitoring informtion submitted in the BMR.

6. Any industrial user subject to a Categorical Pretreatment Standard must submit periodic sampling and analysis reports to the Control Authority on continued compliance in June and December of each year, unless the Pretreatment Standards or the Control Authority requires more frequent submissions. 40 C.F.R. § 403.12(e). Monitoring performed using approved methods and conducted more frequently than required must be included in the report. 40 C.F.R. § 403.12(g)(5). Note that if a facility is subject to a categorical standard, it will be classified as an SIU and also subject to the additional SIU reporting requirements described above.

7. The reports identified in 4-6 above are not required when the POTW itself collects all the information required. 40 C.F.R. § 403.12(g).

8. Twenty-four hour reporting. If sampling performed by an Industrial User in 4-6 above indicates a violation, the user must notify the Control Authority within 24 hours of becoming aware of the violation. 40 C.F.R. § 403.12(g)(2). The sampling and analysis must then be repeated and the results submitted within 30 days of becoming aware of the violation, unless the Control Authority undertakes the sampling.

B. <u>Reporting Requirements for Industrial Users Not Subject to Categorical Pretreatment Standards</u>.

1. SIUs are also defined to include cetain dischargers not subject to categorical standards. An SIU also includes an industrial user that discharges an average of 25,000 gallons per day or more of process wastewater or contributes a process wastestream which makes up 5 percent or more of the dry hydraulic or organic capacity of the POTW treatment plant or is designated as such by the Control Authority as specified in 40 C.F.R. § 403.3(t)(1)(ii)).

2. The POTW <u>must</u> now control SIUs (including non-categorical SIUs) through permits or other similar individual control mechanisms. 40 C.F.R. § 403.8(f)(1)(iii). The permits must include self-monitoring, sampling, reporting, notification and recordkeeping requirements, including identification of pollutants to be monitored, sampling frequency, type and location, based on applicable categorical pretreatment standards, local limits, state and local law.

3. Noncategorical SIUs must submit at least every 6 months (on dates specified by the POTW) a description of the nature, concentration and flow of pollutants required to be reported to the Control Authority based on sampling and analysis, unless the Control Authority collects all the necessary information. 40 C.F.R. § 403.12(h). The Control Authority will specify what pollutants must be reported when it issues all significant industrial users discharge permits or similar individual control mechanisms as required by 40 C.F.R. § 403.8(f)(1)(ii). This requirement amended the original pretreatment regulations. It also redefined non-categorical SIUs by mandating reporting requirements similar to those imposed on categorical SIUs.

4. The POTW must specifically inspect and sample the effluent from each SIU at least once a year and evaluate at least once every two years whether the SIU needs a plan to control "slug" discharges. 40 C.F.R. § 403.8(f)(2)(v). If a slug control program is needed procedures must be developed for immediately notifying the POTW of slug discharges, with follow-up written notification within 5 days.

5. The Control Authority must specify "appropriate" reporting requirements for all noncategorical industrial users (not just SIUS). 40 C.F.R. § 403.12(h). These reporting requirements are normally incorporated in your local sewer use code and/or your permit, license or approval. If your facility qualifies as a significant industrial user, the Control Authority must issue you a permit if you do not already have one. See III.D.

C. Reporting Requirements Applicable To All
Industrial Users.

1. All industrial users must immediately notify
the POTW of all discharges that "could cause problems to the
POTW", including slug loadings, as defined by the eight
specific prohibitions listed in 40 C.F.R. § 403.5(b)'s
"specific prohibitions" (e.g., discharges that could cause
"interference" or create a fire or explosion in the POTW). 40
C.F.R. § 403.12(f). EPA noted that it will hold the industrial
user accountable for knowing its discharge activity and the
likely effects of its discharge activity. EPA has stated that
"failure to properly assess the impact or likely effect of a
slug load or to give notification for any other reason is no
defense to an enforcement action for failure to notify". 53
Fed. Reg. 40593 (1988).

2. All industrial users that discharge:

- any amount of RCRA "acute" hazardous
wastes; or

- more than 15 kilograms of any RCRA
hazardous waste in a calendar month;

must report the name of the hazardous waste discharged, the
type of discharge (continuous or batch) and the EPA hazardous
waste number to the POTW, EPA and state hazardous waste
authorities as of February 19, 1991, or, if the discharge
commences after that date, within 180 days of commencing
discharge. 40 C.F.R. § 403.12(p). Dischargers of over 100
kilograms of hazardous waste per month must report additional
information. Moreover, an industrial discharger covered by
this notification requirement must certify that it has a
program in place to reduce the volume or toxicity of wastes
generated to the degree it has determined to be economically
practicable.

3. All industrial dischargers must promptly
notify the POTW in advance of any "substantial change" (not
defined) in the volume or character of pollutants in their
discharge, including the hazardous wastes reported under
40 C.F.R. § 403.12(p) and discussed in 2. above. Only changes
expected to occur "on a regular or routine basis over an
extended period of time (three months or more)" need to be
reported. 53 Fed. Reg. 40600 (1988).

4. All industrial users must maintain records of
all information resulting from any of the monitoring activities
and results for 3 years, whether these monitoring activities

are required by the regulations or not, and a longer period in the event of unresolved litigation regarding the industrial user <u>or</u> POTW. 40 C.F.R. § 403.12(o)(2). Records of monitoring activities required by the provisions discussed above must include the information specified in 40 C.F.R. § 403.12(o)(1).

     5. Upset. Within 24 hours of becoming aware of an upset that violates a Categorical Pretreatment Standard, an industrial user must report on the circumstances of the upset to the POTW, and, if reported orally, follow-up with a written submission within 5 days. 40 C.F.R. § 403.16(c)(3). The written notification must contain certain facts. Consider developing a form letter to insure all elements are included in each letter. This notification is required to maintain an upset defense.

     6. Bypass. If an industrial user knows in advance of the need for a bypass (an anticipated bypass) it shall submit prior notice to the Control Authority, if possible at least 10 days in advance. 40 C.F.R. § 403.17(c)(1). Oral notice of an unanticipated bypass that exceeds applicable Pretreatment Standards must be submitted to the Control Authority within 24 hours of the time the industrial user becomes aware of the bypass. 40 C.F.R. § 403.17(c)(2). A written submission must then be provided within 5 days. These notices are required to maintain a bypass defense. 40 C.F.R. § 403.17(d)(1)(iii).

     7. A POTW pretreatment program must require the submission of all notices and self-monitoring reports from industrial users "as are necessary to assess and assure compliance with all Pretreatment Standards and Requirements, including the specified reporting requirements". 40 C.F.R. § 403.8(f)(1)(iv).

     8. A POTW pretreatment program must also ensure, through inspection, surveillance and monitoring, independent of industrial users reports, compliance with all applicable Pretreatment Standards and requirements by industrial users. 40 C.F.R. § 403.8(f)(1)(v).

     9. A POTW must provide annual public notification in the largest local daily newspaper of industrial users in significant noncompliance over the past 12 months. 40 C.F.R. § 403.8(f)(2)(vii). Significant noncompliance includes failure to provide, within 30 days after the due date, required reports and failure to accurately report noncompliance.

10. POTWs with a design flow greater than 1 mgd or with approved pretreatment programs must now provide in their permit applications results of valid whole effluent biological toxicity testing and other information concerning toxic problems. 40 C.F.R. § 122.21(j). Some states, like New York, have notified POTWs that bioassay results are not needed with their renewal applications. These decisions have been made by states due to personnel shortages. Over time the POTWs that are required to perform these analysis may pass along similar reporting requirements to their SIUs and may be forced to carryout modified toxicity reduction evaluations.

IV. Enforcement and Penalties

A. Sources and Types of Enforcement:

1. There are four general entities that can enforce NPDES or Pretreatment violations under the CWA: EPA, the State, the control authority (POTW), and/or citizen groups. The entity that initiates an enforcement action depends upon whether the state has received approval from EPA to implement the NPDES and/or pretreatment program. It is extremely important to assess the enforcement posture of all involved agencies and/or entities in determining an appropriate response to any enforcement action. In this regard, it should be remembered the government agencies generally focus limited resources on specific enforcement initiatives. For example, EPA is currently devoting significant resources to enforcing against POTWs that do not have adequate control over their industrial dischargers, as well as industrial dischargers to POTWs.

a. EPA can bring a civil action to enforce the CWA and can seek a permanent injunction, a temporary injunction or a civil penalty of up to $25,000 per day for each violation. Atlantic States Legal Foundation, Inc. v. Tyson Foods, Inc., 897 F.2d 1128, 1138 (11th Cir. 1990). EPA has developed a Clean Water Act Civil Penalty Policy to be used in settling civil actions. Environmental Protection Agency Memorandum, Clean Water Act Penalty Policy for Civil Settlement Negotiations (Feb. 16, 1984). The policy emphasizes imposition of a penalty that discourages any economic benefit for non-compliance (e.g., at least the cost avoided by non-compliance) and the gravity of the offense and also attempts to deter the permittee and others from future violations. Not all courts rely on EPA's Civil Penalty Policy, although many do give it some attention. See id.

b. EPA can also bring criminal enforcement actions. "Responsible corporate officers" (e.g., any person with a responsible relationship with the act in question and who can also prevent the act) are the primary individuals who can be found criminally liable under the CWA. EPA may also assess criminal sanctions against a corporation.

(i) For "negligent" violations convicted violators may be subject to a fine not less than $2,500 and not more than $25,000 per day of violation and/or up to 1 year of imprisonment. Criminal negligence can require, variously, only a showing of want of due care or it can require a degree of recklessness.

(ii) For "knowing violations" fines increase to not less than $5,000 and nor more than $50,000 per day of violation, and up to three years imprisonment. The government does not need to prove premediation or malice, the government only need show that the act that violated the law was done knowingly or absent a mistake or inadvertence.

(iii) For "knowing endangerment" when a violator knowingly violates one of the CWA's provisions and "knows at the time that he thereby places another person in imminent danger of death or serious bodily injury" a convicted individual can be fined up to $250,000 per day and jailed for up to 15 years. Organizations can be fined up to $1,000,000 per day.

c. Finally, EPA can assess administrative penalties for violations of the CWA. There are two classes of penalties:

(i) Class I violations carry maximum penalties of $10,000 per violation with a cap of $25,000. EPA has issued a Class I Administrative Penalty Policy. Environmental Protection Agency Memorandum, Guidance on Class I Clean Water Act Administrative Penalty Procedures (July 27, 1987).

(ii) Class II violations carry maximum penalties of $10,000 per violation with a cap of $125,000.

d. Note that all permit applications, reports and information submitted to EPA must be certified under 40 C.F.R. § 122.22(d) or 40 C.F.R. § 122.41(k)(2). The certification states:

I certify under penalty of law that this document and all attachments were prepared under my direction or supervision in accordance with a system designed to assure that qualified personnel properly gather and evaluate the information submitted. Based on my inquiry of the person or persons who manage the system, or those persons directly responsible for gathering the information, the information submitted is, to the best of my knowledge and belief, true, accurate, and complete. I am aware that there are significant penalties for submitting false information, including the possibility of fine and imprisonment for knowing violations.

e. Criminal provisions specifically related to reporting and recordkeeping are also specified by the CWA. The CWA provides that any person who "knowingly" falsifies, tampers with or renders inaccurate any monitoring device or method required to be maintained under a permit can be fined up to $10,000 and jailed up to two years. See 40 C.F.R. § 122.41(j)(5) and 33 U.S.C. § 1319(c)(4). The CWA also provides that any person who "knowingly" makes any false statement, representation or certification in any record or any other document submitted or required to be maintained, including monitoring and compliance/non-compliance reports can be fined up to $10,000 per violation and jailed up to 2 years. See 40 C.F.R. § 122.41(k)(2) and 33 U.S.C. § 1319(c)(4). In a recent case the director of a municipal POTW was convicted on 18 felony counts under the knowing false statement provision for falsifying the POTW's DMRs. U.S. v. Brittain, 931 F.2d 1413 (10th Cir. 1991).

2. In NPDES delegated states, state enforcement programs do not need to be identical to EPA's enforcement authority, although EPA can establish minimum acceptability criteria. The specific mechanisms available to state authorities will depend on the applicable state statutes and regulations.

3. POTWS must have the authority to seek injunctive relief and to assess (either directly or through local courts) civil or criminal penalties of at least $1,000 per day for each pretreatment violation. 40 C.F.R. § 403.8(f)(1)(vi)(A). A POTW need not have administrative penalty authority. Specific penalties and penalty authority will either be found in the local sewer use code or in the permits issued by the POTW. POTWs must now also develop an enforcement response plan, detailing procedures to investigate and respond to industrial user noncompliance. 40 C.F.R. § 403.8(f)(5).

4. Section 505 of the CWA also allows any person "having an interest which is or may be adversely affected" to bring a civil enforcement action against a discharger for violation of any "effluent standard or limitation" under the Act (citizen suits). 33 U.S.C. § 1365(c). Citizen suits may pray for injunctive relief, civil penalties ($25,000 per day per violation) and attorney and expert witness fees. Since the CWA is a strict liability statute, citizen suits often succeed simply by introducing a dischargers DMRs showing reported effluent violations, and moving for summary judgment. See Sierra Club v. Union Oil Co., 813 F.2d 1480, 1491-92 (9th Cir. 1987) (discharger's DMR is conclusive evidence of a violation, absent a valid affirmative defense). Failure to submit monitoring reports due to inoperative meters was found to be a violation of the CWA, since the CWA requires that reports be made. Sierra Club v. Union Oil Co., 716 F.Supp. 429, 434 (N.D. Cal. 1988). There are two significant limitations on the scope of citizen suits. First, a citizen suit cannot be commenced if EPA or the state is currently prosecuting an enforcement action for the violation alleged. 33 U.S.C. § 1365(b)(1)(B). Second, the Supreme Court has arguably restricted the ability of citizen suits to recover for "wholly past violations," requiring that citizen suits may be brought only for violations that are "ongoing". Gwaltney of Smithfield, Ltd. v. Chesapeake Bay Foundation, Inc., 484 U.S. 49 (1987).

Case law further defines the application of a citizen suit for reporting violations. Sierra Club v. Simkins Industries, Inc., 847 F.2d 1109 (4th Cir. 1988); cert. denied, 488 U.S. 992. In Simkins, a citizen suit was filed alleging that the discharger failed to file complete DMRS for a number of years, in violation of the reporting requirements in its NPDES permit, and praying for the previous civil penalty maximum of $10,000 per day per violation. The court found that reporting requirements contained in an NPDES permit were a type of obligation that could be enforced in a citizen suit and that the permittee had failed to conduct all the sampling required in its permit and to report the results in its DMRs. The number of days of violation, for purposes of assessing penalties, was calculated not from the first date a DMR was due, but from the effective date of the permit. The court reasoned that the permittee had an obligation as of the effective date of the permit to take actions, such as required sampling, which would make timely filing of complete DMRs possible. Id. at 1611 n. 11. Consequently, the court found 977 violations, one for each day from the date of the issuance of the permit to the date the permittee first filed a complete DMR, which exposed the permittee to a maximum penalty of $10,000 x 977 = $9,700,000. The court then reduced this penalty to $977,000. You may not be so fortunate.

APPENDIX A

SAMPLE

**DOCUMENT RETENTION
POLICY AND PROCEDURE**[1]

1. **POLICY**

Corporate policy is to "destroy all records except those specifically authorized to be preserved." Those records "authorized to be preserved" are listed in the attached schedule. This schedule has been approved by the Records Management Committee as the only corporate authority for the detention of records. Official retention periods listed in the schedule are as short as possible in order to minimize our records inventory. Longer periods are based upon positive legal, audit, or management requirements.

---

[1]   This sample document retention policy was adapted from one prepared some years ago for a major corporation. In addition to the general policy guidelines presented here, the actual policy included 40 pages of itemized retention periods for specified documents.

2. DEFINITIONS

(a) <u>A positive legal requirement</u> means that: a specific federal or state law requires us to keep the record; important property rights which the corporation has legal obligations to protect are involved, such as patents, employee pension equities, etc.; or we are aware of a specific, impending claim or legal action. The mere fact that a record is potentially useful in the event of a lawsuit does <u>not</u> constitute a positive legal requirement. Each month the corporation enters into numerous sales, purchase, and freight transactions involving significant quantities of records. Most of these records would need to be retained for fifteen years or more to address every possible legal problem that could arise. As a practical matter, the retention of such records must simply be based on sound business procedure. Such records will normally be kept for one to two years--a period long enough to verify performance, to make or receive payment, and to furnish support for the audit of accounts. If probable claims or legal situations are identified during this period, the records directly concerned with the specific transaction can be set aside. After this period, if unanticipated legal problems still arise, the corporation knowingly assumes the risk of any loss caused by not having records--a loss that should in any event be less expensive than massive records storage.

(b) <u>Auditing requirements</u> refer to state and federal tax audits, particularly the federal government's review of corporate income tax returns. All records needed for a federal tax audit are retained for a period long enough to cover the statutory limitation on such audits plus whatever extensions may be arranged by separate agreement.

(c) <u>Management requirements</u> refer to the needs of corporate departments producing records of proprietary, technical, or economic value to future operations of the company, e.g. technological research and development, market research and analysis, facilities engineering, etc. The mere fact that people at upper levels of management "might ask for certain records" does <u>not</u> constitute a positive management requirement nor an acceptable reason for saving records that are otherwise disposable.

Most corporate records do not fit into the legal, audit, or management requirement classifications described above. They may be vital to current goals and useful for analysis of current operations, but they are of little or no value to the corporation by the time they are over one year old.

Therefore, the Records Management Committee has assigned short term retention categories of "current plus 1 year" or less to ninety percent of the corporation's records.

3. <u>**RETENTION AND DISPOSAL PROCEDURE**</u>

(a) <u>The Records Schedule</u> is divided into sections by the corporation's management functions rather than its organization. Each section applies to the records at all locations where that functional activity is officially performed. Some sections, such as "Sales," apply to many locations. Others, such as "Market Research," apply to only a few. As general rule, records are listed in the order of permanence. Retention periods are expressed in terms of the number of calendar years plus the current calendar year.

If a record is classified as "C plus 2 years," this means that during 1981 all 1980 and 1979 copies will be kept; 1979 copies will be destroyed in January, 1982, and 1980 copies will be destroyed in January 1983. In other words, there will always be at least two full prior calendar years of a "C plus 2" record on hand, and at least one full prior year of a "C plus" record.

"Active" means that the <u>record should be kept as long as it is actively used, is pertinent or in effect, and has not been superseded by receipt of more up-to-date material</u>. In a few instances, the meaning of "Active" has been slightly changed for a particular record and the modified definition shown in a footnote.

(b) <u>Annual Records Disposal.</u> The most important records housekeeping task is the year-end disposal. Each January, a year's collection of records in all categories except "Permanent" should be discarded by all company offices and locations. The records schedule will be the guide to "Permanent" records, most of which are found in research and technical locations or in certain headquarters departments. Records classified as "Active" should also be reviewed even though the life span of "Active" material is not necessarily related to its chronological age. <u>CAUTION:</u> <u>Accounting records should not be destroyed without clearance from the Tax Department</u>.

4. <u>**PROCEDURE FOR AMENDING THE RECORDS SCHEDULE**</u>

In order to assist the Records Management Committee to keep abreast of developments that warrant amendments or changes to the records schedule, anyone in the corporation who feels that a retention period should be changed because of changes in legal, auditing, or management requirements, or who feels that a new item should be added to the schedule, should submit the following information to the Records Coordinator for referral to the Committee:

(a) Department or location that has the record.

(b) Name and present schedule number of record, or a brief description if it is a proposed new item on the schedule.

(c) Proposed retention period.

(d) Reason for the proposed retention including specific citation to the law or regulation and the government body, and an explanation of the need for the record, who uses it and for what purposes, together with enough detail to give the Committee a clear picture of the value of the record.

5. FILING

Refer to Corporate File Manual for detailed information on the subject of filing.

6. RECORDS CENTER PROCEDURE

The Corporate Records Center provides a records storage service to offices that do not have file space for long term records. Because the Center has limited room for expansion, only records with retention periods of at least "C plus 2 years" will be accepted. In addition, "Active" records cannot be accepted because, by definition, these should be destroyed when they become inactive.

(a) Procedure for Using Records Center Services

(i) Consult the records schedule to make sure the material to be transferred is eligible for Records Center storage.

(ii) Call the Records Center and request the number of records transfer cartons needed - approximately two are required for each full file drawer of records. The Records Center will furnish transfer cartons and copies of the Records Transfer Form.

(iii) Follow instructions on the Records Transfer form for packing records, preparing the form, and delivering records to the Center.

(iv) Assuming the records are eligible for storage, a box number (which is also a shelf location number) will be assigned to each box, and the month and year the records are scheduled for destruction unless "permanent") will be shown on each box and on the Records Transfer form. One copy of the Transfer Form will be returned. Records received by the Center that are ineligible for storage will be returned to the sender, or will be destroyed if they have passed the authorized retention time.

(v) Accepted records will be held until their retention period expires. During this time, you may obtain reference or charge-out service by giving the box number and name of the record concerned.

(vi) When the destruction month arrives, a ten-day advance notice of the exact date destruction is to occur will be sent to the parent office. This gives the parent office a chance to notify the Center if a legal claim or legal action has arisen. If notice of a special legal claim or action is then given, it will be referred by the Center to the Legal Department, and, if confirmed, the destruction date will be postponed for one year. At the end of such year, the ten-day notice and postponement procedure will be repeated if the claim has not been settled.

(vii) In the event any record is released from the Record Center, such action shall be recorded. If the file or box has not been returned within six months, the Record Center shall automatically be absolved of further responsibility and the record may be placed in the Record Center only by following the procedure outlined in paragraphs (i) through (iv).

<u>Records in the Records Center will be destroyed when the authorized period has expired unless there is a specific claim or legal action pending</u>.

ENVIRONMENTAL PROTECTION AGENCY

40 CFR

7.85 Recipients of EPA assistance in the operation of programs or activities receiving such assistance beginning February 13, 1984.

To keep nondiscrimination compliance information.

Retention period: 3 years after completion of project or until complaint is resolved when any complaint or other action for alleged failure to comply with nondiscrimination provision is brought before the three year period ends.

26.115 Institutions conducting research involving human subjects conducted or otherwise subject to Federal regulations.

See 7 CFR 1c.115.

30.500 Persons awarded EPA grants, and contractors in excess of $10,000.

Grantee shall maintain books, records, documents, and other evidence and accounting procedures necessary to show (a) amount, receipt, and disposition of all assistance received for project, including non-Federal share, and (b) total costs of the project. Contractors of grantees shall maintain books, documents, papers, and records which are pertinent to specific EPA grants.

Retention period: 3 years except that (1) if any litigation, claim, or audit is started before the expiration of the 3-year period, the records shall be retained until all litigations, claims, or audit findings involving the records have been resolved, (2) records for nonexpendable property acquired with Federal funds shall be retained for 3 years after its final disposition, and (3) when records are transferred to or maintained by EPA, 3-year retention requirement is not applicable to the grantee. The 3-year retention period starts (i) from the date of submission of the final financial status report for project grants, or, for grants which are

awarded annually, from the date of the submission of the annual financial status report, (ii) from the date of approval of the final payment request for WWT works, and (iii) for such longer period, if any, as is required by the user charge system.

(i) If a grant is terminated completely or partially, the records relating to the work terminated shall be preserved and made available for a period of 3 years from the date of any resulting final termination settlement.

(ii) Records which relate to (a) appeals under the Subpart L—Disputes of this part, (b) litigation on the settlement of claims arising out of the performance of the project for which a grant was awarded, or (c) costs and expenses of the project to which exception has been taken by EPA or any of, it duly authorized representatives, shall be retained until any appeals, litigation, claims, or exceptions have been finally resolved.

30.900 Persons awarded EPA grants and contractors in excess of $10,000.

See 30.500.

31.20 State and local governments receiving Federal grants and cooperative agreements.

To maintain accounting records which adequately identify the source and application of funds provided for financially-assisted activities. These records must contain information pertaining to grant or subgrant awards and authorizations, obligations, unobligated balances, assets, liabilities, outlays or expenditures, and income.

Retention period: See 7 CFR 3016.2.

31.42 State and local governments receiving Federal grants and cooperative agreements.

To maintain records to comply with the requirements of 40 CFR 35.6700, 35.6705, and 35.6710 and requirements of source documentation described in 40 CFR 31.20(b)(6).

Retention period: 10 years following submission of the final Financial Status Report for the site, or until resolu-

Environmental Protection Agency

35.929-3 Persons awarded grants to assist in the construction of waste treatment works in compliance with the Clean Water Act.

To maintain records as are necessary to document compliance with regulations upon approval and implementing the user charge system.

Retention period: Not specified.

35.4066 Recipients of technical assistance grants under the Superfund Program.

To document all procurement activities with written records that furnish sufficient documentation for cost recovery purposes. In addition, to comply with the requirements regarding records described in 40 CFR 31.20, 35.6700, 35.6705, and 35.6710.

Retention period: See 40 CFR 35.4105.

35.4105 Recipients of technical assistance grants under the Superfund Program.

(a) To keep and preserve full written financial records accurately disclosing the amount and disposition of any funds; whether in cash or in-kind, applied to the technical assistance grant project.

Retention period: 10 years from date of final Financial Status Report or until any audit, litigation, cost-recovery and/or any disputes initiated before the end of the 10-year retention period are settled, whichever is longer.

(b) The recipient shall require its contractor(s) to keep and preserve detailed records in connection with the contract, reflecting acquisitions, work progress, reports, expenditures, and commitments and indicating their relationship to established costs and schedules.

Retention period: 10 years after the termination or end of the contract.

35.6250 Recipients of CERCLA-funded cooperative agreements and Superfund State Contracts.

(a) To maintain a recordkeeping system that consists of complete site-specific files containing documentation of costs incurred.

(b) To maintain records to comply with the requirements of 40 CFR 35.6700, 35.6705, and 35.6710 and requirements of source documentation described in 40 CFR 31.20(b)(6).

Retention period: 10 years following submission of the final Financial Status Report for the site, or until resolu-

35.6700

tion of all issues arising from litigation, claim, negotiation, audit, cost recovery, or other actions, whichever is later. Written approval must be obtained from the EPA award official before destroying any records.

35.6270 Recipients of CERCLA-funded cooperative agreements and Superfund State Contracts.

To maintain records that enable site specific documentation for cost recovery, as applicable, and provides sufficient documentation for cost recovery purposes. In addition, to comply with the requirements regarding records described in 40 CFR 31.20, 35.6700, 35.6705, and 35.6710.

35.6335 Recipients of CERCLA-funded cooperative agreements and Superfund State Contracts.

To maintain property records for CERCLA-funded property which include the contents specified in 40 CFR 35.6700.

35.6700 Recipients of CERCLA-funded cooperative agreements and Superfund State Contracts.

To maintain an administrative record consistent with section 113 of CERCLA, the National Contingency Plan, and relevant EPA policy and guidance. In addition:

(a) To maintain project records by site, activity, and operable unit, as applicable.

(b) To maintain property, financial and procurement records.

(c) To maintain time and attendance records and supporting documentation; documentation of compliance with statutes and regulations that apply to the project; and the number of site-specific technical hours spent to complete each pre-remedial product.

Retention period: 10 years following submission of the final Financial Status Report for the site, or until resolution of all issues arising from litigation, claim, negotiation, audit, cost recovery or other actions, whichever is later. Written approval must be obtained from the EPA award official before destroying any records.

35.6705 Recipients of CERCLA-funded cooperative agreements and Superfund State Contracts.

To maintain all financial and programmatic records, supporting documents, statistical records, and other records which are required by 40 CFR 35.6700, program regulations, or the cooperative agreement, or are otherwise reasonably considered as pertinent to program regulations or the cooperative agreement.

Retention period: 10 years following submission of the final Financial Status Report for the site, or until resolution of all issues arising from litigation, claim, negotiation, audit, cost recovery, or other actions, whichever is later. Written approval must be obtained from EPA award official before destroying any records.

35.6710 Recipients of CERCLA-funded cooperative agreements and Superfund State Contracts.

To maintain records as required by 40 CFR 35.6705. To also comply with records access requirements described in 40 CFR 31.36 (i)(10) and 31.42(e).

35.6815 States and political subdivisions of Indian Tribes; Cooperative Agreements and Superfund State Contracts for Superfund Responses Actions.

To maintain records on a site-specific basis. See also 40 CFR 35.6705 and 35.6710.

35.10035 Indian tribal governments receiving grants for environmental protection programs. [Added]

To document all procurement activities with written records that furnish reasons for decisions.

39.115 Persons applying for a loan guarantee for construction of treatment work.

(a) To maintain financial reports and records necessary to reflect the planned and actual receipt of revenue for repayment.
(b) To keep accurate books, records, and accounts relating to the loan, the loan guarantee, and the funds and accounts used to pay the amounts due on the loan.

Guide to Record Retention 1994

Retention period: (a) 3 years; (b) not specified.

51.102 States conducting public hearings on air pollution control implementation plans.

To maintain a record of each hearing. The record must contain, at a minimum, a list of witnesses together with the text of each presentation. Retention period: Not specified.

51.214 Owners or operators of each source subject to continuous emission monitoring and recording requirements.

To maintain a file of all pertinent information (emission measurements, continuous monitoring system, performance evaluations, calibration checks, and adjustments and maintenance performed on such monitoring systems) and other reports as required by 40 CFR part 51, appendix P. Retention period: 2 years following the date of collection of information.

51.359 States participating in the motor vehicle inspection and maintenance (I/M) programs.

To maintain quality control compliance records.

Part 51, Appendix P Owners or operators of affected facilities subject to continuous emission monitoring and recording requirements.

To maintain a file of all information reported in the quarterly summaries, and all other data collected either by the continuous monitoring system or as necessary to convert monitoring data to the units applicable standard. Retention period: For a minimum of two years from the date of collection of such data or submission of such summaries.

Part 52 Owners and operators of stationary sources emitting air pollutants for which a national standard is in effect.

See 51.214 and specific State plans.

Environmental Protection Agency

52.145 Owners or operators of fossil fuel-fired steam-generating equipment designated as Units 1, 2, and 3 at the Navajo Generating Station in the Northern Arizona Intrastate Air Quality Control Region.

To maintain records according to the procedures in 40 CFR 60.7.

52.535 Owner(s) or operator(s) of stationary sources of lead facilities.

To maintain continuous records of plant process and emission control operations as necessary to determine continuous compliance. Retention period: 2 years.

52.689 Owner(s) or operator(s) of the bunker limited smelters.

See 40 CFR 52.535.

52.741 Affected facilities; control strategy ozone control measures in certain counties in Illinois.

To maintain a copy of the results of the appropriate test methods and capture efficiency protocols. Retention period: 3 years.

52.741 Owners or operators of coating operations.

To maintain each day at the facility the following records on:
(a) The name and identification number of each coating as applied on each coating line;
(b) The weight of VOM per volume of each coating (minus water and any compounds which are specifically exempted from the definition of VOM) as applied each day on each coating line; and
(c) All records necessary to calculate the daily-weighted average VOM content from the coating line in accordance with the proposal submitted and other such information as specified in cited section.
Retention period: 3 years.

52.741 Owners or operators of paint or ink manufacturing plants.

(a) To keep at the plant records of leak when detected. Such records shall contain the date of detection and repair.
(d) Maintenance and inspection records for emission sources; and other such information as specified in cited section.
Retention period: 2 years from the date of each detection or each repair attempt.
Retention period: 3 years.

(a) The name and identification number of each coating and ink as applied on each printing line;
(b) The VOM content of each coating and ink as applied each day on each printing line;
(c) Any record showing violation of 40 CFR 52.741(h)(1)(i);
(d) Control device monitoring data;
(e) A log of operating time for the capture system, control device, monitoring equipment, and the associated printing line; and
(f) A maintenance log for the capture system, control device, and monitoring equipment detailing all routine and nonroutine maintenance performed including dates and duration of any outages.
Retention period: 3 years.

52.741 Owners or operators of pharmaceutical manufacturing facilities.

To maintain the following records on:
(a) Air pollution control parameters;
(b) Vapor pressure of VOM being controlled;
(c) For any leak which cannot be readily repaired within one hour after detection: (1) The name of the leaking equipment; (2) the date and time the leak is detected; (3) the action taken to repair the leak; and (4) the date and time the leak is repaired.
(d) Maintenance and inspection records for emission sources, and other such information as specified in cited section.
Retention period: 2 years.

52.741 Owners or operators of subject flexographic, packaging rotogravure or publication rotogravure printing lines.

To maintain each day for each coating line the following records on:
(a) To keep at the facility records necessary to demonstrate compliance with emission source requirements.
Retention period: 3 years.
(b) To maintain at the facility records necessary to demonstrate compliance with emission source requirements.
Retention period: 3 years.
(c) To maintain records which include (but are not limited to) the percent of water (by weight) in the paint and the quantity

Environmental Protection Agency

60.49b Owners or operators of industrial-commercial-institutional steam generating facilities.

(a) If monitoring of steam generating unit operating condition plan is approved, to maintain records of predicted nitrogen oxide emission rates, and the monitored operating conditions, including steam generating unit load, identified in the plan.

(b) To maintain records of the amounts of all fuels fired during each day and calculate the annual capacity factor individually for coal, distillate oil, residual oil, natural gas, wood, and municipal-type solid waste for each calendar year.

(c) To maintain records of the nitrogen content of the oil residual combusted in the affected facility and calculate the average fuel nitrogen content on a per calendar quarter basis.

(d) To maintain records of opacity for facilities subject to the opacity standards under 40 CFR 60.43b.
Retention period: 2 years following date of record.

(e) To maintain records on the calendar date, the average hourly nitrogen oxides emission rates measured or predicted and other information as specified in section cited for each steam generating unit operating day for facilities subject to nitrogen oxide standards under 40 CFR 60.44(b).

(f) To maintain records of the following information for each steam generating unit operating day: (1) Calendar date; (2) the number of hours of operation; and (3) a record of the hourly steam load.

60.56a Owners or operators of affected facilities located within large municipal waste combustor (MWC) plants.
To maintain in a readily accessible location operating manual and records of training.

60.59a Owners or operators of affected facilities located within large municipal waste combustor (MWC) plants.
To maintain records on the calendar date, emission rates, and parameters measured using CEMS, annual performance tests conducted to determine compliance with the particulate matter, dioxin/furan and hydrogen chloride limits, and other such records as specified in section cited if subject to municipal waste combustor for organics acid gases, and nitrogen oxides.
Retention period: 2 years.

60.63 Owners or operators of Portland cement plants.
To maintain records of visible emissions.
Retention period: 2 years.

60.107 Owners or operators subject to the sulfur oxides emission standards.
To maintain all data and calibration from continuous monitoring systems located at the inlet and outlet to the control device, including the results of the daily drift tests and quarterly accuracy assessments, written procedures for the quality control program, and other such information as specified in cited section.
Retention period: At least 2 years following the date of measurement.

60.113a Owners or operators of volatile organic liquid storage vessels (including petroleum liquid storage vessels).
To maintain records of each gap measurement at the plant.
Retention period: 2 years following the date of measurement.

60.115b Owners or operators of volatile organic liquid storage vessels (including petroleum liquid storage vessels.)

(a) To maintain a record of each inspection performed identifying the storage vessel on which the inspection was performed; the date the vessel was inspected; and the observed condition of each component of the control equipment (seals, internal floating roof, and fittings).
Retention period: At least 2 years.

(b) To keep a record of each gap measurement performed as required by 40 CFR 60.113(b).
Retention period: 2 years.

(c) After installing control equipment in accordance with 40 CFR 60.112b(a)(3) or (b)(1) (closed vent system and control device other than a flare), to keep a copy of the operating plan and record of the measured values of Magie oil, glycol, and other solvents in the ink being produced.
Retention period: 3 years.

52.741 Owners or operators of non-CTG sources-exempt emission sources.
To maintain the following information at the facility:
(a) Control devices monitoring data;
(b) A log of operating time for the capture system, control device, monitoring equipment and the associated emission source; and
(c) A maintenance log for the capture system, control device and monitoring equipment detailing all routine and non-routine maintenance performed including dates and duration of any outages.
Retention period: 3 years.

52.1113 Owners or operators of stationary sources.
See 40 CFR 52.535.

52.1224 Owners or operators of stationary sources.
See 40 CFR 52.535.

52.1277 Owners or operators of stationary sources.
See 40 CFR 52.535.

52.1324 Owners or operators of stationary sources.
See 40 CFR 52.535.

52.1378 Owners or operators of stationary sources.
See 40 CFR 52.535.

52.1473 Owners or operators of stationary sources.
See 40 CFR 52.535.

52.1574 Owners or operators of stationary sources.
See 40 CFR 52.535.

53.9 Applicants offering analyzers for sale as ambient air monitoring or equivalent methods.
To maintain an accurate and current list of the names and mailing addresses of all ultimate purchasers of such analyzer.
Retention period: 2 years following date of such records.

Guide to Record Retention 1994

57.404 Primary nonferrous smelter owners.
To maintain records of the air quality measurements made, meterological information acquired, emission curtailment ordered (including the identity of the persons making such decisions), and calibration and maintenance performed on SCS (supplementary control system) during the operation of the SCS.
Retention period: Duration of the NSO.

60.7 Owners or operators of any building, structure, facility, or installation emitting air pollutants.
To maintain records of the occurrence and duration of any startup, shutdown, or malfunction in operation of any affected facility, any malfunction of the air pollution control equipment, or any periods during which a continuous monitoring system or device is inoperative; a file of all measurements, including monitoring and performance testing measurements; performance, evaluation; and any other records which may be required by applicable subparts.
Retention period: 2 years.

60.23 States adopting plans for control of designated facilities.
To maintain a record of each public hearing for inspection by any interested party.
Retention period: 2 years.

60.48c Owners or operators of affected facilities subject to the sulfur dioxide emission limits, fuel oil sulfur limits, or percent reduction requirements.
To keep records, as applicable, on control devices; excess emission; results of emission tests, fuel sampling and analysis results; date of construction or reconstruction; anticipated startup and actual startup; fuel supplier certification; and fuel combusted during each day; amounts of each other such information as specified in cited section.
Retention period: 2 years following date of such records.

60.116b

of the parameters monitored in accordance with 40 CFR 60.113b(c)(2).

(a) To keep readily accessible records showing the dimension of the storage vessel and an analysis showing the capacity of the storage vessel.

Retention period: For the life of the source.

(b) To maintain a record of the VOL stored, the period of storage, and the maximum true vapor pressure of that VOL during the respective storage period.

Retention period: At least 2 years.

60.153 Owners or operators of sewage treatment plants.

(a) To maintain for incinerators equipped with a wet scrubbing device, records of the measured pressure drop of the gas flow through wet scrubbing.

(b) To maintain records of the measured oxygen content of the incinerator exhaust gas.

(c) To maintain records of the rate of sludge charged to the incinerator, the measured temperatures of the incinerator, and the fuel flow to the incinerator, and the total solids and volatile solids content of the sludge charged to the incinerator.

Retention period: 2 years.

60.223 Owners or operators of any granular diammonium phosphate plants.

To maintain a daily record of equivalent P₂O₅ feed by first determining the total mass rate in metric ton/hr. of phosphorus-bearing feed using a flow monitoring device and proceeding according to 40 CFR 60.224(b)(3).

60.233 Owners or operators of any triple superphosphate plants.

See 40 CFR 60.233.

60.243 Owners or operators of any granular triple superphosphate storage facilities.

See 40 CFR 60.223.

Guide to Record Retention 1994

60.116b Owners or operators of volatile organic liquid storage vessels (including petroleum liquid storage vessels).

60.265 Owners or operators of electric submerged arc furnaces.

To maintain a permanent record fo the fan performance curve (prepared for a specific temperature).

Retention period: 2 years.

60.273 Owners or operators of facilities in steel plants that produce carbon, alloy, or specialty steels: Electric arc furnaces and dust-handling systems.

To maintain records of any 6-minute average that is in excess of the emission limit specified in 40 CFR 60.272(a).

Retention period: 2 years.

60.274a Owners or operators of steel plants that produce carbon, alloy, or specialty steels: Electric arc furnaces and dust-handling systems.

To maintain data on monitoring, measurement, and monthly operational status.

Retention period: 2 years.

60.276a Owners or operators of steel plants that produce carbon, alloy, or specialty steels: Electric arc furnaces, argon-oxygen decarburization vessels, and dust-handling systems.

To maintain records of measurements required in 40 CFR 60.274a.

Retention period: 2 years.

60.310 Owners or operators of affected facilities in metal furniture surface coating operations in which organic coatings are applied.

To keep purchase or inventory records and other data necessary to substantiate annual coating usage.

Retention period: 2 years.

60.343 Owners or operators of lime manufacturing plants.

To maintain records of any 6-month average that is in excess of the emissions specified in 40 CFR 60.342.

Retention period: Not specified.

60.344 Owners or operators of lime manufacturing plants.

See 60.343.

Environmental Protection Agency

60.434 Owners or operators of affected facilities using waterborne ink systems or solvent-borne ink systems with solvent recovery system.

To maintain records on the amount of solvent and water used, solvent recovered, and estimated emission percentage for each performance averaging period.

Retention period: 2 years.

60.445 Owners or operators of affected facilities controlled by pressure sensitive tape and label surface coating devices.

(a) To maintain records of all coatings used, the results of the reference test method or the manufacturer's formulation data used for determining, the VOC content of those coatings.

(b) To maintain records of the amount of solvent applied in the coating at each affected facility.

(c) To maintain records of the amount of solvent recovered by the monitoring device.

(d) To maintain records of the amount of solvent applied in the coating at the facility.

(e) To maintain records of the measurements required by sections 60.443 and 60.445.

Retention period: (a)-(c) 1 month; (d) 12 months; and (e) 2 years.

60.455 Owners or operators of affected facilities in surface coating operation in large appliance surface coating operations.

(a) To maintain records of all data and calculations used to determine VOC emissions from each affected facility.

(b) Where compliance is achieved through the use of thermal incineration, to maintain records of the incinerator combustion chamber temperature.

(c) If catalytic incineration is used, to maintain source daily records of the gas temperature, both upstream and downstream of the incinerator catalyst bed.

(d) Where compliance is achieved through the use of a solvent recovery system, to maintain records of the amount of solvent recov-

60.495

ered by the system for each affected facility.

Retention period: Not specified.

60.465 Owners or operators of affected facilities in metal surface coating operations.

(a) To maintain records of all data and calculations used to determine monthly VOC emissions from each affected facility and to determine the monthly emission limit, where applicable.

(b) Where compliance is achieved through the use of thermal incineration, to maintain source daily records of the gas temperature, both upstream and downstream of the incinerator catalyst bed.

Retention period: Not specified.

60.473 Owners or operators of affected facilities in asphalt processing and asphalt roofing manufacture operations.

To maintain a file of the monitoring results of the temperature of the gas at the inlet of the control device.

Retention period: 2 years.

60.486 Owners or operators of affected leaks in the VOC in the synthetic organic chemicals manufacturing industries.

(a) To keep records of equipment leaks (equipment identification information, dates of leaks, and repair methods.

(b) To keep records on design requirements for closed vent systems and control devices and equipments and valves.

Retention period: 2 years.

60.495 Owners or operators of affected facilities in the beverage can surface coating industries.

(a) To maintain records of all data and calculations used to determine VOC emissions from each affected facility in the initial and monthly performance tests.

(b) To maintain daily records of the incinerator combustion chamber temperature where compliance is achieved through the use of thermal incineration.

(c) To maintain daily records of the gas temperature, both upstream and downstream of the incinerator catalyst bed if catalytic incineration is used.

(d) To maintain daily records of the amount of solvent recovered by the system for each affected facility where compliance is achieved through the use of a solvent recovery system.
Retention period: Not specified.

60.505 Owners or operators of bulk gasoline terminals.

(a) To maintain tank truck vapor tightness documentation.
Retention period: Permanent.

(b) To maintain records of each monthly leak inspection and to keep documentation of all notifications to owners or operators of each nonvapor-tight gasoline tank truck loaded at the affected facility.
Retention period: At least 2 years.

(c) To keep records of all replacements or additions of components performed on an existing vapor processing system.
Retention period: At least 2 years.

60.537 Accredited laboratories testing new residential wood heaters.

To maintain records of all documentation pertaining to each certification test, including the full test report and raw data sheets, technician notes, calculations, and tests results for test runs.
Retention period: For at least 5 years.

60.537 Commercial owners who sell used residential wood heaters (stoves).

To maintain records of the names and addresses of the previous owners.
Retention period: At least 5 years.

60.537 Manufacturers of new residential wood heaters.

To maintain records of certification testing data, quality assurance (QA) program results, production volumes and information needed to support a request for a waiver or exemption.
Retention period: For at least 5 years.

Guide to Record Retention 1994

60.545 Owners or operators of undertread cementing operations, sidewall cementing operations, green tire spraying operations where organic solvent-sprays are used or Michelin-B operations that use carbon absorbers.

To maintain continuous records of the organic concentration level of the carbon bed exhaust.
Retention period: 2 years.

60.545 Owners or operators of affected facilities that use catalytic incinerators in the rubber tire manufacturing industries.

To maintain continuous records of the temperature before and after the catalyst bed for catalytic incinerators.
Retention period: 2 years.

60.545 Owners or operators of affected facilities that use thermal incinerators in the rubber tire manufacturing industries.

To maintain continuous records of the thermal incinerator combustion temperature.
Retention period: 2 years.

60.545 Owners or operators of undertread cementing operations, sidewall cementing operations, green tire spraying operations where organic solvent-based sprays are used, Michelin-A operations, Michelin-B operations, or Michelin-C automatic operations seeking to comply with specified kg/mo uncontrolled VOC use limit.

To maintain records of monthly VOC use and the number of days in each compliance period.
Retention period: 2 years.

60.545 Owners or operators of affected facilities in the rubber tire manufacturing industries required to conduct monthly performance tests as required by 40 CFR 60.543(b)(1).

To maintain records of the results of the monthly tests.
Retention period: 2 years.

60.625 Owners or operators of affected facilities in the petroleum dry cleaner operations.

To maintain records of the performance tests for measuring the flow rate of recovery solvent.
Retention period: Not specified.

60.635 Owners or operators of affected facilities in onshore natural gas processing plants.

To maintain pressure relief devices leak repair information in a log in a readily accessible location.
Retention period: 2 years.

Environmental Protection Agency

60.545 Owners or operators of tread end cementing operation and green tire spraying operation using water-based cements or sprays containing less than 1.0 percent by weight of VOC.

To maintain records of formulation data or the results of Method 24 analysis conducted to verify the VOC contents of the spray.
Retention period: Not specified.

60.565 Owners or operators of polypropylene, polyethylene, poly(ethylene terephthalate) and poly(ethylene) manufacturing plants.

To maintain up-to-date, readily accessible records of the performance tests and other such information as specified in cited section.
Retention period: 2 years.

60.615 Owners or operators of new, modified, and reconstruction air oxidation facilities.

To keep up-to-date, readily accessible continuous records of (a) the equipment operating parameters specified to be monitored under 40 CFR 60.613(a) and (c) as well as up-to-date, readily accessible records of periods of operation during which the parameter boundaries established during the most recent performance data are exceeded; (b) the flow indication specified under 40 CFR 60.613(a)(2), 60.613(b)(2), 60.613(c)(1), and (c) records of all periods when the vent stream is diverted from the control device or has no flow rate; and other such records as specified in cited section.

60.647 Owners or operators of affected facilities that process natural gas; Sulfur dioxide emissions.

To maintain records of the calculations and measurements required by the standards for sulfur dioxide and operation monitoring of emission and operation requirements.
Retention period: 2 years following the date of the measurements.

60.665 Owners or operators of new, modified, and reconstituted distillation facilities.

See 40 CFR 60.615.

60.684 Owners or operators of wool fiberglass insulation manufacturing plants.

To maintain records of measurements required to comply with the mass emission standards.
Retention period: 2 years.

60.697 Owners or operators of petroleum refinery wastewater systems.

To maintain records of (a) the design and operating specifications for all equipment used to comply to applicable standards in a readily accessible locations; (b) each inspection where a water seal is dry or breached, a cap or plug is out of place, emissions are detected, or a problem is identified, including information about the repairs or corrective action taken; (c) for facilities using a thermal incinerator, continuous records must be maintained of the temperature of the gas stream in combustion zone of the incinerator. Also, to maintain records of all 3-hour periods during which the average temperature of the gas stream in the combustion zone of the thermal incinerator is more than 28 degree C (50 degree F) below the temperature; and other such records as specified in cited section.
Retention period: 2 years unless otherwise noted.

60.705 Owners or operators complying with the volatile organic compound (VOC) emissions from the synthetic organic chemical manufacturing industry (SOCMI) reactor processes.
[Added]

To keep an up-to-date, readily accessible record (a) of the data measured...

during each performance test; (b) of the equipment operating parameters specified to be monitored as well as up-to-date readily records of periods of operation during which the parameter boundaries established during the most recent performance test are exceeded; and other records as specified in cited section.

60.714 Owners or operators of affected coating operations or affected coating mix preparation equipments.

To maintain records of the monthly weighted average mass of VOC contained in the coating per volume of coating solids applied to each coating.

Retention period: 2 years following the date of the measurements and calculations.

60.724 Owners or operators of facilities that surface coat plastic parts for business machines.

To maintain at the source, records of all data and calculations used to determine monthly VOC emissions from each coating.

Retention period: For a period of at least 2 years.

60.735 Owners or operators of calciner and dryer at mineral processing plants.

To maintain a record, once each day, from the recording of the monitoring devices and arithmetic average over a 2-hour period of both the change in pressure of the gas stream across the scrubber and the flowrate of the scrubbing liquid.

Retention period: 2 years.

60.744 Owners or operators of new, modified and reconstructed facilities that perform polymeric coating of supporting substrates.

To maintain records of the measurements and calculations required in 40 CFR 60.743 and 60.744.

Retention period: For at least 2 years following the date of the measurements and calculations.

60.747 Owners or operators of new, modified and reconstructed facilities that perform polymeric coating of supporting substrates.

To retain records of all measurements from the CEM as required by 40 CFR 60.7.

Retention period: At least 2 years.

Part 60, Appendix F Owners or operators of any building, structure, facility, or installation emitting air pollutants.

Retention period: At least 2 years.

Part 60, Appendix G Plant owners or operators; Newton Power Stations of Central Illinois Public Service Co. [Added]

(a) To maintain record of each hourly SO_2 CEMs value and hourly flow rate value, and each hourly Btu heat input rate, hourly steam rate, or hourly electrical power output, and a record of each hourly weighted average emission rate.

Retention period: For all periods of operation of Unit 1 or 2 under provisions of 40 CFR 60.43(e), including operations of DAFGDS startup, shutdown, and malfunction when HI and EI are assumed to be zero (0).

(b) To keep a record of each hourly gas flow rate through DAPGOSstack, each hourly stack gas flow rate through the bypass stack during any period that the DAFGDS bypass is opened or flow is indicated, and reason for bypass operation.

Guide to Record Retention 1994

61.25 Owners or operators of underground uranium mines.

To maintain records documenting the source of input parameters including the results of all measurements upon which they are based, the calculations and/or analytical methods used to derive values for input parameters, and the procedure used to determine compliance. In addition, the documentation should be sufficient to allow an independent auditor to verify the accuracy of the determination made concerning the facility's compliance with the standard.

Retention period: 5 years and records must be made available for inspection by the Administrator or his authorized representative.

61.33 Owners or operators of any stationary sources emitting hazardous pollutants for which a national standard is in effect.

To maintain record of emission test results from stack sampling needed to determine total emissions, as specified in the sections cited.

Retention period: 2 years.

61.34 Owners or operators of any stationary sources emitting hazardous pollutants for which a national standard is in effect.

To maintain records of concentrations at all sampling sites and other data needed to determine such concentrations.

Retention period: 2 years.

61.43 Owners or operators of rocket motor test sites.

Retention period: 2 years.

61.44 Owners or operators of rocket motor test sites.

To retain records of air sampling test results and other data needed to determine integrated intermittent concentrating.

Retention period: 2 years.

Environmental Protection Agency

61.53 Owners or operators of any stationary sources which process mercury ore to recover mercury, use mercury chlor-alkali cells to produce chlorine gas and alkali metal hydroxide, and incinerate or dry wastewater treatment plant sludge.

To maintain records of emission test results and other data needed to determine total emissions.

Retention period: 2 years.

61.54 Owners or operators of sludge incineration plants, sludge drying plants, etc.

(a) To maintain daily records of all of the emission monitoring.

Retention period: 2 years.

(b) To maintain at the chlor-alkali plant records of the certifications and calibrations.

Retention period: Certification- For as long as the device is used for this purpose. Calibration- For a minimum of 2 years.

(c) To maintain records of all leaks and spills of mercury.

61.55 Owners or operators of mercury-cell chlor-alkali plants.

To maintain records of sludge, sampling, charging rate determination and other data needed to determine mercury content of wastewater treatment plant sludges.

Retention period: 2 years.

61.67 Owners or operators of plants which produce vinyl chloride.

To maintain records of emission test results and other data needed to determine mine emissions.

Retention period: 3 years.

61.70 Owners or operators of plants which produce vinyl chloride.

To maintain records of all data, needed to determine average emissions.

Retention period: 3 years.

61.71 Owners or operators of plants which produce vinyl chloride.

To maintain records of: (a) The leaks detected by the vinyl chloride monitoring system; (b) leaks detected during routine monitoring with the portable hydrocarbon detector and the action

taken to repair the leaks; and (c) emission monitoring. To also keep a daily operating record for each polyvinyl chloride reactor, including pressures and temperatures.
Retention period: 3 years.

61.124 Owners or operators of calciners and nodulizing kilns at elemental phosphorus plants.
See 40 CFR 61.25.

61.126 Owners or operators of elemental phosphorus plants subject to national emission standards for radionuclide emissions.
To maintain continuous measurement recordings of the primary and secondary current and the voltage in each electric field when using an electrostatic precipitator control device.
Retention period: For a minimum of 5 years.

61.138 Owners or operators of coke by-product recovery plants.
(a) To maintain records pertaining to the design of control equipment installed to comply with 40 CFR 61.132 through 61.134.
(b) To maintain records pertaining to sources subject to 40 CFR 61.132 and 61.133. Such records shall contain the date of the inspection and the name of the inspector; a brief description of each visible defect in the source or control equipment and the method and date of repair of the defect; the date of repair of the leak; and a brief description of any system abnormalities found during the annual maintenance inspection, the annual maintenance inspection, the repairs made, the date of attempted repair, and the date of actual repair.
Retention period: 2 years following each semiannual (and other) inspection and each annual maintenance inspection.

61.139 Owners and operators of coke by-product recovery plants (National emission standards for hazardous air pollutants for benzene emissions from coke).
To maintain records on design, operation, testing and monitoring to assure that each add-on control device used as

alternative mean of complying with the standards of process vessels, storage tanks and intercepting sumps achieves emission reductions equivalent to gas blanketing.
Retention period: (a) Control device: for the life of the control device; (b) for carbon adsorber and vapor incinerator for the life of the control device; (c) vapor incinerator, the average firebox temperature of the incinerator (or the average temperature upstream and downstream of the catalyst bed for a catalytic incinerator), measured and averaged over the most recent compliance test shall be recorded for at least 2 years or until the most recent compliance test on the incinerator, whichever is longer; (d) carbon adsorber—the date of the determination of the maximum concentration point, and the data needed to make the determination shall be recorded for at least 2 years or until the next maximum concentration point determination on the carbon adsorber, whichever is longer; and (e) carbon adsorber and vapor incinerator monitoring records—2 years.

61.142 Owners or operators of asbestos mills.
To maintain records of the results of visible emission monitoring and air cleaning device inspections.
Retention period: 2 years.

61.144 Manufacturers of operations using commercial asbestos.
See 40 CFR 61.142.

61.145 Owners or operators of asbestos demolition and renovation operations.
To keep daily temperature records during periods when wetting operations are suspended due to freezing temperature. The owner or operator must record the temperature in the area containing the facility components at the beginning, middle, and end of each workday.
Retention period: 2 years.

61.147 Owners or operators of demolition and renovation operations-asbestos emission control.
See 40 CFR 61.142.

61.149 Owners or operators of asbestos mills.
(a) To keep records temperatures recorded at hourly intervals, during periods when wetting operations are suspended.
Retention period: At least 2 years in a form suitable for inspection.
(b) To retain a copy of all waste shipment records, including a copy of the waste shipment record signed by the owner or operator of the designated waste disposal site.
Retention period: 2 years.
See 40 CFR 61.149.

61.150 Owners or operators of asbestos manufacturing, fabricating, demolition, renovation, and spraying operations.
Retention period: 2 years.

61.154 Owners or operators of active waste disposal sites receiving asbestos-containing waste material.
(a) To maintain waste shipment records.
Retention period: 2 years.
(b) To maintain records of the location, depth and area, and quantity in cubic meters (cubic yards) of asbestos-containing waste material within the disposal site on a map or diagram of the disposal area.
Retention period: Until closure.

61.155 Owners or operators of operations that convert regulated asbestos-containing material (RACM) into nonasbestos (asbestos-free) material.
To maintain on-site records of (a) the results of start-up performance testing and all subsequent performance testing, including operating parameters, feed characteristic, and analyses of output materials; (b) results of the composite analyses required during the initial 90 days of operation; (c) results of the monthly composite analyses; (d) results of continuous monitoring and logs of process operating parameters; (e) the information on waste shipments received; and (f) for output materials where no analyses were performed to determine the presence of asbestos, records of the name and location of the purchaser or disposal site to which the

output materials were sold or deposited, and the date of sale or disposal.
Retention period: 2 years.

61.165 Owners or operators of glass melting furnaces which use commercial arsenic as raw materials.
To maintain records to meet the emission limit requirements.
Retention period: 2 years.

61.176 Owners or operators of copper converters.
To maintain records of the visual inspections, maintenance, and repairs performed on each secondary hood systems.
Retention period: 2 years.

61.185 Owners or operators of arsenic trioxide and metal arsenic production facilities.
To maintain records of all measurements, maintenance and repairs made to the continuous monitoring system or monitoring device, ambient concentrations at all sampling sites, other data needed to determine such concentrations and other information as specified in section cited.
Retention period: 2 years.

61.209 Owners or operators of phosphogypsum stacks.
(a) To maintain records for each stack documenting the procedure used to verify compliance with the flux standard including all measurements, calculations, and analytical methods on which input parameters were based. The required documentation shall be sufficient to allow an independent auditor to verify the correctness of the determination made concerning compliance of the stack with flux standard.
(b) To maintain records documenting the procedures used to determine the average radium - 226 concentration, including all measurements, calculations, and analytical methods on which input parameters were based, and other such information as specified in cited section.
Retention period: For at least 5 years from the date of use of the phosphogypsum.

61.224

Owners and operators of all sites that are used for the disposal of uranium mill tailings.

See 40 CFR 61.25.

61.246

Owners or operators of sources intended to operate in volatile hazardous air pollutant (VHAP) service.

(a) To keep records in a log of each leak as specified in 40 CFR 61.242-2, 61.242-3, 61.242-7.

Retention period: 2 years.

(b) To maintain records, in a log, pertaining to all equipment subject to the requirements in 40 CFR 61.242-1 to 40 CFR 61.242-11 and all other records as specified in cited section.

61.255

Owners or operators of facilities byproduct materials during and following the processing of uranium ores, commonly referred to as uranium mills and their associated tailings.

See 40 CFR 61.25

61.276

Owners or operators with a storage vessel subject to the national emission standard for benzene emissions.

(a) To keep readily accessible records showing the dimensions of the storage vessel and an analysis showing the capacity of the storage vessel.

Retention period: As long as the storage vessel is in operation.

(b) To keep records pertaining to closed vent system and control devices in a readily accessible location.

Retention period: 2 years.

61.305

Owners or operators of affected facilities subject to the standards for benzene waste operations and benzene transfer operations.

To maintain an up-to-date readily accessible records of data measured during the performance test, equipment operating parameters, and flare pilot flame monitoring.

Retention period: 2 years from the date the information is recorded.

61.356

Owners or operators of facilities subject to the standards for benzene waste operations. [Amended]

(a) To maintain records that identify each waste stream (records shall include all test results, measurements, calculations, and other necessary documentation).

(b) To maintain documentation for each waste shipment that includes the date waste is shipped offsite, quantity of waste shipped offsite, name and address of the facility receiving the waste, and a copy of the notice sent with the waste shipment.

(c) To maintain engineering design documentation for all control equipment that is installed on the waste management unit, and other such information as specified in cited section.

Retention period: (a) and (b) 2 years from the date the information is recorded unless otherwise specified. (c) For the life of the control equipment.

62.4622

Owners or operators of stationary sources emitting air pollutants for which a national standard is in effect.

To maintain records of the nature and amounts of emissions from such source and any other information as may be deemed necessary to determine whether such source is in compliance with applicable emission limitations or other control measures that are part of the plan.

Retention period: 2 years.

63.324

Owners or operators of dry cleaning facilities. [Added]

To keep (a) receipts of perchloroethylene purchases and log on site of the volume of perchloroethylene purchased each month by the dry cleaning facility as recorded from perchloroethylene purchases; If no perchloroethylene is purchased during a given month then the owner or operator would enter zero gallons into the log; (b) the calculation and result of the yearly perchloroethylene consumption determined on the first day of each month; (c) the date when the dry system components are inspected for perceptible leaks and the name or location or dry cleaning system components where perceptible leaks are de-

Guide to Record Retention 1994

70.4

Permittees; State Operating Permit Programs.

To maintain documentation for those changes.

70.6

Permittees; State Operating Permit Programs.

To keep a record describing changes made at the source that result in emissions of a regulated air pollutant subject to an applicable requirement, but not otherwise regulated under the permit, and the emissions resulting from those changes.

72.7

New utility units serving one or more generators with total nameplate capacity of 25 MWe or less and burns only fuels with a sulfur content of 0.05 percent or less under the Acid Rain Program; exemption. [Added]

To retain at the source that includes the unit, records of the results of the tests performed and a copy of the purchase agreements for the fuel stating the sulfur content of such fuel.

Retention period: 5 years.

72.9

Owners and operators of the source and each affected source under the Acid Rain Program. [Added]

To maintain on site at the source (a) the certificate of representation for the designated representative for the source and each affected unit at the source and all documents that demonstrate the truth of the statements in the certificate of representation: (b) all emission monitoring information in accordance with 40 CFR part 75; (c) copies of all reports, compliance certifications, and other submissions and all records made or require; and any other information as specified in cited section.

Environmental Protection Agency

tected; (d) the dates of repair and date the document is created; This period of written or verbal orders for repair parts to demonstrate compliance and other such information as specified in cited section.

Retention period: 5 years.

Retention period: 5 years from the date the document is created. This period may be extended for cause, at any time, prior to the end of 5 years; in writing by the Administrator or permitting authority. The certificate of representation and documents shall be retained on site at the source beyond such 5 years period until such documents are superseded because of the submission of a new certificate of representation, changing the designated representative.

73.75

Applicants for and holders of independent power producer written guarantees for SO₂ allowances.

(a) *Applicants.* To maintain copies of the $750 written offers to Phase I utilities, any responses to such offers, and copies of documents showing the project milestones.

(b) *Holders.* To retain copies of bids in the annual auctions and any written offers made of other allowance holders.

73.82

Applicants for conservation and renewable energy reserve allowances. [Added]

To maintain a file of all measurements, data, reports, and other information as specified in cited section.

Retention period: 3 years.

75.50

Owners or operators of affected sources subject to continuous emission monitoring requirements. [Added]

To maintain records of verification of energy savings.

Retention period: 3 years. The Administrator may extend this period for cause by notifying the applicant in writing.

75.51

Owners or operators of affected sources subject to continuous emission monitoring requirements. [Added]

To maintain specific SO₂ emission records for units with qualifying Phase I technology; specific parametric data record for calculating substitute emissions data for units with add-on emission controls; and specific NOₓ emission records for gas-fired peaking units or oil-fired peaking units using optional protocol.

75.52

Retention period: See 40 CFR 72.50.

75.52 Owners or operators of affected sources subject to continuous emission monitoring requirements. [Added]

To maintain certification, quality assurance and quality control records. Retention period: 6 months.

80.7 Refiners, distributors, and retailers of gasoline.

To maintain information on bulk shipments and annual gallonage sales of unleaded gasoline as specified in section.

Retention period: See 40 CFR 75.50.

80.27 Distributors, resellers, carriers, retailers, and wholesale purchaser-consumers of gasoline and alcohol blends volatility.

To maintain each invoice, loading ticket, bill lading, delivery ticket and other documents which accompany the shipment of such gasoline. Such documents shall be available for inspection by the Administrator or authorized representative during such period. Retention period: 1 year.

82.13 Producers of Class I controlled substances (ozone depleting chemicals) during control period. [Revised]

To maintain the following records:
(a) Dated records of the quantity of each control substance produced at each facility;
(b) Dated records of the quantity of controlled substances produced for use in processes that result in their transformation or for use in processes that result in their destruction and quantity sold for use in processes that result in their transformation or for use in processes that result in their destruction;
(c) Copies of invoices or receipts documenting sales of controlled substance for use in processes resulting in destruction;
(d) Dated records of the quantity of each controlled substance used at each facility as feedstocks or destroyed in the manufacture of any substance, or in the manufacture of any substance, and any controlled substance introduced into the production process of the same

controlled substance at each facility; and all other records as specified in cited section. Retention period: 3 years.

82.13 Importers of Class I controlled substance (ozone depleting chemicals). [Revised]

To maintain the following records:
(a) The quantity of each controlled substance imported, either alone or in mixtures, including the percentage of each mixture which consists of a controlled substance;
(b) The quantity of controlled substances other than transhipments or used or recycled substances imported for use in processes resulting in their transformation or destruction and quantity sold for use in processes that result in their destruction or transformation;
(c) The date on which the controlled substances were imported;
(d) The commodity code for the controlled substances shipped;
(e) The importer number for the shipment;
(f) A copy of the bill of lading for the import;
(g) The invoice for the import;
(h) Dated records documenting the sale or transfer of controlled substances for use in process resulting in transformation or destruction; and other such records as specified in cited section. Retention period: 3 years.

82.13 Persons transshipping controlled substances. [Revised]

To maintain records that indicate that the controlled substance shipment originated in one country destined for another country, and does not enter interstate commerce with the U.S. Retention period: 3 years.

82.166 Persons requesting additional production allowances or consumption allowances or who transform or destroy Class I controlled substances not produced by them. [Revised]

To maintain dated records of the quantity and level of controlled substances used and entirely consumed in the manufacture of another chemical; the mass of waste products. Retention period: 3 years unless otherwise indicated.

Guide to Record Retention 1994

menting the sale of the controlled substance to the person; dated records of the names, commercial use, and quantities of the resulting chemical(s); dated records of shipments to purchasers of the resulting chemical(s); addresses of the resulting chemical(s); and other such information as specified in cited section. Retention period: 3 years.

82.42 Persons who own approved refrigerated recycling equipment certified under 40 CFR 82.36(a)(2).

To maintain records of the name and address of any facility to which refrigerant is sent. Retention period: 3 years.

82.65 Persons selling or distributing or offering to sell or distribute emission reductions and non-essential products. [Added]

To retain proof that such product was manufactured and placed into initial inventory before the relevant specified date. Such proof may take the form of shipping forms, lot numbers, manufacture date stamps, invoices or equivalent business records. Retention period: Not specified.

82.166 Persons disposing of small appliances MVAC and MVAC-like appliances. [Added]

To maintain copies of signed statement verifying that the refrigerant has been evacuated from the appliances previously. Retention period: 3 years unless otherwise indicated.

82.166 Reclaimers; class I and class I substance for use as a refrigerant. [Added]

To maintain records of the quantity of material sent to them for reclamation, the mass of refrigerant reclaimed, and the mass of waste products. Retention period: 3 years unless otherwise indicated.

Environmental Protection Agency 85.1403

82.166 Programs certifying technicians; class I or class II substance for use as a refrigerant. [Added]

To maintain records which include but are not limited to the names and addresses of all individuals taking the test, and scores of all certification tests administered, and the dates and locations of all tests administered. Retention period: 3 years.

82.166 Owners/operators of appliances normally containing 50 or more pounds of refrigerant. [Added]

(a) To keep servicing records documenting the date and type of service, as well as the date(s) when refrigerant is added.
(b) To keep records of refrigerated purchased and added to such appliances in cases where owners add their own refrigerant. Such records should indicate the date(s) when refrigerant is added. Retention period: 3 years unless otherwise indicated.

82.166 Approved equipment testing organizations; class I or class II substance for use as a refrigerant. [Added]

To maintain records of equipment testing and performance and a list of equipment that meets EPA requirements. Retention period: 3 years, unless otherwise indicated.

82.166 Persons selling or distributing any class I or class II substance for use as a refrigerant. [Added]

To maintain invoices that indicate the name of the purchaser, the date of sale, and the quantity of refrigerant purchased. Retention period: 3 years unless otherwise indicated.

Part 82, Subpart F, Appendix D Certifying programs for technicians. [Added]

See 40 CFR 82.166.

85.1403 Operators of pre-1994 model year urban buses effective at time of engine rebuild or engine replacement. [Added]

To keep records of all engine rebuilds and replacement performed on urban

85.1404

buses as required by 40 CFR 85.1404 and to maintain evidence that urban buses are in compliance with applicable requirements.

85.1404 Operators of 1993 and earlier model year (MY) urban buses whose engines are rebuilt or replaced after Jan. 1, 1995. [Added]

(a) To keep all purchase records, receipts, and part numbers for parts and components used in the rebuilding of urban bus engines.

(b) To keep individual records containing a brief history of each urban bus subject to the rebuild provisions.

(c) To maintain fuel purchase records consisting of all purchase records of fuels for which the operator is claiming additional emission reductions; purchase records for fuels, other than diesel fuel, which are used with dual-fueled engines.

Retention period: Until the 5 year anniversary of a rebuild or until the engine is rebuilt again, whichever occurs first.

85.1412 Retrofit/rebuild equipment certifiers. [Added]

To maintain the following adequately organized and index records:

(a) Detailed production drawings showing all dimensions, tolerances, performance requirements and material specifications and any other information necessary to completely describe the equipment;

(b) All data obtained during testing of the equipment and subsequent analysis based on that data, including the mileage and the vehicle or engine configuration determinants;

(c) All information used in determining those vehicles or engine for which the equipment is represented as being equivalent from an emissions standpoint to the original equipment being replaced.

(d) A description of the quality control plan used to monitor production and assure compliance of the equipment with the applicable certification requirements;

(e) All data taken in implementing the quality control plan, and any subsequent analyses of that data; and

(f) All in-service data, analyses performed by the equipment certifier and correspondence with vendors, distributors, consumers, retail outlets or engine manufacturers regarding any design, production or in-service problems associated with 25 or more pieces of any certified equipment.

Retention period: 5 years from the date of certification.

85.1507 Certificate holders importing nonconforming motor vehicles and motor vehicle engines into the U.S.

To maintain adequately organized and index records, correspondence and other documents relating to the certification, modification, test, purchase, sale, storage, registration and importation of that vehicle or engine, including but not limited to specified information required in section cited.

Retention period: 6 years from the date of entry of a nonconforming vehicle or engine imported by the certificate holder.

85.1508 Certificate holders importing non-conforming motor vehicles and motor vehicle engines into the U.S.

To maintain a list of owners of all vehicles or engines imported.

Retention period: 6 years.

85.1510 Certificate holders importing non-conforming motor vehicles and motor vehicle engines into the U.S.

(a) To maintain a record of having furnished written maintenance instructions.

(b) To maintain in a file copies of emission warranties and fuel economy labeling.

85.1706 Manufacturers of new and in-use motor vehicles and motor vehicle engines.

To maintain records which provide each vehicle identification or engine serial number, indicate the use of the vehicle or engine on exempt status and indicate the final disposition of any vehicle or engine removed from exempt status.

Guide to Record Retention 1994

85.1806 Manufacturers of new motor vehicles or new motor vehicle engines who have been notified that such vehicles or engines are not in conformity with applicable emission standards and regulations.

To maintain records to permit the analysis of recall campaigns as specified in the section cited.

Retention period: 5 years.

85.1904 Manufacturers of motor vehicles or motor vehicle engines who have initiated voluntary emissions recalls.

To maintain records relating to notifications and remedial repairs.

Retention period: Not specified.

85.1906 Manufacturers of new motor vehicles or new motor vehicle engines subject to defect reporting requirements.

To maintain information gathered by the manufacturer to compile emissions defect information reports and voluntary emissions recall reports.

Retention period: 5 years from date of manufacture of the affected vehicles.

86.078-7 Manufacturers of new motor vehicles or new motor vehicle engines subject to air pollution control regulations.

To maintain general and specific records including routine emission test records relating to such vehicles as specified in the section cited.

Retention period: 6 years after issuance of all related certificates of conformity; routine emission test records—1 year after issuance of all certificates of conformity to which they relate.

86.080-7 Manufacturers of new motor vehicles (or new motor vehicle engines) subject to the emission standards or procedures.

To maintain general and individual records consisting of:

(a) Identification and description and certification vehicles (or certification engines) for which testing is required;

(b) A description of all emission control systems which are installed on or incorporated in each certification vehicle (or certification engine);

Environmental Protection Agency

(c) A description of all procedures used to test each certification vehicle (or certification engine);

Note: A properly filed application for certification following the format prescribed by the EPA for the appropriate model year may be considered records.

(d) A brief history of each motor vehicle (or motor vehicle engine) used for certification;

(e) All emission tests performed (except tests performed by EPA directly), including tests results, the date and purpose of each test, and the number of miles accumulated on the vehicle or the number of hours accumulated on the engine;

(f) The date of each mileage (or service) accumulation run, listing the mileage (or the number of operating hours) accumulated.

Retention period: 6 years after issuance of all certificates of conformity. Routine emission test records-1 year after issuance of all certificates.

86.090-7 Manufacturers (or contractors for the manufacturers, if applicable) of new vehicles or engines certified under any of the averaging or banking programs.

To maintain adequately organized and indexed records containing the following:

(a) EPA engine family;

(b) Vehicle (or engine) model year and build date;

(c) Vehicle (or engine) identification number;

(d) BHP rating (heavy duty only);

(e) Purchaser and destination;

(f) Assembly plant; and other such information as specified in cited section.

Retention period: 6 years from the due date for the end-of-model year report.

86.090-14 Small-volume manufacturers of light-duty vehicles, light-duty trucks, and heavy-duty engines subject to air pollution controls.

To maintain records of all the information required by 40 CFR 86.090-21.

Guide to Record Retention 1994 Environmental Protection Agency

86.090-24 Manufacturers of new motor vehicles and new motor vehicle engines subject to air pollution controls.

To maintain and make available to EPA Administrator upon request, the engineering evaluation, including any test data used to support the deletion of optional equipment from the test vehicles.

86.090-26 Manufacturers of light-duty vehicles subject to air pollution controls.

(a) To maintain and provide to EPA Administrator, a record of the rationale used in making for engine family, the mileage at which the engine-steam combination is stabilized for emission-data testing determination.

(b) To retain records of all information concerning all emission tests and maintenance, including vehicle alterations to represent other vehicle selections whenever a manufacturer intends to operate and test a vehicle which may be used for emission or durability data.

86.091-7 Manufacturers of new motor vehicles (or new motor vehicle engines) subject to the emission standards or procedures.

See 40 CFR 86.090-7.

86.091-15 Manufacturers of heavy-duty engines eligible for the nitrogen and particulate averaging, trading, and banking programs.

To maintain the quarterly records required by 40 CFR 86.091-7(c)(8).

86.093-35 Manufacturers of heavy-duty engines.

In lieu of including the date of manufacture on the engine label, to maintain a record of the engine manufacture dates.

86.094-7 Manufacturers of any new model year 1994 through 1997 light-duty vehicle or light light-duty trucks, or model year 1996 through 1998 heavy light-duty trucks. [Amended]

(a) To retain the following adequately organized and indexed records for each such vehicle: (1) EPA engine

family; (2) Vehicle identification number; (3) Model year and production volume for the actual U.S. sales for the model year for each engine family.

(b) To also retain adequately organized records of the actual U.S. sales volume for the model year for each engine family.

Retention period: 8 years from the due date for the applicable end of-model year report.

(c) To maintain routine emission test records.

Retention period: 1 year after issuance of all certificates of conformity.

86.094-24 Manufacturers of model year 1994, 1995, and 1996 light-duty vehicles (LDVs) and light-duty truck (LDTs). [Revised]

To maintain engineering evaluation, including any test data, used to support the deletion of optional equipment from test vehicles.

86.094-26 Manufacturers of model year 1994, 1995, and 1996 light-duty vehicles (LDVs) and light-duty trucks (LDTs). [Added]

To maintain records on mileage and service accumulation and emission requirements compliance.

86.094-35 Manufacturers (or contractors for the manufacturers, if applicable) of any model year 1994 through 1997 light-duty vehicle or light-duty truck or model year 1994 through 1998 heavy light-duty trucks.

In lieu of including the date of manufacture on the engine label, to maintain a record of the engine manufacture dates.

86.096-7 Manufacturers (or contractors for the manufacturers, if applicable) of any new model 1996 through 1998 light-duty vehicles, light-duty trucks or heavy-duty vehicles. [Added]

See 40 CFR 86.094-7.

86.096-26 Manufacturers of gasoline-and-methanol-fueled light-duty vehicles, light-duty trucks and heavy-duty vehicles. [Added]

To maintain a record of the rationale used in making the determination for

each engine family and the number of hours at which the engine system combination is stabilized for emission-data testing.

86.107-90 Manufacturers of petroleum-fueled and methanol-fuel light-duty vehicles and light-duty trucks.

(a) To maintain permanent records of results at the initiation and termination of each diurnal or hot soak in measuring hydrocarbon (hydrocarbons plus methanol as appropriate).

(b) For the methanol sample to maintain permanent records of the following: (1) The volumes of deionized water introduced into each impinger; (2) the rate and time of sample collection; (3) the volumes of each sample introduced into the gas chromatograph; (4) the flow rate of carrier gas through the carrier; and (5) the chromatogram of the analyzed sample.

86.129-94 Manufacturers of gasoline-and methanol-fueled light-duty vehicles, light-duty trucks and heavy-duty vehicles. [Added]

In addition to the vehicle data recording, to document the following parameters for the determination of the fuel temperature profile: (a) Date and time of vehicle fueling; (b) odometer reading at vehicle fueling; (c) date and time vehicle was parked, parking location and orientation; (d) odometer reading at parking; (e) date and time engine was started; and other such information as specified in cited section.

86.142-90 Manufacturers of 1977 and later motor year new light-duty vehicles and new light-duty trucks subject to emission test procedures. [Amended]

To maintain for each test: (a) Test number; (b) system or device tested (brief description); (c) date and time of day for each part of the test schedules; (d) instrument operated; (e) driver or operator; (f) vehicle ID number, manufacturer, model year, standard, engine family, evaporative emissions family, basic engine description; and such other information as cited in section.

86.440-78 Manufacturers of new gasoline-fueled motorcycles subject to emission control standards.

To maintain general and specific records relating to such vehicles as specified in section cited.

Retention period: 6 years; routine emission test records—1 year.

86.605-88 Manufacturers of new gasoline-fueled and diesel light-duty vehicles and new gasoline-fueled and dieseled light-duty trucks subject to selective enforcement auditing procedures required by air pollution control regulations.

To maintain general and individual records relating to vehicle emission tests performed pursuant to test orders as specified in the section cited.

Retention period: 1 year after completion of tests.

86.608-88 Manufacturers of new gasoline-fueled and diesel light-duty vehicles and new gasoline-fueled and dieseled light-duty trucks subject to selective enforcement auditing procedures required by air pollution control regulations.

See 40 CFR 86.608-88.

86.608-90 Manufacturers of new gasoline-fueled and diesel light-duty vehicles and new gasoline-fueled and dieseled light-duty trucks subject to selective enforcement auditing procedures required by air pollution control regulations.

To maintain equivalency documentation if using an equivalent method when measuring the temperature of the test fuel at other than the approximate mid-volume of the fuel tank and when draining the test fuel from other than the lowest point of the tank.

Retention period: 1 year after completion of all testing in response to a test order.

86.1005-88 Manufacturers of new gasoline-fueled and diesel heavy-duty vehicles and new gasoline-fueled and diesel heavy-duty trucks subject to selective enforcement auditing procedures required by air pollution control regulations.

To maintain general and individual records relating to vehicle emission tests performed pursuant to test orders as specified in the section cited.
Retention period: 1 year after completion of tests.

86.1005-90 Manufacturers of new petroleum-fueled or methanol-fueled heavy duty or engine or light-duty trucks.

To maintain testing and auditing records as specified in section cited.
Retention period: 1 year after completion of all testing in response to a test order.

86.1008-88 Manufacturers of new gasoline-fueled and diesel heavy-duty vehicles and new gasoline-fueled and diesel heavy-duty trucks subject to selective enforcement auditing procedures required by air pollution control regulations.
See 40 CFR 86.608-88.

86.1008-90 Manufacturers of new petroleum-fueled or methanol-fueled heavy-duty engines or light-duty trucks.

To maintain general records pertaining to description of all equipment used to test engines or vehicles pursuant to Production Compliance Audit (PCA) testing; individual records on each PCA; and test equipment description records for each test cell that was used to perform emission testing.
Retention period: 6 years after completion of all testing.

86.1108-87 Manufacturers of new gasoline-fueled or diesel heavy-duty engine or heavy-duty vehicle.

To maintain general records pertaining to description of all equipment used to test engines or vehicles pursuant to Production Compliance Audit (PCA) testing; individual records on each PCA; and records of all data used to complete application.
Retention period: 3 years from date of the sample, measurement, report or application.

Guide to Record Retention 1994

86.1227-76 Manufacturers of gasoline- and methanol-fueled light-duty vehicles, light-duty trucks and heavy-duty vehicles.
See 40 CFR 86.129-94.

86.1242-90 Manufacturers of new gasoline-fueled and methanol-fueled heavy duty vehicles.
See 40 CFR 86.142-90.

88.205-94 Vehicle manufacturers required to participate in the California Pilot Test Program.
To maintain quarterly records.

112.7 Owners and operators of onshore or offshore facilities engaged in oil activities.
To maintain written procedures developed for prevention of oil pollution and record of inspection required in 40 CFR, part 112.
Retention period: 3 years.

122.21 Persons holding or applying for permits to discharge wastes pursuant to the national pollutant discharge elimination program.
To maintain records of all information resulting from monitoring activities and relating to all sludge-related application data and other such information as indicated in section cited.
Retention period: 5 years (or longer as required by 40 CFR, part 403), except for records of monitoring information: 3 years.

122.41 Persons holding permits to discharge wastes pursuant to the national pollutant discharge elimination program.
To maintain records of all monitoring information, including all calibration and maintenance records and all original strip chart recordings for continuous monitoring instrumentation, copies of all reports required by the permit, and records of all data used to complete application.
Retention period: Not specified.

Part 136, App. A Laboratories performing tests for the organic chemical analysis of municipal and industrial waste-water.
To maintain performance records to document the quality of data that is generated.
Retention period: Not specified.

Environmental Protection Agency

123.43 State agencies administering national pollutant discharge elimination system permit programs.
To maintain records and information as the Administrator of EPA may reasonably require to ascertain whether the State program complies with the requirements of the Clean Water Act.
Retention period: Not specified.

122.44 Persons holding permits to discharge wastes pursuant to the national pollutant discharge elimination program.
To maintain a record summarizing the results of the inspection and a certification that the facility is in compliance with the plan and the permit, and identifying any incidents of non-compliance.
Retention period: 3 years.

125.26 Dischargers submitting applications for a compliance extension for facilities installing innovative technology under the national pollutant discharge elimination program.
To keep records of all data used to complete the request for a compliance extension.
Retention period: For the life of the permit containing the compliance extension.

141.33 Owners or operators of public water systems.
To maintain records of (a) bacteriological analyses; (b) chemical analyses; (c) actions taken to correct violations of primary drinking water regulations; (d) copies of written reports, summaries or communications relating to sanitary surveys of the system; and (e) records concerning variances or exemptions granted to the system.
Retention period: (a) 5 years; (b) 10 years; (c) 3 years after last action taken for each violation; (d) 10 years;

and (e) 5 years after expiration of variance or exemption.

141.80 Owners or operators of public water systems.
See 40 CFR 141.91.

141.81 Owners or operators of public water systems.
To maintain information to support applicable corrosion control treatment requirements. See also 40 CFR 141.91.

141.82 Owners or operators of public water systems.
To maintain data and documentation describing corrosion control treatment requirements. See also 40 CFR 141.91.

141.83 Owners or operators of public water systems.
To maintain information to demonstrate in compliance with the source water treatment requirements. See also 40 CFR 141.91.

141.84 Owners or operators of public water systems.
To maintain information to demonstrate compliance with the lead service line replacement requirements. See also 40 CFR 141.91.

141.85 Owners or operators of public water systems.
To maintain information to demonstrate compliance with the public education and supplemental monitoring requirements. See also 40 CFR 141.91.

141.86 Owners or operators of public water systems.
To maintain information to demonstrate compliance with the monitoring requirements for lead and copper in tap water. See also 40 CFR 141.91.

141.87 Owners or operators of public water systems.
To maintain information to demonstrate compliance with the monitoring requirements for water quality parameters. See also 40 CFR 141.91.

Guide to Record Retention 1994

Environmental Protection Agency

141.88

141.88 Owners or operators of public water systems.

To maintain information to demonstrate compliance with the monitoring requirements for lead and copper in source water. See also 40 CFR 141.91.

141.91 Owners or operators of public water systems.

To retain on premises original records of all sampling data and analyses, reports, surveys, letters, evaluations, schedules, State determinations and other information required by 40 CFR 141.81 through 141.88.

Retention period: No fewer than 12 years.

142.14 State agencies having primary enforcement responsibilities over public water.

To maintain records of tests, measurement, analyses, decisions, and determinations performed on each public water system to determine compliance with applicable provisions of State primary drinking water regulations. To also maintain records of the currently applicable or most recent State determinations including all supporting information and an explanation of the technical basis for each decision for the control of lead and copper.

Retention period: (a) Records of turbidity measurements-for less than 1 year; (b) records of disinfectant residual measurements and other parameters necessary to document disinfection effectiveness and applicable reporting requirements-not less than 1 year; (c) records of decisions-40 years or until 1 year after the decision is reversed or revised; (d) records of any determination that a public water system supplied by a surface water source or a ground water source under the direct influence of surface water is not required to provide filtration treatment-40 years or until withdrawn; (e) records of analyses for contaminants other than microbiological contaminants (including total coliform, fecal coliform, and heterotrophic plate concentration, and other parameters necessary to determine disinfection effectiveness (including temperature and pH measurements and turbidity—not less than 12 years; (f) records of microbiological analyses and maintenance records and all origi-

the form of actual laboratory reports or in an appropriate summary form; (g) records of decisions made pursuant to the total coliform provisions of 40 CFR part 141–5 years; (h) records on state determinations— 12 years; and (i) records of the most recent vulnerability determination, all monitoring requirements and asbestos repeat monitoring decisions and other supporting data-in perpetuity or until more recent vulnerability, monitoring frequency decision or repeat monitoring determination have been made.

144.28 Owners or operators of Class I, II, and III wells authorized by underground injection control program.

To maintain records of all monitoring information, including all calibration and maintenance records and all original strip chart recordings for continuous monitoring instrumentation, and copies of all reports required by this permit.

Retention period: 3 years. This period may be extended by request of the Director at any time.

144.31 Persons applying for permit to operate underground injection wells.

To keep all data used to complete permit applications and any supplemental information.

Retention period: 3 years.

144.51 Persons holding underground injection control permits.

To retain records of all monitoring information, including all calibration and maintenance records and all original strip chart recordings for continuous monitoring instrumentation, copies of all reports required by this permit, and records of all data used to complete the application for the permit.

Retention period: 3 years. This period may be extended by request the State Director at any time.

146.13 Owners and operators of underground wells disposing of fluids.

To retain records of all monitoring information, including all calibration and maintenance records and all origi-

nal strip chart recordings for continuous monitoring instrumentation, copies of all monitoring reports required by this permit, and records of all data used to complete the application for the permit.

Retention period: 3 years.

146.23 Owners and operators of underground wells disposing of fluids.

Retention period: Not specified.

146.33 Owners and operators of underground wells disposing of fluids.

See 146.13.

146.72 Owners or operators of Class I hazardous waste wells.

To retain records reflecting the nature, composition, and volume of all injected fluids.

Retention period: 3 years following well closure.

147.2913 Owners and operators of Class II injection wells located on the Osage Mineral Reserve, Oklahoma.

To maintain monitoring records on the injection pressure and rate.

Retention period: 3 years or 3 years after enforcement action has been resolved.

147.2922 Owners/operators of Class II injection wells authorized by permit.

To retain all monitoring records on injection pressure and rate.

Retention period: 3 years or if enforcement action is pending, 3 years after enforcement action has been resolved.

157.36 Registrants of pesticide products required to be in child-resistant packaging.

To maintain records on description of the packages, copies of certification statements required by section 157.34, and other information as specified in the section.

Retention period: As long as the child-resistant packaging is in effect.

160.120

nal strip chart recordings for continuous monitoring instrumentation, copies of all monitoring reports required by this permit, and records of all data used to complete the application for the permit.

Retention period: —

160.29 Testing facilities conducting studies that support applications for research or marketing permits for pesticides regulated by EPA.

To maintain a current summary of training and experience and job description for each individual engaged in or supervising the conduct of a study.

Retention period: 5 years.

160.35 Testing facility quality assurance units conducting studies that support applications for research or marketing permits for pesticide products regulated by EPA.

To maintain (a) a copy of a master schedule sheet of all studies conducted; (b) copies of all protocols pertaining to all studies; and (c) written and properly signed records of each periodic inspection.

Retention period: (a) and (b) 5 years; (c) 2 years.

160.63 Testing facilities conducting studies that support applications for research or marketing permits for pesticides regulated by EPA.

To maintain written records of all inspection, maintenance, testing, calibrating, and/or standardizing operations. Also to maintain written records of nonroutine repairs performed on equipment as a result of failure and malfunction.

Retention period: 2 years.

160.81 Testing facilities conducting studies that support applications for research or marketing permits for pesticides regulated by EPA.

To maintain historical file of standard operating procedures and all revisions thereof, including the dates of such revisions.

Retention period: In accordance with 40 CFR 160.195.

160.120 Testing facilities conducting studies that support applications for a research or marketing permits for pesticides regulated by EPA.

To maintain with the protocol records of all changes in or revisions of an approved protocol and the reasons therefore.

Retention period: In accordance with 40 CFR 160.195.

160.195 Testing facilities conducting studies that support applications for research or marketing permits for pesticides regulated by EPA.

(a) To maintain documentation records, raw data, and specimens pertaining to a study and required to be retained.

Retention period: (1) In the case of a study used to support an application for a research or marketing permit approved by EPA, the period during which the sponsor holds any research or marketing permit to which the study is pertinent. (2) A period of at least 5 years following the date on which the results of the study are submitted to the EPA in support of an application for research marketing registration. (3) In other situations (e.g. where the study does not result in the submission of the study in support of an application for a research or marketing permit), a period of at least 2 years following the date on which the study is completed, terminated, or discontinued.

(b) Wet specimens, samples of test, control, or reference substances, and specially prepared material which are relatively fragile and differ markedly in stability and quality during storage shall be retained only as long as the quality of the preparation affords evaluation.

(c) To maintain the master schedule sheet, copies of protocols and records of quality assurance inspections in accordance with 40 CFR 160.195(b).

(d) To maintain summaries of training and experience and job description in accordance with 40 CFR 160.195(b).

166.32 State agencies using or applying pesticides pursuant to a specific quarantine and public health exemption.

To maintain records for all treatments involving the first use of a pesticide. Records will include the locations where the pesticide was applied, dates of application (range), and total quantity of the pesticide use.
Retention period: 2 years following the date of expiration of the exemption.

Guide to Record Retention 1994

166.50 State agencies using pesticide under a crisis exemption.
See 40 CFR 166.32.

168.75 Exporters of unregistered pesticides. [Added]
To maintain documentation of any changes to the registered product for export purposes in accordance with CFR 169.2.

168.75 Exporters of unregistered pesticide research and development products. [Added]
To maintain records consisting of the identity of the purchaser and country of intended use of the research product; the amount shipped; and the intended use by the purchaser; including the type of application site, rate of application, and measures taken for protection of humans from direct or dietary exposure.
Retention period: See 40 CFR 169.2.

168.75 Producers of unregistered pesticides. [Added]
To maintain records pertaining to products intended for export.
Retention period: See 40 CFR 169.2.

168.85 Exporters of pesticides, devices and active ingredients used in producing a pesticide. [Added]
To keep records of the product labeling used, including the EPA registered labeling, any foreign labeling on or attached to the product when shipped; and as applicable, any supplemental labeling used; and other such records as specified in cited section.
Retention period: See 40 CFR 169.2.

169.2 Producers of pesticides, devices, or active ingredients used in producing pesticides subject to the Federal Insecticide, Fungicide, and Rodenticide Act, including pesticides produced pursuant to an experimental use permit and pesticides, devices, and pesticide active ingredients produced for export. [Amended]
To maintain records showing product name, EPA Registration Number, Experimental Permit Number if the pesticide is produced under an Experimental Use Permit, amounts per batch

Environmental Protection Agency

and batch identification of all pesticides produced. To also maintain records of production, brand names, receipt, shipment, inventories, advertising, guarantees, disposal, tests, research, and such other records as specified in the section cited.
Retention period: Various.

171.11 Certified commercial pesticides applicators.
To maintain records of specified information relating to the use of restricted use pesticides.
Retention period: 2 years.

172.5 Producers of pesticides produced pursuant to an experimental use permits.
To keep operating records in a daily log.
Retention period: 2 years.

180.31 Persons obtaining an experimental permit for use of a pesticide chemical for which a temporary tolerance is established.
To maintain temporary tolerance records of production, distribution, and performance.
Retention period: 2 years.

180.4725 Persons obtaining an experimental permit for use of the herbicide pentyl 2-chloro-4-fluoro-5-(3,4,5,6-tetrahydrophthalimido)phenoxyacetate. [Added]
To keep records of production distribution, and performance and on request make the records available to any authorized officer or employee of the EPA or FDA.
Retention period: Not specified.

205.172 Manufacturers of new motorcycle exhaust systems subject to noise emission standards.
To maintain general and individual records as specified in section.
Retention period: 3 years.

224.1 Persons holding permits to allow dumping of material into the ocean waters.
To maintain complete records of materials dumped, time and locations of dumping, and such other records as required in section cited.
Retention period: Not specified.

240.211 Owners and operators of thermal processing facilities and land disposal sites.
To maintain records and monitoring data as required by regulations.
Retention period: Not specified.

240.211-1 Owners and operators of thermal processing facilities and land disposal sites.
See 240.211.

240.211-3 Owners and operators of thermal processing facilities and land disposal sites.
See 40 CFR 258.29.

241.212-3 Owners/operators of land disposal sites for solid wastes.
To maintain records on major operational problems, complaints or difficulties; qualitative and quantitative evaluation of the environmental impact of the land disposal site with regard to the effectiveness of gas and leachate control; vector control efforts and other date as required by regulation.
Retention period: Not specified.

258.20 Owners or operators of municipal solid waste landfills (MSWLF).
To maintain records of any inspection incoming loads for regulated hazardous wastes or PCB wastes.
See 40 CFR 258.29

258.23 Owners or operators of municipal solid waste landfill (MSWLF).
See 40 CFR 258.29

258.28 Owners or operators of municipal solid waste landfill (MSWLF).
See 40 CFR 258.29

258.29 Owners or operators of municipal solid waste landfills (MSWLF).
To retain near the facility in an operating record or in an alternative location approved by the Director of an approved State the following information as it becomes available:
(a) Any location restriction restriction demonstration requirement under 40 CFR part 258, subpart B.

Subparts E, F, and G

(b) Inspection records, training procedures, and notification procedures required in 40 CFR 258.20.

(c) Gas monitoring results from monitoring and any remediation plans required by 40 CFR 258.23.

Retention period: For a period of 3 years from the due date of the report.

(d) Any MSWLF unit design documentation for placement of leachate or gas condensate in a MSWLF unit.

(e) Any demonstration, certification, finding, monitoring, testing, or analytical data required by 40 CFR part 258, subpart E.

(f) Closure and post-closure care plans and any monitoring, testing, or analytical data required by 40 CFR part 258, subpart E.

(g) Any cost estimates and financial assurance documentation required by 40 CFR part 258, subpart G.

(h) Any information demonstrating compliance with small community exemption.

Subparts E, F, and G (sections 258.50-258.74) Owners or operators of municipal solid waste landfills (MSWLF).

See 40 CFR 258.29.

259.54 Generators of medical waste, including generators of less than 50 pounds per month.

(a) To keep a copy of each tracking form signed in accordance with 40 CFR 259.52.

Retention period: For at least 3 years from the date the waste was accepted by the initial transporter.

(b) To retain a copy of all exception reports required to be submitted under 40 CFR 259.55(c).

Retention period: 3 years from when the exception report was submitted.

(c) To maintain a shipment log at the original generation point.

Retention period: For a period of 3 years from the date the waste was shipped.

(d) To maintain a shipment log at each central collection point and other such records as specified in cited section.

Retention period: For a period of 3 years from the date that regulated medical waste was accepted from each original generation point.

259.55 Generators of medical waste including generators of less than 50 pounds per month.

To maintain a copy of the exception report.

Retention period: For a period of 3 years from the due date of the report.

259.61 Generators of regulated medical waste who incinerate regulated medical waste on-site.

(a) To keep an operating log at the incineration facility.

Retention period: From June 22, 1989 to June 22, 1991.

(b) To maintain the following information for each shipment of regulated medical waste accepted:

(1) The date the waste was accepted;

(2) The name and State permit or identification number of the generator who originated the shipment. If the State does not issue permit or identification numbers, then the generators' address;

(3) The total weight of the regulated medical waste accepted from the originating generator; and

(4) The signature of the individual accepting the waste.

Retention period: Until at least June 22, 1992.

(c) To keep copies of all tracking forms if subject to the tracking form requirements.

Retention period: 3 years from the date the waste was accepted.

(d) To retain a copy of the on-site incinerator report form.

Retention period: For 3 years from the date of submission.

259.76 Transporters of medical waste.

To retain a copy of each tracking form in accordance with 40 CFR 259.77.

259.77 Transporters of regulated medical waste.

(a) To keep a copy of the tracking form signed by the transporter, the previous transporter (if applicable), and the next party, which may be one of the following: Another transporter or the owner or operator of an intermediate handler, or destination facility.

Retention period: For a period of 3 years from the date the waste was accepted by the next party.

259.55 Generators of medical waste including generators of less than 50 pounds per month.

To maintain a copy of the exception report.

Retention period: For a period of 3 years from the due date of the report.

259.61 Generators of regulated medical waste who incinerate regulated medical waste on-site.

(a) To keep an operating log at the incineration facility.

Retention period: From June 22, 1989 to June 22, 1991.

(b) For regulated medical waste that is not accompanied by a generator-initiated tracking form, to retain a copy of all transporter-initiated tracking forms and consolidation logs.

Retention period: For a period of 3 years from the date the waste was accepted by the transporter.

(c) For any regulated medical waste that was received by the transporter that was accompanied by a tracking form and consolidated by a tracking form and consolidated or remanifested by the transporter to another tracking form, to retain (1) a copy of the generator-initiated tracking form signed by the intermediate handler or destination facility and all associated consolidation logs.

Retention period: (1) 3 years from the date the waste was accepted by the transporter; and (2) 3 years from the date the waste was accepted by the intermediate handler or destination facility.

(d) To retain a copy of each transporter report required by 40 CFR 259.78.

Retention period: 3 years after the date of submission.

259.81 Owners or operators of facilities including destination and intermediate facilities receiving regulated medical waste generated in a Covered State.

(a) To retain a copy of each tracking form in accordance with 40 CFR 259.83.

(b) To retain a copy of the tracking form or shipping papers if signed in lieu of the tracking form.

Retention period: For at least 3 years from the date of acceptance of the regulated medical waste.

259.83 Owners or operators of destination facilities or intermediate handlers receiving regulated medical waste generated in a Covered State.

(a) To maintain (1) copies of all tracking forms and logs; (2) the name and State permit or identification number of each generator who delivered waste to the destination facility or intermediate handler, if the State does not issue permit or identification numbers then the generator's address;

and (3) copies of all discrepancy reports.

(b) To maintain the following information for each shipment of regulated medical waste accepted: (1) The date and State permit or identification number of the generator who originated shipment. If the State does not issue permit or identification numbers, then the generator's address; (3) the total weight of the regulated medical waste accepted from the originating generator; and (4) the signature of the individual accepting the waste.

Retention period: 3 years from the date the waste was accepted.

259.91 Persons engaged in rail transportation of regulated medical waste generated in a Covered State.

To retain a copy of the tracking forms and rail shipping papers in accordance with 40 CFR 259.77.

261.4 Generators of waste samples and owners or operators of laboratories or operators of laboratories conducting or testing facilities conducting treatability studies.

(a) To maintain copies of shipping documents; a copy of the contract with the facility conducting the treatability study; documentation showing the amount of waste shipped under the exemption; the name, address, and EPA identification number of the laboratory or testing facility that received the waste; the date the shipment was made; and whether or not unused samples and residues were returned to the generator or sample collector, or if sent to a designated facility, the name of the facility and the EPA identification number, and other information as specified in section cited.

Retention period: 3 years.

(b) To keep, on site, a copy of the treatability study contract and all shipping papers associated with the transport of treatability study samples to and from the facility.

Retention period: 3 years.

261.31 Hazardous waste generators and treatment, storage, and disposal facilities.

To maintain in operating or other onsite records, documents and data sufficient to prove that the unit is an agrificient to prove that the unit is an aggressive biological treatment unit and the sludges sought to be exempted from the definition of F037 and/or F038 were actually treated in the aggressive biological treatment unit.

261.35 Hazardous waste generators.

To maintain the following records documenting the cleaning and replacement as part of the facilities operating records:

(a) The name and address of the facility;

(b) Formulations previously used and date on which their use ceased in each process at the plant;

(c) Formulations currently used in each process at the plant;

(d) The name and address of any persons who conducted the cleaning and replacement.

(e) The dates on which cleaning and replacement were accomplished;

(f) The dates of sampling and testing; and other information as specified in section cited.

262.34 Hazardous waste generators.

To maintain records on:

(a) A description of procedures that will be followed to ensure that all wastes are removed from the drip pad at least once every 90 days;

(b) Documentation of each waste removal, including the quantity of waste removed from the drip pad and the sump or collection system and the date and time of removal;

(c) A written description of procedures to ensure that each waste volume remains in the unit for no more than 90 days;

(d) A written description of the waste generation and management practices for the facility showing that they are consistent with respecting the 90 day limit, and documentation that the procedures are compiled with; or

(e) Documentation that the unit is emptied at least once every 90 days.

262.40 Hazardous waste generators.

(a) To keep a copy of each manifest signed.

Retention period: 3 years or until receipt of a signed manifest from facility receiving the hazardous waste.

(b) To keep a copy of each Biennial Report and Exception Report.

Retention period: 3 years from due date of report.

(c) To keep records of any test results, waste analyses, or other determinations that the waste is hazardous.

Retention period: 3 years from the date that the waste was last sent to on-site or off-site treatment, storage, or disposal.

262.57 Primary exporters of hazardous waste.

To maintain copies of each notification of intent to export; each EPA Acknowledgement of Consent; each confirmation of delivery of the hazardous waste from consignee; and each annual report.

Retention period: 3 years.

263.20 Hazardous waste transporters.

See 40 CFR 263.22.

263.22 Hazardous waste transporters.

To keep a copy of the manifest signed by the generator, transporter, and the next designated transporter or the owner or operator of a designated facility.

Retention period: 3 years from date initial transporter accepted the hazardous waste.

263.22 Hazardous waste transporters (water bulk shipment transporter).

To retain a copy of shipping paper containing all the information for shipments delivered to designated facility by water (bulk shipment).

Retention period: 3 years from date initial transporter accepted the hazardous waste.

263.22 Hazardous waste transporters (initial and final rail transporter).

Initial rail transporter to keep a copy of manifest and shipping paper for shipments by rail within the U.S.; final rail transporter to keep a copy of paper and manifest signed by the owner or operator (or shipping paper if signed in lieu of manifest by the designated facility) for shipments by rail within the U.S.

Retention period: 3 years from date of delivery.

263.22 Hazardous waste transporters (transporter who transmits hazardous waste out of the U.S.).

To keep a copy of the manifest indicating when the hazardous waste left the U.S.

Retention period: 3 years from date initial transporter accepted the hazardous waste.

264.15 Owners and operators of all hazardous facilities.

To keep inspection records of the date and time of the inspection, the name of the inspector, the observations made, and the date and nature of any repairs or other remedial actions.

Retention period: 3 years.

264.16 Hazardous waste transporters, personnel training records.

To maintain personnel training records.

Retention period: For current personnel, until closure of facility; for former personnel, 3 years from date employee left facility.

264.19 Hazardous waste transporters.

See 40 CFR 264.73.

264.71 Owners and operators of on-site and off-site hazardous waste treatment, storage, and disposal facilities.

To keep a copy of the manifest and shipping paper (if signed in lieu of the manifest at time of delivery) signed by the owner or operator.

Retention period: 3 years from date of delivery.

264.71 Owners and operators of on-site and off-site hazardous waste treatment, storage, and disposal facilities (hazardous waste from a rail or water bulk shipment) transporter.

To keep a copy of each shipping paper and manifest signed by the owner or operator for hazardous waste delivered by rail or water (bulk shipment).

Retention period: 3 years from date of delivery.

264.73 Owners and operators of on-site and off-site hazardous waste treatment, storage, and disposal facilities.

To keep a written operating record of the facility.

Retention period: Until at least closure of the facility; monitoring data at post-closure period; records for inspection: 3 years.

264.97 Owners and operators of hazardous waste treatment, storage, and disposal facilities.

To maintain in the facility operating records, ground-water monitoring data including actual-levels of constituents.

264.98 Owners and operators of hazardous waste treatment, storage, and disposal facilities.

To maintain records of ground-water analytical data as measured and in a form necessary for the determination of statistical significance under 40 CFR 264.97(h).

264.279 Owners or operators of hazardous waste, storage, and disposal facilities.

To maintain operating records including hazardous waste application dates and rates.

Retention period: 3 years.

264.309 Owners and operators of facilities that dispose of hazardous waste in landfills.

To maintain operating records that include (a) on a map, the exact location and dimensions, including depth, of each cell with respect to permanently survey benchmarks; and (b) the contents of each cell and the approximate location of each hazardous waste type within each cell.

Retention period: 3 years.

264.347 Owners or operators of hazardous waste incinerators.

To keep in the operating log monitoring and inspection data.

Retention period: 3 years.

264.571 Owners or operators of hazardous waste treatment, storage and disposal facilities.

To keep on file at the facility a written assessment of the drip pad, reviewed and certified by an independent qualified registered professional engineer that attests to the results of the evaluation.

264.573 Owners or operators of hazardous waste treatment, storage, and disposal facilities.

(a) To maintain records sufficient to document that all treated wood is held on the pad following treatment in accordance with design and operating requirements.

(b) To maintain, as part of the operating and waste handling practices. This must include identification of preservative formulations used in the past, a description of drippage management practices, and a description of treated wood storage and handling practices.

264.574 Owners or operators of hazardous waste treatment, storage, and disposal facilities.

To maintain the design and operating requirements inspection certification as part of the facility operating record.

264.1035 Owners or operators of hazardous waste treatment, storage and disposal facilities.

To maintain (a) an implementation schedule that includes dates by which the closed-vent system and control device will be installed and in operation; (b) up-to-date documentation of compliance with the process vent standards; (c) design documentation and monitoring, operating, and inspection information for each closed-vent system and control device requirement; and other information as specified in section cited.

264.1064 Owners or operators of hazardous waste treatment, storage and disposal facilities.

To maintain in the operating record (a) records on equipment identification number and hazardous waste management unit identification; (b) approxi-

mate locations within the facility; (c) type of equipment; (d) inspection log; (e) design documentation and monitoring, operating, and inspection information for each closed-vent system and control device requirements; and other information as specified in section cited.

264.1101 Owners and operators of hazardous waste treatment, storage, and disposal facilities.

To maintain in the facility's operating log, a written description of the operating procedures used to maintain the integrity of areas without secondary containment.

265.15 Owners or operators of all hazardous waste facilities.

To maintain inspection log or summary of the date and time of the inspection, the name of the inspector, a notation of the observations made, and the date and nature of any repairs or other remedial actions.
Retention period: 3 years.

265.16 Hazardous waste transporters.

To maintain personnel training records.
Retention period: For current personnel, until closure of facility; for former personnel, 3 years from date employee left facility.

265.71 Owners and operators of on-site and off-site hazardous waste treatment, storage, and disposal facilities.

To keep a copy of the manifest and shipping paper (if signed in lieu of the manifest at time of delivery) signed by the owner or operator.
Retention period: 3 years from date of delivery.

265.71 Owners and operators of on-site and off-site hazardous waste treatment, storage, and disposal facilities (hazardous waste from a rail or water bulk shipment) transporter.
See 264.71.

265.73 Owners and operators of on-site and off-site hazardous waste treatment, storage, and disposal facilities.

To keep a written operating record at the facility.

265.94 Owners and operators of on-site and off-site hazardous waste treatment, storage, and disposal facilities.

(a) An owner or operator who does not operate a groundwater quality assessment plan must keep records of analyses of groundwater samples, groundwater surface elevation data, and evaluations of the measurements of groundwater samples.
Retention period: Throughout active life of facility and for disposal facilities, throughout post-closure care period as well.

(b) An owner or operator who operates a groundwater quality assessment plan must keep records of the analyses and evaluations specified in the plan.
Retention period: Throughout the active life of the facility and for disposal facilities, throughout the postclosure care period as well.

265.112 Owners and operators of on-site and off-site hazardous waste treatment, storage, and disposal facilities.

To keep a written closure plan at the facility which identifies the steps necessary to completely close the facility at any point during its intended life and at the end of its intended life.
Retention period: Not specified.

265.118 Owners and operators of on-site and off-site hazardous waste treatment, storage, and disposal facilities.

To keep a written post-closure plan at the facility which identifies the activities which will be carried on after final closure and the frequency of those activities.
Retention period: Not specified.

265.142 Owners and operators of all hazardous waste facilities.

A facility owner or operator must keep a written estimate of facility closure cost at the facility.
See 40 CFR 264.1064.

Retention period: Not specified.

265.144 Owners and operators of hazardous waste disposal facilities.

An owner or operator must keep a written estimate of annual cost of post-closure monitoring and maintenance of the facility at the facility.
Retention period: Not specified.

265.279 Owners and operators of hazardous waste land treatment facilities.

To keep hazardous waste application dates and rates in the operating records.
Retention period: 3 years.

265.309 Owners and operators of facilities that dispose of hazardous waste in landfills.

To keep (a) on a map, the exact location and dimensions, including depth, of each cell with respect to permanently surveyed benchmarks; and (b) the contents of each cell and the approximate location of each hazardous waste type within each cell in the operating records.
Retention period: 3 years.

265.441 Owners or operators of hazardous waste treatment, storage and disposal facilities.
See 40 CFR 264.571.

265.443 Owners or operators of hazardous waste treatment, storage and disposal facilities.
See 40 CFR 264.573.

265.444 Owners or operators of hazardous waste treatment, storage and disposal facilities.
See 40 CFR 264.573.

265.1035 Owners or operators of hazardous waste treatment, storage and disposal facilities.
See 40 CFR 264.1035.

265.1064 Owners or operators of hazardous waste treatment, storage and disposal facilities.
See 40 CFR 264.1064.

265.1101 Owners or operators of hazardous waste treatment, storage, and disposal facilities.

See 40 CFR 264.1101.

266.44 Burners of used oil burned for energy recovery.

(a) To keep a copy of each invoice received.

Retention period: 3 years from the date the invoice is received.

(b) To keep copies of analyses of used oil.

Retention period: 3 years from the date off-specification used oil from that marketer is received.

266.70 Persons storing recycled materials utilized for precious metal recovery.

To maintain records showing the volume of materials stored at the beginning of the calendar year; the amount of materials generated or received during the calendar year; and the amount of materials remaining at the end of the calendar year.

Retention period: 3 years.

(c) To keep a copy of each certification notice sent to a marketer.

Retention period: 3 years from the calendar year.

266.100 Owners or operators of boiler or industrial furnace burning hazardous waste facilities.

To document compliance with applicable provisions including limits on levels of toxic organic constituents and Btu value of the waste, and levels of recoverable metals in the hazardous waste compared to normal nonhazardous waste feedstocks.

Retention period: At least 3 years.

266.102 Owners or operators of boiler or industrial furnace burning hazardous waste facilities (permit standards for burners).

To maintain in the operating record, monitoring and inspection data, and other information as specified in cited section.

Retention period: For not less than 3 years.

266.103 Owners or operators of boiler or industrial furnace burning hazardous waste facilities (interim status standards for burners).

See 40 CFR 266.102.

266.108 Owners or operators of boiler or industrial furnace burning hazardous waste facilities (small quantity on-site burner exemption).

To maintain at the facility sufficient records documenting compliance with the hazardous waste quantity, firing rate, and heating value limits. At a minimum, these records must indicate the quantity of hazardous waste and other fuel burned in each unit per calendar month, and the heating value of the hazardous waste.

Retention period: At least 3 years.

266.111 Owners or operators of boilers or industrial furnace burning hazardous waste facilities (direct transfer standards).

To maintain in the operating record, records of inspection made at least once each operating hour when hazardous waste is being transferred from the transport vehicle (container) to the boiler or industrial furnace.

Retention period: At least 3 years from the date of the inspection.

268.6 Owners or operators of hazardous waste treatment, storage, and disposal facilities.

To maintain and keep on site a copy of the monitoring data collected under the monitoring plan that describes the monitoring program installed at and around the unit to verify continued compliance with the conditions of the variance.

268.7 Owners and operators of hazardous waste treatment, storage, and disposal facilities.

(a) To maintain on-site a copy of the notification and certification required for each waste shipment together with the tolling agreement.

Retention period: For at least 3 years after termination or expiration of the agreement. The 3-year retention requirement is automatically extended during the course of any unresolved enforcement action regarding the regu-

lated activity or as requested by the Administrator.

(b) To keep records of the names and location of each entity receiving the hazardous waste-derived products.

(c) To keep records of all inspections, evaluations, and analysis of treated debris that are made to determine compliance with the treatment standards.

(d) To keep records of any data or information that the treater obtains during treatment of the debris that identifies key operating parameters of the treatment unit.

(e) To keep on-site in the generators' records, a written waste analysis plan which describes the procedures the generator will carry out to comply with the treatment standards.

268.8 Owners or operators of hazardous waste treatment, storage, and disposal facilities.

To retain on-site a copy of the demonstration (if applicable) and certification required for each waste shipment.

Retention period: 5 years from the date that the waste that is the subject of such documentation was last sent to on-site or off-site disposal.

270.10 Applicants applying for the hazardous waste permit.

To keep records of all data used to complete permit applications and any supplemental information.

Retention period: 3 years from the date the application is signed.

270.30 Persons holding RCRA permits.

To maintain records of all monitoring information, including all calibration and maintenance records and all original strip chart recordings for continuous monitoring instrumentation, copies of all reports required by permit, and records of all data used to complete the application for the permit.

Retention period: 3 years.

279.44 Used oil transporters.

To retain records of analyses conducted or information used to determine that the total halogen content of used oil being transported or stored at a transfer facility is above or below

1,000 ppm under the rebuttable presumption.

Retention period: 3 years.

279.46 Used oil transporters.

(a) To keep a record of each used oil shipment accepted for transport. Records for each shipment must include: (1) The name and address of the generator, transporter, or processor/re-finer who provided the used oil for transport; (2) the EPA identification number (if applicable) of the generator, transporter, or processor/re-refiner who provided the used oil for transport; (3) the quantity of used oil accepted; (4) the date of acceptance; and (5) the signature, dated upon receipt of the used oil, of a representative of the generator, transporter, or processor/refiner who provided the used oil for transport.

(b) To keep a record of each shipment of used oil that is delivered to another used oil transporter, or to a used oil burner, processor/re-refiner, or disposal facility. Records of each delivery must include (1) the name and address of the receiving facility or transporter; (2) the EPA identification number of the receiving facility or transporter; (3) the quantity of used oil delivered; (4) the date of delivery; and (5) the signature, dated upon receipt of the used oil, of a representative of the receiving facility or transporter; and

(c) To keep record for each shipment of used oil exported to any foreign country.

Retention period: 3 years.

279.55 Owners or operators of used oil processing and re-refining facilities.

To keep at the facility a written analysis plan describing the procedures that will be used to comply with the analysis requirements of 40 CFR 279.53 (Rebuttal presumption for used oil) and 40 CFR 279.72 (Tracking).

Retention period: 3 years.

279.56 Used oil processor/re-refiners.

To keep a record of each used oil shipment that is accepted for processing/re-refining and shipped to a used oil burner, processor/re-refiner, or disposal facility. These records may take the form of a log, invoice, manifest, bill of lading or other shipping documents.

Retention period: 3 years.

279.57

279.57 Owners or operators of used oil transfer facilities.

To keep a written operating record at the facility of records and results of used oil analyses performed as described in 40 CFR 279.55 and summary reports and details of all incidents that require implementation of the contingency plan as specified in 40 CFR 279.52(b).

Retention period: Until closure of the facility.

279.63 Used oil burners who burn off-specification used oil for energy recovery.

See 40 CFR 279.55.

279.65 Used oil burners who burn off-specification used oil for energy recovery.

See 40 CFR 279.56.

279.66 Used oil burners who burn off-specification used oil for energy recovery.

To maintain the one-time written and signed record certifying that (a) the burner has notified EPA stating the location and general description of used oil management activities and (b) the burner will burn the used oil only in industrial furnace or boiler.

Retention period: 3 years from the date the burner last receives shipment of off-specification used oil from the generator, transporter, or processor/re-refiner.

279.72 Used oil fuel marketers.

To keep copies of analyses of the used oil (or other information) used to make the determination that the used oil that is to be burned for energy recovery meets the specifications for used oil fuel under 40 CFR 279.11.

Retention period: 3 years.

279.74 Used oil generators.

See 40 CFR 279.56.

Retention period: 3 years.

279.75 Used oil generators, transporters, or processors/re-refiners.

See 40 CFR 279.66.

Guide to Record Retention 1994

280.20 Owners and operators of new underground storage tank systems.

To maintain records that demonstrate compliance with design, construction, installation, and notification performance standards.

Retention period: Remaining life of the tank and piping.

280.31 Owners and operators of steel underground storage tank system with corrosion protection.

For UST systems using cathodic protection, to maintain records of the operation of the cathodic protection to demonstrate compliance with performance standards. These records must provide (a) the results of the last three inspections to ensure the equipment is running properly and (b) the results of testing for proper operation by a qualified cathodic protection tester.

280.33 Owners and operators of underground storage tank systems.

To maintain records of each repair.

Retention period: For the remaining operating life of the UST.

280.34 Owners and operators of underground storage tank systems.

See 40 CFR 280.20, 280.31, 280.33, 280.45, and 280.74.

280.45 Owners and operators of underground storage tank systems.

(a) To maintain all written performance claims pertaining to any release detection system used, and the manner in which these claims have been justified or tested by the equipment manufacturer or installer.

Retention period: 5 years or for a reasonable period of time determine by the implementing agency, from the date of installation.

(b) To maintain records on the results of any sampling, testing, or monitoring.

Retention period: 1 year, or for a reasonable period of time determined by the implementing agency, except that the results of tank tightness testing must be retained until the next test is conducted.

(c) To maintain written documentation of all calibration, maintenance,

and repair of release detection equipment permanently located on-site.

Retention period: 1 year or for a reasonable time period determined by the implementing agency. Any schedules of required calibration and maintenance provided by the release detection equipment must be retained for 5 years from the date of installation.

280.74 Owners and operators of underground storage tank systems.

To maintain records on the results of the site investigation conducted at permanent closure.

Retention period: 3 years after completion of permanent closure or change-in-service in one of the following ways: (a) By the owners and operators who took the UST system out of service; (b) by the current owners and operators of the UST system site; or (c) by mailing these records to the implementing agency if they cannot be maintained at the closed facility.

280.107 Owners and operators of underground storage tanks containing petroleum. [Redesignated as 280.111]

280.111 Owners and operators of underground storage tanks containing petroleum. [Redesignated from 280.107 and revised]

(a) To maintain a copy of the instrument worded as specified when using an assurance mechanism.

(b) To maintain a copy of the chief financial officer's letter based on year-end financial statement for the most recent completed financial year when using a financial test or guarantee, or a local government guarantee supported by the local government.

(c) To maintain a copy of the signed standby trust fund agreement and copies of any amendments to the agreement when using a guarantee, surety bond, or letter of credit.

(d) To maintain a copy of bond rating published within the last twelve months by Moody's or Standard & Poor's; and other information as specified in cited section.

Retention period: Not specified.

Environmental Protection Agency

372.10

281.32 Owners and operators of approved underground storage tank systems.

To maintain records of monitoring, testing, repairs, and closure that are sufficient to demonstrate recent facility compliance status.

Retention period: Records demonstrating compliance with repair and upgrading requirements must be maintained for the remaining operating life of the facility, these records must be readily available when requested by the implementing agency.

281.40 Owners and operators of State approved underground storage tank systems.

To maintain records on operation.

Retention period: Unspecified.

302.8 Persons in charge of vessels or facilities from which hazardous substances have been released in quantities that are equal to or greater than their reportable quantities (RQs).

To maintain on file at the facilities or in the case of vessels at the offices within the U.S., in either ports or calls, places of regular berthing, or the headquarters of the businesses operating the vessels, all notification supporting documents, materials and other information.

Retention period: 1 year.

372.10 Persons subject to the toxic chemical release reporting; community-right-to-know requirements.

To maintain a copy of each report submitted; and supporting documentation and materials.

Retention period: 3 years from date of the submission of the report under 40 CFR 372.30.

(a) To maintain a copy of each report submitted; and supporting documentation and materials.

Retention period: 3 years from date of the submission of the report under 40 CFR 372.30.

(b) To maintain all supporting materials and documentation used to determine whether a notice is required and used to developed each required notice under 40 CFR 372.45 and a copy of each notice.

Retention period: 3 years from the date of the submission of a notification under 40 CFR 372.45. Records must be maintained at the facility to which the notification applies or from which a notification was provided. Such records must

be readily available for purposes of inspection by EPA.
To maintain records of monitoring activities and results.
Retention period: 3 years.

403.12 Publicly owned treatment works (POTW's) and industrial users subject to pretreatment requirements.
To maintain records of all data used to complete permit applications and any supplemental information.
Retention period: 5 years from the date the application is signed or as required by 40 CFR part 503.

501.15 Applicants for the State sludge management program.
To retain records of all monitoring information, copies of all reports required by the permit, and records of all data used to complete the application for the permit.
Retention period: At least 5 years from the date of the sample, measurement, report or application, or longer as required by 40 CFR part 503. This period may be extended by request of the Director at any time. [Added]

501.15 Persons holding permits under the State Sludge Management Program.
To retain records of all monitoring information, copies of all reports required by the permit, and records of all data used to complete the application for the permit.
Retention period: 5 years from the date the application is signed or as required by 40 CFR part 503.

503.17 Publicly and privately owned treatment works that generate or treat domestic sewage sludge and persons who uses or disposes of sewage sludge from such treatment works. [Added]
To maintain records on the concentration of each pollutant listed in Table 3 of 40 CFR 503.13; certification statements; a description of how Class A pathogen requirements are met; and other such information as specified in cited section.
Retention period: 5 years.

503.20 Persons preparing sewage sludge for the period that the sewage sludge remains on the surface disposal site. [Added]
To maintain records containing the name and address of the person who prepares the sewage sludge, the name and address of the person who either owns the land or leases the land; the location, by either street address or latitude and longitude, of the land; and explanation of why sewage sludge needs to remain on the land for longer than two years prior to final use or disposal; and the approximate time period when the sewage sludge will be used or disposed.

503.27 Persons preparing sewage sludge and/or owners/operators of the surface disposal site. [Added]
To maintain records on the concentration of each pollutant listed in Table 1 of 40 CFR 503.23 in the sewage sludge when the pollutant concentrations in Table 1 of 40 CFR 503.23 are met; certificate statements; a description of how the pathogen and vector attraction reduction requirements are met; and other such information as specified in cited section.
Retention period: 5 years.

503.47 Persons firing sewage sludge in sewage sludge incinerators. [Added]
To maintain records on the concentration of lead, arsenic, cadmium, chromium, and nickel in the sewage sludge fed to the sewage sludge incinerator; the total hydrocarbons concentrations in the exit gas from the sewage sludge incinerator stack; information that indicates the requirements in the National Emission Standard for beryllium in subpart C of 40 CFR part 61 are met; and other such information as specified in cited section.
Retention period: 5 years.

600.005-81 Manufacturers of new motor vehicles subject to fuel economy regulations.
To maintain general and individual records related to the sections cited.
Retention period: 5 years after the end of the model year to which the records relate.

600.105-78 Manufacturers of new motor vehicles subject to fuel economy regulations.
See 40 CFR 600.005-81.

600.205-77 Manufacturers of new motor vehicles subject to fuel economy regulations.
See 40 CFR 600.005-81.

600.305-77 Manufacturers of new motor vehicles subject to fuel economy regulations.
See 40 CFR 600.005-81.

600.505-78 Manufacturers of new motor vehicles subject to fuel economy regulations.
See 40 CFR 600.005-81.

704.11 Manufacturers, importers, and processors of chemical substances and mixtures.
To retain (a) a copy of each report submitted by the person in response to the requirements of section 8 (a) of the Toxic Substances Control Act (TSCA); (b) materials and documentation sufficient to verify or reconstruct the values submitted in the report; (c) a copy of each notice sent by the person, return receipt requested, to that person's customers for the purpose of notifying their customers of the person's reporting obligations; and (d) all return receipts signed by the person's customer's who received the notice.
Retention period: 3 years.

704.25 Persons who manufacture, import, and process Aminoundecanoic acid.
To retain documentation of information contained in the chemical-specific report.
Retention period: 5 years from the date of submission of the report.

704.33 Persons who manufacture, import or process P-tert-butylbenzoic acid (P-TBBA), p-tert-butyltoluene (P-TBT) and p-tert-butylbenzaldehyde (P-TBB).
To maintain documentation of information contained in report on data under section 8(a), including information on chemical identity and structure, production, use, exposure, disposal, and health and environmental effects.
Retention period: 5 years from the date of submission of the report.

704.95 Manufacturers and importers of the chemical substances phosphoric acid, (1,2-ethanediyl)-bis (nitrilo-bis (methylene))tetrakis-(EDTMPA)) and its salts.
To retain documentation of information contained in reports.
Retention period: 5 years from the date of the submission of the report.

704.102 Manufacturers, importers, and processors of hexachloronorbornadiene (HEX-BCH) for use as an intermediate in the production of isodrin or endrin, on or after January 2, 1986.
To retain documentation of information contained in reports.
Retention period: 5 years from the date of the submission of the report.

704.104 Persons who manufacture, import, or process hexafluoropropylene oxide.
See 40 CFR 704.95.

710.37 Manufacturers and importers of certain substances included in the Toxic Substances Control Act (TSCA) Inventory.
To maintain records that document any information reported to EPA. For substances that are manufactured or imported at less than 10,000 pounds annually, volume records must be maintained as evidence to support a decision not to submit a report.
Retention period: 4 years beginning with effective date of that reporting period.

717.15 Firms manufacturing or processing chemical substances and mixtures.
To maintain records of significant adverse reactions to human health or the environment alleged to have been caused by chemical substances or mixtures.
Retention period: 30 years for employee health related allegations, and 5 years for all other allegations.

720.78 Manufacturers and importers of new chemical substances subject to the provisions of the Toxic Substances Control Act.
(a) To maintain documentation of information reviewed and evaluated to determine the need to make any notification of risk.

721.40

Retention period: 5 years.

(b) To maintain documentation of the nature and method of notification concerning the health and environmental effect of a substance including copies of any labels or written notices used.

(c) To maintain documentation of prudent laboratory practices used instead of notification and evaluation.

Retention period: 5 years.

(d) To maintain the names and addresses of any persons other than the manufacturer or importer to whom the substance is distributed, the identity of the substance to the extent known, the amount distributed, and copies of notification required under section 720.36(c)(2).

(e) Persons manufacturing or importing substance in quantities greater than 100 kilograms per year must maintain records of the identity of the substance to the extent known, the production volume of the substance, and the disposition of the substance.

Retention period: 5 years.

721.40 Manufacturers, importers, or processors submitting a significant new use notice to EPA.

To maintain documentation of information contained in the significant new use notice.

Retention period: 5 years from the date of the submission of the significant new use notice.

721.47 Persons manufacturing, importing, or processing chemical substances for significant uses in small quantities solely for research and development.

To retain (a) copies of citations to information reviewed and evaluated to determine the need to make any notification of risk; (b) documentation of the nature and method of notification including copies of any labels or written notices used; (c) documentation of prudent laboratory practices used instead of notification and evaluation; and (d) the names and addresses of any persons other than the manufacturer, importer, or processor, to whom the substance is distributed, the identity of the sub-

stance, the amount distributed, and copies of the notification required.

Retention period: 5 years.

721.72 Manufacturers, importers, and processors of substances; significant new use rules.

To maintain records documenting establishment and implementation of a hazard communication program. The hazard communication program will at a minimum, describe how the requirements of this section for labels, MSDSs, and other forms of warning material will be satisfied.

Retention period: 5 years from the date of creation.

721.125 Manufacturers, importers, and processors of substances; significant new use rules.

(a) To maintain records documenting the manufacture and importation volume of the substance and the corresponding dates of manufacture and import.

(b) To maintain records documenting volumes of the substance purchased in the United States by processors of the substance, names, and addresses of suppliers, and corresponding dates of purchases.

(c) To maintain records documenting the establishment and implementation of a program for the use of any applicable personal protective equipment required under 40 CFR 721.63; and other such information as specified in cited section.

Retention period: 5 years from the date of their creation.

721.224 Manufacturers, importers, and processors of 2-chloro-N-methyl-N-substituted acetamide (generic name). [Redesignated from 721.224.]

See 40 CFR 721.125.

721.225 Manufacturers, importers, and processors of 2-chloro-N-methyl-N-substituted acetamide (generic name). [Redesignated from 721.225.]

721.235 Manufacturers, importers, and processors of halogenated-N-(2-(pentyloxy)phenyl)-N-(substituted phenyl) acetamide. [Redesignated as 721.275]

721.263 Manufacturers, importers, and processors of substituted aliphatic acid halide (generic name). [Redesignated as 721.530]

721.264 Manufacturers, importers, and processors of acrylamide, polymer with substituted alkylacrylamide salt (generic name). [Redesignated as 721.6520]

721.270 Manufacturers, importers, and processors of alanine, N-(2-carboxyethyl)-N-alkyl-, salt-. [Redesignated as 721.520]

721.273 Manufacturers, importers, and processors of aliphatic diurethane acrylate ester. [Redesignated as 721.415]

721.275 Manufacturers, importers, and processors of alkyldicarboxylic acids, polymers with alkanepolyol and TDI, alkanol blocked, acrylate. [Redesignated as 721.6720]

721.278 Manufacturers, importers, and processors of amino acrylate monomer. [Redesignated as 721.460]

721.285 Manufacturers, importers, and processors of certain acrylates. [Re-

721.296

721.285 Manufacturers, importers, and processors of acetamide, N-[4-[2-nitro-4-(pentyloxy)phenyl]-, N-[2-amino-4-(pentyloxy)phenyl]-. [Added]

See 40 CFR 721.125.

721.287 Manufacturers, importers, and processors of dialkylamino alkanoate metal salt. [Redesignated as 721.4620]

721.289 Manufacturers, importers, and processors of alkenoic acid, trisubstituted-phenyl ester. [Redesignated as 721.3040]

721.290 Manufacturers, importers, and processors of alkenoic acid, trisubstituted-phenylalkyl-disubstituted-phenyl ester. [Redesignated as 721.3080]

721.291 Manufacturers, importers, and processors of monosubstituted alkoxyaminotriazines (generic name). [Redesignated as 721.9700]

721.293 Manufacturers, importers, and processors of amide of polyamine and organic acid (generic name). [Redesignated as 721.8180]

721.295 Manufacturers, importers, and processors of reaction products of secondary alkyl amines with a substituted benzenesulfonic acid and sulfuric acid (generic name). [Redesignated as 721.9220]

721.296 Manufacturers, importers, and processors of alkylphenoxypolyalkoxyamine (generic name). [Redesignated as 721.540]

721.305

Guide to Record Retention 1994

Environmental Protection Agency

721.305 Manufacturers, importers, and processors of aminophenol. [Redesignated as 721.5820]

721.315 Manufacturers, importers, and processors of ethylated aminophenol. [Redesignated as 721.5840]

721.320 Manufacturers, importers, and processors of acrylamide-substituted epoxy. [Added]

See 40 CFR 721.125.

721.325 Manufacturers, importers, and processors of certain acrylates. [Redesignated from 721.285]

See 40 CFR 721.125.

721.370 Manufacturers, importers, and processors of substituted diacrylate. [Added]

See 40 CFR 721.125.

721.377 Manufacturers, importers, and processors of tert-Amyl peroxy alkylene ester (generic name). [Redesignated as 721.2920]

See 40 CFR 721.125.

721.390 Manufacturers, importers, and processors of monoacrylate. [Redesignated from 721.1454]

See 40 CFR 721.125.

721.400 Manufacturers, importers, and processors of polyalkylpolysilazane, bis (substituted acrylate). [New; redesignated from 721.1617]

See 40 CFR 721.125.

721.400 Manufacturers, importers, and processors of aliphatic diurethane acrylate ester. [Redesignated from 721.273]

721.415 Manufacturers, importers, and processors of aliphatic diurethane acrylate ester. [Redesignated from 721.273]

721.425 Manufacturers, importers, and processors of anilino ether. [Redesignated as 721.3380]

721.430 Manufacturers, importers, and processors of oxo-substituted aminoalkanoic acid derivative. [Added]

See 40 CFR 721.125

721.435 Manufacturers, importers, and processors of aromatic amine compound. [Redesignated as 721.750]

721.440 Manufacturers, importers, and processors of aromatic nitro compound. [Redesignated as 721.875]

721.445 Manufacturers, importers, and processors of sodium salt of an alkylated, sulfonated aromatic (generic name). [Redesignated as 721.950]

721.445 Manufacturers, importers, and processors of substituted alkenamide. [Added]

See 40 CFR 721.125.

721.450 Manufacturers, importers, and processors of substituted aromatic (generic). [Redesignated as 721.925]

721.454 Manufacturers, importers, and processors of alkyl alkenoate, azobis-. [Redesignated as 721.2380]

721.460 Manufacturers, importers, and processors of benzenamine, 3-chloro-2,6-dinitro-N,N-dipropyl-4-(trifluoromethyl)-. [Redesignated as 721.1000]

721.460 Manufacturers, importers, and processors of amino acrylate monomer. [New; redesignated from 721.278]

See 40 CFR 721.125.

721.462 Manufacturers, importers, and processors of benzenamine, 4-chloro-2-methyl-; benzenamine, 4-chloro-2-methyl-, hydrochloride; and benzenamine,2-chloro-6-methyl-. [Redesignated as 721.1025]

721.464 Manufacturers, importers, and processors of benzene, 1,2-di-methyl-, polypropene derivative, sulfonated, potassium salts. [Redesignated as 721.1225]

721.466 Manufacturers, importers, and processors of benzene, (1-methylethyl)(2-phenylethyl)-. [Redesignated as 721.1350]

721.467 Manufacturers, importers, and processors of benzene, substituted, alkyl acrylate derivative (generic name). [Redesignated as 721.1175]

721.470 Manufacturers, importers, and processors of aliphatic difunctional acrylic acid ester. [Added]

See 40 CFR 721.125.

721.480 Manufacturers, importers, and processors of benzenediazonium, 4-(dimethylamino)-, hydroxy-5-sulfobenzoic acid with 2-. [Redesignated as 721.1650]

721.490 Manufacturers, importers, and processors of modified acrylic ester (generic name). [New; redesignated from 721.977]

See 40 CFR 721.125.

721.500 Manufacturers, importers, and processors of benzenepropanoic acid, 3-(2H-benzotriazol-2-yl)-5-(1,1-dimethylethyl)-4-hydroxy-, C₇-₉-branched and linear alkyl esters. [Redesignated as 721.1600]

721.505 Manufacturers, importers, and processors of halogenated acrylonitrile. [Redesignated from 721.1130]

See 40 CFR 721.125.

721.520 Manufacturers, importers, and processors of alanine, N-(2-carboxyethyl)-N-alkyl-, salt-. [New; redesignated from 721.1150]

721.520 Manufacturers, importers, and processors of substituted polyglycidyl benzeneamine (P-83-394). [Redesignated as 721.1150]

721.523 Manufacturers, importers, and processors of brominated aromatic compound (generic name). [Redesignated as 721.775]

721.530 Manufacturers, importers, and processors of substituted aliphatic acid halide (generic name). [Redesignated from 721.263]

See 40 CFR 721.125.

721.536 Manufacturers, importers, and processors of halogenated phenyl alkane. [Added]

See 40 CFR 721.125.

721.540 Manufacturers, importers, and processors of alkylphenoxypolyalkoxyamine (generic name). [Redesignated from 721.296]

See 40 CFR 721.125.

721.550 Manufacturers, importers, and processors of alkyl alkenoate, azobis-. [New; redesignated from 721.454]

721.550 Manufacturers, importers, and processors of benzenediazonium, 4-(dimethylamino)-, salt with 4-hydroxy-5-sulfonbenzoic acid(1:1). [Redesignated as 721.1500]

721.555 Manufacturers, importers, and processors of 1,3-benzenediamine, 4-(1,1-dimethylethyl)-ar-methyl complying with the significant new use rule requirements. [Redesignated as 721.1450]

721.555

721.557 Manufacturers, importers, and processors of mixture of 1, 3-benzenediamine, 2-methyl-4,6-bis (methylthio)- and 4-methyl-2,6-bis (methylthio); significant new uses; Toxic Substances Control Act. [Redesignated as 721.1525]

721.564 Manufacturers, importers, and processors of substituted benzenedicarboxylic acid, poly (alkyl acrylate) derivative. [Redesignated as 721.1575]

721.566 Manufacturers, importers, and processors of substituted benzenesulfonic acid, alkali metal salt. [Redesignated as 721.4640]

721.567 Manufacturers, importers, and processors of disulfonic acid rosin amine salt of a benzidine derivative (generic name). [Redesignated as 721.1675]

721.570 Manufacturers, importers, and processors of benzoate ester. [Redesignated as 721.2940]

721.575 Manufacturers, importers, and processors of benzoic acid, 3,3'-methyl-enebis (6 amino, di-2-propenyl ester. [Redesignated as 721.1725]

721.580 Manufacturers, importers, and processors of alkylbisoxyalkyl (substituted 1,1-dimethylethylphenyl) benzotriazole (generic name). [Redesignated as 721.1735]

See 40 CFR 721.125.

721.588 Manufacturers, importers, and processors of 2-substituted methylenebistrisubstituted vinyl thiazolinium salt (generic name). [Redesignated from 721.1765]

721.600 Manufacturers, importers, and processors of 3-alkyl-2-(2-anilino) vinyl thiazolinium salt (generic name). [Redesignated from 721.2585]

See 40 CFR 721.125.

721.605 Manufacturers, importers, and processors of polymer of bisphenol A diglycidal ether, substituted alkenes, and butadiene. [Redesignated as 721.6900]

721.609 Manufacturers, importers, and processors of bisphenol A, epichlorohydrin, polyalkylenepolyol and polyisocyanato derivative. [Redesignated as 721.1825]

721.611 Manufacturers, importers, and processors of toluene sulfonamide bisphenol A epoxy adduct. [Redesignated as 721.1850]

721.612 Manufacturers, importers, and processors of N,N'-Bis (2,(2-(3-alkyl) thiazoline) vinyl)-1,4-phenylene diamine methyl sulfate double salt (generic name). [Redesignated as 721.5960]

721.617 Manufacturers, importers, and processors of boric acid, alkyl and substituted alkyl esters (generic name). [Redesignated as 721.1875]

721.625 Manufacturers, importers, and processors of alkylated diarylamine, sulfurized (generic name). [Redesignated from 721.792]

See 40 CFR 721.125.

721.660 Manufacturers, importers, and processors of substituted bromothiophene. [Redesignated from 721.1900]

721.700 Manufacturers, importers, and processors of methylenebistrisubstituted aniline (generic name). [Redesignated from 721.1395]

See 40 CFR 721.125.

721.740 Manufacturers, importers, and processors of phosphorylated caprolactone, alkyloxoheteromonocycle polyalkylene polyol alkyl ether (generic name). [Redesignated as 721.2000]

721.750 Manufacturers, importers, and processors of aromatic amine compound. [Redesignated from 721.435]

721.756 Manufacturers, importers, and processors of E-Caprolactone modified 2-hydroxyethyl acrylate monomer. [Redesignated as 721.6960]

721.757 Manufacturers, importers, and processors of polyoxyalkylene substituted aromatic azo colorant. [Added]

See 40 CFR 721.125.

721.759 Manufacturers, importers, and processors of carprolactone, polymer with hexamethylene diisocyanate hydroxyalkyl acrylate ester, reaction products with substituted alkanoic acid and metal heteromonocycle. [Redesignated as 721.6940]

721.766 Manufacturers, importers, and processors of bis(substituted) carbomonocyclic azocarbomocyclic name). [Removed]

721.767 Manufacturers, importers, and processors of carbamic acid, (trialkyloxy silyalkyl)-substituted acrylate ester. [Redesignated as 721.2050]

721.770 Manufacturers, importers, and processors of coconut oil, reaction products with tetrahydroxy branched alkane esters of benzenepropanoic acid (generic name). [Removed]

721.775 Manufacturers, importers, and processors of brominated aromatic compound (generic name). [Redesignated from 721.523]

See 40 CFR 721.125.

721.783 Manufacturers, importers, and processors of dialkenylamide (generic name). [Redesignated as 721.625]

721.792 Manufacturers, importers, and processors of alkylated diarylamine, sulfurized (generic name). [Redesignated as 721.625]

721.800 Manufacturers, importers, and processors of dicarboxylic acid monoester. [Redesignated as 721.3000]

721.805 Manufacturers, importers, and processors of benzenamine, 4,4'-[1,3-phenylenebis(1-methylethylidene)]bis[2,6-dimethyl-.

See 40 CFR 721.125.

721.818 Manufacturers, importers, and processors of dimer acids, polymer with polyalkylene glycol, bisphenol A-diglycidyl ether, and alkylenepolyols polyglycidyl ethers (generic name). [Redesignated as 721.6960]

721.821 Manufacturers, importers, and processors of 2,5-dimercapto-1,3,4-thiadiazole, alkyl polycarboxylate (generic name). [Redesignated as 721.2460]

721.840 Manufacturers, importers, and processors of alkyl substituted diaromatic hydrocarbons.

See 40 CFR 721.125.

721.850

721.850 Manufacturers, importers, and processors of [(dinitrophenyl)azo]-[2,4-diamino-5-methoxybenzene] derivatives. [Redesignated as 721.1300]

721.853 Manufacturers, importers, and processors of alkylated diphenyl oxide (generic name). [Redesignated as 721.2560]

721.875 Manufacturers, importers, and processors of aromatic nitro compound. [Redesignated from 721.440]

See 40 CFR 721.125.

721.880 Manufacturers, importers, and processors of distillates (petroleum), C(3–8), polymers with styrene and mixed terpenes (generic name). [Redesignated as 721.7020]

721.925 Manufacturers, importers, and processors of substituted aromatic (generic). [Redesignated from 721.450]

See 40 CFR 721.125.

721.950 Manufacturers, importers, and processors of epibromohydrin. [Redesignated as 721.2600]

721.950 Manufacturers, importers, and processors of sodium salt of an alkylated, sulfonated aromatic (generic name). [New; redesignated from 721.445].

See 40 CFR 721.125.

721.953 Manufacturers, importers, and processors of reaction product of alkanediol and epichlorohydrin. [Redesignated as 721.2625]

721.958 Manufacturers, importers, and processors of substituted bis(hydroxy alkane) polymer with epichlorohydrin, acrylate. [Redesignated as 721.6840]

Guide to Record Retention 1994

721.960 Manufacturers, importers, and processors of acid modified acylated epoxide. [Redesignated as 721.2650]

721.976 Manufacturers, importers, and processors of perfluoroalkyl epoxide (generic name). [Redesignated as 721.2675]

721.977 Manufacturers, importers, and processors of modified acrylic ester (generic name). [Redesignated as 721.490]

721.978 Manufacturers, importers, and processors of alkyl ester (generic name). [Redesignated as 721.2825]

721.979 Manufacturers, importers, and processors of substituted amino-benzoic acid ester (generic name). [Redesignated as 721.2900]

721.980 Manufacturers, importers, and processors of unsaturated amino ester salt (generic name). [Redesignated as 721.2860]

721.983 Manufacturers, importers, and processors of unsaturated amino alkyl salt (generic name). [Redesignated as 721.2880]

721.990 Manufacturers, importers, and processors of methacrylic ester. [Redesignated as 721.4800]

721.1000 Manufacturers, importers, and processors of benzenamine, 3-chloro-2,6-dinitro-N,N-dipropyl-4-(trifluoromethyl)-. [Redesignated from 721.460]

721.1005 Manufacturers, importers, and processors of vinyl epoxy ester. [Redesignated as 721.3140]

Environmental Protection Agency

721.1007 Manufacturers, importers, and processors of ethane, 1,1-dichloro-1 fluoro-. [Redesignated as 721.3200]

721.1025 Manufacturers, importers, and processors of ethanol, 2-amino-, compound with N-hydroxy-N-nitrosobenzenamine (1:1). [Redesignated as 721.3320]

721.1025 Manufacturers, importers, and processors of benzenamine, 4-chloro-2-methyl-; benzenamine, 4-chloro-2-methyl-, hydrochloride; and benzenamine, 2-chloro-6-methyl-. [New; redesignated from 721.462]

See 40 CFR 721.125.

721.1027 Manufacturers, importers, and processors of aliphatic polyglycidyl ether. [Redesignated as 721.3520]

721.1028 Manufacturers, importers, and processors of di(alkanepolyol) ether, polyacrylate. [Redesignated as 721.7400]

721.1029 Manufacturers, importers, and processors of brominated arylalkyl ether. [Redesignated as 721.3420]

721.1030 Manufacturers, importers, and processors of diglycidyl ether of disubstituted carbopolycycle (generic name). [Redesignated as 721.3480]

721.1032 Manufacturers, importers, and processors of perhalo alkoxy ether. [Redesignated as 721.3500]

721.1033 Manufacturers, importers, and processors of phosphorylated polyoxyethylene alkyl ether (generic name). [Redesignated as 721.3540]

721.1036 Manufacturers, importers, and processors of polyalkylene glycol alkyl ether acrylate. [Redesignated as 721.4020]

721.1040 Manufacturers, importers, and processors of fatty acid amine salt (generic name). [Redesignated as 721.3625]

721.1050 Manufacturers, importers, and processors of benzenamine,2,5-dibutoxy-4-(4-morpholinyl)-, sulfate. [Redesignated as 721.7040]

See 40 CFR 721.125.

721.1064 Manufacturers, importers, and processors of formaldehyde, polymer with (chloromethyl)oxirane, 4,4'-(1-methylethylidene)bis[2,6-dibromophenol] and phenol, 2-methyl-2-propenoate. [Redesignated]

721.1068 Manufacturers, importers, and processors of benzenamine, 4-isocyanato-, N,N-bis(4-isocyanatophenyl)2-5-dimethoxy-. [Added]

See 40 CFR 721.125.

721.1075 Manufacturers, importers, and processors of benzenamine,4-(1-methylbutoxy)-, hydrochloride. [Redesignated as 721.3440]

721.1078 Manufacturers, importers, and processors of haloalkyl substituted cyclic ethers. [Redesignated]

721.1078

721.1082

Guide to Record Retention 1994

Environmental Protection Agency

721.1300

721.1082 Manufacturers, importers, and processors of substituted ethylene diamine, methyl sulfate quaterized (generic name). [Redesignated as 721.3580]

721.1100 Manufacturers, importers, and processors of glycol monobenzoate. [Redesignated as 721.3860]

721.1105 Manufacturers, importers, and processors of glycols, polyethylene-, hydroxypropyl-p-(1,1,3,3-tetramethylbutyl) phenyl ether, sodium salt. [Redesignated as 721.4040]

721.1120 Manufacturers, importers, and processors of benzenamine, 4,4''-[1,4-phenylenebis(1-methylethylidene)]bis[2,6 dimethyl-. See 40 CFR 721.125.

721.1125 Manufacturers, importers, and processors of substituted alkyl halide. [Redesignated as 721.575]

721.1130 Manufacturers, importers, and processors of halogenated acrylonitrile. [Redesignated as 721.505]

721.1137 Manufacturers, importers, and processors of 3,6,9,12,15,18,21-heptaoxatetratriaoctanoic acid, sodium salt. [Redesignated as 721.5400]

721.1140 Manufacturers, importers, and processors of tris(disubstituted alkyl) heterocycle. [Redesignated as 721.4100]

721.1143 Manufacturers, importers, and processors of alkylenebis (substituted epichlorohydrin, disubstituted heteromonocycle, acrylate polymer. [Redesignated as 721.6760]

721.1150 Manufacturers, importers, and processors of substituted polyglycidyl benzeneamine (P-83-384). [Redesignated from 721.520]

In addition to the requirements of section 721.40, to maintain records which include the names of persons informed of the hazards associated with the substance, the names of any transferee and the dates of any transfers of containers which are labeled, and the method used to determine that protective gloves are impervious to the substance and the date and results of the determination. Retention period: 5 years from the date of creation of the record.

721.1175 Manufacturers, importers, and processors of benzene, substituted, alkyl acrylate derivative (generic name). [Redesignated from 721.467]
See 40 CFR 721.125.

721.1204 Manufacturers, importers, and processors of hexanedioic acid, polymer with 1,2-ethanediol and 1,6-diisocyanato-2,2,4(or 2,4,4)-trimethylhexane, 2-hydroxyethyl-acrylate-blocked. [Redesignated as 721.4220]

721.1208 Manufacturers, importers, and processors of alkyl peroxy-2-ethyl hexanoate. [Redesignated as 721.4240]

721.1210 Manufacturers, importers, and processors of benzene, (2-chloroethoxy)-. See 40 CFR 721.125.

721.1225 Manufacturers, importers, and processors of benzene, 1,2-di methyl-, polypropene derivatives sulfonated, potassium salts. [Redesignated from 721.464]

721.1232 Manufacturers, importers, and processors of nitrophenoxyalkanoic acid substituted thiazino hydrazide (generic name). [Redesignated as 721.4270]

721.1233 Manufacturers, importers, and processors of substituted hydrazine. [Redesignated as 721.4280]

721.1234 Manufacturers, importers, and processors of hydrazinecarboxamide, hexanediylbis[2,2-dimethyl]-. [Redesignated as 721.4300]

721.1235 Manufacturers, importers, and processors of hydrazinecarboxamide, N,N'-(methylenedi-4,1-phenylene)bis[2,2-dimethyl]-. [Redesignated as 721.4320]

721.1237 Manufacturers, importers, and processors of substituted hydroxyalkyl alkenoate, [(1-oxo-2-propenyl)oxy]alkoxy]carbonylamino substituted]aminocarbonyloxy--. [Redesignated as 721.4400]

721.1243 Manufacturers, importers, and processors of substituted hydroxylamine. [Redesignated as 721.4420]

721.1245 Manufacturers, importers, and processors of heterocyclic aldehyde imine. [Removed]

721.1247 Manufacturers, importers, and processors of reaction product of alkyl carboxylic acids, alkane polyols, alkyl acrylate, and isophorone diisocyanate. [Redesignated as 721.9240]

721.1261 Manufacturers, importers, and processors of alcohol, alkali metal salt. [Redesignated as 721.4660]

See 40 CFR 721.125.

721.1265 Manufacturers, importers, and processors of metal salts of complex inorganic oxyacids (generic name). [Redesignated as 721.4680]

721.1272 Manufacturers, importers, and processors of metalated alkylphenol copolymer (generic name). [Redesignated as 721.4700]

721.1282 Manufacturers, importers, and processors of reaction product of a monoalkyl succinic anhydride with an ω-hydroxy methacrylate. [Redesignated as 721.9360]

721.1285 Manufacturers, importers, and processors of hydroxyalkyl methacrylate, alkyl ester. [Redesignated as 721.4780]

721.1287 Manufacturers, importers, and processors of 2-(2-Hydroxy-3-tert-butyl-5-methyl-6-tert-butylbenzyl)-4-methyl-6-tert-butylphenyl methacrylate. [Redesignated as 721.4790]

721.1290 Manufacturers, importers, and processors of substituted oxide alkylene polymer, metacrylate. [Redesignated as 721.7180]

721.1296 Manufacturers, importers, and processors of methane, bromodifluoro- [Redesignated as 721.4820]

721.1298 Manufacturers, importers, and processors of methanol, trichloro-, carbonate (2:1). [Redesignated as 721.4880]

721.1300 Manufacturers, importers, and processors of [(dinitrophenyl)azo]-[2,4-diamino-5-methoxybenzene] derivatives. [Redesignated from 721.850]
See 40 CFR 721.125.

721.1325

721.1325 Manufacturers, importers, and processors of benzene, 1-(1-methylbutoxy)-4-nitro-.
See 40 CFR 721.125.

721.1350 Manufacturers, importers, and processors of benzene, (1-methyethyl)(2-phenylethyl)-. [Redesignated from 721.466]
See 40 CFR 721.125.

721.1372 Manufacturers, importers, and processors of substituted nitrobenzene. [Added]
See 40 CFR 721.125.

721.1375 Manufacturers, importers, and processors of carbamodithioic acid, methyl-compound with methanamine (1:1). [Redesignated as 721.2075]

721.1375 Manufacturers, importers, and processors of disubstituted nitrobenzene (generic name). [New; redesignated from 721.1477]
See 40 CFR 721.125.

721.1390 Manufacturers, importers, and processors of methylenebis (4-isocyanato benzene), polymer with polycaprolactone triol and alkoxylated alkanepolyol, hydroxyalkyl methacrylate ester. [Redesignated as 721.1740]

721.1395 Manufacturers, importers, and processors of methylenebistrisubstituted aniline (generic name). [Redesignated as 721.700]

721.1425 Manufacturers, importers, and processors of methylphenol, bis(substituted) alkyl. [Redesignated as 721.5600]

721.1430 Manufacturers, importers, and processors of pentachlorobenzene. [Added]
See 40 CFR 721.125.

Guide to Record Retention 1994

721.1435 Manufacturers, importers, and processors of 1,2,4,5-tetrachlorobenzene. [Added]
See 40 CFR 721.125.

721.1440 Manufacturers, importers, and processors of 1,3,5-trinitrobenzene. [Added]
See 40 CFR 721.125.

721.1450 Manufacturers, importers, and processors of 1, 4-(1,1-dimethylethyl)-an-methyl benzenediamine, comply with the significant new use rule requirements. [Redesignated from 721.555]

721.1454 Manufacturers, importers, and processors of monoacrylate. [Redesignated as 721.390]

721.1456 Manufacturers, importers, and processors of monomethoxy neophenyl glycol propoxylate monacrylate. [Redesignated as 721.3870]

721.1480 Manufacturers, importers, and processors of naphthalene, 1,2,3,4-tetrahydro (1-phenylethyl) (specific name). [Redesignated as 721.5225]

In addition to the requirements of 40 CFR 721.40, to maintain the following records:

(a) Any determination that gloves are impervious to the substance;

(b) Names of persons who have attended safety meetings, the dates of such meetings, and copies of any written information provided;

(c) Copies of any MSDSs used;

(d) Names and addresses of all persons to whom the substance is sold or transferred including shipment destination address, if different, the date of each transfer, the quantity of substance sold or transfer on such date; and other such information as specified in cited section.

Retention period: 5 years after the records are created.

Environmental Protection Agency

721.1465 Manufacturers, importers, and processors of 2-Naphthalenecarboxamide-N-aryl-3-hydroxy4 arylazo (generic name). [Redesignated as 721.5275]

721.1470 Manufacturers, importers, and processors of nickel acrylate complex. [Redesignated as 721.5325]

721.1475 Manufacturers, importers, and processors of substituted nitrile (generic name). [Redesignated as 721.5350]

721.1477 Manufacturers, importers, and processors of disubstituted nitrobenzene (generic name). [Redesignated as 721.1375]

721.1478 Manufacturers, importers, and processors of halonitribenzoic acid, substituted (generic name). [Redesignated as 721.1700]

721.1483 Manufacturers, importers, and processors of 6-Nitro-2(3H)-benzoxazolone. [Redesignated as 721.1775]

721.1489 Manufacturers, importers, and processors of unsaturated organic compound. [Redesignated as 721.9870]

721.1490 Manufacturers, importers, and processors of 7-Oxabicyclo [4,1.0] heptane, 3-ethenyl, homopolymer, ether with 2-ethyl-2-(hydroxymethyl)-1,3-propanediol (3:1), epoxidized. [Redesignated as 721.5600]

721.1491 Manufacturers, importers, and processors of substituted oxazolone (generic name). [Redesignated as 721.5550]

721.1525

721.1495 Manufacturers, importers, and processors of 2-Oxepanone, polymer with 4,4'-(1,methylethylidene) bisphenol and 2,2-(1-methylethylidene) phenyleneoxymethylene)(bis(4,1-phenylene oxymethylene) bisoxirane, graft. [Redesignated as 721.7160]

721.1497 Manufacturers, importers, and processors of bisallkylated fatty alkyl amine oxide. [Redesignated as 721.3740]

721.1500 Manufacturers, importers, and processors of reaction product of hydroxyethyl acrylate and methyl oxirane. [Redesignated as 721.9320]

721.1502 Manufacturers, importers, and processors of oxirane, 2,2'-(1,6-hexanediylbis (oxymethylene)bis-. [Redesignated as 721.5575]

721.1504 Manufacturers, importers, and processors of substituted oxirane. [Redesignated as 721.5600]

721.1525 Manufacturers, importers, and processors of pentacholoroethane. [Redesignated as 721.3220]

721.1525 Manufacturers, importers, and processors of mixture of 1, 3-benzenediamine, 2-methyl-4,6-bis (methylthio)- and benzenediamine, 4-methyl-2,6-bis (methylthio); significant new uses; Toxic Substances Control Act. [New; redesignated from 721.557]

In addition to the requirements of 40 CFR 721.17, to maintain the following records: (a) Any determination that gloves are impervious to the substance; (b) names of persons who have attended safety meetings; the dates of such meetings, and copies of any written information provided; copies of any MSDs used, names and addresses of all persons to whom the PMN substance is

721.1536

sold or transferred including shipment destination address if different, the date of each sale or transfer, the quantity of substance sold or transferred on such date; copies of any labels used; and other information as specified in cited section.

Retention period: 5 years after the date the records are created.

721.1537 Manufacturers, importers, and processors of phenol, 4,4'-methylene-bis(2,6-dimethyl-. [Redesignated as 721.5740]

721.1538 Manufacturers, importers, and processors of phenol, 4,4'(oxybis(2,1-ethanediylthio))bis-. [Redesignated as 721.5780]

721.1540 Manufacturers, importers, and processors of phenol, 4,4'-[methylenebis(oxy-2,1-ethanediylthio)] bis-. [Redesignated as 721.5760]

721.1541 Manufacturers, importers, and processors of sulfurized alkylphenol. [Redesignated as 721.5800]

721.1542 Manufacturers, importers, and processors of trisubstituted phenol (generic name). [Redesignated as 721.5900]

721.1544 Manufacturers, importers, and processors of sulfur bridged substituted phenols (generic name). [Redesignated as 721.5880]

721.1550 Manufacturers, importers, and processors of benzenediazonium, 4-(dimethylamino)-, salt with 2-hydroxy-5-sulfobenzoic acid (1:1). [Redesignated from 721.490]

721.1536 Manufacturers, importers, and processors of phenol, 4,4-(9H-fluoren-9-ylidene)bis-. [Removed]

721.1555 Manufacturers, importers, and processors of substituted benzenediazonium salt. [Added]
See 40 CFR 721.125.

721.1560 Manufacturers, importers, of 1,1-dimethylpropyl peroxyester (generic name). [Redesignated as 721.3020]

721.1565 Manufacturers, importers, and processors of substituted alkyl peroxyhexane carboxylate (mixed isomers) (generic name). [Redesignated as 721.4200]

721.1568 Manufacturers, importers, and processors of substituted benzenediazonium. [Added]
See 40 CFR 721.125.

721.1575 Manufacturers, importers, and processors of substituted benzenedicarboxylic acid, poly (alkyl acrylate derivative. [Redesignated from 721.564]
See 40 CFR 721.125.

721.1582 Manufacturers, importers, and processors of dialkyl phosphorodithioate phosphate compounds. [Redesignated as 721.5980]

721.1585 Manufacturers, importers, and processors of substituted phosphate ester (generic). [Redesignated as 721.3080]

721.1600 Manufacturers, importers, and processors of benzenepropanoic acid, 3-(2H-benzotriazol-2-yl)-5-(1,1-dimethylethyl)-4-hydroxy-,C7-9-branched and linear alkyl esters. [New; redesignated from 721.500]
See 40 CFR 721.125.

721.1608 Manufacturers, importers, and processors of phosphonium salt (generic name). [Redesignated as 721.6080]

721.1610 Manufacturers, importers, and processors of phosphoric acid, compounds with 2-(dibutylamino) ethanol. [Redesignated as 721.6100]

721.1611 Manufacturers, importers, and processors of phosphoric acid, 1,2-ethanediyl tetrakis(2-chloro-1-methylethyl) ester. [Redesignated as 721.6120]

721.1612 Manufacturers, importers, and processors of polymer of alkyl carbomonocycle diisocyanate with alkanepolyol polyacrylate. [Redesignated as 721.6740]

721.1614 Manufacturers, importers, and processors of oxyalkanepolyol polyacrylate. [Redesignated as 721.7420]

721.1616 Manufacturers, importers, and processors of polyalkylenepolyol alkylamine (generic name). [Redesignated as 721.7440]

721.1617 Manufacturers, importers, processors of polyalkylpolysilazane, bis (substituted acrylate). [Redesignated as 721.400]

721.1619 Manufacturers, importers, processors of polyfluorosulfonic acid salt. [Redesignated as 721.9630]

721.1620 Manufacturers, importers, and processors of hydrogenated arylated polydecene. [Redesignated as 721.6480]

721.1621 Manufacturers, importers, and processors of epoxidized polybutene. [Removed]

721.1622 Manufacturers, importers, and processors of polymer. [Redesignated as 721.6500]

721.1624 Manufacturers, importers, and processors of polymer of adipic acid, alkyldiisocyanatocarbomonocycle, alkanepolyol, hydroxyalkyl acrylate ester. [Redesignated as 721.6580]

721.1625 Manufacturers, importers, and processors of alkylbenzene sulfonate, amine salt. [Redesignated from 721.1897]
See 40 CFR 721.125.

721.1630 Manufacturers, importers, and processors of polymer of alkanepolyol, polyalkylpolyisocyanatocarbomonocycle, acetone oxime-blocked (generic name). [Redesignated as 721.8680]

721.1632 Manufacturers, importers, and processors of alkanoic acid, butanediol and cyclohexanealkanol polymer (generic name). [Redesignated as 721.6680]

721.1634 Manufacturers, importers, and processors of polymer of alkenoic acid, alkylacrylate sodium salt (generic name). [Redesignated as 721.6700]

721.1638

721.1638 Manufacturers, importers, and processors of polymer of substituted alkylphenol formaldehyde and phthalic anhydride, acrylate (generic name). [Redesignated as 721.6780]

721.1641 Manufacturers, importers, and processors of hydroxyethyl acrylate polyisocyanate. [Redesignated as 721.7080]

721.1643 Manufacturers, importers, and processors of polymer of isophorone diisocyanate, trimethylolpropane, polyalkylenepolyol, polyalkylenepolyol, disubstituted alkanes and hydroxyethyl acrylate. [Redesignated as 721.7100]

721.1646 Manufacturers, importers, and processors of polyethylenepolyamine and alkanediol diglycidyl ether. [Redesignated as 721.7260]

721.1648 Manufacturers, importers, and processors of polymer of styrene, substituted alkyl methacrylates, 2-ethylhexyl methacrylate, methacrylic acid and substituted bis(benzene). [Redesignated as 721.7340]

721.1650 Manufacturers, processors, and importers of alkylbenzenesulfonic acid and sodium salts.

See 40 CFR 721.125.

721.1675 Manufacturers, importers, and processors of disulfonic acid rosin amine salt of a benzidine derivative (generic name). [Redesignated from 721.567]

See 40 CFR 721.125.

Guide to Record Retention 1994

Environmental Protection Agency

721.1700 Manufacturers, importers, and processors of poly(oxy-1,4-butanediyl),α-(1-oxo-2-propenyl)-ω[(1-oxo-2-propenyl)oxy]-. [Redesignated as 721.7660]

721.1702 Manufacturers, importers, and processors of poly(oxy-1,2-ethanediyl)-α-hydro-ω hydroxy-2-ethyl-2-(hydroxymethyl)-1,3-propanediol, methyl ether. [Redesignated as 721.7680]

721.1704 Manufacturers, importers, and processors of poly[oxy(methyl-1,2-ethanediyl)]α,α'-(2,2-dimethyl-1,3-propanediyl)bis[ω-(oxiranylmethoxy)-. [Redesignated as 721.7780]

721.1706 Manufacturers, importers, and processors of poly(oxy-1,2-ethanediyl),α,α'-[(1-methylethylidene)di-4,1-phenylene] bis[ω-(oxiranylmethoxy)-. [Redesignated as 721.7720]

721.1708 Manufacturers, importers, and processors of poly(oxy-1,2-ethanediyl),α-hydro-ω-(oxiranylmethoxy)-, ether with 2-ethyl-2-(hydroxymethyl)-1,3-propanediol (3:1). [Redesignated as 721.7700]

721.1710 Manufacturers, importers, and processors of polyol carboxylate ester. [Redesignated as 721.7460]

721.1711 Manufacturers, importers, and processors of polyol polyols. [Redesignated as 721.7480]

See 40 CFR 721.125.

721.1712 Manufacturers, importers, and processors of nitrate polyether polyol (generic name). [Redesignated as 721.7500]

721.1715 Manufacturers, importers, and processors of alkoxylated alkane polyol, polyacrylate ester. [Redesignated as 721.7560]

721.1725 Manufacturers, importers, and processors of polysubstituted polyol. [Redesignated as 721.7540]

721.1728 Manufacturers, importers, and processors of benzoic acid, 3,3'-methyl-enebis (6-amino-, di-2-propenyl ester. [New; redesignated from 721.575]

See 40 CFR 721.125.

721.1732 Manufacturers, importers, and processors of nitrobenzoic acid octyl ester. [Added]

See 40 CFR 721.125.

721.1735 Manufacturers, importers, and processors of alkylbisoxyalkyl (substituted dimethylethylphenyl) benzotriazole (generic name). [Redesignated from 721.580]

See 40 CFR 721.125.

721.1740 Manufacturers, importers, and processors of substituted acrylated alkoxylated aliphatic polyol. [Redesignated as 721.7580]

721.1740 Manufacturers, importers, and processors of substituted dichlorobenzothiazoles. [Added]

721.1745 Manufacturers, importers, and processors of ethoxybenzothiazole disulfide.

See 40 CFR 721.125.

721.1790

721.1750 Manufacturers, importers, and processors of 1H-Benzotriazole, 5-(pentyloxy)-and benzotriazole, 5-(pentyloxy)-, sodium and potassium salts. [Added]

See 40 CFR 721.125.

721.1760 Manufacturers, importers, and processors of alkyl (heterocyclic) phenylazohetero monocyclic polyone (generic name). [Redesignated as 721.7600]

721.1763 Manufacturers, importers, and processors of alkyl (heterocyclic) phenylazohetero monocyclic polyone, (alkylimidazolyl) methyl derivative (generic name). [Redesignated as 721.7620]

721.1765 Manufacturers, importers, and processors of 2-substituted benzotriazole. [Redesignated as 721.1483]

721.1775 6-Nitro-2(3H)-benzoxazolone. [Redesignated as 721.1483]

721.1778 Manufacturers, importers, and processors of poly(oxo-1,2-ethanediyl),α-(2-methyl-1-oxo-2-propenyl)-ω-hydroxy-C_{10-16}-alkyl ethers. [Redesignated as 721.7740]

721.1780 Manufacturers, importers, and processors of poly(oxy-1,2-ethanediyl),α-(1-oxo-2-propenyl)-ω-hydroxy-C_{10-16}-alkyl ethers. [Redesignated as 721.7760]

721.1790 Manufacturers, importers, and processors of polyurethane. [Redesignated as 721.8075]

721.1795 Manufacturers, importers, and processors of 1,3-propanediamine, N,N'-1,2-ethanediylbis-, polymer with 2,4,6-trichloro-1,3,5-triazine, reaction products with N-butyl-2,2,6,6-tetramethyl-4-piperidinamine. [Redesignated as 721.7280]

721.1796 Manufacturers, importers, and processors of 2-propenamide, N-[3-(dimethylamino)propyl]-. [Redesignated as 721.8225]

721.1797 Manufacturers, importers, and processors of 2-propenenitrile, polymer with 1,3-butadiene, carboxy-1-cyano-1-methylpropyl-terminated, polymers with bisphenol A, epichloro-hydrin, and 4,4'-(1-methylethylidene)bis[2,6-dibromophenol], dimethacrylate. [Redesignated as 721.7300]

721.1798 Manufacturers, importers, and processors of 2-propenenitrile, polymer with 1,3-butadiene, carboxy-1-cyano-1-methylpropyl-terminated, polymers with epichlorohydrin, formaldehyde 4,4'-(1-methylethylidene)bis-dibromophenol], 2-methyl-2-propenoate, and phenol. [Redesignated as 721.7320]

721.1800 Manufacturers, importers, and processors of 3,3',5,5'-tetramethylbiphenyl-4,4'-diol. [Redesignated from 721.2155]

See 40 CFR 721.125.

721.1805 Manufacturers, importers, and processors of 2-propenoic acid, 3-(dimethylamino)propyl ester. [Redesignated as 721.8275]

721.1810 Manufacturers, importers, and processors of 2-propenoic acid, 2-hydroxybutyl ester. [Redesignated as 721.8300]

See 40 CFR 721.125.

721.1814 Manufacturers, importers, and processors of 2-propenoic acid, 2-methyl-,1,(hydroxymethyl) propyl ester. [Redesignated as 721.8325]

721.1815 Manufacturers, importers, and processors of 2-propenoic acid, 7-oxabicyclo [4.1.0] hept-3-ylmethyl ester. [Redesignated as 721.8350]

721.1816 Manufacturers, importers, and processors of 2-propenoic acid, 3,3,5-trimethylcyclohexyl ester. [Redesignated as 721.8400]

721.1817 Manufacturers, importers, and processors of 2-propenoic acid, 2-methyl-, 2-[3-(2H-benzotriazol-2-yl)-4-hydroxyphenyl]ethyl ester. [Redesignated as 721.8450]

721.1818 Manufacturers, importers, and processors of 2-propenoic acid, 2-methyl-1,1-dimethylethyl ester. [Redesignated as 721.8475]

721.1820 Manufacturers, importers, and processors of bisphenol A derivative. [Added]

See 40 CFR 721.125.

721.1822 Manufacturers, importers, and processors of 2-propenoic acid, 2-methyl-7-oxabicyclo [4.1.0] hept-3-ylmethyl ester. [Redesignated as 721.8500]

721.1824 Manufacturers, importers, and processors of 2-propenoic acid, 2-methyl-3,3,5-trimethylcyclohexyl ester. [Redesignated as 721.8525]

721.1825 Manufacturers, importers, and processors of bisphenol A, epichlorohydrin, polyalkylenepolyol and polyisocyanato derivative. [Redesignated from 721.609]

See 40 CFR 721.125.

721.1828 Manufacturers, importers, and processors of 2-propenoic acid, 2-methyl-,7,7,9-trimethyl-4,13-dioxo-3,14-dioxo-5,12-diazahexadecane, 1,16-diyl ester. [Redesignated as 721.8550]

721.1830 Manufacturers, importers, and processors of 2-propenoic acid [octahydro-4,7-methano-1H-indene-1,5(1,6 or 2,5)-diylbis (methyl-ene) ester. [Redesignated as 721.8575]

721.1832 Manufacturers, importers, and processors of 2-propenoic acid, octahydro-4,7-methano-1H-indenyl ester. [Redesignated as 721.8600]

721.1835 Manufacturers, importers, and processors of halogenated pyridines. [Redesignated as 721.8675]

721.1840 Manufacturers, importers, and processors of halogenated substituted pyridine. [Redesignated as 721.8750]

721.1845 Manufacturers, importers, and processors of substituted pyridines. [Redesignated as 721.8775]

721.1850 Manufacturers, importers, and processors of toluene sulfonamide bisphenol A epoxy adduct. [Redesignated from 721.611]

See 40 CFR 721.125.

721.1858 Manufacturers, importers, and processors of halogenated alkyl pyridine. [Redesignated as 721.8700]

721.1875 Manufacturers, importers, and processors of boric acid, alkyl esters (generic name). [New; redesignated from 721.617]

See 40 CFR 721.125.

721.1880 Manufacturers, importers, and processors of disubstituted halogenated pyridinol. [Redesignated as 721.8850]

721.1883 Manufacturers, importers, and processors of substituted halogenated pyridinol. [Redesignated as 721.8875]

721.1886 Manufacturers, importers, and processors of substituted halogenated pyridinol, alkali salt. [Redesignated as 721.8900]

721.1887 Manufacturers, importers, and processors of epoxy resin. [Redesignated as 721.2750]

721.1888 Manufacturers, importers, and processors of polymer of substituted phenol, formaldehyde, epichlorohydrin, and disubstituted benzene. [Redesignated as 721.7220]

721.1889 Manufacturers, importers, and processors of resoicinol, form-aldehyde substituted carbomonocycle resin. [Redesignated as 721.9480]

721.1890 Manufacturers, importers, and processors of carboxy silyl salt (generic name). [Removed, 1992]

721.1895 Manufacturers, importers, and processors of silane, (1,1-dimethylethoxy) dimethoxy (2-methyl propyl)-. [Redesignated as 721.9500]

721.1896

721.1896 Manufacturers, importers, and processors of bis (2,2,6,6-tetramethylpiperidinyl) ester of cycloalkyl spiroketal. [Redesignated as 721.9530]

721.1897 Manufacturers, importers, and processors of alkylbenzene sulfonate, amine salt. [Redesignated as 721.1625]

721.1898 Manufacturers, importers, and processors of α-Olefin sulfonate, potassium salts. [Redesignated as 721.5425]

721.1900 Manufacturers, importers, and processors of substituted bromothiophene. [Redesignated from 721.660]

See 40 CFR 721.125.

721.1920 Manufacturers, importers, and processors of 1,4-Bis(3-hydroxy-4-benzoylphenoxy)butane. [Added]

721.1925 Manufacturers, importers, and processors of substituted carboheterocyclic tetracarboxylate. [Redesignated from 721.2094]

See 40 CFR 721.125.

721.1950 Manufacturers, importers, and processors of 2-butenedioic acid (Z), mono(2-((1-oxopropenyl)oxy)ethyl ester.

See 40 CFR 721.125.

721.2000 Manufacturers, importers, and processors of phosphorylated caprolactone, alkyloxoheteromonocycle polyalkylene polyol alkyl ether (generic name). [Redesignated from 721.740]

See 40 CFR 721.125.

721.2025 Manufacturers, importers, and processors of substituted phenylimino carbamate derivative.

See 40 CFR 721.125.

721.2050 Manufacturers, importers, and processors of carbamic acid, tetrachloroethylene (triallkyloxy silylalkyl)-substituted acrylate ester. [Redesignated from 721.767]

See 40 CFR 721.125.

721.2070 Manufacturers, importers, and processors of alkylene glycol terephthalate and substituted benzoate esters (generic name). [Redesignated as 721.4060]

721.2075 Manufacturers, importers, and processors of terpenes and terpenoids, limonene fraction, polymer with substituted carbopolycycles (generic name). [Redesignated as 721.7360]

721.2085 Manufacturers, importers, and processors of reaction product of alkylphenol, tetraalkyl titanate and tin complex. [Redesignated as 721.9260]

See 40 CFR 721.125.

721.2092 Manufacturers, importers, of 3-methylcholanthrene. [Added]

721.2094 Manufacturers, importers, and processors of substituted butane tetracarboxylate. [Redesignated as 721.1925]

721.2100 Manufacturers, importers, and processors of derivative of tetrachloroethylene (P-82-684). [Redesignated as 721.3560]

721.2120 Manufacturers, importers, and processors of cyclic amide.

See 40 CFR 721.125.

721.2132 Manufacturers, importers, and processors of tetraglycidalamines (generic name). [Redesignated as 721.3840]

721.2140 Manufacturers, importers, and processors of carbopolycyclic azoalkylaminoalkylcarbomono-cyclic ester, halogen acid salt.

See 40 CFR 721.125.

721.2150 Manufacturers, importers, and processors of N,N,NN'-Tetrakis(oxiranylmethyl)-1,3-cyclohexane-dimethanamine. [Redesignated as 721.2275]

721.2155 Manufacturers, importers, and processors of 3,3',5,5'-tetramethylbiphenyl-4,4'-diol. [Redesignated as 721.1800]

See 40 CFR 721.125.

721.2170 Manufacturers, importers, and processors of cyclic phosphazene, methacrylate derivative. [Added]

721.2175 Manufacturers, importers, and processors of salt of cyclodiamine and mineral acid.

See 40 CFR 721.125.

721.2180 Manufacturers, importers, and processors of substituted thiazino hydrazine salt (generic name). [Redesignated as 721.4340]

721.2184 Manufacturers, importers, and processors of titanate [Ti_6O_{13}(2-)], dipotassium. [Redesignated as 721.9675]

721.2270

721.2188 Manufacturers, importers, and processors of 1,3,5-triazine,2,4,6-triamine, hydrobromide. [Redesignated as 721.9780]

721.2192 Manufacturers, importers, and processors of disubstituted alkyl triazines (generic name). [Redesignated as 721.9720]

721.2194 Manufacturers, importers, and processors of poly(substituted triazinyl) piperazine (generic name). [Redesignated as 721.9760]

721.2196 Manufacturers, importers, and processors of substituted triazine isocyanurate (generic name). [Redesignated as 721.9800]

721.2225 Manufacturers, importers, and processors of cyclohexanecarbonitrile, trimethyl-5-oxo-.

See 40 CFR 721.125.

721.2250 Manufacturers, importers, and processors of 1,4-cyclohexanediamine, cis- and trans-.

See 40 CFR 721.125.

721.2260 Manufacturers, importers, and processors of 1,2-Cyclohexanedicarboxylic acid, 2,2-bis[[[2-(oxiranylmethoxy)carbonyl]cyclohexyl]carbonyl]oxy]methyl]1,3-propanediyl bis(oxiranylmethyl) ester. [Added]

721.2270 Manufacturers, importers, and processors of aliphatic dicarboxylic acid salt. [Added]

See 40 CFR 721.125.

721.2275 Manufacturers, importers, and processors of N,N,N',N'-Tetrakis(oxiranylmethyl)-1,3-cyclohexane-dimethanamine. [Redesignated from 721.2150]

721.2287 Manufacturers, importers, and processors of DDT (Dichlorodiphenyltri-chloroethane. [Added]
See 40 CFR 721.125.

721.2340 Manufacturers, importers, and processors of dialkenylamide (generic name).
See 40 CFR 721.125.

721.2380 Manufacturers, importers, and processors of disubstituted diamino anisole.

In addition to the requirements of section 721.40, to maintain records which include the results of any determination that gloves are impervious, the names of persons required to wear gloves, and copies of labels. Retention period: 5 years from the date of creation of the record.

721.2420 Manufacturers, importers, and processors of alkoxylated dialkyldiethylenetriamine, alkyl sulfate salt.
See 40 CFR 721.125.

721.2460 Manufacturers, importers, and processors of 2,5-dimercapto-1,3,4-thiadiazole, alkyl polycarboxylate (generic name). [Redesignated from 721.821]
See 40 CFR 721.125.

721.2475 Manufacturers, importers, and processors of dimetridazole.
See 40 CFR 721.125

721.2480 Manufacturers, importers, and processors of urea, condensate with poly[oxy(methyl-1,2ethanediyl)]-α-2-aminomethylethyl)]-μ-(2-aminoethylethoxy) (generic name). [Redesignated as 721.9900]

721.2490 Manufacturers, importers, and processors of urea, (hexahydro-6-methyl-2-oxopyrimidinyl)-. [Redesignated as 721.9920]

721.2500 Manufacturers, importers, and processors of polyamine ureaformaldehyde condensate (specific name). [Redesignated as 721.6440]

721.2520 Manufacturers, importers, and processors of alkylated diphenyls. [Added]
See 40 CFR 721.125.

721.2540 Manufacturers, importers, and processors of diphenylmethane diisocyanate (MDI) modified.
See 40 CFR 721.125.

721.2555 Manufacturers, importers, and processors of urethane acrylate. [Redesignated as 721.9940]

721.2560 Manufacturers, importers, and processors of alkylated diphenyl oxide (generic name). [Redesignated from 721.853]
See 40 CFR 721.125.

721.2565 Manufacturers, importers, and processors of alkylated sulfonated diphenyl oxide, alkali and amine salts. [Added]
See 40 CFR 721.125.

721.2568 Manufacturers, importers, and processors of polyaromatic urethane. [Removed, 1992]

721.2575 Manufacturers, importers, and processors of disubstituted diphenylsulfone. [Added]
See 40 CFR 721.125.

721.2585 Manufacturers, importers, and processors of 3-alkyl-2-(2-anilino) vinyl thiazolinium salt (generic name). [Redesignated as 721.800]

721.2625 Manufacturers, importers, and processors of reaction product of alkanediol and epichlorohydrin. [Redesignated from 721.853]

721.2650 Manufacturers, importers, and processors of acid modified epoxide. [Redesignated from 721.960]
See 40 CFR 721.125.

721.2675 Manufacturers, importers, and processors of perfluoroalkyl epoxide (generic name). [Redesignated as 721.978]
See 40 CFR 721.125.

721.2750 Manufacturers, importers, and processors of epoxy resin. [Redesignated as 721.1887]
See 40 CFR 721.125.

721.2825 Manufacturers, importers, and processors of alkyl ester (generic name). [Redesignated from 721.978]

721.2840 Manufacturers, importers, and processors of alkylcarbamic acid, alkynyl ester.
See 40 CFR 721.125.

721.2860 Manufacturers, importers, and processors of unsaturated amino ester salt (generic name). [Redesignated from 721.980]

721.2880 Manufacturers, importers, and processors of unsaturated amino alkyl salt (generic name). [Redesignated from 721.983]
See 40 CFR 721.125.

721.2900 Manufacturers, importers, and processors of substituted aminobenzoic acid ester (generic name). [Redesignated from 721.979]

721.2920 Manufacturers, importers, and processors of tert-Amyl peroxy alkylene ester (generic name). [Redesignated from 721.377]
See 40 CFR 721.125.

721.2940 Manufacturers, importers, and processors of benzoate ester. [Redesignated from 721.570]
See 40 CFR 721.125.

721.2980 Manufacturers, importers, and processors of substituted cyclohexyldiamino ethyl esters.
See 40 CFR 721.125.

721.3000 Manufacturers, importers, and processors of dicarboxylic acid monoester. [Redesignated from 721.800]

In addition to the requirements of section 721.40, to maintain records including the names of persons required to wear protective clothing, and the name and address of each person to whom the substance is sold or transferred and the date of such sale or transfer. Retention period: 5 years from the date of creation of the record.

721.3020 Manufacturers, importers, and processors of 1,1-dimethylpropyl peroxyester (generic name). [Redesignated from 721.1560]
See 40 CFR 721.125.

721.3040 Manufacturers, importers, and processors of alkenoic acid, trisubstituted-benzyl-disubstituted-phenyl ester. [Redesignated from 721.289]
See 40 CFR 721.125.

721.3060 Manufacturers, importers, and processors of alkenoic acid, trisubstituted-phenylalkyl-disubstituted-phenyl ester. [Redesignated from 721.290]
See 40 CFR 721.125.

721.3080 Manufacturers, importers, and processors of substituted phosphate ester (generic). [Redesignated from 721.1585]
See 40 CFR 721.125.

721.3100 Manufacturers, importers, and processors of oligomeric silicic acid ester compound with a hydroxylalkylamine.
See 40 CFR 721.125.

721.3120 Manufacturers, importers, and processors of Propenoate-ter-minated alkyl substituted silyl ester.

See 40 CFR 721.125.

721.3140 Manufacturers, importers, and processors of vinyl epoxy ester. [Redesignated from 721.1005]

See 40 CFR 721.125.

721.3180 Manufacturers, importers, and processors of ethane, 2-chloro-1,1,1,2-tetrafluoro-.

See 40 CFR 721.125.

721.3200 Manufacturers, importers, and processors of ethane, 1,1-dichloro-1 fluoro-. [Redesignated from 721.1007]

See 40 CFR 721.125.

721.3220 Manufacturers, importers, and processors of pentacholoroethane. [Redesignated from 721.1525]

See 40 CFR 721.125.

721.3240 Manufacturers, importers, and processors of ethane, 1,1,1,2,2-pentafluoro-.

See 40 CFR 721.125.

721.3248 Manufacturers, importers, and processors of ethane, 1,2,2-trichlorodifluoro-. [Added]

See 40 CFR 721.125.

721.3254 Manufacturers, importers, and processors of ethane, 1,1,1-trifluoro-. [Added].

See 40 CFR 721.125.

721.3260 Manufacturers, importers, and processors of ethanediimidic acids.

See 40 CFR 721.125.

721.3320 Manufacturers, importers, and processors of ethanol, 2-amino-, compound with N-hydroxy-N-nitrosobenzenamine (1:1). [Redesignated from 721.1025]

See 40 CFR 721.125.

721.3340 Manufacturers, importers, and processors of ethanol, 2,2'-(hexylamino) bis-.

See 40 CFR 721.125.

721.3350 Manufacturers, and processors of N-itrosodiethanolamine. [Added]

See 40 CFR 721.125.

721.3360 Manufacturers, importers, and processors of substituted etha-nolamine.

See 40 CFR 721.125.

721.3367 Manufacturers, importers, and processors of alkenyl ether of alkanetriol polymer. [Added]

See 40 CFR 721.125.

721.3374 Manufacturers, importers, and processors of alkylenediolalkyl ether. [Added]

See 40 CFR 721.125.

721.3380 Manufacturers, importers, and processors of anilino ether. [Redesignated from 721.425]

See 40 CFR 721.125.

721.3390 Manufacturers, importers, and processors of aromatic amino ether. [Added]

See 40 CFR 721.125.

721.3420 Manufacturers, importers, and processors of brominated arylalkyl ether. [Redesignated from 721.1029]

See 40 CFR 721.125.

721.3435 Manufacturers, importers, and processors of butoxy-substituted ether alkane. [Added]

See 40 CFR 721.125.

721.3440 Manufacturers, importers, and processors of haloalkyl substituted cyclic ethers. [Redesignated from 721.1078]

See 40 CFR 721.125.

721.3460 Manufacturers, importers, and processors of diglycidyl ether of disubstituted carbopolycyle (generic name). [Redesignated from 721.1030]

See 40 CFR 721.125.

721.3480 Manufacturers, importers, and processors of halogenated biphenyl glycidyl ethers.

See 40 CFR 721.125.

721.3500 Manufacturers, importers, and processors of perhalo alkoxy ether. [Redesignated from 721.1032]

See 40 CFR 721.125.

721.3520 Manufacturers, importers, and processors of aliphatic polyglycidyl ether. [Redesignated from 721.1027]

See 40 CFR 721.125.

721.3540 Manufacturers, importers, and processors of phosphorylated oxoheteromonocycle polyoxyethylene alkyl ether (generic name). [Redesignated from 721.1033]

See 40 CFR 721.125.

721.3560 Manufacturers, importers, and processors of derivative of tetrachloroethylene (P-62-684). [Redesignated from 721.2100]

See 40 CFR 721.125.

721.3580 Manufacturers, importers, and processors of substituted ethyl-enediamine, methyl sulfate quaterized (generic name). [Redesignated from 721.1082]

See 40 CFR 721.125.

721.3620 Manufacturers, importers, and processors of fatty acid amine condensate, polycarboxylic acid salts.

See 40 CFR 721.125.

721.3625 Manufacturers, importers, and processors of fatty acid amine salt (generic name). [Redesignated from 721.1040]

See 40 CFR 721.125.

721.3629 Manufacturers, importers, and processors of triethanolamine salts of fatty acids. [Added]

See 40 CFR 721.125.

721.3640 Manufacturers, importers, and processors of trimethylolpropane fatty acid diacrylate. [Redesignated from 721.1045]

See 40 CFR 721.125.

721.3680 Manufacturers, importers, and processors of ethylene oxide adduct of fatty acid ester with pen-taerythritol.

See 40 CFR 721.125.

721.3700 Manufacturers, importers, and processors of fatty acid, ester with styrenated phenol, ethylene oxide adduct.

See 40 CFR 721.125.

721.3720 Manufacturers, importers, and processors of fatty amide.

See 40 CFR 721.125.

721.3740 Manufacturers, importers, and processors of bisalkylated fatty alkyl amine oxide. [Redesignated from 721.1497]

See 40 CFR 721.125.

721.3764 Manufacturers, importers, and processors of fluorene sub-stituted aromatic amine.

See 40 CFR 721.125.

721.3800 Manufacturers, importers, and processors of formaldehyde, condensed polyoxyethylene fatty acid, ester with styrenated phenol, ethylene oxide adduct.

See 40 CFR 721.125.

721.3840 Manufacturers, importers, and processors of tetraglycidalamines (generic name). [Redesignated from 721.2132]

See 40 CFR 721.125.

721.3860 Manufacturers, importers, and processors of glycol monobenzoate. [Redesignated from 721.1100]

See 40 CFR 721.125.

721.3870

721.3870 Manufacturers, importers, and processors of monomethoxy neopentyl glycol propoxylate monacrylate. [Redesignated from 721.1456]

See 40 CFR 721.125.

721.3880 Manufacturers, importers, and processors of polyalkylene glycol substituted acetate.

See 40 CFR 721.125.

721.3900 Manufacturers, importers, and processors of alkyl polyethylene glycol phosphate, potassium salt. [Redesignated from 721.1590]

See 40 CFR 721.125.

721.4000 Manufacturers, importers, and processors of polyoxy alkylene glycol amine.

See 40 CFR 721.125.

721.4020 Manufacturers, importers, and processors of polyalkylene glycol alkyl ether acrylate. [Redesignated from 721.1036]

See 40 CFR 721.125.

721.4040 Manufacturers, importers, and processors of glycols, polyethylene-, hydroxypropyl-p-(1,1,3,3-tetramethylbutyl) phenyl ether, sodium salt. [Redesignated from 721.1105]

See 40 CFR 721.125.

721.4060 Manufacturers, importers, and processors of alkylene glycol terephthalate and substituted benzoate esters (generic name). [Redesignated from 721.2070]

See 40 CFR 721.125.

721.4080 Manufacturers, importers, and processors of MNNG (N-methyl N'-nitro-N-nitrosoguanidine).

See 40 CFR 721.125.

721.4100 Manufacturers, importers, and processors of tris(disubstituted alkyl) heterocycle. [Redesignated from 721.1140]

See 40 CFR 721.125.

Guide to Record Retention 1994

721.4128 Manufacturers, importers, and processors of dimethyl-3-substituted heteromonocycle (generic name). [Added]

See 40 CFR 721.125.

721.4133 Manufacturers, importers, and processors of dimethyl-3-substituted heteromonocyclic amine. [Added]

See 40 CFR 721.125.

721.4156 Manufacturers, importers, and processors of hexachloropropene. [Added]

See 40 CFR 721.125.

721.4200 Manufacturers, importers, and processors of substituted alkyl peroxyhexane carboxylate (mixed isomers) (generic name). [Redesignated from 721.1565]

See 40 CFR 721.125.

721.4215 Manufacturers, importers, and processors of hexanedioic acid, diethenyl ester. [Added]

See 40 CFR 721.125.

721.4220 Manufacturers, importers, and processors of hexanedioic acid, polymer with 1,2-ethanediol and 1,6-diisocyanato-2,2,4(or 2,4,4)-trimethylhexane, 2-hydroxyethyl-acrylate-blocked. [Redesignated from 721.1204]

See 40 CFR 721.125.

721.4240 Manufacturers, importers, and processors of alkyl peroxy-2-ethyl hexanoate. [Redesignated from 721.1208]

See 40 CFR 721.125.

721.4250 Manufacturers, importers, and processors of hexanoic acid, 2-ethyl-, ethenyl ester. [Added]

See 40 CFR 721.125.

721.4260 Manufacturers, importers, and processors of hydrazine, [4-1-methylbutoxy) monohydrochloride.

See 40 CFR 721.125.

Environmental Protection Agency

721.4270 Manufacturers, importers, and processors of nitrophenoxyalkanoic acid substituted thiazino hydrazide (generic name). [Redesignated from 721.1232]

See 40 CFR 721.125.

721.4280 Manufacturers, importers, and processors of substituted hydrazine. [Redesignated from 721.1233]

See 40 CFR 721.125.

721.4300 Manufacturers, importers, and processors of hydrazinecarboxamide, N,N'-1,6-hexanediylbis[2,2-dimethyl-]. [Redesignated from 721.1234]

See 40 CFR 721.125.

721.4320 Manufacturers, importers, and processors of hydrazinecarboxamide, N,N'-(methylenedi-4,1-phenylene)bis[2,2-dimethyl-]. [Redesignated from 721.1235]

See 40 CFR 721.125.

721.4340 Manufacturers, importers, and processors of substituted thiazino hydrazine salt (generic name). [Redesignated from 721.2180]

See 40 CFR 721.125.

721.4380 Manufacturers, importers, and processors of modified hydro-carbon resin.

See 40 CFR 721.125.

721.4390 Manufacturers, importers, and processors of trisubstituted hydroquinone diester. [Added]

See 40 CFR 721.125.

721.4400 Manufacturers, importers, and processors of substituted hydroxyalkyl alkenoate, [(1-oxo-2-propenyl)oxy]alkoxycarbonylamino substituted[aminocarbonyl]oxy-. [Redesignated from 721.1237]

See 40 CFR 721.125.

721.4640

721.4420 Manufacturers, importers, and processors of substituted hydroxylamine. [Redesignated from 721.1243]

See 40 CFR 721.125.

721.4460 Manufacturers, importers, and processors of amidinothiopropionic acid hydrochloride.

See 40 CFR 721.125.

721.4480 Manufacturers, importers, and processors of 2-imino-1,3-thiazin-4-one-5,6-dihydromonohydrochloride.

See 40 CFR 721.125.

721.4520 Manufacturers, importers, and processors of isopropylidene, bis (1,1-dimethylpropyl) derivative.

See 40 CFR 721.125.

721.4550 Manufacturers, importers, and processors of diperoxy ketal. [Added]

See 40 CFR 721.125.

721.4568 Manufacturers, importers, and processors of methylpolychloro aliphatic ketones. [Added]

See 40 CFR 721.125.

721.4590 Manufacturers, importers, and processors of mannich-based adduct. [Added]

See 40 CFR 721.125.

721.4600 Manufacturers, importers, and processors of recovered metal hydroxide.

See 40 CFR 721.125.

721.4620 Manufacturers, importers, and processors of dialkylamino alkenoate metal salt. [Redesignated from 721.287]

See 40 CFR 721.125.

721.4640 Manufacturers, importers, and processors of substituted benzenesulfonic acid, alkali metal salt. [Redesignated from 721.566]

See 40 CFR 721.125.

721.4660

721.4660 Manufacturers, importers, and processors of alcohol, alkali metal salt. [Redesignated from 721.1261]

See 40 CFR 721.125.

721.4680 Manufacturers, importers, and processors of metal salts of complex inorganic oxyacids (generic name). [Redesignated from 721.1265]

See 40 CFR 721.125.

721.4700 Manufacturers, importers, and processors of metalated alkylphenol copolymer (generic name). [Redesignated from 721.1272].

See 40 CFR 721.125.

721.4720 Manufacturers, importers, and processors of disubstituted phenoxazine, chlorometalate salt.

See 40 CFR 721.125.

721.4780 Manufacturers, importers, and processors of hydroxyalkyl methacrylate, alkyl ester. [Redesignated from 721.1285]

See 40 CFR 721.125.

721.4790 Manufacturers, importers, and processors of 2-(2-Hydroxy-3-tert-butyl-5-methylbenzyl)-4-methyl-6-tert-butylphenyl methacrylate. [Redesignated from 721.1287]

See 40 CFR 721.125.

721.4800 Manufacturers, importers, and processors of methacrylic ester. [Redesignated from 721.990]

See 40 CFR 721.125.

721.4820 Manufacturers, importers, and processors of methane, bromodifluoro— [Redesignated from 721.1296]

See 40 CFR 721.125.

721.4840 Manufacturers, importers, and processors of substituted triphenylmethane. [Redesignated as 721.2188]

See 40 CFR 721.125.

Guide to Record Retention 1994

721.4880 Manufacturers, importers, and processors of methanol, trichloro—, carbonate (2:1). [Redesignated from 721.1298]

See 40 CFR 721.125.

721.5050 Manufacturers, importers, and processors of 2,2'-((1-methylethylidene)bis(4,1-phenyloxy(1-butoxymethyl)-2,1-ethanediyl)oxymethylene))bisoxirane, reduction product with a diamine.

See 40 CFR 721.125.

721.5075 Manufacturers, importers, and processors of mixed methyltin mercaptoester sulfides. [Added]

See 40 CFR 721.125.

721.5200 Manufacturers, importers, and processors of disubstituted naphthalene.

See 40 CFR 721.125.

721.5225 Manufacturers, importers, and processors of naphthalene, 1,2,3,4-tetrahydro (1-phenylethyl) phenylazo trisubstituted naphthalene (specific name). [Redesignated from 721.1460]

See 40 CFR 721.125.

721.5250 Manufacturers, importers, and processors of trimethyl spiropolyheterocyclic naphthalene compound.

See 40 CFR 721.125.

721.5275 Manufacturers, importers, and processors of 2-Napthalenecarboxamide-N-aryl-3-hydroxy4 arylazo (generic name). [Redesignated from 721.1465]

See 40 CFR 721.125.

721.5285 Manufacturers, importers, and processors of ethoxylated substituted napthol. [Added]

See 40 CFR 721.125.

721.5300 Manufacturers, importers, processors of neodecaneperoxoic acid, 1,1,3,3-tetramethylbutyl ester.

See 40 CFR 721.125.

Environmental Protection Agency

721.5310 Manufacturers, importers, and processors of neononanoic acid, ethenyl ester. [Added]

See 40 CFR 721.125.

721.5325 Manufacturers, importers, and processors of nickel acrylate complex. [Redesignated from 721.1470]

See 40 CFR 721.125.

721.5330 Manufacturers, importers, and processors of nickel salt of an organo compound containing nitrogen. [Added]

See 40 CFR 721.125.

721.5350 Manufacturers, importers, and processors of substituted nitrile (generic name). [Redesignated from 721.1475]

See 40 CFR 721.125.

721.5375 Manufacturers, importers, and processors of nitrothiophene-carboxylic acid, ethyl ester, bis [[[(subsituted)]amino] lkylphenyl]azo] (generic name). [Redesignated from 721.1488]

See 40 CFR 721.125.

721.5385 Manufacturers, importers, and processors of octanoic acid, hydrazide. [Added]

See 40 CFR 721.125.

721.5400 Manufacturers, importers, and processors of 3,6,9,12,15,18,21-heptaoxatetratriaoctanoic acid, sodium salt. [Redesignated from 721.1137]

See 40 CFR 721.125.

721.5425 Manufacturers, importers, and processors of α-olefin sulfonate, potassium salts. [Redesignated from 721.1898]

See 40 CFR 721.125.

721.5450 Manufacturers, importers, and processors of α-olefin sulfonate, sodium salt.

See 40 CFR 721.125.

721.5475 Manufacturers, importers, and processors of azaspiro[4,5]decane, dichloroacetyl.

See 40 CFR 721.125.

721.5705

721.5500 Manufacturers, importers, and processors of 7-oxabicyclo [4.1.0] heptane, 3-ethenyl, homopolymer, ether with 2-ethyl-2-(hydroxymethyl))-1,3-propanediol (3:1), epoxidized. [Redesignated from 721.1490]

See 40 CFR 721.125.

721.5525 Manufacturers, importers, and processors of substituted spiro oxazine.

See 40 CFR 721.125.

721.5550 Manufacturers, importers, and processors of substituted dialkyl oxazolone (generic name). [Redesignated from 721.1491]

See 40 CFR 721.125.

721.5575 Manufacturers, importers, and processors of oxirane, 2,2'-(1,6-hexanediylbis (oxymethylene)bis—. [Redesignated from 721.1502]

See 40 CFR 721.125.

721.5600 Manufacturers, importers, and processors of substituted oxirane. [Redesignated from 721.1504]

See 40 CFR 721.125.

721.5625 Manufacturers, importers, and processors of oxiranemethanamine, N,N'-[methylenebis(2-ethyl-4,1-phenylene)]bis[N-(oxiranylmethyl)]-. [Redesignated from 721.6625]

See 40 CFR 721.125.

721.5660 Manufacturers, importers, and processors of pentaerythritol, mixed esters with carboxylic acids.

See 40 CFR 721.125.

721.5700 Manufacturers, importers, and processors of pentanenitrile, 3-amino-.

See 40 CFR 721.125.

721.5705 Manufacturers, importers, and processors of 2,5,8,10,13-Pentaoxahexadec-15-enoic acid, 9,14-dioxo-2-[(1-oxo-2-propenyl)oxy]ethyl ester. [Added]

See 40 CFR 721.125.

721.5710

721.5710 Manufacturers, importers, and processors of phenacetin. [Added]
See 40 CFR 721.125.

721.5740 Manufacturers, importers, and processors of phenol, 4,4'-methylenebis(2,6-dimethyl-. [Redesignated from 721.1537]
See 40 CFR 721.125.

721.5760 Manufacturers, importers, and processors of phenol, 4,4'-[methylenebis(oxy-2,1-ethanediylthio)]bis-. [Redesignated from 721.1540]
See 40 CFR 721.125.

721.5780 Manufacturers, importers, and processors of phenol, 4,4'(oxybis(2,1-ethanediylthio)bis-. [Redesignated from 721.1538]
See 40 CFR 721.125.

721.5800 Manufacturers, importers, and processors of sulfurized alkylphenol. [Redesignated from 721.1541]
See 40 CFR 721.125.

721.5820 Manufacturers, importers, and processors of aminophenol. [Redesignated from 721.305]
See 40 CFR 721.125.

721.5840 Manufacturers, importers, and processors of ethylated aminophenol. [Redesignated from 721.315]
See 40 CFR 721.125.

721.5860 Manufacturers, importers, and processors of methylphenol, bis(substituted) alkyl. [Redesignated from 721.1425]
See 40 CFR 721.125.

721.5880 Manufacturers, importers, and processors of sulfur bridged substituted phenols (generic name). [Redesignated from 721.1544]
See 40 CFR 721.125.

721.5900 Manufacturers, importers, and processors of trisubstituted phenol (generic name). [Redesignated from 721.1542]
See 40 CFR 721.125.

Guide to Record Retention 1994

721.5910 Manufacturers, importers, and processors of phenolic resin. [Added]
See 40 CFR 721.125.

721.5915 Manufacturers, importers, and processors of polysubstituted phenylazopolysubstitutedphenyl dye. [Added]
See 40 CFR 721.125.

721.5920 Manufacturers, importers, processors of phenyl(disubstitutedpolycyclic). [Added]
See 40 CFR 721.125.

721.5960 Manufacturers, importers, and processors of N,N'-bis(2,2-(3-alkyl) thiazoline) vinyl)-1,4-phenylenediamine methyl sulfate double salt (generic name). [Redesignated from 721.612]
See 40 CFR 721.125.

721.5980 Manufacturers, importers, and processors of phosphorodithioate phosphate compounds. [Redesignated from 721.1582]
See 40 CFR 721.125.

721.5990 Manufacturers, importers, and processors of halogenated phosphate ester. [Added]
See 40 CFR 721.125.

721.6020 Manufacturers, importers, and processors of phosphine, dialkylphenyl. [Redesignated from 721.1600]
See 40 CFR 721.125.

721.6060 Manufacturers, importers, and processors of alkylaryl substituted phosphite.
See 40 CFR 721.125.

721.6070 Manufacturers, importers, and processors of alkyl phosphonate ammonium salts. [Added]
See 40 CFR 721.125.

721.6080 Manufacturers, importers, and processors of phosphonium salt (generic name). [Redesignated from 721.1608]
See 40 CFR 721.125.

Environmental Protection Agency

721.6085 Manufacturers, importers, and processors of phosphonocarboxylate [Added]
See 40 CFR 721.125.

721.6090 Manufacturers, importers, and processors of phosphoramide. [Added]
See 40 CFR 721.125.

721.6100 Manufacturers, importers, and processors of phosphoric acid, C_{6-12}-alkyl esters, compounds with 2-(dibutylamino) ethanol. [Redesignated from 721.1610]
See 40 CFR 721.125.

721.6120 Manufacturers, importers, and processors of phosphoric acid, 1,2-ethanediyl tetrakis(2-chloro-1-methylethyl) ester. [Redesignated from 721.1611]
See 40 CFR 721.125.

721.6140 Manufacturers, importers, and processors of dialkyldithiophosphoric acid, aliphatic amine salt.
See 40 CFR 721.125.

721.6160 Manufacturers, importers, and processors of piperazinone, 1,1''-[1,3,5-triazine-2,4,6-triyltris[(cyclohexylimino)-2,1-ethanediyl]tris[3,3,4,5,5-pentamethyl]-.
See 40 CFR 721.125.

721.6180 Manufacturers, importers, and processors of polyamine and organic acid. [Redesignated from 721.293]
See 40 CFR 721.125.

21.6186 Manufacturers, importers, and processors of polyamine dithiocarbamate. [Added]
See 40 CFR 721.125.

21.6193 Manufacturers, importers, and processors of polyallylene polyamine. [Added]
See 40 CFR 721.125.

721.6580

721.6200 Manufacturers, importers, and processors of fatty acid polyamide condensate, phosphoric acid ester salts.
See 40 CFR 721.125.

721.6220 Manufacturers, importers, and processors of aryl sulfonate of a fatty acid mixture, polyamine condensate.
See 40 CFR 721.125.

721.6440 Manufacturers, importers, and processors of polyamine ureaformaldehyde condensate (specific name). [Redesignated from 721.2500]
See 40 CFR 721.125.

721.6480 Manufacturers, importers, and processors of hydrogenated arylated polydecene. [Redesignated from 721.1620]
See 40 CFR 721.125.

721.6500 Manufacturers, importers, and processors of polymer. [Redesignated as 721.6522]
See 40 CFR 721.125.

721.6520 Manufacturers, importers, and processors of acrylamide, polymer with substituted alkylacrylamide salt (generic name). [Redesignated from 721.264]
See 40 CFR 721.125.

721.6540 Manufacturers, importers, and processors of acrylamide, polymers with tetraalkyl ammonium salt and polyalkyl, aminoalkyl methacrylamide salt.
See 40 CFR 721.125.

721.6560 Manufacturers, importers, and processors of acrylic acid, polymer with substituted ethene.
See 40 CFR 721.125.

721.6580 Manufacturers, importers, and processors of polymer of adipic acid, alkyldiisocyanatocarbomonocycle, hydroxyalkyl acrylate ester. [Redesignated from 721.1624]
See 40 CFR 721.125.

721.6600 Manufacturers, importers, and processors of adipic acid, polymer with 1,4-cyclohexane-dimethanol, dipropylene glycol, and TDI, alkanol blocked, substituted carbomonocyclic dicarboxylic acid (generic name). [Redesignated from 721.266]

See 40 CFR 721.125.

721.6620 Manufacturers, importers, and processors of alkanaminium, polyalkyl-[(2-methyl-1-oxo-2-propenyl)oxy]salt, polymer with acrylamide and substituted alkyl methacrylate.

See 40 CFR 721.125.

721.6625 Manufacturers, importers, and processors of oxiranemethanamine, N,N'-[methylenebis(2-ethyl-4,1-phenylene)]bis[N-(oxiranylmethyl)]-. [Redesignated as 721.5625]

721.6640 Manufacturers, importers, and processors of alkanedioic acid, methylenebiscarbomonocyclic diisocyanate, and alkylene glycols, hydroxyalkyl acrylate ester.

See 40 CFR 721.125.

721.6660 Manufacturers, importers, and processors of polymer of alkanepolyol polyalkylpolyisocyanatocarbomonocycle, acetone oxime-blocked (generic name). [Redesignated from 721.1630]

See 40 CFR 721.125.

721.6680 Manufacturers, importers, and processors of alkanoic acid, butanediol and cyclohexanealkanol polymer (generic name). [Redesignated from 721.1632]

See 40 CFR 721.125.

721.6700 Manufacturers, importers, and processors of polymer of alkenoic acid, substituted alkylacrylate sodium salt (generic name). [Redesignated from 721.1634]

See 40 CFR 721.125.

721.6720 Manufacturers, importers, and processors of alkyldicarboxylic acids, polymers with alkanepolyol and TDI, polymer with substituted alkanepolyol polyacrylate. [Redesignated from 721.1612]

See 40 CFR 721.125.

721.6740 Manufacturers, importers, and processors of polymer of alkyl carbomonocycle diisocyanate with alkanepolyol polyacrylate. [Redesignated from 721.275]

See 40 CFR 721.125.

721.6760 Manufacturers, importers, and processors of alkylenebis substituted alkylphenol epichlorohydrin, heteromonocycle, and phthalic anhydride, acrylate polymer. [Redesignated from 721.1638]

See 40 CFR 721.125.

721.6780 Manufacturers, importers, and processors of polymer of substituted alkylphenol formaldehyde epichlorohydrin, acrylate. [Redesignated from 721.1143]

See 40 CFR 721.125.

721.6820 Manufacturers, importers, and processors of polymer of substituted aryl olefin.

See 40 CFR 721.125.

721.6840 Manufacturers, importers, and processors of substituted bis(hydroxy alkane) polymer with epichlorohydrin, acrylate. [Redesignated from 721.956]

See 40 CFR 721.125.

721.6880 Manufacturers, importers, and processors of bisphenol A, epichlorohydrin, methylenebis (substituted carbomonocycle), polyalkylene glycol, alkanol, methacrylate polymer. [Redesignated from 721.607]

See 40 CFR 721.125.

721.6900 Manufacturers, importers, and processors of polymer of bisphenol A diglycidal ether, substituted alkenes, and butadiene. [Redesignated from 721.605]

See 40 CFR 721.125.

721.6920 Manufacturers, importers, and processors of butyl acrylate, polymer with substituted methyl styrene, methyl methacrylate, and substituted silane.

See 40 CFR 721.125.

721.6940 Manufacturers, importers, and processors of carprolactone, polymer with hexamethylene diisocyanate hydroxyalkyl acrylate polyalkylenepolyol, disubstituted alkanes and hydroxyalkyl acrylate. [Redesignated from 721.759]

See 40 CFR 721.125.

721.6960 Manufacturers, importers, and processors of E-Caprolactone modified 2-hydroxyethyl acrylate monomer. [Redesignated from 721.756]

See 40 CFR 721.125.

721.6980 Manufacturers, importers, and processors of dimer acids, polymer with polyalkylene glycol, bisphenol A-diglycidyl ether, and alkylenepolyols polyglycidyl ethers (generic name). [Redesignated from 721.818]

See 40 CFR 721.125.

721.7000 Manufacturers, importers, and processors of polymer of disodium maleate, allyl ether, and ethylene oxide.

See 40 CFR 721.125.

721.7020 Manufacturers, importers, and processors of distillates (petroleum), C(3–6), polymers with styrene and mixed terpenes (generic name). [Redesignated from 721.880]

See 40 CFR 721.125.

721.7040 Manufacturers, importers, and processors of formaldehyde, polymer with (chloromethyl)oxirane, 4,4'-(1-methylethylidene)bis[2,6-dibromophenol] and phenol, methyl-2-propenoate. [Redesignated from 721.1064]

See 40 CFR 721.125.

721.7080 Manufacturers, importers, and processors of polymer of hydroxyethyl acrylate and polyisocyanate. [Redesignated from 721.1641]

See 40 CFR 721.125.

721.7100 Manufacturers, importers, and processors of isophorone diisocyanate, trimethylolpropane, polyalkylenepolyol, disubstituted alkanes and hydroxyalkyl acrylate. [Redesignated from 721.1643]

See 40 CFR 721.125.

721.7140 Manufacturers, importers, and processors of methylenebis (4-isocyanato benzene), polymer with polycaprolactone triol and alkoxylated alkanepolyol, methacrylate ester. [Redesignated from 721.1390]

See 40 CFR 721.125.

721.7160 Manufacturers, importers, and processors of 2-oxepanone, polymer with 4,4'-(1-methylethylidene)bisphenol and 2,2-[1-methylethylidene)(bis(4,1-phenyleneoxymethylene)] bisoxirane, graft. [Redesignated from 721.1495]

See 40 CFR 721.125.

721.7180 Manufacturers, importers, and processors of substituted oxide-alkylene polymer, methacrylate. [Redesignated from 721.1290]

See 40 CFR 721.125.

721.7200 Manufacturers, importers, and processors of perfluoroalkyl aromatic carbamate modified methacrylate copolymer.

See 40 CFR 721.125.

721.7210 Manufacturers, importers, and processors of epoxidized copolymer of phenol and substituted phenol.

See 40 CFR 721.125.

721.7220 Manufacturers, importers, and processors of polymer of substituted phenol, formaldehyde, epichlorohydrin, and disubstituted benzene. [Redesignated from 721.1888]

See 40 CFR 721.125.

721.7240 Manufacturers, importers, and processors of polymer of phthalate, disubstituted dioxoheteropolycycle, and methacrylic acid.

See 40 CFR 721.125.

721.7260 Manufacturers, importers, and processors of polyethylenepolyamine and alkanediol diglycidyl ether. [Redesignated from 721.1646]

See 40 CFR 721.125.

721.7280 Manufacturers, importers, of propanediamine, N,N'-1,2-ethanediylbis-, polymer with 2,4,6-trichloro-1,3,5-triazine, reaction products with N-butyl-2,2,6,6-tetramethyl-4-piperidinamine. [Redesignated from 721.1795]

See 40 CFR 721.125.

721.7300 Manufacturers, importers, and processors of 2-propenenitrile, polymer with 1,3-butadiene, carboxy-1-cyano-1-methylpropyl-terminated, polymers with bisphenol A, epichlorohydrin, and 4,4'-(1-methylethylidene)bis[2,6-dibromophenol], dimethacrylate. [Redesignated from 721.1797]

See 40 CFR 721.125.

721.7320 Manufacturers, importers, and processors of 2-propenenitrile, polymer with 1,3-butadiene, 3-carboxy-1-cyano-1-methylpropyl-terminated, polymers with epichlorohydrin, formaldehyde 4,4'-(1-methylethylidene)bis phenol, 2-methyl-2-propenoate. [Redesignated from 721.1798]

See 40 CFR 721.125.

721.7340 Manufacturers, importers, and processors of polymer of styrene, substituted alkyl methacrylate, 2-ethylhexyl acrylate, methacrylic acid and substituted bis(benzene). [Redesignated from 721.1848]

See 40 CFR 721.125.

721.7360 Manufacturers, importers, and processors of terpenes and terpenoids, limonene fraction, polymer with substituted alkane polycycles (generic name). [Redesignated from 721.2075]

See 721.125.

721.7370 Manufacturers, importers, and processors of acrylates of aliphatic polyol. [Added]

See 40 CFR 721.125.

721.7400 Manufacturers, importers, and processors of di(alkanepolyol) ether, polyacrylate. [Redesignated from 721.1614]

See 40 CFR 721.125.

721.7420 Manufacturers, importers, and processors of oxyalkanepolyol polyacrylate. [Redesignated from 721.1616]

See 40 CFR 721.125.

721.7440 Manufacturers, importers, and processors of polyalkylenepolyol alkylamine (generic name). [Redesignated from 721.1763]

See 40 CFR 721.125.

721.7450 Manufacturers, importers, and processors of aromatic amine polyols. [Added]

See 40 CFR 721.125.

721.7460 Manufacturers, importers, and processors of polyol carboxylate ester. [Redesignated from 721.1710]

See 40 CFR 721.125.

721.7480 Manufacturers, importers, and processors of isocyanate terminated polyols. [Redesignated from 721.1711]

See 40 CFR 721.125.

721.7500 Manufacturers, importers, and processors of nitrate polyether polyol (generic name). [Redesignated from 721.1712]

See 40 CFR 721.125.

721.7540 Manufacturers, importers, and processors of polysubstituted polyol. [Redesignated from 721.1725]

See 40 CFR 721.125.

721.7560 Manufacturers, importers, and processors of alkoxylated alkane polyol, polyacrylate ester. [Redesignated from 721.1715]

See 40 CFR 721.125.

721.7580 Manufacturers, importers, and processors of substituted alkoxylated aliphatic polyol. [Redesignated from 721.1740]

See 40 CFR 721.125.

721.7600 Manufacturers, importers, and processors of alkyl (heterocyclic) phenylazohetero monocyclic polyone, (generic name). [Redesignated from 721.1760]

See 40 CFR 721.125.

721.7620 Manufacturers, importers, and processors of alkyl (heterocyclic) phenylazohetero monocyclic polyone, (alkylimidazlyl) methyl derivative (generic name). [Redesignated from 721.1763]

See 40 CFR 721.125.

721.7660 Manufacturers, importers, and processors of poly(oxy-1,4-butanediyl),α-(1-oxo-2-propenyl)oxy)-ω[(1-oxo-2-propenyl)oxy]-. [Redesignated from 721.1700]

See 40 CFR 721.125.

721.7680 Manufacturers, importers, and processors of poly(oxy-1,2-ethanediyl),α-hydro-ω-ether with 2-ethyl-2-(hydroxymethyl)-1,3-propanediol (3:1) di-2-propenoate, methyl ether. [Redesignated from 721.1702]

See 40 CFR 721.125.

721.7700 Manufacturers, importers, and processors of poly(oxy-1,2-ethanediyl),α-hydro-ω-(oxiranylmethoxy)-, ether with 2-ethyl-2-(hydroxymethyl)-1,3-propanediol (3:1). [Redesignated from 721.1708]

See 40 CFR 721.125.

721.7720 Manufacturers, importers, and processors of poly(oxy-1,2-ethanediyl),α,α'-[(1-methylethylidene) di-4,1-phenylene]bis[ω-(oxiranylmethoxy)-. [Redesignated from 721.1706]

See 40 CFR 721.125.

721.7740 Manufacturers, importers, and processors of poly(oxo-1,2-ethanediyl),α-(2-methyl-1-oxo-2-propenyl)-ω-hydroxy-C_{10-16}-alkyl ethers. [Redesignated from 721.1778]

See 40 CFR 721.125.

721.7760 Manufacturers, importers, and processors of poly(oxy-1,2-ethanediyl),α-(1-oxo-2-propenyl)-ω-hydroxy-C_{10-16}-alkyl ethers. [Redesignated from 721.1780]

See 40 CFR 721.125.

721.7770 Manufacturers, importers, and processors of alkylphenoxypoly(oxyethylene) sulfuric acid ester, substituted amine salt. [Added]

See 40 CFR 721.125.

721.7780 Manufacturers, importers, and processors of poly[oxy(methyl-1,2-ethanediyl)],α,α'-(2,2-dimethyl-1,3-propanediyl)bis[ω-(oxiranymethoxy)-. [Redesignated from 721.1790]

See 40 CFR 721.125.

721.8075 Manufacturers, importers, and processors of polyurethane. [Redesignated from 721.1790]

See 40 CFR 721.125.

721.8125 Manufacturers, importers, and processors of propane, 1,1,1,2,3,3,3-heptafluoro-.

721.8082

721.8082 Manufacturers, importers, and processors of polyester polyurethane acrylate. [Added]

See 40 CFR 721.125.

721.8160 Manufacturers, importers, and processors of propanoic acid, 2,2-dimethyl-, ethenyl ester.

See 40 CFR 721.125.

721.8225 Manufacturers, importers, and processors of 2-propenamide, N-[3-(dimethylamino)propyl]–. [Redesignated from 721.1796]

See 40 CFR 721.125.

721.8260 Manufacturers, importers, and processors of 1-propanol, 3,3′-oxybis[2,2-bis(bromomethyl)-.

See 40 CFR 721.125.

721.8265 Manufacturers, importers, and processors of 2-propenoic acid, C₁₈–₂₆ and C₇₀alkyl esters. [Added]

See 40 CFR 721.125.

721.8275 Manufacturers, importers, and processors of 2-propenoic acid, 3-(dimethylamino)-2,2-dimethylpropyl ester. [Redesignated from 721.1805]

See 40 CFR 721.125.

721.8290 Manufacturers, importers, and processors of propenoic acid, docosyl ester. [Added]

See 40 CFR 721.125.

721.8325 Manufacturers, importers, and processors of 2-propenoic acid, 1,(hydroxymethyl) propyl ester. [Redesignated from 721.1814]

See 40 CFR 721.125.

721.8300 Manufacturers, importers, and processors of 2-propenoic acid, 2-hydroxybutyl ester. [Redesignated from 721.1810]

See 40 CFR 721.125.

721.8325 Manufacturers, importers, and processors of 2-propenoic acid, 1-(hydroxymethyl)propyl ester. [Redesignated from 721.1814]

See 40 CFR 721.125.

Guide to Record Retention 1994

721.8335 Manufacturers, importers, and processors of 2-propenoic acid, 2-[[[(1-methylethoxy)carbonyl]amino]ethyl ester. [Added]

See 40 CFR 721.125.

721.8350 Manufacturers, importers, and processors of 2-propenoic acid, 7-oxabicyclo [4.1.0] hept-3-ylmethyl ester. [Redesignated from 721.1815]

See 40 CFR 721.125.

721.8375 Manufacturers, importers, and processors of 2-propenoic acid, 2-(2-oxo-3-oxazolidinyl)ethyl ester.

See 40 CFR 721.125.

721.8400 Manufacturers, importers, and processors of 2-propenoic acid, 3,3,5-trimethylcyclohexyl ester. [Redesignated from 721.1816]

See 40 CFR 721.125.

721.8425 Manufacturers, importers, and processors of 2-propenoic acid, 2-[[[(1,3,3-trimethyl-5-[[2-(1-oxo-2-propenyl)oxy] ethoxy] carbonyl] amino] cyclohexyl] methyl]amino carbonyl] oxy]ethyl ester.

See 40 CFR 721.125.

721.8450 Manufacturers, importers, and processors of 2-propenoic acid, 2-methyl-, 2-[3-(2H-benzotriazol-2-yl)-4-hydroxyphenyl]ethyl ester. [Redesignated from 721.1817]

See 40 CFR 721.125.

721.8475 Manufacturers, importers, and processors of 2-propenoic acid, 2-methyl-1,1-dimethylethyl ester. [Redesignated from 721.1818]

See 40 CFR 721.125.

721.8500 Manufacturers, importers, and processors of 2-propenoic acid, 2-methyl-7-oxabicyclo [4.1.0] hept-3-ylmethyl ester. [Redesignated from 721.1822]

See 40 CFR 721.125.

721.8525 Manufacturers, importers, and processors of 2-propenoic acid, 2-methyl-3,3,5-trimethylcyclohexyl ester. [Redesignated from 721.1824]

See 40 CFR 721.125.

Environmental Protection Agency

721.8550 Manufacturers, importers, and processors of 2-propenoic acid, 2-methyl-1,7,7,9-trimethyl-4,13-dioxo-3,14-dioxo-5,12-diazahexadecane, 1,16-diyl ester. [Redesignated from 721.1828]

See 40 CFR 721.125.

721.8575 Manufacturers, importers, and processors of 2-propenoic acid [octahydro-4,7-methano-1H-indene-1,5(1,6 or 2,5)-diyl]bis (methylene) ester. [Redesignated from 721.1830]

See 40 CFR 721.125.

721.8600 Manufacturers, importers, and processors of 2-propenoic acid, octahydro-4,7-methano-1H-indenyl ester. [Redesignated from 721.1832]

See 40 CFR 721.125.

721.8650 Manufacturers, importers, and processors of 2-propenoic acid, reaction product with 2-oxepanone and alkyltriol. [Added]

See 40 CFR 721.125.

721.8675 Manufacturers, importers, and processors of halogenated pyridine. [Redesignated from 721.1835]

See 40 CFR 721.125.

721.8700 Manufacturers, importers, and processors of halogenated alkyl pyridine. [Redesignated from 721.1858]

See 40 CFR 721.125.

721.8750 Manufacturers, importers, and processors of halogenated substituted pyridine. [Redesignated from 721.1840]

See 40 CFR 721.125.

721.8775 Manufacturers, importers, and processors of substituted pyridines. [Redesignated from 721.1863]

See 40 CFR 721.125.

721.8825 Manufacturers, importers, and processors of substituted 2-methylpyridine and substituted 2-phenoxypyridine. [Redesignated from 721.1875]

See 40 CFR 721.125.

721.8850 Manufacturers, importers, and processors of disubstituted halogenated pyridinol. [Redesignated from 721.1880]

See 40 CFR 721.125.

721.8875 Manufacturers, importers, and processors of substituted halogenated pyridinol. [Redesignated from 721.1883]

See 40 CFR 721.125.

721.8900 Manufacturers, importers, and processors of substituted halogenated pyridinol, alkali salt. [Redesignated from 721.1886]

See 40 CFR 721.125.

721.8965 Manufacturers, importers, and processors of 1H-Pyrole-2, 5-dione, 1-(2,4,6-tribromophenyl)-. [Added]

See 40 CFR 721.125.

721.9000 Manufacturers, importers, and processors of N-Nitrosopyrrolidine. [Added]

See 40 CFR 721.125.

721.9075 Manufacturers, importers, and processors of quaternary ammonium salt of fluorinated alkylaryl amide. [Added]

See 40 CFR 721.125.

721.9075

In addition to the requirements of section 721.40, to maintain records including the names of persons required to wear protective clothing and/or equipment, records of respirator fit tests for each person required to wear a respirator, and the names and addresses of persons to whom any of these substances are sold or transferred and the date of such sale or transfer.

Retention period: 5 years from the date of creation of the record.

721.9220 Manufacturers, importers, and processors of reaction products of secondary alkyl amines with a substituted benzenesulfonic acid and sulfuric acid (generic name). [Redesignated from 721.2295]

See 40 CFR 721.125.

721.9240 Manufacturers, importers, and processors of reaction product of alkyl carboxylic acids, alkane polyamines, alkyl substituted.

See 40 CFR 721.125.

721.9260 Manufacturers, importers, and processors of reaction product of alkylphenol, tetraallyl titanate and tin complex. [Redesignated from 721.2085]

See 40 CFR 721.125.

721.9280 Manufacturers, importers, and processors of ethoxylated fatty acid oils and a phenolic pentaerythritol tetraester.

See 40 CFR 721.125.

721.9300 Manufacturers, importers, and processors of substituted hydroxyalkanes and polyalkylpolyisocyanatocarbomonocycle.

See 40 CFR 721.125.

721.9320 Manufacturers, importers, and processors of reaction product of hydroxyethyl acrylate and methyl oxirane. [Redesignated from 721.1500]

See 40 CFR 721.125.

721.9360 Manufacturers, importers, and processors of reaction product of a monoalkyl succinic anhydride with an ω-hydroxy methacrylate. [Redesignated from 721.1282]

See 40 CFR 721.125.

721.9400 Manufacturers, importers, and processors of reaction product of phenolic pentaerythritol tetraesters with fatty acid esters and oils, and glyceride triesters.

See 40 CFR 721.125.

Guide to Record Retention 1994

721.9420 Manufacturers, importers, and processors of polymethylcarbomonocycle, reaction product with 2-hydroxyethyl acrylate.

See 40 CFR 721.125.

721.9460 Manufacturers, importers, and processors of tall oil fatty acids, reaction products with polyamines, alkyl substituted.

See 40 CFR 721.125.

721.9480 Manufacturers, importers, and processors of resoicinol, formsubstituted aldehyde carbomonocycle resin. [Redesignated from 721.1889]

See 40 CFR 721.125.

721.9500 Manufacturers, importers, and processors of silane, (1,1-dimethylethoxy) dimethoxy (2-methyl propyl)-. [Redesignated from 721.1895]

See 40 CFR 721.125.

721.9510 Manufacturers, importers, and processors of silicone esterpolyacrylate. [Added]

See 40 CFR 721.125.

721.9525 Manufacturers, importers, and processors of acrylate substituted siloxanes and silicones.

See 40 CFR 721.125.

721.9527 Manufacturers, importers, and processors of bis(1,2,2,6,6-pentamethyl-4-piperidin-4-ol) ester of cycloaliphatic spiroketal. [Added]

See 40 CFR 721.125.

721.9530 Manufacturers, importers, and processors of bis (2,2,6,6-tetramethyl-4-piperidinyl) ester of cycloalkyl spiroketal. [Redesignated from 721.1896]

See 40 CFR 721.125.

721.9570 Manufacturers, importers, and processors of halophenyl sulfonamide salt. [Added]

See 40 CFR 721.125.

721.9580 Manufacturers, importers, and processors of ethyl methanesulfonate. [Added]

See 40 CFR 721.125.

721.9620 Manufacturers, importers, and processors of aromatic sulfonic acid compound with amine. [Added]

See 40 CFR 721.125.

721.9630 Manufacturers, importers, and processors of polyfluorosulfonic acid salt. [Redesignated from 721.1619]

See 40 CFR 721.125.

721.9650 Manufacturers, importers, and processors of tetramethylammonium salts of alkylbenzenesulfonic acid. [Added]

See 40 CFR 721.125.

721.9660 Manufacturers, importers, and processors of methylthiouracil. [Added]

See 40 CFR 721.125.

721.9665 Manufacturers, importers, and processors of organotin catalysts. [Added]

See 40 CFR 721.125.

721.9675 Manufacturers, importers, and processors of titanate [Ti,O,]3,(2-)), dipotassium. [Redesignated from 721.2184]

See 40 CFR 721.125.

721.9700 Manufacturers, importers, and processors of monosubstituted alkoxyaminotriazines (generic name). [Redesignated from 721.291]

See 40 CFR 721.125.

721.9720 Manufacturers, importers, and processors of disubstituted alkyl triazines (generic name). [Redesignated from 721.2192]

See 40 CFR 721.125.

Environmental Protection Agency

721.9730 Manufacturers, importers, and processors of 1,3,5-triazin-2-amine, 4-dimethylamino-6-substituted-. [Added]

See 40 CFR 721.125.

721.9740 Manufacturers, importers, and processors of brominated triazine derivative.

See 40 CFR 721.125.

721.9760 Manufacturers, importers, and processors of substituted triazine isocyanurate (generic name). [Redesignated from 721.2194]

See 40 CFR 721.125.

721.9780 Manufacturers, importers, and processors of 1,3,5-triazine-2,4,6-triamine, hydrobromide. [Redesignated from 721.2188]

See 40 CFR 721.125.

721.9800 Manufacturers, importers, and processors of poly(substituted triazinyl) piperazine (generic name). [Redesignated from 721.2196]

See 40 CFR 721.125.

721.9820 Manufacturers, importers, and processors of substituted triazole.

See 40 CFR 721.125.

721.9850 Manufacturers, importers, and processors of 2,4,8,10-tetraoxa-3,9-diphosphaspiro[5.5]undecane,3,9-bis[2,4,6-tris(1,1-dimethylethyl)phenoxy]-.

See 40 CFR 721.125.

721.9870 Manufacturers, importers, and processors of unsaturated organic compound. [Redesignated from 721.1489]

See 40 CFR 721.125.

721.9900 Manufacturers, importers, and processors of urea, condensate with poly[oxy(methyl-1,2-ethanediyl)]-α-(2-aminomethylethyl)-μ-(2-aminomethylethoxy) (generic name). [Redesignated from 721.2480]

See 40 CFR 721.125.

721.9920 Manufacturers, importers, and processors of urea, (hexahydro-6-methyl-2-oxopyrimidinyl)-. [Redesignated from 721.2490]
See 40 CFR 721.125.

721.9925 Manufacturers, importers, and processors of urea, aminoethylethylene methacrylamide. [Added]
See 40 CFR 721.125.

721.9940 Manufacturers, importers, and processors of urethane acrylate. [Redesignated from 721.2555]
See 40 CFR 721.125.

721.9957 Manufacturers, importers, and processors of N-Nitroso-N-methylurethane. [Added]
See 40 CFR 721.125.

721.9975 Manufacturers, importers, and processors of zirconium(IV),[2,2-bis[(2-propenyloxy)methyl]-1-butanolato-01,02]tris(2-propenoato-0-)-.
See 40 CFR 721.125.

723.50 Manufacturers of new chemical substances manufactured in quantities of 1,000 kilograms or less per year under low volume exemption.
To maintain records of (a) the annual production volume of the new chemical substance under the exemption and (b) documentation of information in the exemption notices and compliance with the terms of the regulations.
Retention period: 5 years.

723.175 Manufacturers and processors of new chemical substances used in or for the manufacture of processing of instant photographic and peel-apart film articles under instant photographic chemical exemption.
To keep records on annual production volume, exposure monitoring, worker's training and exposure, and method of treatment.
Retention period: 30 years.

723.250 Manufacturers of new polymers under polymer exemption.
To maintain records of production volume for the first 3 years of manufacture, the date of commencement of manufacture, and documentation of concentration of this information and any other information provided in the limited premanufacture notice.
Retention period: 5 years.

749.68 Persons distributing in commerce hexavalent chromium-based water treatment chemicals for use in cooling systems after February 20, 1990.
To retain in one location at the headquarters of the distribution documentation showing (a) the name, address, contact, and telephone number of the cooling system owners/operations to whom the chemicals were shipped and (b) the chemicals included in the shipment, the amount of each chemical shipped, and the location(s) at which the chemical will be used.
Retention period: 2 years from the date of shipment.

761.30 Owners or operators of PCB transformers in use or stored for reuse.
To maintain records of inspections and maintenance history, including leaks, repairs, replacement, cleanup and containment.
Retention period: 3 years after disposal of transformer.

761.30 Owners or operators of railroad transformers using PCBs.
(a) To maintain records of concentration of PCBs in dielectric fluid after servicing railroad transformer for purposes of reducing PCB concentration in dielectric fluid.
Retention period: Until January 1, 1991.
(b) To maintain at the facility documentation to support the reason for the emergency installation of a PCB transformer. Documentation must be completed within 30 days after installation of the PCB transformer.
Retention period: Not specified.

761.30 Owners or operators of heat transfer systems that ever contained PCBs in heat fluid in concentrations greater than 50 ppm.
To maintain annual records on disposal, storage, chemical waste landfills, incineration, high efficiency broilers, and other documentation as specified in section.

Guide to Record Retention 1994 Environmental Protection Agency

ties.
Retention period: 5 years.

761.125 Owners of spilled PCBs.
(a) At the completion of cleanup, to document the cleanup with records and certification of decontamination.
Retention period: 5 years.
(b) If cleanup is delayed because of adverse weather conditions, lack of access due to physical impossibility or emergency operating conditions, to maintain records documenting the fact that circumstances precluded rapid response.
Retention period: 5 years.

761.180 Owners or operators of facilities used to dispose of PCBs.
To maintain records of PCB activities.
Retention period: 5 years.

761.60 Owners or operators of high efficiency boilers used to dispose of mineral oil dielectric fluid and other liquids containing between 50 and 500 ppm PCBs.
To maintain records of quantities of mineral oil dielectric fluid burned each month, and data from monitoring of combustion.
Retention period: 5 years.

761.75 Owners or operators of facilities used to dispose of PCBs.
To maintain records of all disposal operations.
Retention period: 5 years.

761.80 Processors and distributors of PCB in small quantities for research and development having commercial exemption.
To maintain records of PCB activities.

761.30 Owners or operators of hydraulic systems that ever contained PCBs at concentrations above 50ppm.
To maintain records of data obtained from required test sampling of PCB concentration in hydraulic fluid.
Retention period: 5 years after PCB concentration in fluid reaches 50 ppm.

761.193 Persons importing, manufacturing, processing, distributing in commerce or using chemicals containing inadvertently generated PCBs.
Retention period: 3 years; chemical waste landfill data 20 years.

761.183 Persons importing, manufacturing, processing, distributing in commerce or using chemicals containing inadvertently generated PCBs.
To maintain records of actual monitoring of PCB concentrations.
Retention period: 3 years after a process ceases operation or importing ceases, or for 7 years, whichever is shorter.

761.209 Transporters of PCB waste.
To maintain a copy of the manifest, signed by the generator, transporter, and the next designated transporter, if applicable, or the owner or operator of the designated commercial storage or disposal facility.
Retention period: 3 years from the date the PCB waste was accepted by the initial transporter. Record retention period may be extended automatically during the course of any outstanding enforcement action regarding the regulated activity.

761.209 Generators of PCB waste.
To keep a copy of each manifest signed until a signed copy from the designated commercial storage or disposal facility which received the PCB waste is received.
Retention period: 3 years from the date the PCB waste was accepted by the designated commercial storage or disposal facility. Record retention period may be extended automatically during the course of any outstanding enforcement action regarding the regulated activity.

761.209 Water (bulk shipment) transporters of PCB waste.
To retain a copy of the shipping papers for shipments of PCB waste delivered to designated commercial storage or disposal facility by water (bulk shipment).
Retention period: 3 years from the date the PCB waste was accepted by the initial transporter. Record retention period may be extended automatically during the course of any outstanding enforcement action regarding the regulated activity.

761.209

761.209 Initial rail transporters of PCB waste.

To maintain a copy of the manifest and the shipping paper required to accompany the PCB waste.

Retention period: 3 years from the date the PCB waste was accepted by the initial transporter. Record retention period may be extended during the course of any outstanding enforcement action regarding the regulated activity.

761.209 Final rail transporters of PCB waste.

To keep a copy of the signed manifest, or the required shipping paper if signed by the designated facility in lieu of the manifest.

Retention period: 3 years from the date the PCB waste was accepted by the initial transporter. Record retention period may be extended automatically during the course of any outstanding enforcement action regarding the regulated activity.

763.93 Local educational agencies identifying asbestos-containing materials in schools.

To maintain in its administrative office a complete updated copy of the management plan. In addition, to maintain records on response actions, operations and maintenance, and training and periodic surveillance as part of the management plan.

Retention period: 3 years.

763.94 Local educational agencies identifying asbestos-containing materials in schools.

To maintain records on response actions, operations and maintenance, training and periodic surveillance, and management plans.

Retention period: 3 years.

763.114 Local education agencies identifying friable-asbestos-containing materials in schools.

To maintain results of inspections and analyses; copies of Notice to School Employees; blueprint, diagram or written description of the buildings and other information as specified in the section.

Retention period: Not specified.

Guide to Record Retention 1994

763.121 Employers of employees covered by the EPA asbestos abatement worker protection rule.

(a) To maintain records of objective data for exempted data when relying on objective data that demonstrate that products made from or containing asbestos are not capable of releasing fibers of asbestos in concentrations at or above the action level under the expected conditions of processing, use, or handling to exempt such operations from the initial monitoring requirements.

Retention period: Duration of the employer's reliance upon such objective data.

(b) To maintain records of all measurements taken to monitor employee exposure to asbestos.

Retention period: At least 30 years.

(c) To maintain employee medical surveillance records.

Retention period: Duration of employee employment plus 30 years.

(d) To maintain all employee training records.

Retention period: 1 year beyond the last date of employment.

763.121 Appendix C Employers of employees covered by the EPA asbestos abatement worker protection rule.

To maintain summary of all qualitative fit test results.

Retention period: 3 years.

763.178 Persons producing an asbestos-containing product that is subject to a labeling requirement.

To maintain a copy of the label used in compliance.

Retention period: 3 years after the effective date of the ban on distribution in commerce for the product which the labeling requirements apply.

763.178 Persons producing an asbestos-containing product that is subject to a manufacture, importation and/or processing ban.

To maintain the results of the inventory for the banned product.

Retention period: 3 years after the effective date of the ban on manufacture, importation, and processing.

Environmental Protection Agency

763.178 Persons whose asbestos-producing activities are subject to manufacture, importation, processing and distribution in commerce bans.

To maintain all commercial transactions regarding the product including the date of purchases and sale and the quantities purchased or sold.

Retention period: 3 years after the effective date of the ban on distribution in commerce for a product.

Part 763, Appendix A to Subpart E Laboratories which analyze asbestos bulk samples and asbestos air samples.

To maintain log of all pertinent sampling information and appropriate logs or records verifying compliance with the mandatory quality insurance procedures.

Retention period: Not specified.

Part 763, Appendix D to Subpart E Transporters of asbestos waste.

To maintain as evidence of receipt at the disposal site a copy of the chain of custody form signed by the disposal site operator.

Retention period: Not specified.

792.29 Toxic substances control testing facilities.

To maintain a current summary of training and experience and job description for each individual engaged in or supervising the conduct of a study.

Retention period: Not specified.

792.31 Toxic substances control testing facility management.

To document and maintain such action as raw data, records on the replacement of the study director if it becomes necessary to do so during the conduct of a study.

Retention period: 10 years.

792.33 Toxic substances control testing facilities study directors.

To maintain and verify (a) all experimental data, including observations of unanticipated responses of test systems; (b) notes on unforeseen circumstances that may affect the quality and integrity of the study when they

---

792.105

occur; and (c) documentation of the corrective action taken.

Retention period: In accordance with 40 CFR 792.195.

792.35 Toxic substances control testing facility quality assurance units.

To maintain a copy of a master schedule sheet of all studies conducted at the testing facility; copies of all protocols pertaining to all studies for which the unit is responsible; and copies of written and properly signed records of each periodic inspection.

Retention period: Indefinitely.

792.63 Toxic substances control testing facility quality assurance units.

To maintain records of all inspection, maintenance, testing, calibrating, and/or standardizing operations, and standardizing operations, and nonroutine repairs performed on equipment as a result of failure and malfunction.

Retention period: 10 years.

792.81 Toxic substances control testing facilities.

To maintain a historical file of standard operating procedures and all revisions thereof, including the dates of such revisions.

Retention period: In accordance with 40 CFR 792.195.

792.90 Toxic substances control testing facilities.

To maintain as raw data documentation of the analyses of feed and water used for the animals to ensure that contaminants known to be capable of interfering with the study and reasonably expected to be present in such feed or water are not present at levels above those specified in protocol and to maintain documentation of any use of pest control materials.

Retention period: In accordance with 40 CFR 792.195.

792.105 Toxic substances control testing facilities.

(a) For each batch, to maintain documentation on the indentity, strength, purity, and composition or other characteristics which will appropriately define the test or control substance.

792.185

(b) To maintain documentation on the methods, fabrication, or derivation of the test and control substances.

(c) For studies of more than 4 weeks' duration, to reserve samples from each batch of test-control substances.

Retention period: In accordance with 40 CFR 792.195.

792.185 Sponsors and toxic substances control testing facilities.

For each study, to maintain a copy of the final report and of any amendments to it.

Retention period: In accordance with 40 CFR 792.195.

792.190 Toxic substances control testing facilities.

(a) To maintain all raw date, documentation, records, protocols, specimens, and final reports generated as a result of a study.

(b) To maintain correspondence and other documents relating to interpretation and evaluation of data, other than those documents contained in the final report.

Retention period: See 40 CFR 792.195.

792.195 Toxic substances control testing facilities—retention period.

(a) Documentation records, raw data, and specimens pertaining to a study and required to be retained by 40 CFR part 792 shall be retained in the archive(s) for a period of at least 10 years following the effective date of the applicable final test rule.

(b) In the case of negotiated testing agreement, documentation records, raw data, and specimens pertaining to a study and required to be retained by 40 CFR part 792 shall be retained in the archive(s) for a period of at least 10 years following the publication date of

the acceptance of a negotiated test agreement.

(c) In the case of testing submitted under section 5, documentation records, raw data, and specimens pertaining to a study and required to be retained under 40 CFR part 792 shall be retained in the archive(s) for a period of at least 5 years following the date on which the results of the study are submitted to the agency.

(d) Wet specimens, samples of test, control or reference substances, and specially prepared material which are relatively fragile and differ markedly in stability and quality during storage shall be retained only as long as the quality of the preparation affords evaluation. Specimens obtained from municipal water-plants, and wet specimens of soil, blood, urine, feces, biological fluids, do not need to be retained after quality assurance verification.

(e) Master schedule sheet, copies of protocols, records of quality assurance inspections, summaries of training, experience and job description, and records and reports of the maintenance and calibration shall be retained for the length of time specified in 40 CFR 792.195(b).

799.10 Persons who manufacture or intend to manufacture (including import and/or persons who process or intend to process a chemical substance or mixture (DETA) under the specific chemical test rule.

To maintain all raw data, documentation, records, protocols, specimens and reports generated as a result of study in accordance with the TSCA Good Laboratory Practice Standards (GLP's) in 40 CFR part 792.

Retention period: In accordance with 40 CFR 792.195.

Wage and Hour Division

29 CFR

500.60 Farm labor contractors, agricultural employers and agricultural associations using migrant or seasonal agricultural workers.

To maintain payroll records and copies of all records for places of employment.

Retention period: 3 years.

500.80 Farm labor contractors, agricultural employers and agricultural associations employing migrant or seasonal agricultural workers.

To maintain payroll records.
Retention period: 3 years.

502.11 Employers of reportable workers employed in seasonable agricultural services.

(a) For each replenishment agricultural worker, to maintain records containing the name in full; INS Alien Registration Number and Social Security Account Number; local address including zip code and permanent address (if any); crop(s) and task(s) performed; and hours work each day.

(b) To maintain a complete copy of dated and signed Work-Day Report (Form ESA-92) submitted to the Federal Government and report provided to any replenishment agricultural worker of the number of work-days employed in seasonal agricultural services, including the period covered by the report.

Retention period: 3 years. If subject to the requirements of MSPA, see 29 CFR 500.80. If subject to the requirements of FLSA, see 29 CFR part 516.

502.12 Persons employing reportable workers in seasonal agricultural services.

To keep a copy of the completed EAS-92s furnished to the Federal Government.

Retention period: 3 years.

502.13 Persons employing reportable workers who are replenishment agricultural workers.

To keep a copy of each completed WH-501R (or whatever form is used to report) furnished to an replenishment agricultural worker.

Retention period: 3 years.

504.310 Facilities using non-immigrant aliens as registered nurses (H-1 or H-1A).

See 20 CFR 655.310.

504.350 Facilities using nonimmigrant aliens as registered nurses (H-1 or H-1A).

See 20 CFR 655.350.

504.400 Facilities using nonimmigrant aliens as registered nurses (H-1 or H-1A).

See 20 CFR 655.350.

505.5 Persons receiving grants from the National Endowment for the Arts—Labor Standard on Projects or Production.

To maintain and preserve sufficient records as an assurance of compliance with the National Foundation on the Arts and the Humanities Act of 1965 and other information as specified in the section cited.

Retention period: 3 years after the end of the grant period to which records pertain.

506.510 Employers using alien crew-members for longshore activities in U.S. ports.

See 20 CFR 655.510.

507.705 Employers using aliens on H-1B visas in specialty occupations.

See 20 CFR 655.705.

507.730 Employers using aliens on H-1B visas in specialty occupations.

See 20 CFR 655.730.

Guide to Record Retention 1994

507.760 Employers using aliens on H-1B visas in specialty occupations—retention period.

See 20 CFR 655.760.

508.900 Employers using F-1 students in off-campus work.

See 20 CFR 655.900.

508.910 Employers using F-1 students in off-campus work.

See 20 CFR 655.910.

508.940 Employers using F-1 students in off-campus work.

See 20 CFR 655.910.

Appendix A to part 508, subpart J Employers using F-1 students in off-campus work.

See appendix A to 20 CFR part 655, subpart J.

515.6 State agencies having agreements with Secretary of Labor, or Administrator of Wage and Hour Division, for utilization of their services in making investigations and inspections under Fair Labor Standards Act and Public Contracts Act.

To keep accounting records and supporting data pertaining to expenditures for investigations and inspections.

Retention period: Not specified.

516.1 Employers subject to any provisions of the Fair Labor Standards Act of 1938, as amended.

To maintain records containing the information and data required by specific sections of 29 CFR part 516.

Retention period: Various.

Part 516 Employers subject to the Fair Labor Standards Act including special recordkeeping rules that apply to employers who employees fall within various minimum wage and /or overtime pay exemptions in the Act.

To maintain records as indicated in 29 CFR part 516.

Retention period: Various.

508.520 Employers using alien crew-members for longshore activities using automated vessels.

See 20 CFR 655.510.

516.2 Employers subject to Fair Labor Standards Act whose employees are subject to minimum wages and overtime provisions pursuant to section 6 or 7(a) of the Fair Labor Standards Act.

To maintain and preserve payroll records; records of retroactive payments of wages; records on employees working on fixed schedules; and other such records as specified in section cited.

Retention period: (a) Payroll records and certificates, agreements, plans, notices, etc.– 3 years; (b) basic employment and earning records and wage rate tables, order, shipping, and billing records and records of additions to or deductions from wages paid–2 years.

516.3 Employers subject to Fair Labor Standards Act employing bona fide executive, administrative, and professional employees (including academic administrative personnel and teachers in elementary or secondary schools), and outside sales employees.

To maintain and preserve records containing all the information and data required by 29 CFR 516.2(a) except paragraphs (a)(6) through (10) and, in addition, the basis on which wages are paid in sufficient detail to permit calculation for each pay period of the employee's total remuneration for employment including fringe benefits and prerequisites.

Retention period: 3 years.

516.5—516.9 Employers subject to Fair Labor Standards Act.

See part 516.

516.11 Employers subject to Fair Labor Standards Act whose employees are exempt from both minimum wage and overtime requirements under section 13(a)(2), (3), (4), (8), (10), (12), or (13)(d) of the Act.

See 516.2.

516.12 Employers subject to Fair Labor Standards Act whose employees are exempt from overtime pay requirements.

(a) See 516.2 with exceptions.

516.13 Employers subject to Fair Labor Standards Act employing livestock auction employees exempt from overtime pay requirements under section 13(b)(13) of the Act.

(a) See 516.2 with exceptions.

(b) To maintain records containing employment and earning information for each workweek in which the employee is employed both in agriculture and in connection with livestock operations.

Retention period: (a) 3 years; (b) 2 years.

516.14 Employers subject to Fair Labor Standards Act employing country elevator employees exempt from overtime pay requirements under section 13(b)(14) of the Act.

(a) See 516.2 with exceptions.

(b) To maintain records containing for each workweek, the names and occupations of all persons employed in the country elevator, whether or not covered by the Act, and information demonstrating that 'area of production' requirements of 29 CFR part 536 are met.

Retention period: (a) 3 years; (b) 2 years.

516.15

(b) To maintain information and data regarding the basis on which wages are paid (such as the monetary amount paid, expressed as earnings per hour, per day, per week, etc.)

Retention period: (a) 3 years; (b) 2 years.

516.16 Retail or service establishment subject to Fair Labor Standards Act employing Commission employees exempt from overtime pay requirements pursuant to section 7(i).

(a) See 516.2 with exceptions.

(b) To also maintain other information as specified in section cited.

Retention period: (a) 3 years; (b) 2 years.

516.17 Employers subject to Fair Labor Standards Act employing seamen exempt from overtime pay requirements pursuant to section 13 (b)(6) of the Act.

(a) See 516.2 with exceptions.

(b) To maintain other information as specified in section cited.

(a) 3 years; (b) 2 years.

516.18 Employers subject to Fair Labor Standards Act employing employees in certain tobacco, cotton, sugar care, or sugar beet services who are partially exempt from overtime pay requirements pursuant to section 7(m), 13(h), 13(i) or 13(j) of the Act.

(a) See 516.2.

(b) To maintain and preserve a record of the daily and weekly overtime compensation paid. Also to note in the payroll records the beginning date of each workweek during which the establishment operates under the particular exemption.

Retention period: (a) 3 years; (b) 2 years.

516.20 Employers subject to Fair Labor Standards Act employing employees under certain collective bargaining agreements who are partially exempt from overtime pay requirements as provided in section 7(b)(1) or section 7(b)(2) of the Act.

(a) See 516.2.

(b) To keep copies of collective bargaining agreement and National Labor Relations Board certifications as part of the record and a copy of each amendment or addition thereto. To also keep other records as specified in section cited.

Retention period: (a) 3 years; (b) 2 years.

516.16

516.21 Employers subject to Fair Labor Standards Act employing bulk petroleum employees partially exempt from overtime pay requirements pursuant to section 7(b)(3) of the Act.

(a) See 516.2(a).

(b) To maintain daily as well as weekly overtime compensation records.

Retention period: (a) 3 years; (b) 2 years.

516.22 Employers subject to Fair Labor Standards Act employing employees engaged in charter activities for a street, suburban or interurban electric railway or local trolley or motorbus carrier pursuant to section 7(n) of the Act.

(a) See 516.2(a).

(b) In addition, to maintain records of the hours worked each workweek in charter activities and a copy of the employment agreement or understanding.

Retention period: (a) 3 years; (b) 2 years.

516.23 Employers subject to Fair Labor Standards Act employing employees of hospitals and residential care facilities compensated for overtime work on the basis of a 14-day work period pursuant to section 7(j) of the Act.

(a) See 516.2 with exceptions.

(b) To maintain records on time of day and day of week on which the employee's 14-day work period begins and total hours worked each workday and total hours worked each 14-day work period: total straight-time wages paid for hours worked during the 14-day period total overtime excess compensation paid for hours worked in excess of 8 in a workday and 80 in the work period; a copy of the agreement or understanding with respect to using the 14 day period for overtime pay computations and other such records as specified in section cited.

Retention period: (a) 3 years; (b) 2 years.

Labor Department

Guide to Record Retention 1994

516.24 Employers subject to Fair Labor Standards Act hiring employees under section 7(f) 'Belo' contracts.

(a) To maintain and preserve payroll or other records containing all the information and data required by 29 CFR 516.2(a) with exceptions.

(b) To also maintain records on the total weekly guaranteed earning; total weekly compensation in excess of weekly guaranty; and a copy of the bona fide individual contract or the agreement made as a result of collective bargaining or where such contract or agreement is not in writing, a written memorandum summarizing its term.

Retention period: (a) 3 years; (b) 2 years.

516.25 Employers subject to Fair Labor Standards Act employing employees paid for overtime on the basis of 'applicable' rates provided in sections 7(g)(1) and 7 (g)(2) of the Act.

To maintain and preserve records containing all the information and data required by 29 CFR 516.2(a) with some exceptions, and other such records as specified in section cited.

Retention period: 2 and 3 years.

516.26 Employers subject to Fair Labor Standards Act employing employees paid for overtime at premium rates computed on a 'basic' rate authorized in accordance with section 7(g)(3) of the Act.

To maintain and preserve records containing all the information and data required by 29 CFR 516.2 with exceptions and other information as specified in section cited.

Retention period: 2 and 3 years.

516.27 Employers subject to Fair Labor Standards Act who make deductions from the wages of employees for 'board, lodging, or other facilities' under section 3 (m) of the Act.

(a) See part 516.

(b) To maintain and preserve records substantiating the cost of furnishing each class of facility with exceptions.

(c) To keep records on additional information as specified in cited section.

516.28 Employers subject to Fair Labor Standards Act employing tipped employees.

(a) To maintain and preserve payroll or other records containing all the information and data required in 29 CFR 516.2(a).

(b) To maintain records on additional information as specified in section cited.

Retention period: (a) 3 years; (b) 2 years.

516.29 Private entities operating amusements or recreational establishments located in national parks or national forests or on lands in National Wildlife Systems employing employees who are partially exempt from overtime pay requirements pursuant to section 13(b)(29) of the Act.

To maintain and preserve records required in 29 CFR 516.2, except that the records of regular hourly rate of pay in 29 CFR 516.2(a)(6) shall be required only in a workweek when overtime compensation is due under section 13(b)(29).

Retention period: 2 and 3 years.

516.30 Employers of learners, apprentices, messengers, students, or handicapped workers employed under special certificates as provided in section 14 of the Fair Labor Standards Act.

To maintain and preserve records containing the same information and data required with respect to other employees employed in the same occupations. In addition, each employer shall segregate on the payroll or pay records the names and required information and data with respect to those learners, apprentices, messengers, handicapped workers and students employed under Special Certificates.

Retention period: 2 and 3 years.

516.31 Employers of industrial homeworkers.

To maintain and preserve payroll or other records containing the following information and data: (a) Date on which work is given out or begun by worker, and amount of such work given out or begun; (b) date on which work is turned in by worker, and the amount of such work; (c) kind of articles worked on and operation performed; (d) piece rates paid; (e) hours worked on each lot of work turned in; (f) wages paid for each lot of work turned in; (g) name and address of each agent, distributor, or contractor through whom homework is distributed or collected and the name and address of each homeworker or from whom it is collected by each such agent, distributor, or contractor; and (h) homeworkers handbook.

Retention period: 2 and 3 years.

516.33 Employers subject to Fair Labor Standards Act employing employees in agriculture pursuant to section 13(a)(6) or 13(b)(12) of the Act.

(a) To maintain and preserve all the information and data required by 29 CFR 516.2(a) with exceptions.

Retention period: For the entire year following the year in which the employer used more than 500 man-days of agricultural labor in any calendar year.

(b) To maintain and preserve records containing name in full, place where minor lives while employed. If the minor's permanent address is elsewhere, give both address; and date of birth if employing in agriculture any minor under 18 years of age on days where school is in session or on any day if the minor is employed in an occupation found to be hazardous by the Secretary.

Retention period: 2 and 3 years.

516.34 Employers subject to Fair Labor Standards Act whose employees received remedial education under specified conditions.

To maintain and preserve records containing all the information and data required by 29 CFR 516.2 and, in addition, to make and preserve a record, either separately or as a notation on the payroll, showing the hours spent each workday and total hours each workweek that the employee is engaged in receiving such remedial education that does not include any job-specific training but that is designed to provide reading and other basic skills at or below the eighth-grade level or to fulfill the requirements for a high school diploma (or

517.206 Employers subject to the training wage provisions of Fair Labor Standards Amendments Act of 1989.

For second 90—day period of eligibility, to maintain the original or a copy of the training program(s), including any revisions.

Retention period: 2 years after the last day on which an individual was employed at the training wage pursuant to such training program(s).

519.7 Agriculture, retail, or service establishments and institutions of higher education subject to Fair Labor Standards Act employing full-time students under special full-time student certificates.

See 516.5.

519.17 Agriculture, retail, or service establishments and institutions of higher education subject to Fair Labor Standards Act employing full-time students outside of their school hours under special full-time student certificates.

See 516.5.

520.7 Employers subject to Fair Labor Standards Act employing student-learners as learners under certificates.

See 516.5.

521.8 Employers subject to Fair Labor Standards Act employing apprentices in skilled trade at wages lower than minimum wage applicable.

See 516.5.

521.8 Joint apprenticeship committees holding certificates issued by Administrator.

See 516.5.

522.7 Employers subject to Fair Labor Standards Act employing special learners certificates.

See 516.5.

Labor Department

525.16 Employers, referring agencies or facilities of workers employed under special minimum wage certificates.

To maintain records indicating (a) verification of the workers' disabilities; (b) evidence of the productivity of each worker with a disability gathered in a continuing basis or at periodic intervals (not to exceed six months in the case of employees paid hourly wage rates); (c) the prevailing wages paid workers not disabled for the job performed who are employed in industry in the vicinity for essentially the same type of work using similar methods and equipment as that used by each worker with disabilities employed under a special minimum wage certificate; (d) the production standards and supporting documentation for non-disabled workers for each job being performed by workers with disabilities employed under special certificates; and (e) certain records required under all of the applicable provisions of 29 CFR part 526.

Retention period: See 29 CFR part 526.

527.7 Educational institutions employing student-workers as learners under certificates.

See 516.

530.8 Homeworkers and employers in the women's apparel industry, the jewelry manufacturing industry, the knitted outerwear industry, the gloves and mittens industry, the button and buckle manufacturing industry, the handkerchief manufacturing industry, and the embroideries industry.

See 516.5.

530.9 Homeworkers and employers in the women's apparel industry, the jewelry manufacturing industry, the knitted outerwear industry, the gloves and mittens industry, the button and buckle manufacturing industry, the handkerchief manufacturing industry, and the embroideries industry.

See 516.5.

530.12 Employers of industrial homeworkers engaged in making hand-fashioned jewelry on the Navajo, Pueblo, and Hopi Indian Reservations.

To keep records, including name, address, and date of birth of the homeworker, if under 19 years of age, and description of work performed, amount and date of cash payments for each pay period, and a schedule of piece rates paid, and all records required by 29 CFR part 516, except those required by 516.2 and 516.31.

Retention period: 3 years.

530.202 Employers who pay homeworkers based on piece rates.

To maintain documentation of the work measurements used to establish the piece rates, and the circumstances under which such measurements were conducted.

Retention period: 3 years and records shall be made available on request to the Wage and Hour Division.

551.9 Employers of local delivery drivers and helpers.

See 516.15.

552.100 Employers of domestic service employees.

See 516.34.

552.110 Employers of domestic service employees.

See 516.34.

553.50 Public agencies employees subject to the compensatory time and compensatory time off provisions of section 7(o) of the Fair Labor Standards Act.

To maintain and preserve records pursuant to section 7(k) of the Fair Labor Standards Act.

Retention period: Not specified.

553.51 Public agencies employees paid pursuant to section 7(k) of the Fair Labor Standards Act.

To maintain and preserve records and data required by 29 CFR 553.50.

Retention period: Not specified.

570.35a State educational agencies concerned with work experience and career exploration programs.

To maintain names and addresses of each school enrolling students in such programs, and the number of enrollees in each unit.

Retention period: 3 years from date of enrollment.

570.6 Employers subject to child-labor provisions of the Fair Labor Standards Act.

Retention period: 3 years.

570.72 Employers subject to child-labor provisions of the Fair Labor Standards Act.

See 516.5.

575.8 Employers granted waivers for employment of 10- and 11-year-old minors in hand harvesting of short-season crops under section 13(c)(4) of the Fair Labor Standards Act.

The employer or group of employers granted such waiver to maintain (a) employment records as required by 29 CFR 516.33(b); (b) date of birth, and name and address of school in which each minor is enrolled; and (c) the number of hours worked each day and each week by each minor.

Retention period: 2 years.

778.603 Employers subject to Fair Labor Standards Act whose employees received remedial education under specified conditions.

To maintain a record of the hours that an employee is engaged each workday and each workweek in receiving remedial education, and the compensation paid each pay period for the time so engaged, as described in 29 CFR 516.34.

779.420 Employers subject to Fair Labor Standards Act.

To maintain records on employees for whom the overtime pay exemption under section 7(i) is taken as specified in 29 CFR 516.16.

794.144 Employers subject to Fair Labor Standards Act.

See 516.2 and 516.21.

801.12 Employers/examiners subject to the Employee Polygraph Protection Act of 1988.

See 29 CFR 801.30.

801.30 Employers/examiners subject to the Employee Polygraph Protection Act of 1988.

(a) To retain a copy of the statement that sets forth the specific incident or activity under investigation and the basis for testing that particular employee if an employee is requested to submit to a polygraph examination in connection with an ongoing investigation involving economic loss or injury. (b) To maintain records specifically identifying the loss or injury in question and the nature of the employee's access to the person or property that is the subject of the investigation. (c) To maintain all opinions, lists, and other records relating to polygraph tests of such persons. In addition, to maintain records of the number of examinations conducted each day and, with regard to tests administered to persons identified by their employer, and the duration of each test period and other such records as specified in cited section.

Retention period: 3 years.

825.500 Employers subject to the Family and Medical Leave Act. [Added]

To make, keep, and preserve records pursuant to the Fair Labor Standards Act. (a) basic payroll and identifying employee data, including name, address, and occupation; rate or basis of pay and terms of compensation; daily and weekly hours worked per pay period; additions to or deductions from wages, and total compensation paid; (b) dates FMLA leave is taken by employees (e.g., available from time records, requests for leave, etc., if so designated). Leave must be designated in records as FMLA leave; (c) If FMLA leave is taken in increments of less than one full day, the hours of the leave; (d) copies of em-

Labor Department

ployee notice of leave furnished to the employer under FMLA, if in writing, regarding designation of leave as FMLA leave, including any written statement from the employer or employee of the reasons for the designation and for the disagreement; (g) any documents (including written and electronic records) describing employee benefits or employer policies and practices regarding the 'aking of paid and unpaid leave; (f) records of any dispute between the employer and an employee

825.500

regarding designation of leave as FMLA leave, including any written statement from the employer or employee of the reasons for the designation and for the disagreement; (g) any documents (including written and electronic records) relating to medical certifications, recertifications or medical histories of employees or employees' family members; and (h) and other such records as specified in cited section.

Retention period: 3 years.

Occupational Safety and Health Administration

29 CFR

Part 1904 Contractors subject to Public Contracts Act (contracts with U.S. agencies or District of Columbia).

To keep a log, a supplementary record, and an annual summary of occupational illnesses and accidents.

Retention period: 5 years following the end of the year to which they relate.

Part 1904 Contractors or subcontractors subject to Service Contract Act of 1965.

To keep a log, a supplementary record, and an annual summary of occupational illnesses and accidents.

Retention period: 5 years following the end of the year to which they relate.

1904.2 Employers subject to the Occupational Safety and Health Act of 1970.

To maintain in each establishment a log and summary of all recordable occupational injuries and illnesses.

Retention period: 5 years.

1904.4 Employers subject to the Occupational Safety and Health Act of 1970.

To maintain in each establishment a supplementary record for each occupational injury or illness for that establishment.

Retention period: 5 years.

1904.6 Contractors or subcontractors subject to Service Contract Act of 1965.

See 4.6.

1904.6 Employers subject to the Occupational Safety and Health Act of 1970.

See 1904.2 and 1904.4.

LABOR DEPARTMENT

1910.20 Employers subject to record access rule on the preservation of employee exposure and medical records.

To make available to employees and their designated representatives and the Assistant Secretary of Labor for OSHA: (a) exposure; (b) medical records for examination and copying; and (c) analyses using exposure or medical records.

Retention period: Unless a specific time period: (a) 30 years, except for certain background data—1 year; (b) and

OSHA standard provides a different time period: (a) 30 years, except for certain background data—1 year; (b) and (c) 30 years.

1910.38 Employers subject to fire prevention standards.

To maintain written records of emergency action plans.

Retention period: Not specified.

1910.66 Building owners of all powered platform installations.

To maintain certification record which contains the date the work was performed, the signature of the person who performed the work, and an identifier for the equipment or installation which was tested or inspected. Records shall be kept readily available for review by the Assistant Secretary's representatives and by the employee.

1910.68 Employers subject to manlifts standards.

To maintain certification records of findings of manlift inspections.

Retention period: Not specified.

1910.95 Employers subject to occupational noise exposure standards.

(a) To maintain noise exposure measurement records.

Retention period: 2 years.

(b) To maintain audiometric test records.

Retention period: For the duration of the affected employee's employment.

1910.96 Employers subject to the ionizing radiation standard.

To maintain records of all employees who are personally monitored.

Retention period: Not specified.

1910.181 Employers subject to derrick standards.

To maintain monthly written report running and idle ropes.
Retention period: Not specified.

1910.184 Employers subject to industrial slings standards.

To maintain record of most recent month in which each alloy steel chain sling was thoroughly inspected and proof test certificates for each new, repaired or reconditioned sling; also, to attach permanent tag or mark, or keep a record in order to indicate date and nature of repairs to metal mesh slings.
Retention period: Not specified.

1910.217 Employers subject to mechanical power presses standard.

To maintain records of the safety system installation certification and validation and the most recent recertification and revalidation as long as the press is in use. The records shall include the manufacture and model number of each component and subsystem, the calculations of the safety distance and the stopping time measurements. The most recent records shall be made available to OSHA upon request.

1910.218 Employers subject to forging machine standards.

To maintain records of the periodic and regular maintenance safety checks.
Retention period: Not specified.

1910.255 Employers subject to welding, cutting, and brazing standards.

To maintain certification records. The certification records shall include the date of inspection, the signature of the person who performed the inspection and the serial number, or other identifier, for the equipment inspected.
Retention period: Not specified.

1910.268 Employers, telecommunications.

To maintain on file certification records which include the identity of the person trained, the signature of the person trained, the signature of employer, or the person who conducted the training, and the date the training was completed.
Retention period: Duration of the employee's employment.

1910.272 Employers in grain handling facilities.

(a) To maintain on file hot work and entry into bins, silos, and tanks permits.
(b) To maintain certification record of each equipment inspection containing the date of the inspection, the name of the person who performed the inspection and the serial number, or other identifier of the equipment inspected.
Retention period: Not specified.

1910.423 Employers subject to post-dive procedure standards.

To record and maintain information for each diving operation and for each dive outside the no-decompression limits, deeper than 100 fsw or using mixed gas.
Retention period: Not specified.

1910.440 Employers subject to commercial diving operations standard.

To maintain records of (a) occupational injuries and illnesses in accordance with 29 CFR part 1904; (b) any diving-related injury or illness requiring hospitalization—until completion of hospitalization as required; (c) medical records; (d) safe practice manuals; (e) depth-time profiles; (f) diving records; (g) decompression procedure assessments; and (h) equipment inspections and testing records.
Retention period: (a) Medical records—5 years; (b) safe practices manual-current document only; (c) depth-time profile—until completion of recording of dive or decompression procedure assessment; (d) dive—1 year except 5 years where decompression sickness; (e) decompression procedure assessment—5 years; (f) equipment inspections and testing records—current entry or until withdrawn from service; (g) records of hospitalization—5 years.

Retention period: Indefinite.

1910.119 Employers; process safety management of highly hazardous chemicals; explosives and blasting agents.

To maintain records on process safety: technology of the process; equipment in the process; process hazard analysis and updates or revalidations for each process covered; operating procedures; employee training; contract employer responsibilities; mechanical integrity: management of change, incident investigation; and emergency planning and response; and also contract employee injury and illness log related to the contractor's work in process areas.
Retention period: Incident investigation—5 years.

1910.120 Employers engaged in the hazardous waste operations and emergency response operations under the Comprehensive Environmental Response, Compensation, and Liability Act of 1980, as amended (42 USC 9601 et. seq.).

To maintain records of the medical surveillance of (a) all employees who are or may be exposed to hazardous substances or health hazards at or above the established permissible exposure limits for these substances, without regard to the use of respirators, for 30 days or more a year; (b) all employees who wear a respirator; and (c) HAZMAT employees engaged in hazardous waste operations.
Retention period: As specified in 29 CFR 1910.20.

1910.134 Employers subject to respiratory protection standards.

To maintain records of inspection dates and findings for respirators maintained for emergency use.
Retention period: Not specified.

1910.146 Employers subject to the permit-required confined space standard. [Added]

To retain each cancelled entry permit to facilitate review of the permit-required confined space program.
Retention period: 1 year.

1910.146, Appendix C Employers subject to the permit-required confined space standard. [Added]

To maintain a written records of the pre-entry test results for the existence of dangerous air contamination and/or oxygen deficiency.
Retention period: For the duration of the job.

1910.156 Employers subject to fire protection standards.

To maintain written records of the fire brigade training policy.
Retention period: Not specified.

1910.157 Employers subject to fire protection standards.

To maintain evidence of the required hydrostatic testing or portable fire extinguishers.
Retention period: Until hydrostatically retesting at stated intervals or until taken out of service, whichever comes first.

1910.159 Employers subject to fire protection standards.

To maintain central records of location, number of sprinklers and basis of design in lieu of signs at sprinkler valves.
Retention period: Not specified.

1910.160 Employers subject to fire protection standards.

To maintain records of the last semi-annual checks of fixed extinguishing systems.
Retention period: Lesser of until the container is rechecked or its life.

1910.179 Employers subject to materials handling and storage standards.

To maintain monthly maintenance and test inspection reports and records on critical items such as brakes, crane hooks, and ropes.
Retention period: Not specified.

1910.180 Employers subject to crawler locomotive and truck cranes.

To maintain monthly certification inspection reports and records concerning rated load test results and ropes idle for a month or more.
Retention period: Not specified.
Ropes shall be kept readily available.

1910.1001 Employers subject to asbestos standards.
(a) To maintain accurate records of all employee exposure measurements.
Retention period: 30 years.
(b) To maintain accurate record of objective data reasonably relied upon in support of exempted operations.
Retention period: Duration of employer's reliance upon objective data.
(c) To maintain accurate record for each employee subject to medical surveillance.
Retention period: Duration of employment plus 30 years.
(d) To maintain all employee training records.
Retention period: 1 year beyond last date of employment of the employee.

1910.1003 Employers subject to certain carcinogen standards.
To maintain records of medical examinations.
Retention period: Duration of employee's employment.

1910.1004 Employers subject to certain carcinogen standards.
See 1910.1003.

1910.1006 Employers subject to certain carcinogen standards.
See 1910.1003.

1910.1007 Employers subject to certain carcinogen standards.
See 1910.1003.

1910.1008 Employers subject to certain carcinogen standards.
See 1910.1003.

1910.1009 Employers subject to certain carcinogen standards.
See 1910.1003.

1910.1010 Employers subject to certain carcinogen standards.
See 1910.1003.

1910.1011 Employers subject to certain carcinogen standards.
See 1910.1003.

1910.1012 Employers subject to certain carcinogen standards.
See 1910.1003.

Guide to Record Retention 1994

1910.1013 Employers subject to certain carcinogen standards.
See 1910.1003.

1910.1014 Employers subject to certain carcinogen standards.
See 1910.1003.

1910.1015 Employers subject to certain carcinogen standards.
See 1910.1003.

1910.1016 Employers subject to certain carcinogen standards.
See 1910.1003.

1910.1017 Employers subject to vinyl chloride standards.
To maintain (a) monitoring and measuring records; (b) authorized personnel rosters; and (c) medical records.
Retention period: (a) Not less than 30 years; (b) not specified; and (c) duration of employment plus 20 years, or 30 years, whichever is longer.

1910.1018 Employers subject to inorganic arsenic standard.
To maintain records of (a) employee exposure monitoring and (b) medical records.
Retention period: 40 years or the duration of employment plus 20 years, whichever is longer.

1910.1025 Employers subject to lead standard.
To maintain records of (a) employee exposure monitoring; (b) medical records; and (c) medical removal records for employees removed from current exposure to lead.
Retention period: (a) and (b) 40 years or the duration of employment plus 20 years, whichever is longer; (c) duration of employee's employment.

1910.1027 Employers subject to the cadmium standards.
(a) To maintain an accurate records of all air monitoring for cadmium in the workplace. The record shall include (1) the monitoring data, duration, and results in terms of an 8-hour TWA of each sample taken; (2) the name, social security number, and job classification of the employees monitored and of all other employees whose exposures the monitoring is intended to represent; (3) a description of the sampling and analytical methods used and evidence of their accuracy; (4) the type of respiratory protective device, if any, worn by the monitored employee; and (5) a notation of any other conditions that might have affected the monitoring results.
Retention period: For at least 30 years.
(b) To maintain a record of the objective data for exemption from requirement for initial monitoring.
Retention period: 30 years.
(c) To maintain medical surveillance records.
Retention period: Duration of employment plus 30 years.

1910.1027, Appendix C Employers subject to cadmium standards.
To maintain a record of the qualitative and quantitative fit test administered to any employee.
Retention period: Until the next fit test is administered.

1910.1028 Employers subject to benzene standards.
To maintain accurate employee exposure monitoring, measurement, and medical records.
Retention period: 30 years in accordance with 29 CFR 1910.20. All records shall be made available upon request to the Assistant Secretary and the Director for examination and copying.

1910.1029 Employers subject to coke oven emissions standard.
To maintain records of (a) all measurements taken to monitor employee exposure required by section cited, and (b) employee medical surveillance programs required by section cited.
Retention period: At least 40 years or the duration of employment plus 20 years, whichever is longer.

Labor Department

1910.1030 Employers subject to occupational exposure to bloodborne pathogens standard.
To maintain medical and training records. (a) Medical records shall include (1) the name and social security number of the employee; (2) a copy of the employee's hepatitis B vaccination status including the dates of all the hepatitis B vaccinations and any medical records relative to the employee's ability to receive vaccination; (3) a copy of all results of examinations, medical testing, and follow-up procedures; (4) employer's copy of the healthcare professional's written opinion; and (5) copy of the information provided to the healthcare professional. (b) Training records shall include (1) the dates of the training sessions; (2) the contents or a summary of the training sessions; (3) the names and qualifications of persons conducting the training; and (4) the names and job titles of all persons attending the training sessions.
Retention period: (a) Medical records–duration of employment plus 30 years in accordance with 29 CFR 1910.20; (b) training records–3 years from the date on which the training occurred.

1910.1043 Employers subject to cotton dust standard.
To maintain records of (a) sample exposure levels which would occur if the employee were not using a respirator and (b) medical records.
Retention period: At least 20 years.

1910.1044 Employers subject to 1, 2, dibromo-3-chloropropane (DBCP).
To maintain records of (a) employee exposure monitoring and (b) medical records.
Retention period: 40 years or the duration of employment plus 20 years, whichever is longer.

1910.1045 Employers subject to acrylonitrile (vinyl cyanide) standard.
To maintain records of (a) objective data relied upon in support of exemptions in the use of materials made from or containing acrylonitrile (AN); (b) employee exposure monitoring; and (c) medical records.

Labor Department

1915.1001 Employers subject to occupational exposures to asbestos standard applicable to shipyards. [Added]

To maintain records on exposure measurements; objective data for exempted operations; medical surveillance; and training.

Retention period: (a) Exposure measurements – For at least 30 years; (b) objective data, for exempted operations – duration of reliance upon such objective data; (c) medical surveillance records – duration of employment plus 30 years; and (d) training records – 1 year beyond the last date of employment of that employee.

1915.1003 Employers subject to occupational exposures to 4-Nitrobiphenyl standard applicable to shipyards. [Added]

To maintain complete and accurate records of all medical examinations.
Retention period: Duration of the employee's employment.

1915.1004 Employers subject to occupational exposures to Alpha-Naphthylamine standard applicable to shipyards. [Added]

See 29 CFR 1915.1003.

1915.1006 Employers subject to occupational exposures to methyl chloromethyl ether standard applicable to shipyards. [Added]

See 29 CFR 1915.1003.

1915.1007 Employers subject to occupational exposures to 3'3'-Dichlorobenzidine (and its salts) standard applicable to shipyards. [Added]

See 29 CFR 1915.1003.

1915.1008 Employers subject to occupational exposures to bis-chloromethyl ether standard applicable to shipyards. [Added]

See 29 CFR 1915.1003.

1915.1009 Employers subject to occupational exposures to beta-Naphthylamine standard applicable to shipyards. [Added]

See 29 CFR 1915.1003.

1915.1010 Employers subject to occupational exposures to benzidine standard applicable to shipyards. [Added]

See 29 CFR 1915.1003.

1915.1011 Employers subject to occupational exposures to 4-Aminodiphenyl standard applicable to shipyards. [Added]

See 29 CFR 1915.1003.

1915.1012 Employers subject to occupational exposures to Ethyleneimine standard applicable to shipyards. [Added]

See 29 CFR 1915.1003.

1915.1013 Employers subject to occupational exposures to beta-Propiolactone standard applicable to shipyards. [Added]

See 29 CFR 1915.1003.

1915.1014 Employers subject to occupational exposures to 2-Acetylaminofluorene standard applicable to shipyards. [Added]

See 29 CFR 1915.1003.

1915.1015 Employers subject to occupational exposures to 4-Dimethylaminoazobenzene standard applicable to shipyards. [Added]

See 29 CFR 1915.1003.

1915.1016 Employers subject to occupational exposures to N-Nitrosodimethylamine standard applicable to shipyards. [Added]

See 29 CFR 1915.1003.

1915.1017 Employers subject to occupational exposures to vinyl chloride standard applicable to shipyards. [Added]

To maintain required monitoring and medical records.
Retention period: Monitoring and measuring records – For not less than 30 years; medical records – for the duration of the employment of each employee plus 20 years, or 30 years, whichever is longer.

1915.1017

Retention period: (a) Duration of employer's reliance upon such objective data; (b) and (c) 40 years or the duration of employment plus 20 years, whichever is longer.

1910.1047 Employers subject to the ethylene oxide standard.

To maintain records of (a) all measurements taken to monitor employee exposure to EEO and (b) medical surveillance of employees.
Retention period: (a) 30 years and (b) for the duration of employment for thirty years.

1910.1048 Employers subject to formaldehyde standards.

To maintain records on exposure measurements, exposure determinations, medical surveillance, and respirator fit testing.
Retention period: (a) Exposure records– For the duration of employment plus 30 years. (b) Medical records – For the duration of employment plus 30 years. (c) Respirator fit testing records–Until replaced by a more recent record.

1910.1200 Employers subject to hazard communication standards.

To maintain (a) a written hazard communication program for the workplace, including lists of hazardous chemicals present; labeling of containers of chemicals as well as of containers of chemicals being shipped to other workplaces; (b) material safety data sheets that are received with incoming shipments of hazardous chemicals, and ensure that they are readily accessible to laboratory employees; and (c) copies of any material safety data sheets that are received with incoming shipments of the sealed containers of hazardous chemicals and shall ensure that the material safety data sheets are readily accessible during each work shift to employees when they are in their work areas. Material safety data sheets shall also be made readily available, upon request, to designated representatives and to the Assistant Secretary, in accordance with the requirements of 29 CFR 1910.20(e). The Director shall also be given access to material safety data sheets in the same manner.

Guide to Record Retention 1994

1910.1450, Appendix A. Employers engaged in laboratory use of hazardous chemicals.

To maintain records of (a) the amounts of chemicals of moderate, chronic or high acute toxicity on hand, amounts used and the names of the workers involved; (b) amounts of these substances stored and used, the dates of use, and names of users; (c) accidents; (d) chemical hygiene plan that document that the facilities and precautions were compatible with current knowledge and regulations; (e) inventory and usage records for high-risk substances and medical records in accordance with state and federal requirements.

1915.7 Employers subject to shipyard standards.

To maintain record or a copy of inspections and tests on file for each vessel.
Retention period: 3 months.

1915.12 Employers subject to explosive and other dangerous atmosphere standards.

To keep on file and make available for inspection a record of tests and inspections of atmosphere in the space to be entered.
Retention period: Not specified.

1915.99 Employers subject to hazard communication standards.

See 1910.1200.

1915.113 Employers subject to shackles and hooks standards.

To maintain certification records of tests on all hooks for which no applicable manufacturer's recommendations are available before use.
Retention period: Not specified.

1915.172 Employers of maritime employees.

To maintain certification records of the hydrostatic pressure tests on portable unfired pressure vessels.
Retention period: Not specified.

1915.1018

1915.1018 Employers subject to occupational exposures to inorganic arsenic standard applicable to shipyards. [Added]

To maintain records on exposure monitoring and medical surveillance.

Retention period: (a) Exposure monitoring records – for at least 40 years or for the duration of employment plus 20 years, whichever is longer; (b) medical records – for the duration of employment plus 20 years whichever is longer.

1915.1025 Employers subject to occupational exposures to lead standard applicable to shipyards. [Added]

See 29 CFR 1915.1018.

1915.1027 Employers subject to the cadmium standard.

See 29 CFR 1910.1027.

1915.1027, Appendix C Employers subject to cadmium standards.

See 29 CFR 1910.1027.

1915.1028 Employer subject to occupational exposures to benzene standard applicable to shipyards. [Added]

To maintain exposure measurements and medical surveillance records.

Retention period: Exposure measurements records – 30 years; and medical surveillance records – for at least the duration of employment plus 30 years.

1915.1030 Employers subject to occupational exposures to bloodborne pathogens standard applicable to shipyards. [Added]

To maintain medical and training records.

1915.1044 Employers subject to occupational exposures to 1,2-dibromo-3-chloropropane. [Added]

See 29 CFR 1915.1018.

Guide to Record Retention 1994

1915.1045 Employers subject to occupational exposures to acrylonitrile standard applicable to shipyards. [Added]

To maintain records on exposure monitoring and medical surveillance.

Retention period: (a) Objective data records for exempted operations data records – for the duration of the employer's reliance upon such objective data; (b) medical monitoring records – for at least the duration of employment plus 20 years, whichever is longer; for the duration of employment of employment plus 20 years, whichever is longer.

1915.1047 Employers subject to occupational exposures to ethylene oxide standard applicable to shipyards. [Added]

See 29 CFR 1915.1003.

1915.1048 Employers subject to occupational exposures to formaldehyde standard applicable to shipyards. [Added]

To maintain an accurate record of all exposures, measurements, exposure determinations; medical surveillance; and respirator fit testing.

Retention period: (a) Exposure records and determinations – for at least 30 years; medical records – duration of employment plus 30 years; and respirator fit testing records – until replaced by a more recent record.

1915.1050 Employers subject to occupational exposures to methylenedianiline standard applicable to shipyards. [Added]

To maintain records on monitoring data for exempted employers; objective data for exempted employers; exposure measurements; medical removals.

Retention period: (a) Monitoring data for exempted employers – duration of the employer's reliance upon such objective data; (b) exposure measurement records – for at least 30 years; (c) medical surveillance records – for at least the duration of employment plus 30 years; and (d) medical removal records – for at least the duration of employment plus 30 years.

1915.1450 Employers engaged in the laboratory use of hazardous chemicals applicable to shipyards. [Added]

To maintain for each employee an accurate record of any measurements taken to monitor employee exposures and any medical consultation and examinations including tests or written opinions.

Retention period: See 29 CFR 1915.1120.

Labor Department

1915.1120 Employers; access to employee exposures and medical records; compliance requirements. [Added]

Unless a specific occupational safety and health standard provide a different period of time, each employer shall assure the preservation and retention of records as follows:

(a) Employee medical records – for at least the duration of employment plus 30 years.

(b) Employee exposure records – for at least 30 years.

(c) Analyses using exposure or medical records – for at least 30 years.

1917.23 Employers subject to marine terminal standards.

To maintain results of any tests on space which contains or has contained a hazardous atmosphere.

Retention period: 30 days.

1917.24 Employers of employees with- in marine terminals.

To maintain records of the dates, locations, and results of carbon monoxide concentration tests.

Retention period: 30 days.

1917.25 Employers subject to marine terminal standards.

To maintain test results to determine the atmospheric concentration of chemicals used to treat cargo.

Retention period: 30 days.

1917.28 Employers subject to hazard communication standards.

See 1910.1200.

1919.11

1917.45 Employers of employees operating cranes and derricks.

To keep records of the monthly inspections of all functional components and accessible structural features of each crane or device.

Retention period: 6 months.

1917.117 Employers of employees with- in marine terminals.

To maintain manlifts inspection records.

Retention period: 1 year.

1918.61 Employers of maritime employees.

To maintain records of tests of strength of stevedoring gear.

Retention period: As long as such gear is in use.

1918.66 Employers subject to longshoring standards.

To maintain records of all hooks for which no applicable manufacturer's recommendations are available.

Retention period: Not specified.

1918.90 Employers subject to hazard communication standards.

See 1910.1200.

1918.93 Employers of maritime employees under the Longshoremen's and Harbor Workers' Compensation Act.

To keep records of the dates, times, and locations of tests for carbon monoxide made when internal combustion engines exhaust into the hold or intermediate deck.

Retention period: 30 days after work is completed.

1919.10 Persons accredited for vessel cargo gear certification.

To maintain records of all work performed on gear certification, including tests, proof loads, and heat treatment; of the status of the certification of each vessel issued a register by such accredited person.

Retention period: Permanent.

1919.11 Persons accredited for vessel cargo gear certification.

See 1919.10.

1919.12

1919.12 Operators or officers of vessels.

To keep vessel's register and certificates relating to cargo gear.

Retention period: 4 years after date of the latest entry except for nonrecurring test certificates concerning gear which is kept in use for a longer period, in which case certificates are retained as long as that gear is in use.

1925.3 Contractors or subcontractors subject to Service Contract Act of 1965.

See 4.6, and part 1904.

1926.33 Employers subject to safety and health regulations for construction. [Added]

(a) To maintain employee medical records.

Retention period: For at least the duration of employment plus 30 years.

(b) To maintain employee exposure records.

Retention period: For at least 30 years.

(c) To maintain using exposure or medical records.

Retention period: At least 30 years.

1926.53 Employers subject to ionizing radiation standard. [Added]

To maintain adequate past and current exposure records which show that the addition of such dose will not cause the individual to exceed the authorized amount. To also maintain records of the radiation exposure of all employees for whom personnel monitoring is required.

1926.58 Employers subject to asbestos, tremolite, anthophyllite and actinolite standards.

See 1910.1001.

1926.59 Employers subject to hazard communication standards.

See 1910.1200.

1926.60 Employers subject to methylenedianiline standards.

(a) To maintain records of the initial monitoring results or objective data supporting exemption.

Retention period: Duration of the reliance upon such objective data.

(b) To maintain an accurate record of historical monitoring data reasonably relied upon in support of the exception.

Retention period: Duration of the employer's reliance upon such historical monitoring data.

(c) To maintain records of all measurements taken to monitor employee exposure to MDA.

Retention period: For at least 30 years.

(d) To maintain medical surveillance records.

Retention period: Duration of employment plus 30 years.

(e) To maintain training records.

Retention period: 1 year beyond the last date of employment.

1926.60, Appendix E Employers subject to methylenedianiline standards.

Retention period: To maintain a summary of all test results.

Retention period: 3 years.

1926.64 Employers subject to the process safety management of highly hazardous chemical standard. [Added]

To maintain process hazards analyses and updates or revalidation for each process covered as well as the documented resolution of recommendations.

1926.65 Employers subject to hazardous waste operations and emergency response regulations. [Added]

To maintain an accurate record of the medical surveillance. The record shall include at least the following information: (a) The name and social security number of the employees; (b) physician's written opinions, recommended limitations, and results of examinations and tests; (c) any employee medical complaints related to exposure to hazardous substances; and (d) a copy of the information provided to the examining physician by the employers, with the exception of the standard and its appendices.

Retention period: See 29 CFR 1926.33.

Guide to Record Retention 1994 — Labor Department

1926.150 Employers subject to the fire protection standard. [Added]

To retain the record of the annual maintenance check date of portable fire extinguishers.

Retention period: 1 year after the last entry or life of the shell, whichever is less.

1926.156 Employers subject to fixed fire extinguishing systems except for automobile sprinklers systems. [Added]

To maintain a record of the last semi-annual check.

Retention period: Until the container is checked again or for the life of the container, whichever is less.

1926.251 Employers subject to rigging equipment for material handling standards.

(a) To maintain records of tests on all hooks for which no applicable manufacturer's recommendations are available.

Retention period: Not specified.

(b) To maintain a record of the most recent month in which each alloy steel chain sling was thoroughly inspected and to make such record available for examination.

1926.550 Employers subject to crane and derrick standards.

To maintain on file the most recent certification records which include the date the crane items were inspected; the signature of the person who inspected the crane items; and a serial number or other identifier, for the crane inspected.

Retention period: Until a new certification is prepared.

1926.552 Employers subject to material hoists, personnel hoists and elevators standards.

To maintain on file the most recent certification records which include the date of the inspection and test of all functions and safety devices were performed; the signature of the person who performed the inspection and test; and a serial number, or other identifier, for the hoist that was inspected and tested.

Retention period: Not specified.

1926.903

1926.652 Employers subject to the excavation occupational safety and health standards.

To maintain at the jobsite one copy of the tabulated data which identifies the registered professional engineer who approved the data and at least one copy of the design.

Retention period: During the construction of the protective system and may be stored off the jobsite, but a copy shall be made available to the Secretary upon request.

1926.800 Employers subject to underground construction standards.

(a) To maintain record of all air quality tests above ground at the workshop and make available these records to the Secretary upon request. The records shall include the location, date, time, substance and amount monitored.

Retention period: Until completion of the project.

1926.803 Employers subject to compressed air standards.

(a) A physician shall at all times maintain complete and full records of examinations made by him.

(b) To also maintain permanent records of all identification badges issued.

(c) To maintain on file at the place where the work is in progress records of air tested in the workplace.

Retention period: Not specified.

1926.900 Employers subject to blasting and the use of explosives standards.

(a) To maintain inventories and use records of all explosives.

(b) To also maintain written descriptions of alternatives designed to prevent premature firing of electric blasting caps.

Retention period: (a) Not specified; (b) For the duration of the project.

1926.903 Owners of trucks used for underground transportation of explosives.

To maintain on file the most recent certification records which include the date of the inspection; the signature of

1926.905

the person who performed the inspection; and a serial number or other identifier, of the truck inspected.
Retention period: Not specified.

1926.905 Employers subject to loading of explosives or blasting agents standards.

To maintain an accurate up-to-date records of explosives and accurate running inventory of all explosives and blasting agents stored on the operation.
Retention period: Not specified.

1926.1076 Employers subject to standard applicable to diving and related support operations conducted in connection with all types of work and employment, including general industry, construction, ship repairing, shipbuilding, shipbreaking and longshoring. [Added]

To maintain dive members medical records (physician's reports).
Retention period: 5 years.

1926.1080 Employers subject to standard applicable to diving and related support operations conducted in connection with all types of work and employment, including general industry, construction, ship repairing, shipbuilding, shipbreaking and longshoring. [Added]

To maintain a diving safe practices manual.
Retention period: Current.

1926.1082 Employers subject to standard applicable to diving and related support operations conducted in connection with all types of work and employment, including general industry, construction, ship repairing, shipbuilding, shipbreaking and longshoring. [Added]

To maintain a depth-time profile, including when appropriate, any breathing gas changes.
Retention period: Until completion of dive, or until completion of the recording of any injuries or illnesses; or until completion of the recording of decompression procedure assessment where there has been an incident of decompression sickness.

1926.1078 Employers subject to standard applicable to diving and related support operations conducted in connection with all types of work and employment, including general industry, construction, ship repairing, shipbuilding, shipbreaking and longshoring. [Added]

To maintain for each diving operation the following information: (a) Names of dive team members including designated person-in-charge; (b) date, time, and location; (c) diving modes used; (d) general nature of work performed; (e) approximate underwater and surface conditions (visibility, water temperature and current); and (f) maximum depth and bottom time for each diver.
Retention period: 1 year, except 5 years where there has been an incident of decompression sickness.

1926.1090 Employers subject to standard applicable to diving and related support operations conducted in connection with all types of work and employment, including general industry, construction, ship repairing, shipbuilding, shipbreaking and longshoring. [Added]

To maintain equipment inspections and testing records.
Retention period: Current entry or tag or until equipment is withdrawn from service.

1926.1091 Employers subject to standard applicable to diving and related support operations conducted in connection with all types of work and employment, including general industry, construction, ship repairing, shipbuilding, shipbreaking and longshoring. [Added]

To maintain records of the occurrence of any diving-related injury or illness which requires any dive team member to be hospitalized for 24 hours or more, specifying the circumstances of the incident and the extent of any injuries or illnesses.
Retention period: 5 years; see also 29 CFR 1926.1076, 1926.1080, 1926.1082, 1926.1083, and 1926.1090.

Guide to Record Retention 1994

Labor Department

1926.1103 Employers subject to occupational exposures to 4-Nitrobiphenyl standard. [Added]

To maintain complete and accurate records of all employees medical examinations.
Retention period: Duration of the employee's employment.

1926.1104 Employers subject to occupational exposures to alpha-Naphthylamine standard.
See 29 CFR 1926.1103.

1926.1106 Employers subject to occupational exposures to methyl chloromethyl ether standard.
See 29 CFR 1926.1103.

1926.1107 Employers subject to occupational exposures to 3,3'-Dichlorobenzidine (and its salts) standard [Added]
See 29 CFR 1926.1103.

1926.1108 Employers subject to occupational exposures to bis-Chloromethyl ether standard [Added]
See 20 CFR 1926.1103.

1926.1110 Employers subject to occupational exposures to benzidine standard. [Added]
See 29 CFR 1926.1103.

1926.1111 Employers subject to occupational exposures to 4-Aminodiphenyl standard. [Added]
See 29 CFR 1926.1103.

1926.1112 Employers subject to occupational exposures to ethyleneimine standard. [Added]
See 29 CFR 1926.1103.

1926.1113 Employers subject to occupational exposures to beta-Propiolactone standard. [Added]
See 29 CFR 1926.1103.

1926.1114 Employers subject to occupational exposures to 2-Acetylaminofluorene standard. [Added]
See 29 CFR 1926.1103.

1926.1115 Employers subject to occupational exposures to 4-Dimethylaminoazobenzene standard. [Added]
See 29 CFR 1926.1103.

1926.1116 Employers subject to occupational exposures to N-Nitrosodimethylamine standard. [Added]
See 29 CFR 1926.1103.

1926.1117 Employers subject to occupational exposures to vinyl chloride standard [Added]

To maintain records of required monitoring and measuring and medical records.
Retention period: For not less than 30 years; medical records – duration of the employment of each employee plus 20 years, or 30 years, whichever is longer.

1926.1118 Employers subject to occupational exposures to inorganic arsenic standard. [Added]

To maintain records on exposure monitoring and medical surveillance. Monitoring records.
Retention period: For at least 40 years or for the duration of employment plus 20 years, whichever is longer; medical records – duration of the employment of each employee plus 20 years, or for the duration of employment plus 20 years, whichever is longer.

1926.1110 Employers subject to occupational exposures to coke oven emissions standard. [Added]
See 29 CFR 1926.1118.

1926.1110 Employers subject to occupational exposures to benzene standard. [Added]
See 29 CFR 1926.1118.

1926.1145

1926.1145 Employers subject to occupational exposures to acrylonitrile standard. [Added]

To maintain accurate records of objective data for exempted operations and on exposure monitoring and medical surveillance.

1926.1147

Retention period: (a) Objective data for exempted operations records – duration of reliance upon such objective data; (b) exposure monitoring records – for at least 40 years or for the duration of employment plus 20 years, whichever is longer; (c) medical surveillance records – for at least 40 years or for the duration of employment plus 20 years, whichever is longer.

See 29 CFR 1926.1145.

1926.1147 Employers subject to occupational exposures to ethylene oxide standard. [Added]

See 29 CFR 1926.1147.

1926.1148 Employers subject to occupational exposures to formaldehyde standard. [Added]

To maintain records (a) of all measurements taken to monitor employee exposure; (b) for each employee subject to medical surveillance; (c) for employee subject to negative pressure fit testing; and (d) of the objective data relied upon to support the exposure determinations.

Retention period: (a) Exposure records and determinations – duration of employment plus 30 years; (b) medical records – duration of employment plus 30 years; and (c) respirator fit testing records – until replaced by a more recent record.

1928.1027 Employers subject to the cadmium standards. [Added]

See 29 CFR 1910.1027.

1928.1027, Appendix C Employers subject to the cadmium standards. [Added]

See 29 CFR 1910.1027, Appendix C.

Guide to Record Retention 1994

1950.11 State agencies receiving development and planning grants for occupational safety and health.

To maintain records consistent with pertinent instructions.

Retention period: Not specified.

1951.47 State agencies receiving grants implementing approved State plans in the occupational health and safety program.

To maintain financial records, supporting documents, statistical records, and all other records pertinent to the grant program.

Retention period: 3 years, or longer if audit findings not resolved; for nonexpendable property, 3 years after final disposition. Microfilm copies may be substituted for the originals.

1952.4 Employers, except small employers as provided in 29 CFR 1904.21, subject to the Occupational Safety and Health Act of 1970.

To maintain records for each occupational injury and illness, including an annual summary, and also a supplemental record in detail according to OSHA Form 103 and such other records as specified in sections cited.

Retention period: 5 years following the end of the year to which they relate for records provided for in 29 CFR 1904.2, 1904.4, and 1904.5 (including forms OSHA No. 200 and its predecessor forms OSHA No. 100 and OSHA No. 102); 5 years for recordkeeping and reporting requirements in those States operating under State plans.

PENSION BENEFIT GUARANTY CORPORATION

29 CFR

2610.11 Pension plan administrators with respect to plan years beginning on or after Jan. 1, 1988).

To retain certain documentation (all plan records including calculations and other data, prepared by an enrolled actuary or, for a plan described in section 412(l) of the Code, by the insurer from which the insurance contracts are purchased) needed to support or to validate premium payments. Records must include but not limited to records that establish the number of plan participants, that reconcile the calculation of the plan's unfunded vested benefits with the actuarial valuation upon which the calculation was based, and for plans that assert entitlement to the cap on the variable rate portion of the premium that demonstrate the methods and assumptions used by the plan during the base period with respect to calculating its maximum deductible contribution pursuant to section 404 of the Code.

Retention period: For a period of 6 years after the premium due date.

2616.9 Contributing sponsor or plan administrator of a terminating plan.

To maintain and preserve all records used to compute benefits with respect to each individual who is a plan participant or a beneficiary of a deceased participant as of the termination date.

Retention period: 6 years after the date the required post-distribution certification is filed with PBGC.

2617.10 Contributing sponsor or plan administrator of a terminating plan.

See 29 CFR 1616.9.

About Government Institutes

Government Institutes, Inc. was founded in 1973 to provide continuing education and practical information for your professional development. Specializing in environmental, health and safety concerns, we recognize that you face unique challenges presented by the ever-increasing number of new laws and regulations and the rapid evolution of new technologies, methods and markets.

Our information and continuing education efforts include a Videotape Distribution Service, over 140 courses held nation-wide throughout the year, and over 150 publications, making us the world's largest publisher in these areas.

Government Institutes, Inc.
4 Research Place, Suite 200
Rockville, MD 20850
(301) 921-2300

Other related books published by Government Institutes:

Federal Spill Reporting Requirements: A Reference Guide — Attorney Ethan S. Naftalin from the Raleigh, North Carolina office of Hunton & Williams explains all the different reporting requirements under CERCLA, EPCRA, TSCA, CWA, RCRA, and DOT Hazmat rules. And, unlike other sources that may just cite the rule itself, **Federal Spill Reporting Requirements: A Reference Guide** walks you through all steps. The author covers in detail the preparation of required forms and provides the names and addresses of contacts for each agency. Spills that are excluded from the various reporting requirements are carefully noted throughout. To make the book even easier to understand, the author defines important terms right in the text itself so these will be no confusion. Included in the appendices are sample reporting forms, tables from the CFRs indicating reportable quantities, and map of EPA regions. *Softcover/286 pages/Jan. '94/$85 ISBN: 0-86587-371-2*

Environmental Law Handbook, 12th Edition — The recognized authority in the field, this invaluable text, written by nationally-recognized legal experts, provides practical and current information on all major environmental areas. *Hardcover/670 pages/Apr '93/$72 ISBN: 0-86587-350-X*

Environmental Statutes, 1994 Edition — All the major environmental laws incorporated into one convenient source.
Hardcover/1,170 pages/Mar '94/$65 ISBN: 0-86587-382-8
Softcover/1,170 pages/Mar '94/$55 ISBN: 0-86587-381-X

Environmental Regulatory Glossary, 6th Edition — This glossary records and standardizes more than 4,000 terms, abbreviations and acronyms, all compiled directly from the environmental statutes or the U.S. Code of Federal Regulations. *Hardcover/544 pages/May '93/$68 ISBN: 0-86587-353-4*

Directory of Environmental Information Sources, 4th Edition — Details hard-to-find Federal Government Resources; State Government Resources; Professional, Scientific, and Trade Organizations; Newsletters, Magazines, and Periodicals; and Databases. *Softcover/350 pages/Nov '92/$78 ISBN: 0-86587-326-7*

Environmental Audits, 6th Edition — Details how to begin and manage a successful audit program for your facility. Use these checklists and sample procedures to identify your problem areas. *Softcover/592 pages/Nov '89/$79 ISBN: 0-86587-776-9*

Prices are subject to change.

Call the above number for our current book/video catalog and course schedule.

RCRA Hazardous Wastes Handbook, 10th Edition — The Washington, D.C. law firm of Crowell & Moring gives you clear, concise answers to take you step-by-step through the maze of RCRA/Hazardous Wastes regulations Includes the RCRA Statute. *Softcover/464 pages/Oct '93/$110   ISBN: 0-86587-355-0*

Clean Water Handbook — Written by attorneys J. Gordon Arbuckle and Russell V. Randle of the Washington, D.C. law firm of Patton, Boggs & Blow, along with a team of other legal and technical experts, this comprehensive handbook offers a straightforward explanation of how the clean water laws and regulations affect your business.
Softcover/446 pages/June '90/$90 ISBN: 0-86587-210-4

Clean Air Handbook, 2nd Edition — Provides a clear explanation of the Clean Air Act including the 1990 Amendments and how they will affect businesses. This handbook covers: regulatory issues and the nonattainment puzzle; NAAQ standards; emerging air quality issues; source performance standards; air toxics regulations; permits and pre-construction review; and stationary and mobile source regulations. *Softcover/340 pages/July '93/$84   ISBN: 0-86587-343-7*

TSCA Handbook, 2nd Edition — The law firm of McKenna & Cuneo provides a comprehensive look at your requirements under the Toxic Substances Control Act (TSCA). Includes a copy of the TSCA law, charts, tables, figures and multiple indexes. *Softcover/490 pages/Nov '89/$95   ISBN: 0-86587-791-2*

Underground Storage Tank Management: A Practical Guide, 4th Edition — This guide will help you develop or maintain UST management programs that will minimize the risk of a release and reduce the potential for costly repercussions. Brings you up-to-date on the latest in tank design, how to predict tank leaks, test tank integrity, avoid costly tank replacement, and more. *Softcover/420 pages/Nov '91/ $84 ISBN: 0-86587-271-6*

Environmental Engineering Dictionary, 2nd Edition — Clearly defines over 12,000 engineering terms relating to pollution control technologies, monitoring, risk assesment, sampling and analysis, quality control, and more!   *Softcover/630 pages/Oct. '92/$72   ISBN: 0-86587-298-8*
Hardcover/630 pages/Oct. '92/$94   ISBN: 0-86587-328-3

Educational Programs

■ Our **COURSES** combine the legal, regulatory, technical, and management aspects of today's key environmental, safety and health issues — such as environmental laws and regulations, environmental management, pollution prevention, OSHA and many other topics. We bring together the leading authorities from industry, business and government to shed light on the problems and challenges you face each day. Please call our Education Department at (301) 921-2345 for more information!

■ Our **TRAINING CONSULTING GROUP** can help audit your ES&H training, develop an ES&H training plan, and customize on-site training courses. Our proven and successful ES&H training courses are customized to fit your organizational and industry needs. Your employees learn key environmental concepts and strategies at a convenient location for 30% of the cost to send them to non-customized, off-site courses. Please call our Training Consulting Group at (301) 921-2366 for more information!

Government Institutes, Inc., 4 Research Place, Suite 200, Rockville, MD 20850, (301) 921-2300